Orthodox by Design

THE S. MARK TAPER FOUNDATION

IMPRINT IN JEWISH STUDIES

BY THIS ENDOWMENT

THE S. MARK TAPER FOUNDATION SUPPORTS

THE APPRECIATION AND UNDERSTANDING

OF THE RICHNESS AND DIVERSITY OF

JEWISH LIFE AND CULTURE

Orthodox by Design

JUDAISM, PRINT POLITICS, AND THE ARTSCROLL REVOLUTION

Jeremy Stolow

UNIVERSITY OF CALIFORNIA PRESS

BERKELEY   LOS ANGELES   LONDON

University of California Press, one of the most
distinguished university presses in the United States,
enriches lives around the world by advancing scholarship
in the humanities, social sciences, and natural sciences. Its
activities are supported by the UC Press Foundation and
by philanthropic contributions from individuals and
institutions. For more information, visit www.ucpress.edu.

University of California Press
Berkeley and Los Angeles, California

University of California Press, Ltd.
London, England

Library of Congress Cataloging-in-Publication Data

Stolow, Jeremy, 1965–
   Orthodox by design : Judaism, print politics, and
the ArtScroll revolution / Jeremy Stolow.
       p.   cm.
   Includes bibliographical references and index.
   ISBN 978-0-520-26425-0 (cloth : alk. paper)—
   ISBN 978-0-520-26426-7 (pbk. : alk. paper)
   1. ArtScroll/Mesorah Publications—History.
2. Jewish publishing—United States—History.
3. Jewish publishers—United States—History.
4. Publishers and publishing—United States—History.
5. Ultra-Orthodox Jews—United States—Intellectual
life.   6. Orthodox Judaism—United States.   I. Title.
Z473.A695S76   2010
070.50973—dc22   2009049282

Manufactured in the United States of America
19   18   17   16   15   14   13   12   11   10
10   9   8   7   6   5   4   3   2   1

This book is printed on Cascades Enviro 100, a 100% post-
consumer waste, recycled, de-inked fiber. FSC recycled
certified and processed chlorine free. It is acid free,
Ecologo certified, and manufactured by BioGas energy.

The publisher gratefully acknowledges the generous support of the Jewish Studies Endowment Fund of the University of California Press Foundation, which was established by a major gift from the S. Mark Taper Foundation.

CONTENTS

FIGURES

TABLES

ACKNOWLEDGMENTS

THIS BOOK COULD NOT HAVE been written without the remarkable community of teachers, colleagues, supporters, friends, and family who accompanied me on my long journey. The debts I have accumulated far outstrip my ability to note them in a few words. Let me begin by thanking my teachers, especially Barbara Godard, who supervised both my master's and doctoral degrees, and whose unswerving faith in me allowed me to risk venturing into a topic for which I had no prior training, let alone "insider" knowledge. Barbara taught me to read and think in entirely new ways, an experience shared by many of her students in the Graduate Programme in Social and Political Thought at York University. During my doctoral studies, I also had the good fortune to study with Ato Sekyi-Otu, Patrick Taylor, Gordon Darroch, Michael Brown, and Stuart Schoenfeld, and I thank each of them for their unflagging support, careful reading, and engaging dialogue. I also wish to thank my fellow graduate students at York for their camaraderie and intellectual generosity, especially the members of the Historiography Reading Group, whose discussions so greatly shaped my own thinking on many issues: Adriana Benzaquén, Jenny Burman, Nergis Canefe, Zoë Druick, Elisabeth Friedman, Victoria Heftler, Peter Ives, and Dennis Soron. As a PhD student, during an extended trip to Jerusalem, I also had the opportunity to meet Michael Silber, David Ellenson, Shaul Stampfer, Charles Liebman, David N. Myers, and Menachem Friedman, each of whom was generous with his time and advice. I very much doubt I would have settled on ArtScroll as a research topic without their insight and encouragement.

From 2000 to 2002, I worked as a postdoctoral fellow and affiliated lecturer in the Faculty of Social and Political Sciences at the University of Cambridge under the supervision of Bryan S. Turner. Together with Bryan, David Lehmann, and another visiting fellow from Israel, Nurit Stadler, I was given an unparalleled opportunity to rethink virtually every assumption that had informed my doctoral research, without the pressure to instrumentalize my thoughts—still very much in flux—by rushing to publish a book about ArtScroll. My thanks to Bryan, David, and Nurit for all their encouragement and engagement, as well as the advice I received from Véronique Mottier, Patrick Baert, Mariane Ferme, Valentina Napoletano, and Ato Quayson, among many others. During my time at Cambridge, it became clear to me that I still had a great deal to learn about ArtScroll and its public impact, a realization that ultimately led me to undertake new field research that would continue for the next several years. This fieldwork, conducted first in London, then in Toronto, and finally in New York City, forced me to revise many of my initial conclusions, and those insights formed the basis of the present book. I was fortunate to have several assistants during my fieldwork: in Toronto, Beth Sapiro; in New York, Rebecca Finkel and Chana Pollack; and subsequently, Elisabeth de Napoli, who tracked down numerous references and sources. I thank each of these assistants for the remarkable work they did helping to organize the survey data, set up interviews, double-check facts, and in several cases conduct interviews on my behalf. Much of the original data in this book would not be present without their diligent work. In particular, I wish to recognize the contributions of Chana Pollack, who played an immensely valuable role helping to open doors for me.

The work I began at Cambridge also brought me into contact with another community of scholars, working at the forefront of the emerging field of interdisciplinary study of religion and media, particularly in the Netherlands and in the United States. Over the past eight years, I have had the incredible fortune to participate in many conferences, research activities, and ongoing conversations that have helped to define "religion and media" as a field of study. Without the enthusiastic support and engagement of this community of scholars, there is no way I would have been able to bring this book to its conclusion. In particular, I wish to recognize the contributions of Jonathan Boyarin, Elizabeth Castelli, Faye Ginsburg,

Barbara Kirshenblatt-Gimblett, Birgit Meyer, Arvind Rajagopal, Jeffrey Shandler, and Angela Zito, each of whom listened to and read countless proposals, articles, draft texts, and "trial versions" of the book. I am profoundly in their debt. Among the many other members of this burgeoning community, I also wish to thank Charles Hirschkind, Stewart Hoover, David Morgan, and Michele Rosenthal for their generosity, advice, encouragement, and support at various times in the past years.

From 2003 to 2004, I was very lucky to be able to formalize my position in this network of scholars through a postdoctoral position at the newly created Center for Religion and Media at New York University, under the direction of Faye Ginsburg and Angela Zito. I have many people to thank for that remarkable, and indeed transformative year, including (but certainly not limited to) Barbara Abrash, Talal Asad, Adam Becker, Omri Elisha, Barry Flood, Michael Gilsenan, Brian Larkin, Mazyar Lotfalian, Fred Myers, Susan Rogers, and Kristen Sands. But above all, I wish to thank the members of the Center's Jews/Religion/Media Working Group, spearheaded by Barbara Kirshenblatt-Gimblett and Jeffrey Shandler and including Jonathan Boyarin, Judah Cohen, Henry Goldschmidt, Judith Goldstein, Jenna Weissman Joselit, Mark Kligman, David Koffman, Faye Lederman, Eddy Portnoy, Lara Rabinovitch, Elissa Sampson, and Brigitte Sion, who created such a lively community and who taught me so much about my own topic. Another member of the working group, Samuel C. Heilman, deserves my special gratitude for having invited me to speak at the Graduate Center at CUNY, and especially for having read and commented incisively on portions of this manuscript.

In 2005 I had the good fortune to be invited by Birgit Meyer to join her research project "Religion, Mass Media, and the Imagination of Community," based at the Amsterdam School for Social Science Research. During my time in Amsterdam, I was given a valuable opportunity to reflect on all the field research I had conducted for the previous four years and to share my thoughts with a remarkable group of interlocutors. My profound thanks to Birgit, and to Maria Jose de Abreu, Francio Guadeloupe, Stephen Hughes, Carly Machado, Martijn Oosterbaan, Mattijs van de Port, Rafael Sanchez, and Marleen de Witte for all their generosity and engagement.

I also have many colleagues, past and present, whom I wish to thank for listening to me talk about my work, sharing ideas, and encouraging me to keep going. At my former institution, McMaster University, I especially wish to recognize the support of William Coleman, Tina Fetner, Dana Hollander, Travis Kroeker, Neil McLaughlin, Celia Rothenberg, Philip

Savage, Alex Sevigny, and Billy Shaffir. And in my present position, in the Department of Communication Studies at Concordia University, I wish to thank all my new colleagues for welcoming me into an incredible and exciting community and giving me time and space to finally bring this book project to its conclusion.

Over the past few years I presented numerous papers that tested various arguments and portions of this book, and these generated for me countless new insights. I thank the organizers and the engaging audience members at more events than I can mention here, but I was especially grateful for the invitations to speak at the conferences "Material Jews" (Center for Religion and Media, New York University, 2006), "Religion, Media, and the Question of Community" (University of Amsterdam, 2006), "The Future of the Religious Past" (Amsterdam, 2005), "Print Culture and the City" (McGill University, 2004), "Religion, Media and the Public Sphere" (University of Amsterdam, 2001), and "After Secularism/Religion" (University of Minnesota, 2000), as well as at the public lectures organized at the University of Kansas, the CUNY Graduate Center, the Center for Religion and Media (New York University), Carleton University, the University of Cambridge, and McMaster University.

Financial support for research leading to this book comes from multiple sources. I am grateful to all these sponsors: the Social Sciences and Humanities Research Council of Canada; the Pew Charitable Trusts; the Arts Research Board of McMaster University; the Pionier Fellowship (Amsterdam School for Social Science Research); the General Research Fund of Trent University; the Myer and Rosaline Feinstein Center for American Jewish History (Temple University); the Advanced Study Center at the University of Michigan; and the Abraham Isaac Scholarship (York University).

In writing this book, I drew upon (but ended up entirely rewriting) a number of earlier publications. These include "Communicating Authority, Consuming Tradition: Jewish Orthodox Outreach Literature and Its Reading Public," in *Religion, Media and the Public Sphere,* ed. Birgit Meyer and Annelies Moors (Bloomington: Indiana University Press, 2006), 73–91; "Holy Pleather: Materializing Authority in Contemporary Orthodox Jewish Publishing," *Material Religion: The Journal of Objects, Art, and Belief* 3 (Autumn 2007): 314–35; "Aesthetics/Ascetics: Visual Piety and Pleasure in a Strictly Kosher Cookbook," *Postscripts: The Journal of Sacred Texts and Contemporary Worlds* 2 (Summer 2006): 5–28; and "Transnationalism and the New Religio-Politics: Reflections on a Jewish Orthodox

Case," *Theory, Culture and Society* 21 (April 2004): 109–37. My thanks to the editors and publishers of each of these texts for publishing these initial forays into my study of ArtScroll. At the University of California Press, I wish to thank all the staff, as well as the anonymous reviewers, who worked so diligently on my manuscript—especially Stan Holwitz, Nick Arrivo, Caroline Knapp, Elisabeth Magnus, and Francisco Reinking.

Finally, I wish to acknowledge two groups of people without whom there would be no book. First, I thank all the people who participated in my field research and who generously gave me their time to share their thoughts about ArtScroll. This includes numerous rabbis, booksellers, librarians, teachers, marketing agents, journalists, authors, webmasters, and others who so enthusiastically responded to my questions. Above all, I thank Rabbi Meir Zlotowitz and Rabbi Nosson Scherman, the presidents and editors-in-chief of ArtScroll and the Mesorah Heritage Foundation. Despite their enormously busy schedules, and without any good reason to trust a complete stranger like myself to have the audacity to write a book about "the ArtScroll phenomenon," they met with me on several occasions in 2003 and 2004, and we corresponded many more times after that. Without their cooperation, this book would have been much thinner. I thank them for their time and willingness to speak to me, as well as for having generously granted me permission to reproduce the images in this book. Finally, I wish to thank my family for all they have given me over so many years. Above all, I thank my true love and lifelong partner, Danielle; my mother, Sari; and my daughter, Malka. Each of you has sustained me in more ways than I can possibly summarize here, and it is to each of you that I dedicate this book, with my humble gratitude and my love.

Introduction

Do you wish you could pray in Hebrew and understand what you are
saying *as you are saying it?* Now you can, with ArtScroll's *Schottenstein
Edition Interlinear Series.* It's easy to pray with meaning in Hebrew
with the new interlinear format developed by ArtScroll to give you
maximum comprehension with minimum effort.

ArtScroll Complete Catalogue (2006)

ARTSCROLL IS A PUBLISHER KNOWN throughout the English-speaking
Jewish world as a purveyor of handsomely designed, accessible, and uncompromisingly Orthodox print commodities, including bilingual prayer
books and Bibles, rabbinic commentaries, legal manuals, historical works,
novels, self-help books, and curricular material for Jewish education. The
advertisement quoted above announces a new edition of ArtScroll's highly
popular Siddur, a liturgical text that in its various formats has sold roughly
one million copies, making it arguably the most successful Jewish prayer
book in the history of publishing. Since its founding in 1976, ArtScroll has
enjoyed a stellar career, in many ways parallel to a broader cultural shift
that has seen an increasingly confident and unapologetic form of Orthodoxy assume a central position on the Jewish public stage. Defined by
some as "Jewish fundamentalism" or "ultra-Orthodoxy" but better referred to as Haredism, this movement promotes stringent interpretations
of Jewish law, intensive study of Jewish texts, and submission to the authority of a narrowly defined rabbinic elite.[1] The expanding influence and
visibility of Haredism in such varied domains as education, philosophy,
law, entertainment, and politics point to one of the most pervasive struggles for legitimacy and authority within contemporary Jewish public life, its
sources of knowledge and imagination, its bonds of affect, and its markets.
The enthusiastic reception of ArtScroll books among diverse constituencies

of Jewish readers can thus be read as a metonym of Haredism's ascendance. For some, the spread of ArtScroll books epitomizes the Haredi assault on Jewish traditions stressing autonomous powers of reason, pluralism, and enlightened acculturation: a dangerous drift toward punctiliousness, interpretive rigidity, and unreflective obedience. But from another point of view, ArtScroll is understood as a vital tool for recuperating an authentic religious tradition and for helping pious Jews navigate the dangerous currents of narcissistic hedonism, empty relativism, and idolatry in the global present.

This book engages with the intellectual and political goals of ArtScroll's Haredi editors and authors as mediated through their books. It is equally concerned with the broader economic, ideological, and affective forces that animate the publisher and define its receptivity in discrete local contexts. What can one hope to gain from such a study? Some readers may find it odd, if not misguided, to devote sustained attention to a single publishing house and its readership. After all, ArtScroll is only one of several institutions dedicated to the expansion and legitimation of Jewish Orthodoxy (a label encompassing a startling array of doctrinal positions and cultural distinctions). Even within the relatively narrow confines of contemporary Jewish print culture, it is not immediately apparent what is so innovative, unprecedented, or consequential about ArtScroll books and the popularity they enjoy. There are many Jewish publishers, Orthodox and non-Orthodox, and many have existed in the past, both distant and recent. Jews are certainly not the only people who produce and read books. And books, for that matter, can hardly be considered the only media with which both Jews and non-Jews interact in their everyday lives. Nevertheless, however parochial the ArtScroll story might at first appear, I propose that there is much to be gained from its close examination. Among other things, this study offers new insight into a phenomenon that has only recently begun to command attention in academic circles and arenas of public debate: the strategically decisive position of institutions, technologies, and practices of mediated communication within the embodied regimens and imagined worlds that constitute religious experience in the global present.

Take a look around the world today and you cannot fail to notice at least some of the ways religious communities, movements, and cultural forms have become deeply reliant upon modern communication technologies and their systems of signification and power. Christian evangelical rap music, video games, and science fiction novels—such as the best-selling

Left Behind series in the United States—are forging new bonds of commodified leisure, apocalyptic fantasy, and moral propriety among an imagined community of "born-again" Americans.[2] The circulation of sermons recorded on audiocassettes in Egypt and elsewhere in the Muslim world is feeding new arenas of public discussion that spill outside the framework of "established" religious and state-sanctioned institutions, fortifying new bases for Islamic community among those ill prepared to participate in "traditional" modes of Qu'ranic interpretation and debate.[3] The production of televised epics such as the *Ramayana* has provided the occasion for Hindu nationalists to reimagine modern India as the legatee of ancient Hindu wisdom, fueling their programs for neoliberal market reform, a "Hinduization" of the Indian state, and even, where need be, the "cleansing" power of anti-Muslim violence.[4] Such instances, which could easily be multiplied or examined in greater depth, dramatize the extent to which religion can no longer (indeed never could) be contained within the confines of traditional social logics of institutional loyalty, the performative demands of face-to-face interaction, the controlled circulation of sacred texts, or the localized boundaries of ritual time. In the context of our contemporary geography of digital information flows, virtual telepresence, panoptical visualization, concentrated media ownership, and fragmented audiences, the field of religious symbols, practices, and modes of belonging has been radically extended along the axes of a dizzying array of technologies, genres, and forms. These range from international radio broadcasts to the spread of mobile phones, trading cards, and bumper stickers, from scientific treatises to popular history and pop psychology books, from Web sites, comic books, and hip-hop music to package tours, museum exhibitions, and mega-rallies in sports stadiums, complete with jumbotron screens and simulcast presentations in distant cities. In increasingly intimate ways, media precede and organize the very conditions of possibility for local, everyday, embodied forms of religious practice and affinity.[5]

So it appears that the religious field is undergoing a phase of radical reconstruction, not only at the level of existing institutions and communities of faith, but also at the level of broader cultural formations haunted by "religious" imagery, including current discourses of transnational belonging and multicultural citizenship, toleration and intolerance, universality and difference, hospitality and war, faith and credit. Perhaps there never has been such a thing as an "unmediated" or "premediated" religion (let us leave aside here the question whether there are good reasons even to hold onto the word *religion*). But in the contemporary moment of ever-expanding horizons and ever-deepening penetrations of mediatic power, the study of technologies, techniques, institutions, and systems of exchange that constitute "media" provides some of the most important clues to an understanding of the ways religion now inhabits public space. How do modern media inscribe religious sensibilities onto the body? How do they reorganize the semantic and discursive possibilities for generating religious "conviction"? How are the social bases of religious authority redistributed in and through media? How do mediated modes of religious affiliation intersect with conditions of transnational migrancy and cultural hybridization that define the global present?

In the spirit of such questions, *Orthodox by Design* aims not only to demonstrate that certain aspects of Jewish publishing merit greater attention than they have been accorded to date but also to shed further light on the increasingly intimate articulations of religion and media in the current historical juncture. Specifically, the case of ArtScroll invites reflection upon the ways in which the medium of the *printed text* has assumed a new status within Jewish public culture.[6] In the coming pages, I hope to demonstrate how ArtScroll evinces this trend. As we shall see, this publisher has had a considerable impact on the contemporary Jewish book market and on a variety of synagogal and communal institutions—to those extents revealing shifts in the structures of symbolic exchange that make up the contemporary English-language Jewish public sphere. While ArtScroll books seem to mark the advance of powerful new expressions of authority emanating from the so-called Religious Right, we shall also see how their consumption and use have empowered a significant Jewish population to attempt, in its own fashion, to reorganize the building blocks of religious imagination and knowledge, their theoretical sources, their modes of legitimation, and their relationship with patterns of everyday conduct and ritual performance. As the proper name for a body of discourse, a financial entity, a community of intellectual producers, and a collection of material artifacts, ArtScroll thus serves as an ideal site for tracking much broader shifts in modes of religious knowledge, practice, agency, and authority.[7] It provides a unique window into the processes whereby the advancing technologies, economic arrangements, and social systems for the production and consumption of texts are redefining the exercise of religious authority and legitimacy. And this in turn provides the basis for revisiting some widely held assumptions about Haredism, its cultural and political influence, and what some take to be its foreboding presence within contemporary Jewish public life.

In particular, by the end of this study, I hope to have convinced my reader of the need to revise the claims commonly made about the "scripturalist" basis of Haredi authority. First coined in 1968 by the anthropologist Clifford Geertz, the term *scripturalism* denotes a prevalent theory about the power of sacred texts to shape the patterns of everyday conduct among members of a religious community and to confer considerable authority onto those who are recognized as expert interpreters of those texts.[8] As we shall see in due course, the notion of scripturalism has played a central role in studies of so-called religious fundamentalisms in the contemporary era, epitomized, in this instance, by the rising popularity of ArtScroll books (and, presumably, the expanding influence of their Haredi authors). But rather than simply assuming that we know what scripturalism must mean in this context, *Orthodox by Design* explores some of the diverse ways ArtScroll texts, as print commodities, actually function in the media-rich universe of contemporary Jewish social life. This exploration will move us beyond simple assumptions about the organization of scripturalist texts and the exercise of scripturalist authority so that we may appreciate how evolving media forms help to reconstitute the very bases of imagination, authority, and agency within diverse cultural and social scenes.

There are, of course, different kinds of Jewish public culture, distinguished, among other things, by historical period, geographic location and scale, repositories of knowledge, and traditions of ritual practice. Many of these are renditions of what one might term "reading publics": that is, forms of publicity that depend on the capacity of circulated texts to address and unite a body of strangers through their concerted attention toward, and their participation within, a network of textually mediated speech acts.[9] *Orthodox by Design* studies a particular type of reading public defined by the activities of consuming, studying, reciting, collecting, and in other ways using texts aimed primarily at Jews living in diaspora who rely upon what has now become the world's dominant vernacular, the English language. As I shall elaborate in the coming pages, the English-speaking Jewish public sphere has long existed as a dynamic site of cultural production in its own right, despite the many ways Jews have oriented themselves to the Hebrew language (as the medium of Jewish discourse and ritual practice) and to Israel (both as "promised land" and as the modern "Jewish state"). Spanning the national territories of the United States, Canada, the United Kingdom, Australia, South Africa, and even Israel—among other places where Jews have written, read, or spoken in English (including, more recently, the deterritorialized space of the Internet)—this public sphere encompasses the demographic majority of world Jewry within a single market, the center of which happens to coincide with one of the core sites of global capitalism and, of particular interest here, the unrivaled capital of the global print and publishing industries: New York City.

Situated within this broad framework, the cadre of authors, editors, patrons, and supporters of ArtScroll are engaged in an intellectual, cultural and political project: to disseminate the voice of Haredi authority within the public culture of English-speaking Jewry, especially among those for whom it is inconvenient, too difficult, or even impossible to engage with strictly Hebrew-language texts. Their project brings together two different intellectual and practical aims under a single institutional rubric. On the one hand, the ArtScroll cadre are concerned to expand the popular base for Haredi authority (translation itself being a mechanism for reaching new populations of consumers and readers, or of reaching more established constituencies in new ways). On the other hand, they understand their role as one of authorizing the "authentic" meaning of key Jewish texts: in other words, of defining the scope of what shall count as their legitimate interpretation and application (which, of course, is the only way their "authenticity" can be produced in the first place). To anticipate one of the key arguments of this study, ArtScroll's twofold project—to popularize and to authorize—unfolds in some counterintuitive, even paradoxical ways. The following pages will demonstrate that ArtScroll books have indeed been appropriated as sources of knowledge, and also as desirable commodities and emblems for public display among diverse constituencies of the contemporary English-language Jewish reading public. It remains to be seen, however, what conclusions can be drawn about the success with which the ArtScroll cadre communicate Haredi authority. Indeed, as we shall see, especially in Chapters 3 and 4, ArtScroll serves as an ideal locus for tracking a series of transformations of this religious authority, according to the logics of popular communication and of commodity exchange, as well as the material constraints that define the circulation and everyday use of printed works.

The title of this book, *Orthodox by Design*, is meant to draw attention to the tensions inherent in ArtScroll's project and in the life of ArtScroll books in the public sphere of English-language Jewry. The word *design* can and should be read here in several ways. From its Latin root, *designare*— to mark out or designate (from *signum*, a sign)—this term has always encompassed a range of activities of "working out," whether in the sense of conceiving in the mind, contriving, planning, or intending (as in "They designed a good excuse not to go to work yesterday," or "This room is not designed for loud music"), or something materialized in the form of a blueprint, a pattern, a sketch or a plan (as in "the design on his shirt," or "She contributed to the design of a new instrument").[10] Running through all these definitions is the idea of aesthetic form but also the idea of *function:* the organization of social relations, embedded in things, that constitutes "society made durable," as Bruno Latour once called it.[11] "Orthodoxy designed" is thus also Orthodoxy as it comes to be known through its material culture—in this case, the materiality of print commodities and the webs of semiosis and social interaction in which they are situated and that they in turn transform. From this perspective, as I shall try to elaborate in this book, "design" is one of the key media in and through which scenarios of conception and production of ArtScroll books are articulated with scenarios of their consumption and use. *Orthodox by Design* therefore seeks to cast the net as widely as possible for the analysis of ArtScroll books: to consider the processes of their conception and authorship; their modes of production and their materialization in specific physical, visual, and typographic registers; their means of distribution, marketing, and public consecration; the work of desire and acquisition; the activities of reading and reciting; and even the less frequently noted practices of transporting, displaying, storing, or disposing of books. As we shall see, each of these arenas is part of a larger process of constituting Jewish Orthodoxy "by design," and each points to some of the deep paradoxes that shape the public life of Haredism and the involvement of Haredi intellectuals and cultural workers in activities of mediation and in the materiality of mediated communication.

ORTHODOXY DESIGNED

Jewish? Speak English? You need this book. Like all of the ArtScroll publications, this is destined to become the standard in the English-speaking world. . . . I recommend that every English-speaking Jewish household acquire a copy of this, regardless of what other publishers' are already owned. This is singular in its quality.

Anonymous reviewer of The Chumash:
The Stone Edition *(ArtScroll), posting on amazon.com*

What is at stake in approaching ArtScroll as a media institution connected with the moral and philosophical outlook and the cultural orientations of Haredi Orthodox Judaism? There is no shortage of controversy in characterizing ArtScroll as a "Haredi" publishing house, since, for one thing, this is not a term used by the press itself. ArtScroll's founding editors prefer to describe it as an "independent Torah publisher," without ties to any of the major institutions or any of the cultural and political movements that make up Jewish public life. They see themselves as engaged in the strictly disinterested business of "Torah scholarship": the redaction and translation of canonical Jewish texts, the production of commentaries based on traditional sources, and the application of the worldview imparted by classical Jewish literature onto other literary genres, such as history, fiction, and pop psychology. As such, the primary goal of ArtScroll's editors, translators, and authors has been to supplant what they regard as inadequate, distorted, or otherwise illegitimate representations of Jewish knowledge, ritual practice, and historical imagination and to replace these with what are presented as corrected, more authentic, more reliable, and better organized translations, commentaries, and interpretations of the Jewish canon and Jewish tradition. In the words of the publisher's cofounder, Rabbi Nosson Scherman, ArtScroll developed out of the "conviction that English-speaking Jews needed an authentic Torah literature in their own language, a literature that was proud and faithful to its origins."[12]

All the same, *pace* ArtScroll's public self-identification, it is difficult to ignore the intimate relations between ArtScroll's key editors, managers, and authors and the world of the Haredi yeshiva,[13] as can be gleaned from their educational background, the social networks in which they participate, and the religious authorities ArtScroll has cultivated as its key intellectual and ideological patrons.[14] Some scholars have pushed the issue further, arguing that ArtScroll's Haredi orientations are evident in the interpretive rigidity with which the publisher has approached canonical Jewish texts or the explicit hostility ArtScroll's editors have shown for "academic" approaches to sacred Jewish literature, rooted in higher criticism and in the sciences of philology and archeology. In this book, I have little to add to ongoing debates about the degree to which ArtScroll fits a Haredi mold. Those debates have tended to revolve around contrasting assessments of ArtScroll's translations of sacred texts into English, the publisher's editorial approach to rabbinic commentaries, or the positions ArtScroll authors appear to endorse in matters of Jewish ethics, law, and ritual conduct.[15] My concerns being somewhat different, I shall take it as given that ArtScroll is a Haredi publisher for the simple reason that it is routinely referred to as such.

"In an ideal world," concedes Rabbi Scherman, "people wouldn't need ArtScroll. They would only need Talmud, Schulchan Aruch, and other classical works."[16] As fully literate and competent masters of Jewish texts, the inhabitants of this ideal world would find it superfluous, if not cumbersome, to use the prostheses of translations, transliterations, summaries, and referential material for which ArtScroll books are so well known. In the real world, however, ArtScroll confronts an amorphous collection of readers and users that make up the contemporary English-language Jewish reading public.[17] This collectivity encompasses both the erudite and the ignorant, the confident and the uncertain, the sympathetic and the dismissive. In the context of this public sphere, marked by an uneven distribution of competencies and commitments, ArtScroll's aim, in the words of Rabbi Meir Zlotowitz, ArtScroll's founder and director, is "to delve deep enough to fathom the true meaning of [classical Jewish texts] as understood by our Sages, and . . . to present [them] to the English-reading audience in a palatable and readable manner."[18] By "removing the language barrier," that is, by rendering Hebrew texts into English and by elucidating their content in an orderly way, ArtScroll "makes the Jewish classics accessible to today's generation."[19] In other words, ArtScroll's editors, and the various Haredi stakeholders in the publisher, seek to instill in their readers a deeper understanding of Jewish tradition, a more intensive engagement with Jewish textual practice, and a stricter observance of Jewish law defined from a "Torah-true" perspective.

The "ArtScroll revolution," as some call it, is rooted in the ability of this publisher to innovate design elements that have not been commonly found among Jewish publishers, including the creation of full-color covers and the employment of a range of advanced typesetting and typographic techniques. Superior design, in other words, lies at the heart of the publisher's mode of address and is the hallmark of its success. "Let's not kid ourselves," writes Rabbi Scherman. "People do judge a book by its cover. If the contents of a book aren't good, then the most beautiful presentation won't sell it. But the outward appearance of a book does help sell it."[20] Aesthetic qualities are in fact among the most frequently mentioned aspects of ArtScroll books. "It's a thrill to see works of this quality available," reports one ardent consumer on the Internet-based book retailer amazon.com. "The illustrations, the typesetting, the layout, they just make the whole thing a meaningful experience. They make a fine gift, an essential addition to any Jewish home—even one that has plenty of Jewish books already."[21] In another such public testimonial to ArtScroll's design, we read:

Like all other ArtScroll products, the typesetting in this Siddur is beautiful. The Hebrew and Aramaic are very readable. The weekly, monthly, and seasonal additions are offsetted [sic] in a shaded background. The service choreography is clearly marked. Important prayer section indicators are bolded. Different type sizes are used to accurately reflect how the letters are represented in the Torah scrolls. . . . Key words and letters are indexed in Hebrew in the English page that faces the Hebrew page, so that even those who are not fluent enough in Hebrew can readily follow the prayers. . . . The readability alone makes this Siddur worth an investment.[22]

Superior design and authoritative scholarship thus constitute the twin paths along which ArtScroll establishes its foothold in the contemporary Jewish imaginary. "By utilizing modern technology," Rabbi Scherman boasts, "we have for the first time presented Torah literature in a format equal to secular books. This has brought a new respect for Torah and has removed the barriers so that Jews today can study in the same way as their grandfathers did."[23]

These words should make us pause. Should we infer that the more ArtScroll books adhere to modern principles of design, the greater their fidelity to a universe of discourse for which these same principles supposedly had no intrinsic significance? After all, as Rabbi Scherman contends, "Traditional Hebrew publishers didn't concern themselves with design. It was all about content. It's really at the level of book design that we are innovators."[24] Rabbi Zlotowitz concurs, adding, "We pride ourselves very much on the fact that, aesthetically, our books look as good as anything available today on the secular market. We really feel that this is one of our accomplishments: that we've raised the level of traditional literature, so its aesthetic aspect is very pronounced."[25] So much for studying "the same way our grandfathers did." The superior design of ArtScroll covers and layout are understood here as helping to secure the authenticity of the text's interior contents, drawing in otherwise uncommitted (or inadequately engaged) readers. But these same design elements also transform the text itself, subjecting it to new interpretive conditions. This paradox informs the fundamental tension within ArtScroll's dual mission to both popularize and render authoritative, and we shall have occasion in the coming pages to examine how this paradox gets inflected in different material, discursive, and performative registers.

At the same time, as I intimated earlier, it is "by design" that the ArtScroll cadre is able to function as a sort of hinge conjoining the cultural milieu of the yeshiva with the more socially diffuse regime of the modern Jewish reading public and, in the process, to redraw the lines dividing elite culture from popular sensibility. In fact, it is important to note here that the cadre of editors, authors, translators, and other figures associated with ArtScroll is not distinguished for having produced any major new interpretations of canonical Jewish texts, nor has it sought such distinction. Instead, ArtScroll's efforts have concentrated on transmitting, legitimating, and in other ways connecting elite ideas with a mass readership, not unlike other "middlebrow" institutions that came to prominence in the twentieth century, such as popular presses, book clubs, and various forms of higher journalism.[26] As Rabbi Zlotowitz describes it, "We see our goal as bringing the insights of the yeshiva to the outside world, giving the 'spiritual innards' of Jewish texts."[27] Through its artful participation in the economic, discursive, and material processes of circulation that constitute textual publication, the ArtScroll cadre acts as both a guardian and a mediator of the "spiritual innards" of the Haredi yeshiva. In so doing, it also comes into contact with a wide range of consumers and readers. Rabbi Zlotowitz imagines this diversity to encompass "a large cross-section of people from the early-teenage day school student to the Hebrew teacher; from the college student seeking a traditional interpretation of a book of the Bible to the housewife; from the 'uninitiated' adult reader with limited Hebrew background to the young kollel [advanced academy devoted to Talmud study] scholar who has neither access to all the sources in their original, nor the time to investigate them individually. . . . [ArtScroll] bridges the gaps and fills the unique individual needs of each reader."[28] Many agree that ArtScroll is distinctive among Haredi publishers, if not all Jewish publishing houses, for its ability to "bridge the gaps" between the different social positions enumerated by Rabbi Zlotowitz. One employee in a Toronto Jewish bookstore attributes ArtScroll's popularity precisely to its capacity to address diverse interlocutors at once:

> The way they can attract people who are not affiliated and people who are affiliated, people who have never thought about being affiliated, and also people who—you know—are interested but they don't know what they want to do. They really have something that everyone can get something out of. To me, that's one of the reasons I've always been impressed with a show like *The Simpsons,* for example. It has something to offer for kids, for adults, for teenagers—like, each person can get something completely different out of it. Which I think is sort of what makes ArtScroll so good is the fact that depending on your age, depending on your level

of affiliation, depending on how much knowledge you have, everyone can get something out of it. And I don't know that I can really say that about some of the other publication houses.[29]

By excavating and distributing a content to which access is normally gained only by entering the yeshiva and participating in its pedagogical methods, disciplinary practices, and hierarchies of value, ArtScroll thus aims to reach out to new audiences, extending the mobilizing horizon of Haredi intellectuals through the circulation of their texts. A once inwardly directed academic culture, isolated behind the walls of the Haredi yeshiva, is thereby transformed into a more portable one: an Orthodoxy that can be transplanted, and can flourish, in a variety of social contexts.[30] Mere access to an ArtScroll library "enables people to continue their program when they are out of the four walls of the study hall."[31] Simply following the instructions from an ArtScroll prayer book communicates the certainty of accuracy and authenticity of ritual performances, since each step has been scrutinized by Haredi rabbinic authorities. In the words of one enthusiast,

> ArtScroll gives you stuff that you wouldn't really know just from reading it unless you have the background for it, and even if you do have the background, you can slip up, I guess. And I'm sure that there are things that have slipped through with ArtScroll. But the chances are much less likely when you are dealing with—I don't know how many rabbis work on each book, I don't know. Like the Talmud. As far as I hear, it's about a dozen on each section. Well, that's pretty good numbers for me. Knowing that I have twelve rabbis teaching me in a very clearly laid out manner. It's comforting.[32]

But what, precisely, does it mean to be "comforted" by an ArtScroll book? What does it mean to be taught by twelve rabbis through the medium of a written text? I propose that it is not possible to answer these questions simply by referring to the fervor of the ArtScroll cadre's commitment to a Haredi form of Jewish Orthodoxy. Nor can we be fully satisfied by noting the degree to which they, or the elites of the yeshiva world from which they emanate, evince a command of the vast literatures concerning traditional forms of Jewish ritual and textual practice. Answers must also be sought by turning to the transformative powers announced in the advertisement quoted in the epigraph of this chapter: "maximum comprehension with minimum effort."

Some readers will immediately see the irony in such a promise, since "comprehension" has never been defined as a strict prerequisite for participation in Jewish ritual life, and the "minimization of effort" certainly does not sound like a "traditional" Jewish value.[33] Why, then, have the ArtScroll editors found it so useful to couch traditional texts in such an untraditional frame? To answer this question, we must first acknowledge that the ArtScroll cadre do not simply uphold established religious categories. Obliged to seek legitimacy and exercise authority in a modern field of cultural production, they participate in a far-reaching reconstruction of the very terms upon which they depend for distinction. In other words, what makes ArtScroll books so valuable, and so desirable, is also what marks their distance from the "traditional" forms of knowledge and learning they seek to instill in their readers. Consider, in this regard, the vocabulary chosen by one fan to describe ArtScroll's virtues:

> They make it basically like *Talmud for Dummies,* or *Praying for Dummies.* ArtScroll is kind of like the *For Dummies* series because it provides everything at a very basic level, but at the same time it really is not for dummies, because of everything it's throwing at you. I mean, it's a lot easier when it's laid out the way they do, but that doesn't mean in any way that they are going to shortchange you in what you're getting out of it. To a certain degree I guess some of their publications end up being a bit of a crutch for some people, but I don't think that—I mean, I suppose it might hinder somebody's ability to be able to learn something for themselves. But the end result with ArtScroll is that it's going to be much easier for them to learn the facts that they need in order to be more observant. It's just much easier to know exactly what you are doing when you are trying to keep a kosher kitchen, for example. You can read a book that breaks everything down and makes everything simple and clear, as opposed to something that just confuses you and leaves you wondering if everything is right at the end of the day.[34]

As suggested here, ArtScroll books participate in new processes of reshuffling the discursive and performative conditions that constituted religious authority in "traditional" Jewish contexts. From the perspective of many readers and users, ArtScroll marks the point of a shift in the balance of power between, on the one hand, locally situated teachers, legal interpreters, and ritual leaders and, on the other hand, the commanding voice of the text. Now it is the text alone that commands, in a voice that is simple, direct and clear. The solitary reader—unencumbered by the disciplining presence of teachers and other communal authority figures—has been afforded a new opportunity to engage in the acquisition of an "authentic" body of Jewish knowledge. "Rabbi ArtScroll" provides instructions so that other rabbis do not have to.[35] Moreover, unlike many other rabbis, Rabbi ArtScroll is remarkably adept at "breaking everything down" so that at the end of the day no one is left wondering whether "everything is right."

For some, Rabbi ArtScroll's voice is anodyne, a helpful and unwavering guide to the perplexed. For others, it is the shrill voice of demagoguery and intolerance of difference. And for others still, ArtScroll's characteristic tone is an object of humor. Consider, for instance, the case of the "ArtScroll chicken," a variant of the old joke, "Why did the chicken cross the road?," in which the author provides a rich parody of the punctilious style of religious instruction associated with ArtScroll books:

> Bend once when the chicken goes onto the road (bending first at the knees, bending fully as it takes its second step); bend again as it reaches the middle of the road (only a half bow); bend a third time as it nears the other side. If it gets across without being run over, say also a *she-hecheyanu* [a blessing for new and unusual experiences] (p. 358); unless the congregation is saying *brochos* [blessings] before and after the *shema* [the basic prayer in affirmation of the one God], in which case no interruption, even for a *brocha,* is permitted. No *brocha* is said on *yontef* [holy day], *rosh chodesh* [first day of the month] or during the entire month of *nissan* [March-April].[36]

These contrasting assessments, we shall see, strike at the heart of debates about Haredism as a mode of scripturalism—that is, debates about the manner and extent of the power of Haredi rabbinic authorities to overtake personal memories, local customs, and autonomous powers of reasoning through the promulgation of new modes of knowledge and practice learned "by the book."

In their defense, the ArtScroll editors insist that their books are simply a remedial technology. "We've always stressed the importance of having a teacher. You can't learn life from a book. Ideally, ArtScroll books shouldn't be stand-alone texts. They are only meant to be adjuncts to rabbis and teachers."[37] But where some see merely adjunction, others attribute a far more expansive role. In the words of its enthusiasts, ArtScroll's Siddur "takes the reader by the hand," it is so "full of information . . . it could almost replace my rabbi," and it will "end up being one of your best and most faithful companions in your attempt at leading an ordered and observant life. Once you've tried it, you'll have a hard time doing without."[38] Similarly, a New York-based Judaica bookseller observes, "it's like having a yeshiva in your own house."[39] Such attributions to the text—as surrogate rabbi and teacher, faithful companion, and holder of hands—are rooted in its unambiguous and explicit mode of address. As one reader puts it, "It basically gives you everything from the beginning without making you feel like something's wrong with you for needing it. It gives you the confidence to tackle situations you otherwise would be scared or apprehensive of, because you're, like, okay, I don't have to worry about not knowing when to stand, sit, when to do this or that, because it says it right there."[40] In other words, ArtScroll's "adjunctive" role is always more than merely supplementary. The activities of purchasing, reading, displaying, or otherwise making use of ArtScroll books point to a deeper process of redistribution of competencies and sources of legitimate authority among written texts, their authors, and their consumers. The succeeding chapters of this book explore how this process of redistribution unfolds, identifying its consequences for the public life of English-speaking diaspora Jews, and inferring some larger lessons with respect to the mediation of religious knowledge and authority in the early twenty-first century. But first, in the remainder of this introduction, a few words are in order to help situate the phenomenon under investigation in a broader social and historical context.

THE ARTSCROLL STORY

Mesorah Publications, popularly known as ArtScroll, was founded in 1976 by Rabbis Meir Zlotowitz and Nosson Scherman. It grew out of an earlier graphics design and print company, also named ArtScroll, which was known in the Brooklyn Orthodox community as a producer of bar mitzvah and wedding invitations and related material. From these modest beginnings, ArtScroll has grown into one of the largest, most financially successful, technically innovative, and culturally pervasive Judaica publishing houses in the English-speaking world.[41] It has well-established markets in the United States, Canada, the United Kingdom, Australia, and South Africa, as well as the Anglophone community in Israel, and it enjoys a growing presence in French-, Spanish-, and Russian-language Judaica markets in the former Soviet Union, France, Argentina, Mexico, and elsewhere.[42] ArtScroll furnishes this international market with a broad range of material of interest to Jewish readers, and especially to participants in the routines of

Jewish ritual life. Expanding at a rate of roughly fifty new titles per year,[43] their booklist encompasses a wide range of material: bilingual Bibles, liturgical and Talmudic texts, translations of rabbinic literature, and increasingly, a host of "non"-religious texts, such as popular history books, biographies and memoirs, youth literature, novels, pop psychology and self-help books, and curriculum materials for primary Jewish education. More recently, the publisher has expanded into other media forms, including audiocassettes, and has experimented with new forms of Web-based communication, such as e-commerce.

ArtScroll's success in the domain of Judaica publishing seems to have been assured from its very inception. Its first publication, *The Megillah: The Book of Esther* (published in 1976 as a memorial volume for a recently deceased friend of the editors), became an instant legend in Jewish book publishing. "Never before had a Judaica book of the Bible sold in excess of 30,000 copies in less than two months, certainly not in an industry that measured best-sellers in numbers like two or three thousand."[44] According to Rabbi Zlotowitz, "We never expected the tremendous response. Our original print run was 500 copies. By now [1995], we have ended up publishing over 50,000."[45] Starting in the mid-1980s, ArtScroll began to break out of its primary market—the Brooklyn-centered Orthodox community—to became a nationally recognized producer of Jewish texts, with numerous best-sellers under its belt. Its Chumash (Pentateuch) was met with such demand that over one hundred thousand copies were distributed in the first ten weeks following its December 1993 release.[46] A similar frenzy was generated leading up to the publication of the *ArtScroll Tanach* (Bible) in 1996.[47] By the late 1990s, it was beyond dispute that ArtScroll had secured a commanding presence in the Jewish book market, enjoying sales unrivaled by any other Orthodox Jewish publisher.[48] And with ArtScroll's growing brand-name recognition, and the publisher's continued commitment to innovations in Judaica publishing, there is little reason to assume that the future will bring any sudden reversals of fortune.

What, precisely, accounts for ArtScroll's business success, and what can this success tell us about the publisher's significance within contemporary Jewish public culture, or indeed within the more global field of print-mediated religious public spheres? Several factors should attract our attention. First, ArtScroll's seemingly unimpeded growth is related to the keen sense the publisher has evinced for capitalizing on specific gaps in the Jewish book market, especially for bilingual liturgical works and other canonical texts. Their prayer books, for instance, have been produced in various formats, including interlinear translations as well as transliterated versions, in different sizes, for daily or weekly usage, as well as slightly modified editions catering to specific congregational needs.[49] This has helped the publisher to consolidate a range of potential customers and even to cultivate a market of clients engaged in repetitive consumption, as it becomes feasible to own different formats of the same book for different occasions and settings.[50] Another factor that explains ArtScroll's prominence is its reputation as a publisher willing and able to embark on large-scale projects that have had little precedent (and not much success) among other English-language Judaica publishers, such as the redaction and commentary on the Babylonian Talmud, a massive project that involved a remarkable array of translators and scholars from both within and outside the Haredi world and has won approval from a broad spectrum of Jewish scholars and intellectuals (a topic to which I shall return in Chapter 1). A third noteworthy strategy Mesorah Publications has deployed to strengthen its position in the Jewish book market is the division of its booklist into distinct genres appearing under different imprimaturs. Thus the name ArtScroll increasingly is associated with "religious" books in the narrow sense of Bibles, prayer books, translations of rabbinic classics, and modern commentaries. Meanwhile, other works published under the Mesorah umbrella are increasingly appearing under another imprimatur, Shaar Press, which is focused mainly on the publication of novels and historical works, as well as on joint publishing ventures with Orthodox organizations such as the National Council of Synagogue Youth. This strategy enables Mesorah, the parent company, to expand its offerings into new generic domains while at the same time preserving the integrity of the original ArtScroll brand name, connoting a serious engagement with Jewish classics.

But ArtScroll's success is not simply a product of their energy for ambitious editorial and translation projects and their marketing savvy. It also rests on the distinctive organizational features the publisher embraces. Many have noted that ArtScroll "is different from other Jewish publishers not only in the sophistication of its book packaging, but also in the professionalism of its marketing and distribution."[51] This "professionalism" is evident in ArtScroll's adherence to a highly advanced, vertically integrated, yet flexible production model, conforming to the most advanced financial, organizational, and industrial trends in the book-publishing business. They do almost everything "in house": from conception to translation, editing, layout, market research, advertising and promotion, distribution, and Web site management. They developed their own typesetting software to meet their particular needs working with bilingual texts with two different scripts (currently managed by their own software division, Compuscribe). They founded and manage the operation of Sefercraft, the only remaining full-service bindery in the entire New York area producing both hardcover and paperback lines of superior quality.[52] Starting in the early 1980s, they developed their own international network of independent distributors. And they rely upon an extensive informal network of yeshiva students, independent scholars, authors, freelance translators, and others within the Haredi community, who are tied together by bonds of trust, sacrifice, and ideological commitment, making it exceedingly difficult to locate the dividing lines between capital and labor that elsewhere define the book-publishing industry. This sense of communal participation in a common goal to produce ArtScroll books affords the publisher considerable flexibility in its financial planning, operational management, and distribution strategies.[53] The freedom to embark upon publishing initiatives without immediate expectations of financial reward is further underscored by the legal status of ArtScroll's parent organization, the Mesorah Heritage Foundation, which has been incorporated in the United States as a nonprofit organization.[54] This arrangement helps to explain how, for instance, ArtScroll has been able to sustain a long-term production cycle of Talmud translations, selling each volume at a significant loss (so the publisher reports), due to the enormous time and energy invested in the project.[55] All these organizational features distinguish ArtScroll from many other publishers, which either are directly profit driven or do not have at their disposal a similarly broad range of intellectual, financial, and material resources.

RELIGION IN PRINT

ArtScroll's rapid expansion within the Jewish book market is also redolent of a broader process of evolution in the global book-publishing industry. The success of this publisher rests on strategies familiar to many publishing houses for accumulating financial as well as symbolic rewards within the existing organizational frameworks for the production and distribution of print commodities. Such strategies reflect the peculiarities of the book-publishing industry, which, in contrast to many other industries and commodity markets, is distinguished, on the one hand, by its enthusiasm for technological innovation and market rationalization and, on the other hand, by its retention of craftlike procedures and long-standing standards of cultural valuation. This tension between innovation and tradition is especially pronounced in the case of religious publishing, one of the most venerated but also one of the most restlessly innovative sectors of the book industry. To clarify how ArtScroll fits into this evolving landscape, it is therefore helpful to devote a few words to the larger field of religious publishing, particularly the history of production and circulation of what we recognize today as "religious" books.[56]

One can of course place religious texts within the *longue durée* of sedimented patterns of textualization, stretching back to antiquity. The production, dissemination, and reception of written texts is indeed an ancient business, and it is hardly incidental that some of the oldest extant examples of writing are in fact works of a "religious" nature, including divinatory texts, ritual instructions, cosmological accounts, myths, legal codes, and other writings inscribed onto stone, clay tablets, tortoise shells, bamboo, leather, or papyrus. Long before the arrival of the printing press, the writing, collection, distribution, storage, and authorized use of texts encompassed a vast arena of activity dominated by religious hierocracies, with their armies of scribes, librarians, scholars, teachers, preachers, and other agents of mediation.[57] But such a long view risks obfuscating the key discontinuities that distinguish present-day religious books from their ancient predecessors. For instance, the invention of movable-type printing, credited to Johannes Gutenberg in mid-fifteenth-century Germany, is often said to have signaled a radical revolution in textual production, according to which increasingly large-scale populations were henceforth defined in and through the incorporation of printed works into their everyday lives.[58] From this perspective, it is important to think of ArtScroll as a producer, not of religious texts per se, but, more precisely, of religious *print matter*.

This is not the place to recount the long and complex history—and considerable debate—surrounding Gutenberg's press and the legacy of the European print revolution of the fifteenth and sixteenth centuries (if indeed it is reasonable to invoke the term *revolution* in this context). But it is nonetheless impossible to ignore the pioneering efforts of early modern religious intellectuals to avail themselves of the new medium, most famously in the case of Martin Luther, Bible translator, pamphleteer, and foremost architect of the Protestant Reformation.[59] Whether for good or ill, Luther provided the prototype for a new form of religious agency, based on relationships being forged between religious intellectuals and printer's shops, stationers, and colporteurs, and their common reliance upon the logics of standardization and public address that inhered in the print medium itself. Through the circulation of printed works, a distinct new arena of possibility was opened up for religious agents to debate opponents, win converts, or consecrate their own legitimacy and authority by claiming to speak in the name of the masses. The development of print markets thus seemed to carry with it the promise of new circulations of knowledge and new ways to imagine community, aligned with the emerging conditions and performative imperatives to "reach the people" through the mechanical reproduction of identical texts and through the networking of individual readers located in an increasingly impersonal public sphere.[60] Just as early modern Christians became enveloped in this universe of print, so too were their Jewish neighbors indelibly transformed by their encounter with the technology, as is evident from the development of a thriving, international Jewish publishing industry—in Rome, Venice, Frankfurt, Amsterdam, Constantinople, and eventually other cities across Europe and the Mediterranean world—catering to rapidly growing, transnational markets of Jewish readers with a seemingly insatiable appetite for works of liturgy, scholarship, law, history, medicine, and other, less lofty topics.[61]

The invention of movable type marks one threshold dividing the modern religious book from its predecessors; the industrialization of print marks another. Indeed, although the advent of the printing press is often hailed as one of the great revolutions of early modern European society, we should not forget that until the nineteenth century print commodities were still based on an artisanal mode of production, organized around the labor of individual master printers, their trusted assistants, and their limited distribution networks of shopkeepers and colporteurs. Within the terms of this craft industry, publishing was largely an activity reserved for learned gentlemen engaged in the transference of symbolic property from authors to readers, and the circulation of printed texts indexed a collocation of private subjects, united by the privilege of their class standing and by their shared commitment to (often overtly masculine) codes for defining literary authority.[62] Starting in the early nineteenth century, however, a series of technological revolutions in book production was sparked by the invention of new techniques for making inexpensive wood-pulp paper, steam power, cylinder presses, and eventually the development of cost-effective stereotypography, as well as the introduction of increasingly efficient and reliable systems of transportation and marketing of print commodities.[63] By the end of the century, the book trade had been transformed by many of the same forces that had been visited on other sectors of advancing industrial economies, driving the expansion of disposable incomes as well as cultivating new techniques of advertising and marketing to feed the emerging societies of consumption. In this context, the ascendancy of the "industrial book"—the mechanically manufactured, casebound product of a corporate publishing entity—represented more than just the extension of written texts to new classes of readers. It also repositioned the markers for "appropriate reading," as printed works began to move beyond their traditional locations of schools or houses of prayer into the public spaces of factories, railway cars, ships, and town squares, and even onto the parlor bookshelf as a centerpiece of bourgeois domestic life.[64] Through their material presence in these diverse social scenes, print commodities could now embody the ideals of religious edification as well as personal ownership and domestic display, reflective of the forces that were redefining print-mediated publicity along the axis of an expanding consumer culture. These rapidly evolving modes of circulation allowed for new possibilities of translation, contact, and exchange, and thereby a repositioning of the lines that both divided and connected "elite" and "popular" culture, the private and the public, the local and the distant, and, for that matter, the imperial metropolis and its colonial periphery.[65]

The expanding scale of production and the changing locations and uses of print commodities in the nineteenth century serve as a sharp reminder that there is no simple continuity between contemporary publishing houses and their fifteenth-century forebears. Indeed, the seeds of change that were planted in the nineteenth century gave rise to a dynamic cultural industry that has shown little sign of withering in the present. Since the twentieth century, and especially since the 1970s, industrial modes of production and dissemination of printed texts have continued to evolve, propelled by a synergy of organizational, technological, financial, and legal forces. These include the intervention of computer technologies at all stages of the writing, production, and marketing processes; the adoption of decentralized, flexible, "just-in-time" production techniques (e.g., the implementation of smaller, more rationalized print runs that respond more directly to demands at the retail level, thereby reducing waste and storage costs); and shifts in the regulatory regimes that govern book production (including international copyright law).[66] In all these respects, ArtScroll typifies a trend that has permitted smaller-scale publishing houses to secure new market niches and to proliferate in an environment of high risk and high reward by situating themselves between the requirements and restraints of commerce and the responsibilities and obligations associated with their guardianship of symbolic capital.

Nowhere are these trends more pronounced, one might argue, than in the field of religious publishing, an area of the book market that has been experiencing considerable diversification and growth in recent years, both within and outside the English-speaking world.[67] Scholars look back to the nineteenth century as a golden age of religious publishing: a time marked by gargantuan press runs of Bibles, tracts, catechisms, hymnals, sermons, and devotional classics, produced by groups such as the American and British Bible and Tract Societies and distributed through globally resonant networks of Christian evangelists and missionaries.[68] But it is hard to avoid the impression that religious publishing today marks another "golden age." Commensurate with the proliferation of religious revivals in the post-World War II period, and the growing capacity of religious consumers to exercise demand for commodities that will meet their ideological and affective expectations and needs, the market for religious print has greatly expanded its range and scope, cementing conditions that have allowed numerous presses—especially small-scale operations and even desktop publishers—to enter into the fray. These producers cater to increasing numbers of evangelical Christians in the United States; Pentecostals in Brazil; Islamic pietists in Egypt, Pakistan, and Indonesia; Hindu nationalists in India; and many others who wish to deepen their understanding, reinforce their commitments, and ignite their imaginations through the consumption of religious print matter.[69] Over the past half century, the United States alone has seen an exponential growth rate of Christian Bibles, recently estimated at over seven thousand different editions, the majority of which constitute an almost completely uncharted territory for the scholarly eye.[70] And beyond such canonical works, markets catering to different faith groups have been shaped by a veritable explosion of publication of legal codices, manuals, and catechisms, as well as a vast array of "substitute products," parasitic upon the genres of writing found in the mainstream market but catering to the needs and sensibilities of religious readers, such as "religious" thrillers, self-help books, and graphic novels. Placed within this comparative context, ArtScroll's successes can be understood as part of a broader shift that has consolidated the position of religious publishing within the global print market and has accorded new prominence to religious print commodities in various arenas of public and private life.

Unfortunately, this dynamic field of religious publishing has failed to attract the sustained attention of many media scholars, journalists, and other observers of contemporary print culture, for whom religious works are presumed (quite groundlessly) to represent an isolated region of the global publishing domain and therefore to be of marginal social significance. One possible reason for this lacuna is that contemporary religious publishing flies in the face of a still-pervasive secularist myth that the power of print to express the will of sovereign peoples, or to summon them to partake in acts of collective deliberation in the court of public reason, contributes to a disintegration of religion as a source of authority and legitimate knowledge in the modern era. The continued existence and indeed the steady expansion of religious print in the current historical moment suggest the need for a radical revision of such accounts of the history of modern publicness and of the role of the print medium within that history. Simply stated, it is not tenable to presume that the spread of journalism, scientific knowledge, "highbrow" literature, and related print-mediated resources somehow has a direct, causal relation to the creation of new arenas for autonomous decision making and collective opinion making, and consequently to the transcendence of clerical and feudal modes of cultural and political authority, as famously postulated by Jürgen Habermas in his account of the birth of "the modern public sphere."[71] There is nothing inherent in the technology or institutional organization of the print medium that leads to a dispelling of religious authority or the fragmentation of religious sources of knowledge or identity. Nor can we suppose that the apparent recrudescence of politicized religious movements and social forms in the current conjuncture somehow signals the end of print culture's (undelivered) promises for a secular modern order. An equally pervasive danger here is to impute direct causal relationships between the expansion of religious print, claims about textual scripturalism, and their social effects among "gullible" populations, eager to find an anchor in a meaningless world and, by that token, susceptible to the demagoguery of "fundamentalist" leaders. As we shall see in due course, there are other ways to construe the public culture of print in modernity and particularly the cultural, intellectual, and social character of religious print markets. The case of ArtScroll is especially instructive in this regard.

To appreciate the place of religious print at the current historical juncture, we must therefore be prepared to dispense with some commonly held assumptions about the secular and secularizing character of textually mediated, modern public spheres. At the same time, we must acknowledge that it is not possible to fully explain the shifting locus of religious printed works in the context of the current culture of consumption, or within the symbolic economy that circumscribes an expanding religious readership, simply by referring to innovations in the financial, technical, and organizational structures governing textual production and dissemination. ArtScroll's market successes are rooted just as much in patterns of consumption and modes of cultural authority that define a specifically *Jewish* appetite for print commodities and in the great importance attached to owning, reading, or simply being familiar with Jewish texts. In other words, if we wish to understand the significance of a publisher like ArtScroll, we must also know something about the particular religious community to which its books are directed and the specific forms of symbolic capital that circulate within this cultural field.

PEOPLE OF THE BOOK: A REEXAMINATION OF TEXT-CENTRISM AND RELIGIOUS AUTHORITY

At the risk of perpetuating a stereotype about Jews and print culture, one could explain the demand for ArtScroll books as the "natural" product of an age-old disposition to the written word and a deeply pervasive cultural bias. After all, Jews, the quintessential "people of the book" *('am ha-Sefer),* are said to enjoy a uniquely intimate relationship with the practices of writing, reading, and interpreting texts, having elevated the status of the book over all other means of communication with the divine. In the rabbinic tradition, the Torah is conceived as the ground, not just for Jewish religious knowledge and practice, but also for the entire order of nature and the cosmos. According to one midrash (commentary), even God Himself had to consult the Torah before creating the universe.[72] For practicing Jews, the Torah represents the definitive record of God's covenant with the Jewish nation. Its holy status requires that this text be transcribed, stored, displayed, and, if need be, destroyed, according to specific regulations and that it be read aloud at prescribed times, according to elaborate rules of biblical prosody. On these terms, Judaism can be distinguished from other traditions where religious authority is defined in terms of a monopoly over the performance of public rituals or where access to the knowledge inscribed in sacred texts is restricted to priestly cadres. Instead, the Jewish tradition is circumscribed within a "text-centered community," defined by a "shared commitment to certain texts and their role in shaping many aspects of Jewish life and endowing the tradition with coherence."[73]

One of the inevitable consequences of Jewish text-centrism is that the possession of *interpretive expertise* in the reading of canonical texts (the Torah, the Mishnah, the Talmud, etc.) becomes closely tied to various forms of cultural and political authority within Jewish communal life. Throughout the long course of Jewish history, especially in the contexts of diaspora, mastery of the canon has almost always been regarded as a key prerequisite for the legitimate exercise of authority within a broad social arena: performative utterances concerning public order (physical comportment, dress, daily habits, etc.); the articulation of moral values; acts of censorship; the establishment (or revision) of educational curricula; the accumulation of personal prestige; and so on. This confers on scholars, rather than priests, prophets, or other kinds of religious leaders, a distinct advantage in the production of religious and cultural authority. After all, scholars are the ones who most readily possess textual mastery and familiarity with the canonized methods of interpretation, and they enjoy a virtual monopoly over the means of innovating new interpretations of this same canon (within the boundaries of "legitimate" interpretation, as defined by the scholarly community itself).[74]

The monopolistic concentration of authoritative discourse in the hands of scholars is greatly facilitated by the high value accorded within Judaism to *Talmud Torah* (the study of canonical texts). In Jewish society, the ability to recite and, even more importantly, to study canonical texts has been established, not just as the basis for common membership, but also as a foremost ideal in its own right, and therefore as a key marker of social distinction. In contemporary Orthodox and Haredi communities, the ideal of *Talmud Torah* plays an important role in the organization of a variety of educational and religious-legal institutions.[75] It is also deeply embedded in the everyday practices, habits, and rhythms that constitute these communities' modes of social reproduction and public legitimation. Moreover, as some have described it, contemporary Orthodoxy evinces a growing reliance upon texts over all other forms of knowledge, such as those learned from lived experience or passed down orally from parents, friends, teachers, and neighbors.[76] In a process that has its roots in the composition of medieval Jewish codices (such as Maimonides' Mishneh Torah, written in the twelfth century, or Joseph Karo's Shulhan Arukh, from the sixteenth century), but that was greatly popularized through mass distribution of popular manuals in the nineteenth century, Orthodox Jews have increasingly turned to written texts that explicate and theoretically legitimate all forms of acceptable and unacceptable behavior, thereby enclosing themselves within communities of practice defined by (increasingly) rigid codes of conduct. The term *scripturalism,* I have already suggested, provides many observers with a convenient (although, as we shall see, ultimately a dissatisfying) theoretical account of the great popularity of instruction manuals among certain sectors of the Jewish Orthodox population, as well as the growing premium that Orthodox Jews place on textual mastery—the acquisition of basic literacy and interpretive insight into Jewish canonical texts, the performative demands of their public recitation, and their study in centers of Jewish education—for Jewish communal life in general.

The practices and ideological investments that constitute Jewish text-centrism—and in particular the rise of so-called scripturalism in the modern era—are among the key forces that have propelled institutions like ArtScroll to the forefront of the Jewish imaginary. It would therefore seem impossible to try to account for the achievements of this publisher without referring to the central (and arguably, increasingly centralizing) status of the text within Jewish culture and society. But how, precisely, ought we to relate ArtScroll's current market success to the long-standing commitment within Jewish communities to canonical works and the associated practices of textual recitation and interpretation? Is it simply a matter of demographic expansion or an increase in disposable incomes among Jewish consumers? Or is ArtScroll the index of a cultural revolution that has seen a growing number of Jews renew or deepen their commitment to Jewish practice and their desire for greater understanding of the Jewish tradition? Is ArtScroll's success commensurate with a victory of Orthodoxy—and particularly of Haredism—over other forms of institutionalized Jewish expression, such as Conservative or Reform Judaism? Is the practice of "brand switching" to ArtScroll the sign of a growing dissatisfaction with the intellectual orientations and practical protocols embedded in the texts of other, more "liberal" Jewish movements? Is it a sign of an impending hegemonic victory of Haredism in the contemporary Jewish imaginary? Or is the ArtScroll revolution a story about the "dumbing down" of Jewish intellectual culture through the proliferation of "user-friendly" formats that risk undermining the very principles that the ArtScroll cadre claim they wish to promote?

To answer these questions, it will be necessary to first dispense with some easy assumptions regarding the supposedly timeless quality of Jewish engagements with texts, religious or otherwise. Indeed, however much the ArtScroll phenomenon invokes the presence of an ancient and venerable relationship between Jews and their books, the institutional, technological, economic, and cultural context is distinctly modern, circumscribed in particular by the history of print and its social logic. ArtScroll must be analyzed within the context of an account of the performative protocols, the legitimating structures, the modes of social address, and the material forces of consumerism, domestication, and communal affiliation that constitute modern religious, print-mediated public spheres. Consequently, in the coming pages, much of our attention will be devoted to the ways ArtScroll authors and publics are co-constituted as horizons of intellectual, cultural, and social mobilization and as arenas of negotiation, improvisation, and interpretive tension.[77]

This contextualizing work is needed to broach some of the key controversies surrounding ArtScroll books and the complex relations of collaboration, competition, and struggle among their various producers, consumers, and critics. Such an analysis will require, however, that we move beyond a more familiar approach to texts, not least sacred texts, as a mere surface of signs, pointing outwards to a universe of intertextual relations. As I shall argue in greater detail in Chapter 4, texts encompass far more than their discursive content; they also exist as the products of varying artisanal and industrial processes, and as material artifacts they carry a semiotic weight that cannot be reduced to the linguistic level. The existence of these multiple levels of meaning and coordinated interaction depends upon, and manifests, a complex constellation of embodied social relationships, technical processes, financial infrastructures, legal frameworks, spatial arrangements, and regimes of circulation.

Among other things, this approach to the social life of texts will lead us to a reevaluation of the Geertzian model of scripturalism. Despite its enormous value for having identified the existence of a "controlling" power enjoyed by written texts in a range of ritual and everyday life contexts, Geertz's notion of scripturalism ultimately fails to account rigorously for the ways such texts actually function in the media-rich contexts of contemporary social life. The term *scripturalism* thus risks obscuring more than it reveals about the processes of distribution and redistribution of competencies, knowledges, and protocols of conduct among authors, readers, consumers, book owners, and, of course, the books themselves, as they have been articulated through evolving technologies and institutional frameworks for the production, dissemination, and reception of print matter. *Orthodox by Design* follows the Geertzian model in treating "the written word" as a strategically decisive source of knowledge and source of religious authority. But, in departure from Geertz, this study shall examine more narrowly how written texts, as bodies of discourse as well as material artifacts, occupy a place in the evolving relationship between Haredi intellectuals and the broader public culture of English-speaking Jews. Chapters 1 and 2 are devoted to painting a picture of the social world in which ArtScroll serves as a metonym for the expanding presence and growing influence of Haredi Orthodox Judaism. Chapters 3 and 4 turn more closely to ArtScroll books themselves, examining the discursive and material agencies that constitute their putatively scripturalist content and functions. Chapter 3 looks at ArtScroll prayer books, cookbooks, and self-help books as key instances of Haredi scripturalism, not least because these particular genres are geared to the performance of both everyday and ritual behaviors—providing, in other words, the "scripts" whereby scripturalism is supposedly activated in the lives of ArtScroll readers. Chapter 4 moves beyond the surface of ArtScroll texts to examine the material agency of typeface and layout, graphic designs, illustrations, book bindings, and complementary technologies relating to the transportation, storage, or use of ArtScroll books, thereby identifying the ways Haredi scripturalism is embedded in the material culture of the books themselves and in the protocols for interaction with these objects. The concluding chapter of this book offers some final reflections on ArtScroll's scripturalism from the perspective of a repositioning of the printed word in our current, so-called digital age. Taken together, these lines of analysis suggest new ways of appreciating how and why ArtScroll books attain their "authentic" and "authoritative" status and therefore their influential role within the contemporary imaginary of English-speaking diaspora Jews, even as they are put to use in diverse ways not necessarily intended by the publisher.

In sum, without resorting to facile oppositions of style and function, form and content, or medium and message, this book argues that the so-called fundamentalist religious authority exercised in and through ArtScroll books needs to be understood as a process that unfolds "by design": that is, as something that gets worked out *both* on a discursive plane of communication *and* at the level of interaction with the material signs of this "authenticity."[78] Rather than treating fundamentalism as simply a matter of ideological indoctrination or directly coerced behavior, *Orthodox by Design* proposes a different approach to the study of religious authority, namely to trace how it is exercised and how it is transformed through the multilayered tissues of affect, technology, and institutionally coordinated action that are redefining the place of media in the world today.

ONE

Authoritative and Accessible

THE YEAR 2005 WAS A big one for ArtScroll. It marked the completion of the seventy-third and final volume of their *Talmud Bavli: The Schottenstein Edition,* a massive work of thirty-five thousand pages, involving over eighty rabbinic scholars for more than fifteen years, at a blistering production rate of one volume every nine weeks.[1] No other publication has more definitively signaled ArtScroll's ascent in the publishing world. Several other ArtScroll books have had a dramatic impact on the English-language Jewish public sphere, such as *The Complete ArtScroll Siddur* (their basic prayer book) and even their best-selling cookbook, *Kosher by Design.*[2] But ArtScroll's Talmud is unique in terms of the intellectual, symbolic, and financial resources at stake for a project of this magnitude, as well as its impact on the relationship of the publisher with its patrons, customers, critics, and even competing publishers.[3]

Let us recall here the status of the Babylonian Talmud as arguably the central text of Rabbinic Judaism. It consists of the written record of what is known in Jewish tradition as the *Torah she be'al peh* (the Oral Law), originally transmitted to Moses on Mt. Sinai alongside the *Torah she bi khtav* (the Written Torah, i.e., the Hebrew Bible), and systematized by a long tradition of authoritative commentators.[4] More than any other text in the Jewish tradition, it symbolizes the shift in ancient Israelite religion from a temple cult organized around sacrificial practices to the religion of a "people of the book," living in diaspora, in the aftermath of the destruction of the Temple at Jerusalem. Over the ensuing centuries, the Talmud has represented the most important source for adjudication within halakhah (Jewish law), while also providing an unparalleled treasure house of legends and anecdotes, philosophical and moral reflections, and historical and scientific observations that mediate the interpretive possibilities of the Torah itself. Mastery over this famously difficult text, written in *leshon hakodesh* (the "holy tongue," a mixture of Aramaic and Hebrew), and laid out on the page in a complex pattern of intertexts, has also provided a key source of symbolic and social distinction throughout the long history of diaspora Jewish communities, dividing an elite of male scholars who are able to "talk in Talmud" from the "lesser world" of women and the ignorant.

ArtScroll is not the first publisher to have embarked upon a translation of this central work in the Jewish canon.[5] But theirs is distinguished as the most thorough and elaborate edition of the Talmud ever produced in the English language, and it is already the most successful. This success is evident from the impressive readership the *Schottenstein Talmud* commands, as measured in the brisk sales of individual volumes, and in the development of a market for entire seventy-three-volume sets.[6] The *Schottenstein Talmud* is also the only English edition to have received the approval of prominent scholars and rabbinic authorities from across the entire Orthodox world, who all praise the ArtScroll text as a remarkable feat of scholarly maturity and exegetical clarity.[7] Its completion thus represents a key moment in the history of this publisher within the larger circulations of knowledge, capital, symbolic power, and religious authority that define the Jewish public sphere.

The completion of the *Schottenstein Talmud* also provides a useful occasion to take stock of a deeper logic that structures ArtScroll's ongoing effort to present simultaneously "authoritative" and "accessible" Jewish books. As I have already suggested in the Introduction, ArtScroll tells a story of how a specific group of intellectuals and cultural producers, embodied in the institutional form of a publishing house, engages in the business of addressing both insiders and outsiders through the medium of books written in the holy tongue and in the vernacular. This effort involves a complex negotiation between the publisher and its imagined public, defined by competing pressures of autonomy and control, custom and innovation, ignorance and erudition, and sacred duty and economic interest. In turn, the ArtScroll story sheds light on the larger intellectual, cultural, and social situation in which Haredi Judaism finds itself today. Located in a public realm defined by increasing diversification of affiliations, cultural patterns, social locations, competencies, and degrees of commitment and interest, Haredim are called upon (and call upon themselves) to posit, and defend, their claim over Jewish tradition. But their efforts invariably transform that tradition, among other things by *redesigning* the corpus of Jewish texts that most "authentically" communicates its meaning. The aim of this chapter is to show how this paradoxical logic of authority and accessibility informs ArtScroll's project, locating the publisher within the intellectual, cultural, and economic ties between Haredi society and the media-rich public culture of English-speaking Jewry.

The powerful, competing pressures to be both authoritative and accessible permeate the entire ArtScroll enterprise, shaping the terms on which the publisher defines itself and addresses others. We can even find them at work in seemingly minor terminological decisions, such as ArtScroll's description of its edition as an "elucidation" of the Talmud rather than a translation. On the one hand, this choice of terms is clearly meant to appease an audience of Orthodox scholars in an intellectual climate that has traditionally been characterized by suspicion of, if not outright hostility toward, translation of the Talmud into the vernacular.[8] On the other hand, ArtScroll's "elucidation" is designed to reach a much larger constituency of readers, from the novice to the most advanced student. In a refrain that has become familiar for the publisher in its publication of religious texts, Rabbi Scherman suggests that the Talmud "really has been a closed book to the vast majority of English-speaking Jews. The idea [behind the *Schottenstein Talmud*] was to create a volume that would elucidate it, make it comprehensible."[9] At the same time, the promise of English to expand the Talmud's readership is also a dangerous index of unauthorized use and intellectual corruption—a concern that further underscores the need for proper training and thorough explanation, not mere translation. As Rabbis Scherman and Zlotowitz elaborate in their preface to *Tractate Makkos,* the very first Talmud volume they published in 1990,

> It is not the purpose of this edition of the Talmud to provide a substitute for the original text or a detour around the classic manner of study. Its purpose is to help the student understand the Gemara [Talmud] itself and improve his ability to learn from the original, preferably under the guidance of a rebbe. The Talmud must be *learned* and not merely read. As clear as we believe the English elucidation to be, thanks to the dedicated work of an exceptional team of Torah scholars, the reader must contribute to the process by himself to think, analyze, and thus to understand.[10]

This cautious description of ArtScroll's Talmud as a "helper" to, but not a substitute for, "real" study (preferably under the watchful eye of a reputable Haredi authority figure) reveals how delicately the publisher is poised in its efforts to promulgate, and to publicly legitimate, new renditions of the Jewish canon in vernacular form. In a press interview around the time of the launching of the final volume of the *Schottenstein Talmud,* Rabbi Scherman admonished prospective readers: "Using the Schottenstein Edition isn't easy—you still have to think. Anyone who reads it will see there is room for further inquiry and discussion. If you pick up a popular magazine which gives you a ten-to-twelve page overview of a particular topic, would any serious person go away saying they're an expert because they've read ten pages in *Reader's Digest?*"[11] One might be tempted to respond to Rabbi Scherman that, just as *Reader's Digest* is a poor substitute for "real" literature, so too might the Schottenstein elucidation serve little purpose other than to comfort a feeble and lazy readership. But that would ignore the actual work performed by such texts: to both vulgarize and enlighten. So designed, they empower readers to negotiate their own paths through the hierarchy of discursive and linguistic registers that demarcate "high" and "low" literary forms. Much like *Reader's Digest,* the *Schottenstein Talmud* is caught up within the twin forces of authorization and popularization that shape all pedagogical literatures. To get a sense of the complexity, the fragility, and also the productive capacities of such work, let us consider four moments that marked the conclusion of ArtScroll's Talmud project and its arrival on the public stage.

FOUR SCENES OF ARRIVAL

At the Library of Congress

The first event occurred on February 9, 2005, when the Mesorah Heritage Foundation (the agency responsible for funding and overseeing the Talmud project) held a special dedication ceremony in the foyer of the Library of Congress in Washington, D.C. Among those in attendance were over twenty senior American politicians, including Senators Frank Lautenberg (D-NJ), Joe Lieberman (D-CT), Hilary Clinton (D-NY), and Sam Brownback (R-KS), Congress Representatives Steny Hoyer (D-MD), Shelly Berkley (D-NV), Eric Cantor (R-VA), and Ralph Regula (D-OH), and an array of journalists from prominent publications, such as the *New York Times.* ArtScroll's ability to muster such an audience says a great deal about the extensive networks of influence that provide the American Orthodox Jewish community with ready access to highly placed cultural, political, and administrative elites. Of equal interest here are the symbolic stakes that ArtScroll has managed to mark in the very act of presenting its Talmud edition to the Library of Congress. In his dedication speech before the assembled lawmakers, library patrons, and distinguished guests, Rabbi Scherman underscored this symbolic victory:

> My friends, this is the most historic day in the Library of Congress since the year 1800. Now if you think that's presumptuous of me, let me explain what I mean. The library was founded in the year 1800, and the collection was started with a gift of two thousand books by Thomas Jefferson. One of those books was a Latin translation of Tractate Bava Kama in the Babylonian Talmud. It is still here some place in the caverns of the library, and on page 140, you will find the initials "T.J.": Thomas Jefferson. And now, after more than 200 years, that edition, that Latin edition of the Bava Kama, is being joined by a full edition of the Talmud in *our* language. And it's an *American* contribution. And it's no exaggeration to say that [in] 350 years of Jews in America, in this blessed country, there has not yet been a literary, religious, cultural publishing effort of this magnitude. It's an astounding effort. Fifteen years of scores of world-class scholars working literally day and night. . . . And tonight we have the great honor to present the complete *Schottenstein Talmud,* this elucidation of the Babylonian Talmud, to the Library of Congress. This library is one of the great gifts of the United States of America. Our culture, our knowledge, our aspirations for the future, are all housed in these magnificent buildings. And now, the complete Talmud, the *Schottenstein Edition of the Talmud,* will take its place with Thomas Jefferson's single Latin volume of Tractate Bava Kama.[12]

The recipient of ArtScroll's gift, Dr. James Hadley Billington, the Librarian of Congress, echoed Rabbi Scherman's characterization of the historical significance of this occasion in his own speech:

> As a lover of books, and with my special responsibilities for this collection, I'm especially pleased to . . . celebrate the completion of this monumental Schottenstein edition of the Talmud, and its donation to the library. . . . The *Schottenstein Talmud* is an example of the deeply sympathetic and intensely creative relationship between America in general and its Jewish community in particular. It is sure to become a classic, and it will join other editions of the Talmud in the library's extraordinary

Hebrew book collections. Scholars can now consult all the great editions of the Talmud, from Bomberg's groundbreaking edition produced in Venice in the first quarter of the sixteenth century, to the late nineteenth-century Vilna edition, upon which the Schottenstein edition is based. So, with this new edition, scholars will now have a remarkable tool with which to understand the deeper meaning of the text, and their continuous resonance for all who value the life of spirit, the world of learning, and the extraordinary record of the people of the book. And for the gift of these precious books to our collection, I give you the sincere thanks, not only of the Library of Congress, but of all lovers of books, and lovers of the deep values that underlie our entire civilization.[13]

What is the significance of this dedication ceremony? Through the staging of this event, ArtScroll presents itself as a bridge between the inner world of Jewish scholarship and the outer world of American intellectual and political life. This bridge is paved with ArtScroll's monopolistic claims over the entire history of the Jewish presence in America, cast here as a history of intellectual contributions consummating in the production of the *Schottenstein Talmud* itself. Rabbi Scherman and Dr. Billington concur in their description of the arrival of ArtScroll's Talmud as the "completion" of a collection first begun by the founding father Thomas Jefferson. In turn, the production, circulation, and preservation of books synecdochally references the collaborative and mutually enriching relationships of Jews and non-Jews, dating back to the foundational moment when Jefferson saw fit to add a Talmud volume to his personal library. In this account, ArtScroll is rhetorically sutured into the fabric of national history and, more precisely, into the history of the American republic's self-appointed *mission civilisatrice* to gather all the world's knowledge and to make it available in the world's most magnificent library. As the dedication speeches make clear, the *Schottenstein Talmud* has now been positioned as a decisive contribution to "our culture" and "our knowledge." Its gift to the library cements the "deep values that underlie our entire civilization." At stake in this first scene of the *Schottenstein Talmud*'s arrival, then, is ArtScroll's status as a contributor to the very order of the "civilized world." The narrative of divine election, of the capacity of a specifically Haredi form of Jewish scholarship to serve as a "light onto the nations," is enacted here through the idiom of American nationalism, through the authorizing power of the library's acquisition practices, and through the presentation of English as the gateway to a truly universal readership.

A second noteworthy event occurred a couple weeks later, on March 1, 2005. In close proximity with the release of the final volume of the *Schottenstein Talmud,* there was a massive public rally of Orthodox Jews: the Siyum haShas (Talmud completion ceremony) that marked the conclusion of the eleventh cycle of Daf Yomi, a popular movement of both religious professionals and laypersons engaged in regular Talmud study. On the night in question, an estimated 120,000 celebrants attended events held simultaneously at Madison Square Gardens in New York City, at the Walt Disney Concert Hall in Los Angeles, at the Yad Eliyahu Stadium in Tel Aviv, at the Binyanei ha-Umah Convention Center in Jerusalem, and at the Ricoh Centre in Toronto, as well as gatherings at over seventy other cities around the world, in order to watch simulcast presentations via satellite television feeds.[14] One of the most dramatic public events in the history of Orthodox Jewry, the eleventh Siyum haShas epitomized the growing strength and confidence of the Haredi movement, expressed here in terms of its success in fostering new practices of reading and popular study of canonical Jewish texts. But this particular ceremony was also marked— even if only tangentially—by the presentation of the *Schottenstein Talmud* as an equally momentous benchmark of the waxing public presence of Haredi Orthodox Judaism.

Daf Yomi (literally, "daily page") is a program of study that was instigated in 1923 by Agudat Israel, one of the preeminent Haredi organizations dedicated to the defense and promotion of Orthodox Judaism.[15] Rabbi Meir Shapiro (1887–1933), then headmaster of the Hakhmei Lublin Yeshivah, proposed the Daf Yomi program as an international effort to encourage all adult male Jews to study one complete page of the Babylonian Talmud each day. In his understanding, this initiative would bring the entire Jewish world together, both laymen and scholars: a unity that would culminate in a *siyum* (completion celebration) every seven years and five months, the duration required to complete all 2,771 tractate pages.[16] Although in its early years, the practice of Daf Yomi was restricted to a relatively small circle of scholars and students, the program has enjoyed growing popularity in the post-World War II period, not least in the English-speaking world.[17] This popularity is registered, for instance, in the exponential growth of *siyum* (completion) ceremonies held in the greater New York area: in 1968, a Siyum haShas held at the Bais Yaakov religious academy of Boro Park (Brooklyn, New York) was attended by a mere 200 participants. In 1984, there were 7,600 participants; in 1990 there were 21,000; in 1997 there were over 70,000; and in 2005 almost double that number again.[18] In between these dramatic and very public moments of mass celebration, the growth of the Daf Yomi movement can also be traced through the spread of Talmud study circles. Across the North American continent, and elsewhere, in virtually every city with a Jewish population, one now finds local Daf Yomi participants gathering at synagogues, schools, community centers, and other sites for *shiurim* (Talmud lessons) held in the early morning hours, at lunchtime, and in the evening. One rather famous study circle, led by Rabbi Pesach Lerner, consists of a group of lawyers, accountants, and other professionals who have been meeting daily since the early 1990s on the 7:51 a.m. commuter train from Far Rockaway to Penn Station in New York City.[19]

The rising popularity of Daf Yomi is also materialized in the rapid expansion of new goods and services catering to existing and potential Talmud students. Starting in the early 1980s, the growing demand for daily Talmud lessons encouraged organizers to develop new telecommunications services, such as Dial-a-Daf, a telephone network enabling callers to access prerecorded lessons by leading *maggidei shiurim* (Talmudic instructors), such as those by Rabbi Eli Teitelbaum of Boro Park (in Brooklyn, New York). The popularity of Dial-a-Daf, administered by the Torah Communications Network, eventually led to the creation of an extensive Torah Phone Library, and other offshoots, such as a growing market of *shiurim* distributed and sold on audiocassette. Not long after, with the personal computing revolution and the emergence of video-conferencing technologies, a new organization, the Torah Conferencing Network, began transmitting recorded *shiurim* of Talmudic "superstars"—such as Rabbi Yisroel Reisman, of Flatbush, New Jersey, and Rabbi Asher Weiss of Sderot, Israel—via satellite to dozens of sites around the world.[20] Since the 1990s, the means for accessing lessons via advanced communication technologies has only continued to expand through the proliferation of Internet databases, chat rooms, Weblogs, and interactive Web sites that offer digitized images of Talmud tractate pages, or lessons in MP3 audio file format, among other electronic tools for enriching Talmud study.[21] Other companies, such as Torah Educational Software (TES) Inc., have developed new learning tools that tap into the rising popularity of Daf Yomi, such as *Gemara Tutor* (in which students compete to learn Talmudic vocabulary and concepts) and *Talmud Master* (an "interactive Talmud trainer" focusing on the text's logical flow and reasoning process).[22] And in March 2005, with much fanfare and considerable media attention, a young entrepreneur named Chaim Shulman launched the ShasPod, a version of Apple's iPod digital recording device that comes preloaded with lessons for the complete Daf Yomi cycle, culled from Talmud lectures by Rabbi Dovid Grossman of Los Angeles.[23] There is little room for doubt that, with the development of new communication technologies, future entrepreneurs will continue to find ways to harness their capabilities and market new products to the Daf Yomi movement.

ArtScroll's Talmud project has played far more than a peripheral role in the success and growing popularity of Daf Yomi in the English-speaking world. This was highlighted during the eleventh Siyum haShas ceremony when the Novominsker Rebbe, Rabbi Yaakov Perlow, current president of Agudath Israel of America and de facto leader of the Daf Yomi movement in the United States, singled out ArtScroll in his address to the gathered mass:

> This *simcha* [joy] tonight is shared by all circles, by those who study in
> the traditional *Shas* [Talmud], in Yiddish. It is also shared, however, by a
> new generation of Torah students, who communicate effectively in the
> spoken language of our country: in English. And therefore, I believe,
> we would all be remiss at this point not to acknowledge, in public, the
> tremendous contributions made by those Torah scholars: the writers,
> the editors, and the benefactors, of a society known as ArtScroll. With-
> out the truth of the *Schottenstein Shas* [Talmud], who have made the
> study of *Gemara* [Talmud] accessible to so many thousands of thirsty
> Jews, eager to drink from the fountain of Torah. The completion of the
> *Schottenstein Shas* in our day is an historic milestone—a sign, I believe,
> from providence, that Torah can and will be advanced, *baruch hashem*
> [thank God], on all frontiers of Jewish life.[24]

As a sign from providence itself, the coincidence in timing of the conclusion of the *Schottenstein Talmud* and the ending of the eleventh Daf Yomi cycle cannot easily be reduced to a mere marketing ploy (although it cannot escape attention that this synchrony presented an ideal opportunity for the press to publicize the availability of the entire edition, just as the new, twelfth cycle of daily Talmud reading was about to begin). The Siyum haShas was simply the most dramatic public moment within what was in fact a deep, symbiotic relationship between ArtScroll and its Daf Yomi audience, running through the entire history of the Talmud translation project. As Rabbi Scherman and Nesanel Kasnett explain, "ArtScroll's publication schedule has revolved around *Daf Yomi* in order to help participants navigate through *daf* after *daf* [page after page] of the sea of the Talmud. The *Daf Yomi* cycle stretches for seven and a half years and in order to coordinate with it as much as possible, new volumes of the Schottenstein Edition were published on a staggered basis to coincide with the *Daf Yomi* schedule, so that it would be in synch with the new *Daf Yomi* volume."[25] If the Library of Congress ceremony addressed the larger, non-Jewish world of lawmakers and library patrons, the Siyum haShas ceremony provided ArtScroll with an occasion to emphasize its links with this popular movement of Orthodox Jewish students, as well as a potential audience of future initiates to the Daf Yomi program. The timing of the completion of ArtScroll's Talmud thus signals a decisive coming of age for both the publisher and the movement in whose name it speaks. The *Schottenstein Talmud* is presented as an ideal vehicle of popular pedagogy in that it promises to sate the thirst for knowledge and understanding, particularly among constituencies of Jewish readers unable to engage in fulltime study and therefore lacking in many of the requisite reading skills. Moreover, as the first edition ever produced that has been designed specifically to accommodate Daf Yomi's modular logic—the reading of one page per day—the ArtScroll text heralds a new regime of interpretive techniques, reading practices, and modes of social organization that has helped to propel Haredi Orthodox Judaism to a dominant position within the popular imagination and within the habitus of everyday life for a growing number of English-speaking Jews.

At the Gala Supper

The third event occurred on March 15, 2005, when the Mesorah Heritage Foundation hosted a gala supper at the New York Hilton Hotel for some 2,700 patrons, supporters, and friends of the publisher.[26] The evening began with a cocktail event that featured kosher sushi, chamber music, and the exhibition of a "Patrons Scroll" projecting the names and faces of prominent donors to the foundation onto the wall of the hotel's Mercury Suite. Afterward, the guests were ushered upstairs to the Grand Ballroom, where they were seated before a long stage upon which sat ArtScroll's principal stakeholders, including the foundation's trustees and board of governors. On a side stage, no less prominently lit, sat an assembly of the key rabbis involved in the translation project. The event was, in the words of one guest with whom I shared a table, a "who's who" of the American Orthodox world and its friends. The stars included prominent financiers and *roshei yeshiva* (headmasters of religious academies), as well as more main-stream celebrities. Even the Hollywood actor John Voight was in attendance.

The supper was followed by a string of speeches and dedications, including those by Rabbi Scherman, Rabbi Zlotowitz, and members of the Schottenstein family, and then the audience was treated to videotaped greetings from Israeli rabbis who were unable to attend in person, as well as a documentary film dramatizing the momentous achievement of the Schottenstein publication and its impact on readers throughout the English-speaking world. At the closing of the evening's events, Rabbi Zlotowitz spoke about the ongoing work of the Mesorah Heritage Foundation, which included the continuation of their Hebrew edition of the Talmud and the inauguration of a new project to translate the Jerusalem Talmud into English. This new effort promised to rival the Babylonian Talmud in terms of its challenges for translators and exegetes and was projected to fill forty-seven volumes in the coming years. The audience was also told about the existing opportunities to dedicate individual volumes in their names and was advised to contact the foundation to arrange for appropriately sized donations. Upon departure, each guest was presented with a deluxe shoulder bag containing copies of the ArtScroll catalog, a limited-edition commemorative volume honoring the scholars and patrons involved in the creation of the Schottenstein Edition of the Babylonian Talmud, a unique ballpoint pen with a pullout miniaturized scroll inscribed with the Tefilah haDerech (the Wayfarer's Prayer, traditionally recited when setting out on a journey), and a copy of the recently completed first volume of the afore-mentioned Jerusalem Talmud.

Through its speeches, food, musical entertainment, and opportunities for socializing, the gala supper was carefully orchestrated to strengthen the bonds of patronage that underpin the Mesorah Heritage Foundation's publishing projects. The gathering of authors, editors, and donors affirmed and helped to further consolidate relationships vital to ArtScroll's success as an institution dedicated both to disinterested scholarship and to the marketing of print commodities. Indeed, the gala supper enacted exchanges in the narrow sense of fundraising and promotionalism, but also through the performance of gift exchanges, in and through which authors, religious leaders, patrons, and curious onlookers (myself included) were invited to perform acts of mutual recognition (Fig. 1). One might say that ArtScroll's stakeholders, by seeing and being seen, speaking and listening to speeches, and participating in the lush festivities, affirmed a principle the sociologist Pierre Bourdieu described as the "interest in disinterestedness": the tacit,

Mesorah Heritage Foundation

4401 SECOND AVENUE
BROOKLYN, NY 11232
(718) 921-9000 / FAX (718) 680-1875
E-MAIL: HERITAGE@MESORAH.COM

February 27, 2005

Mr. Jeremy Stolow

Dear Jeremy,

Thank you for your recent generous contribution of
* * * THREE HUNDRED SIXTY DOLLARS * * *
in support of our Judaic projects. Below is your **official receipt**.

We at the Mesorah Heritage Foundation, an IRS-approved 501(c)(3) not-for-profit publicly supported organization, are grateful for your kind response to our **Patrons Dinner / Commemorative Journal** on March 15, 2005, and for your **reservation for 1 person to that event**. This historic occasion celebrates the completion of the entire 73-volume **Schottenstein Edition of the Talmud and inaugurates other Foundation** projects which make an enormous impact world-wide. Primarily it honors those visionary people who are making these works possible.

Indeed, it is through individuals such as yourself that we can continue our work of sharing Judaism's treasures with the English-speaking world -- for which generations yet unborn will be grateful.

In the merit of your generosity, may you and yours enjoy everything good, and the continued ability to participate in great causes.

Sincerely yours,

Rabbi Meir Zlotowitz
Chairman

Mesorah Heritage Foundation

4401 SECOND AVENUE
BROOKLYN, NY 11232
(718) 921-9000 / FAX (718) 680-1875
E-MAIL: HERITAGE@MESORAH.COM

OFFICIAL RECEIPT
#102641

Many thanks for your contribution
We look forward to your continued support.

Date: February 28, 2005

Received   * * * **THREE HUNDRED SIXTY DOLLARS** * * *

Your gift helps break down the barriers of language and time -- to bring classics of Jewish wisdom to today's English-speaking Jews
... one book at a time.

Mr. Jeremy Stolow

Contributions in excess of $75 per dinner reservation are tax-deductible. Total Dinner Reservations: 1

the WRITTEN WORD IS FOREVER

Figure 1. Receipt for ArtScroll patrons' gala dinner, New York Hilton, March 15, 2005. Here I demonstrate my own implication in the "social alchemy" that enables ArtScroll to convert economic into symbolic value.

and sometimes even disavowed, accumulation of advantages that allows for a "social alchemy," in this case transforming sacred, consecrated objects into objects of commercial value.[27] Without financial donors, ambitious projects such as the translation of the entire Talmud would never have been possible; without the army of editors and authors ready to undertake this work, and the most prominent Haredi rabbinic authorities to bless it with their approval, donors would have no project in which to invest and thus no source of symbolic capital to acquire for themselves. More than just a celebration among insiders, the gala supper dramatized these complex relationships of interdependence and exchange. Unlike the more public events such as the Siyum haShas, which highlighted ArtScroll's resonance with a broad readership, the gala supper threw into relief the *Schottenstein Talmud*'s position at the intersection of a network of financial backers, intellectuals, and guardians of cultural capital, whose partnerships are key to the ArtScroll enterprise.

At the Yeshiva University Museum Exhibit

The fourth and final defining moment pertaining to the completion of the *Schottenstein Talmud* took the form of a major exhibition at the Yeshiva University Museum in New York City from April 12 to August 28, 2005. *Printing the Talmud: From Bomberg to Schottenstein* was an exhibit (and subsequently a catalog publication) that showcased a large range of examples of Talmud texts, from thirteenth-century manuscript fragments to rare original copies of key Talmud editions, beginning with the very first printed edition by the Flemish printer Daniel Bomberg, produced in 1519–23.[28] The exhibit also featured a floor mosaic from the sixth-century synagogue at Rehov, in Israel's Bet Shean Valley, presenting the only known surviving copy of a rabbinic text from the time when the Talmud was redacted, as well as a video installation entitled *The Infinite Sea,* compiled from live video footage of Talmud students sitting and learning in classrooms around the world, from Lima to Moscow to Glasgow.[29] Although, as noted by the museum's director, Sylvia Herskowitz, the initial idea for a show on the history of Talmud publication had preceded the completion of the *Schottenstein Talmud,* the latter event provided the museum an ideal pretext "to try to capture and convey the energy that Talmud represents," not least with respect to *ArtScroll*'s edition, "which has succeeded in making the Talmud accessible to all."[30]

The Yeshiva University Museum show was an important venue for the public arrival of the *Schottenstein Talmud* in at least three respects. First, as suggested by the very title of the exhibit, it defined ArtScroll's Talmud as the latest—and at least for the time being, the *final*—published edition of the Talmud, placing it at the pinnacle of a tradition stretching back to the fifteenth-century Bomberg text. Second, the museum show emphasized the artifactual nature of the Schottenstein edition, presenting it as a valued object to collect and to display. Standing in juxtaposition with displays of older Talmud editions, and even antique relics such as a floor mosaic imported from "the Holy Land," ArtScroll's Talmud acquired an aura of authenticity, as enshrined by the curatorial practices and visual theatrics that underpin the work of museum display.[31] Finally, the show was significant for its location in the Yeshiva University Museum. Founded in 1886, the Yeshiva University has served as the preeminent American school for "modern" Orthodox Jews, and its motto, *Torah u'Maddah* (Torah and secular knowledge), identifies a form of Orthodoxy dedicated to Jewish law and custom, as well as a professed engagement with the "non-Jewish" world. As such, the Yeshiva University represents a cultural and ideological camp that historically has sharply distinguished itself from the Haredi yeshiva world (a topic to which I shall return presently). In this context, the museum's decision to put on a show paying tribute to the *Schottenstein Talmud* can be read as a remarkable concession.[32] In this final moment of ArtScroll's arrival, one catches sight of an emerging terrain of intra-Orthodox consensus and a blurring of formerly rigid dividing lines. The consecration of the *Schottenstein Talmud* within the lineage of legendary printed works, and as a material specimen for display, epitomizes a growing acceptance by non-Haredim of Haredi modes of constructing Orthodox Judaism, in tandem with what some observers have characterized as a tectonic "rightward shift" within Jewish culture and society, and among Orthodox Jews in particular.

The ceremony held at the Library of Congress, the Siyum haShas in Madison Square Garden, the Mesorah Foundation's gala dinner at the Hilton Hotel, and the Yeshiva University Museum exhibition represent four distinct stages of public-making for ArtScroll's most ambitious publishing venture. Taken together, they also delineate some of the key opportunities and constraints that define ArtScroll's mission to affirm and to expand the influence of Haredi rabbinic authority through the medium of canonical religious texts. Each venue materializes one dimension of ArtScroll's success in having produced a "definitive," scrupulously traditionalist, but also pedagogically innovative edition of the Talmud, designed to reach multiple audiences, from the most elementary, part-time student to the advanced scholar. At the same time, the succession of venues for staging the *Schottenstein Talmud*'s public arrival points to the polyvalent character of ArtScroll's mission: driven by the need not only to win customers but also to serve a student movement, to establish legitimacy among intellectual peers, to overtake competitors, and to engage with diverse categories of outsiders, such as journalists, librarians, museum curators, and political elites. The story of the completion of the *Schottenstein Talmud* thus sheds interesting light on a much larger set of shifts that have shaped Haredi Orthodox society over the past several decades and that have transformed the place of Haredi-derived sources of knowledge and religious authority within contemporary Jewish public life. How mediating institutions such as ArtScroll play a decisive role in these transformations is the subject of what follows.

ORTHODOXY, MODERNITY, AND THE RISE OF HAREDISM

Lacking a single, unifying center of authority or an official statement of principles, Orthodox Judaism is made up of several cultural communities, differentiated by their organizational affiliations, their traditions of textual interpretation and ritual practice, and their varying attitudes toward non-Orthodox Jews and, more broadly, the high-tech, culturally hybrid, "non-Jewish" universe in which they find themselves. Broadly speaking, these differences among the Orthodox can be divided into two camps. Those who call themselves "modern" Orthodox (or who in more recent times favor the term *centrist*) accept the authority of the written and oral laws of Jewish tradition but also ascribe inherent value to the "secular" protocols of state citizenship, science, economic interest, and modern cosmopolitan living. By contrast, Haredi Orthodox society—which includes members of the yeshiva world, Hasidic groups, and sectors of the Sephardic community—is characterized by its opposition to all "liberalizing" tendencies in Jewish thought and practice. They are punctilious in their performance of Jewish ritual, dedicated to the intensive study of canonical texts as a religious ideal in its own right, and submissive to a narrow rabbinic elite, to whom Haredi Jews have granted unchallengeable authority in all matters of Jewish law.[33] Haredi society is also characterized by its enclosure within tight cultural enclaves, defined by such things as their geographic concentration (typically in neighborhoods of major urban centers, such as Jerusalem, New York, London, and Toronto), their endogamous kinship patterns, and their distinct forms of speech and dress.[34] Within these confines, Haredim often style themselves as the *she'erit yisrael* (the remnants of Israel), the sole surviving progeny of the original Chosen People, and the unique bearers of Jewish authenticity, who in their everyday lives adhere without compromise to the Jews' covenant with God.[35]

Of course, this enclave society was never fully closed off from the outside world. But in recent years, a combination of centrifugal forces has propelled Haredi Jews well beyond their communities through the creation of Haredi fundraising and lobby groups, political organizations, and media institutions. Likewise, Haredi-trained teachers, missionaries, pulpit rabbis, scribes, kosher licensers, and other agents have been taking up positions in Jewish schools, synagogues, and other institutions throughout the Orthodox community and in the broader public culture of Israel and the Jewish diaspora. One of the effects of this outward movement has been an increasingly emboldened challenge to the authority and legitimacy of modern Orthodox Judaism, the basic outlook of which has been the object of relentless criticism among Haredim. Haredi teachers, rabbis, and other agents have also been at the forefront of pressures within Orthodox Jewry to devalue the practice of socializing with cultural others and the pursuit of secular studies and professional careers.[36] At the same time, they have called upon fellow Orthodox Jews to withdraw from many of the existing arenas of intra-Jewish cooperation, in extreme cases denouncing adherents to Reform, Conservative, and Reconstructionist Judaism as "non-Jews." Some Haredim have likewise refused to accord any legitimacy to the state of Israel, insisting that the Jews remain a people living in divinely prescribed exile, even when living in the Holy Land.[37] In all these ways, the Haredim have involved themselves in a moral mission to expand the frontiers of Haredi authority and to draw the Jewish nation further along a path toward what they define as repentance and redemption. This mission has brought Haredi society into increasingly intimate relationship with the non-Haredi world, precipitating what some refer to as a "slide to the right." But this impression of rightward movement is an effect of the repositioning of the walls separating Haredi enclave culture from the outside world, and consequently the expanding visibility of Haredi Jews in the public sphere, through new channels of mediated communication and new possibilities for the circulation of Haredi forms of Jewish thought and practice.

Like any movement that defines itself as an orthodoxy, Haredism was never a static expression of tradition. Rather, it was a product of (often cataclysmic) social change, precipitating the very need for efforts to systematize, ideologically sharpen, and institutionally reorganize the conditions under which one could claim to uphold traditional Jewish thought, practice, and moral outlook. It is possible to identify historical precedents of religious stringency and asceticism in the Jewish tradition going back to antiquity. Yet Haredi society as we know it today first emerged in the aftermath of a rapidly industrializing, urbanizing, and nationalizing European modernity, within its ensuing regimes of voluntary association and political factionalization and its expanding realms of economic opportunity and cultural choice. "Traditional" European Jewish society had been defined by centuries-old patterns of obligatory membership in geographically and legally constricted corporate communities—known as *kehilot*—that sustained a complex web of local traditions and intercommunal exchanges. These conditions anchored cultural practice, political power, and the formation of Jewish subjects in relatively stable institutions of governance and patterns of daily living.[38] But over the late eighteenth and nineteenth centuries, during the great age of European imperial expansion and nation building, corporate Jewish society was exposed to an evolving set of promises and demands from the project of so-called Emancipation, which aimed to integrate Jewish subjects into the emerging European civil order and to redefine collective Jewish identity on the basis of principles of private confession and voluntary association. A well-known example of the new forms of Jewish public culture that crystallized in and through these shifts is the Haskalah (Jewish Enlightenment), an intellectual and cultural movement first appearing in Germany at the close of the eighteenth century. In their efforts to "rescue" fellow Jews from the privations of corporate life and to bring them into conformity with the sensibilities of modern civil society, Maskilim (enlightened Jews) advocated a series of revisions to liturgical practice (out of which the Reform movement was born) and amendments to Talmudic scholarship and legal reasoning, based on approaches to the Bible that incorporated the emerging scientific discourses of Orientalist historiography and philology. Other trails leading Jews away from the disintegrating world of the *kehila* were blazed by such diverse movements as secular Zionism, Bundism, and communism. And at a more anonymous level, an even wider range of options was made available to post-*kehila* Jews, including the growing opportunities to migrate from countryside to city, or much further abroad—such as to America—and also to reinvent themselves through new patterns of consumerism, fashion, exposure to non-Jewish literature, and even intermarriage and religious conversion.[39]

The rise of Orthodox Judaism is likewise situated in the aftermath of the dismantling of the *kehila* and the circulation of promises—whether near or distant—of a new life and its attendant signs of belonging, in the form of new ideas, new political formations, new commodities, and new relationships with the outside world. This transforming landscape obliged rabbinic leaders to seek out new ways to assert their intellectual, cultural, and political authority. Through their distinctive approaches to rabbinic literature, their ideological pronouncements, and their efforts at institution building—including the creation of sectarian communal organizations, schools, seminaries, philanthropic societies, and political parties—these Orthodox Jewish elites engaged in a dynamic process of reinvention of community, incorporating a wide range of tools to fend off even the mere possibility of influence by liberal and Reform Jews and to inoculate "the faithful" against the contagion of modernity.[40] One of the more dramatic instantiations of this effort was the creation of Agudat Israel (union or band of Israel): the first truly international organization claiming to speak on behalf of all Orthodox Jews in promoting the authority of halakhah in the regulation of both personal conduct and public life.[41] From its foundation in 1912 at Kattowitz (near Cracow, Poland), through the joint efforts of a wide array of German, Polish, and Lithuanian Orthodox rabbis and scholars, Agudat Israel defined itself as an exclusive source of legitimate authority of the Jewish people in its entirety and as a direct legatee of God's covenant at Sinai, faithfully administered in the present by its supreme governing body, the Moetzet Gedolei ha 'Torah (Council of Torah Sages).[42]

Despite its professed goal to "restore" the traditional authority of Orthodox rabbis and Talmud scholars to the pinnacle of Jewish society, in practice Agudat Israel effected a remarkable transformation in the fields of education, political activism, and social service provision, as evident from the multitude of organizations it brought into being: schools and academies, lobby groups, philanthropic societies, political parties, labor unions, agricultural cooperatives, newspapers and publishing houses, orphanages, community outreach groups, a women's movement, a youth movement, and, not least, sponsorship of the aforementioned Daf Yomi initiative. Through these diverse enterprises, Agudat Israel dedicated itself to the defense and cultivation of Haredi values and practices wherever Jews happened to live and wherever questions of legitimate Jewish conduct happened to emerge. Before World War II, when Agudat Israel catered principally to the interests of European Orthodox Jewish communities, the movement articulated its raison d'être with reference to a conception of collective Jewish existence based on cosmological explanations of the state of Jewish exile in the world, as had been elaborated in centuries of canonical writings.[43] Among other things, this vocabulary of exile formed the basis for explicit opposition to the project of Zionism and the prospect of a secular Jewish state in Palestine (which Haredi elites tended to regard as an illegitimate attempt to "hasten the end of time," since it involved the mass return of Jews to the land of Israel without the prior signs of divine approval). Practically speaking, Agudat Israel's principal goals were to legitimate the arrangements of authority and privilege of the existing Orthodox Jewish consistorial bodies and to curtail the spread of *goyish* (non-Jewish) influences among constituencies of "faithful" Jews, including the enticement to emigrate to Palestine, or to America, the consummate *treife medina* ("unholy land").

However, over the course of the twentieth century, even greater changes were visited upon Jewish society, in the wake of which Orthodox Jews had to confront the enormity of the destruction wreaked by the Nazi Holocaust in Europe, the reconfigured geography of a Jewish diaspora now inclined toward the English-speaking world (especially the United States), and the new reality that came with the birth of the modern, secular state of Israel, organized ideologically and institutionally as the "Jewish homeland" and proclaimed as a reversal of the centuries-old condition of exile. Ironically, while the Holocaust had precipitated the annihilation of the majority of European Jewry, it also provided new opportunities for reconstruction and reinvention, injecting new vigor into various strands of Jewish Orthodoxy, not least the Haredim. Once transplanted to foreign soil, the uprooted survivors of the European disaster not only managed to rebuild—demographically as well as institutionally—but were able to flourish in new ways. The history of Agudath Israel of America is particularly instructive in this regard. Founded in New York in 1939 (after a failed attempt in 1922),[44] the American chapter was given new life thanks to the arrival of survivors from eastern Europe, who helped build a considerable network of public relations and political lobby groups, sectarian schools and yeshivot, and periodical publications, in Yiddish (*Dos Yidishe Vort,* since 1952) and in English (the *Jewish Observer,* since 1963), as well as sponsoring publishing initiatives with (ideologically, if not directly) affiliated publishing houses, the most prominent example of which is, in fact, ArtScroll.

Host societies such as the United States, Canada, the United Kingdom, and Australia thus offered the Haredim new opportunities for activism and social mobility and the benefits of a relatively deregulated religious marketplace, allowing for the accumulation of new forms of economic, political, and cultural capital. As evident from the case of Agudath Israel of America and, more broadly, the array of European-styled schools and yeshivot founded by Haredi Jews in the post-World War II period, migration actually enhanced the capacity of Haredi rabbinic authorities to form organizational structures to which affiliation and degree of commitment could now be determined freely by the individuals involved, and for which distinct rules and directives could be formulated that would be binding upon those committed members alone. No longer encumbered by the exigencies of competition with "moderate" elements of the mandatory consistorial bodies to which European Jews had belonged, the postwar generation of Haredi Orthodox elites were able to reposition themselves as an institutionally and intellectually autonomous vanguard, claiming to represent the exclusive, uncorrupted, and authentic version of Jewish identity and practice, both in Israel and in the English-speaking Jewish diaspora.[45]

In the immediate aftermath of World War II, the Haredim were largely preoccupied with the establishment of their own neighborhoods, schools, synagogues, and communal institutions. These activities were undertaken in the face of considerable opprobrium heaped upon Haredi rabbis, ostensibly for having contributed to the casualty count because they had been known for discouraging Jews within their communities from supporting the Zionist project or from migrating out of Europe, or for otherwise failing to actively resist the Nazi onslaught.[46] Haredi society also labored under the shadow of (retrospectively hasty) predictions that the Haredi way of life was simply too ill equipped to offer a viable means of Jewish survival in the postwar global order. In the English-speaking world in particular, the combined forces of suburbanization, upward economic mobility, and a growing confidence that Jews could enjoy a secure place within the hospitable conditions of legally sanctioned religious pluralism and state-sponsored multiculturalism gave little impetus to the legitimacy of Haredi cultural practices and sources of rabbinic authority in the wider circuits of public life.[47] By contrast, modern Orthodoxy, committed to what Samuel Heilman has called a strategy of "contrapuntal accommodation," seemed far more adept at negotiating between the imperatives of maintaining Jewish tradition and of securing economic, cultural, and political success.[48] However, by the late 1960s it had become clear that the Haredim were defying the odds placed against them. They had not only survived but matured into a well-organized bloc, increasingly willing and able to exercise influence in the institutional and cultural domains that lay beyond their communal boundaries, and thereby enjoying an increasingly disproportional impact on the course of public life, not least in the English-speaking Jewish diaspora.[49]

To conclude, the contemporary Haredi enclave is often described as a society of scholars, centered on the yeshiva and its rabbinic leadership and populated by male students and their families, whose lives are organized according to the religious ideal of full-time, lifelong Talmud study. At the same time, this kernel of yeshiva culture is inseparable from a larger, capillary architecture that surrounds the Haredi enclave and defines its various portals of access to the outside world. In fact, through the development of mobile affinity networks, and through the increasingly routine activities of outward-oriented agents, the contemporary Haredi community finds itself in intimate rapport with the economic, political, and communicational contexts of "semi-" and "non-Haredi" Jewish public culture and with the even larger arrangements of territorial nation-states and transnational flows that shape the contemporary global order. One important arena of exchange is defined by the steady pressure placed upon the yeshiva to secure the financial means for its continued existence. In both Israel and the diaspora, Haredi communities struggle to meet such needs through participation in narrowly circumscribed occupational niches so as to minimize contact with the outside, "secular" world) and through a gendered hierarchy of labor, according to which women are considered "freer" to seek paid employment, since, unlike men, they have not been mandated to study Talmud.[50] At an institutional level, yeshivot themselves are relentlessly driven to attract investment from philanthropists and government agencies or through grassroots fundraising. These pressures have only increased in recent years, commensurate with an exploding population of yeshiva students, giving rise in the Haredi community to conditions of growing economic precariousness and, in the worst of circumstances, to a pervasive discourse of fatalism and a new premium placed on the heroism of poverty.[51]

An equally powerful dynamic shaping the relationship between the yeshiva-centered Haredi community and the larger public sphere comes with the growing sense among Haredim that their survival, let alone their success, is tied to their ability to establish a foothold within non-Haredi fields of culture and politics. So, for instance, one can trace a growing preoccupation among Haredi intellectuals with "nonobservant," "lapsed," or "assimilated" Jews, sometimes referred to in Orthodox parlance as *tinokos shenishbu* (children raised in [gentile] captivity). Since the late 1960s, the religious mandate to rescue such "lost souls" has been articulated through a movement known as *kiruv r'hokim* (lit., "bringing clos[er] those who are far").[52] This *kiruv* movement is dedicated to bringing into the Haredi fold nonaffiliated or marginally affiliated Jews by inducing them to become *ba'alei teshuva* (masters of return or repentance), that is, Jews who will voluntarily affiliate with the Haredi community, its prescripts, its discourses, and its cultural practices.[53] Although their numbers are statistically minute, *ba'alei teshuva* play a crucial symbolic role within the Haredi community itself, namely to produce consensus among Haredi interlocutors that "victory is on their side."[54] On these terms, successful converts are paraded as the spoils of a war against secularism and assimilation, and the language of rescue and reclamation serves to legitimate increasingly intensive missionary efforts launched into the non-Haredi world. *Kiruv* activists perform such work by orchestrating a variety of encounters with non-Haredi Jews through such diverse offerings as Hebrew lessons, public lectures, impromptu invitations to Shabbat dinners in Haredi homes, crash courses in Jewish history, and even revival meetings in sports arenas. Not surprisingly, *kiruv* efforts have also been manifested through channels of mediated communication, such as radio shows, circulating audiocassettes, the Internet, and, of course, the distribution of print matter, including editions of key liturgical works designed especially for the novice reader (an arena of publishing in which ArtScroll has in fact played a pioneering role, as we shall see in future chapters).

Alongside the aforementioned army of teachers, pulpit rabbis, and other outward-oriented emissaries of Haredi society, it is therefore crucial to note the role played by institutions such as ArtScroll. Acting as both conduits and filters, such mediating agents perform the work of connecting insiders and outsiders, and in so doing they redefine the very distinctions between inside and outside. And, given the high value Jewish culture has placed on the written word, publishing houses merit special attention. They are synecdoches of Haredism's expanded presence in Jewish public life, evincing the double logic of authority and accessibility that drives this expansion.

THE SCRIPTURAL ECONOMY: THE YESHIVA WORLD AND THE BOOK TRADITION

The making of many books is without limit, and much study is weariness of the flesh.

ECCLESIASTES (12:12)

As I have suggested, Haredi Orthodox Judaism can be characterized by its emphasis on scholastic and legalistic approaches to Jewish textual sources and by its overarching effort to organize, specify, and extend knowledge about legitimate conduct and about the true workings of the social, natural, and cosmic order, as derived from sacred books. This form of religious "scripturalism" is radical and uncompromising in its promotion of continuous, intensive engagement with canonical Jewish literature and in its stringent application in all arenas of life. In Clifford Geertz's classic formulation, based on his comparative study of Islamic modernization in Morocco and Indonesia during the late 1960s, the rise of scripturalism involves a shift in the sources of intellectual and religious authority from the guardians of custom to an elite of textual experts, who have taken it upon themselves to distill the infinite varieties of local knowledge and everyday conduct into an explicit, rationally ordered system of knowledge and codified behavior.[55] In the case of Haredism, one can identify a comparable shift whereby a new scholarly elite has been empowered to exercise authority through its proclaimed monopoly over the true meaning of Jewish texts and through its assertion that these texts must take precedence over all other sources of religious authenticity.

Among other things, this scripturalism has fueled what one might call a "Judaicization" of knowledge, that is, an attempt to impose "Torah-true" standards of verification upon all knowledge claims, religious and scientific, past and present, speculative and practical. This epistemological stance is vividly illustrated in a recent ArtScroll publication, *Our Wondrous World: Wonders Hidden below the Surface,* by Rabbi Avrohom Katz. "The more one studies Torah, the stronger the conviction that the vast, infinite, interconnected edifice that Torah comprises is the work of an Infinite Intelligence," Katz proclaims at the outset of his discussion, which consists of a series of short essays on the miraculous designs of hydraulic machines, birds' beaks, and human hands and on the divine genius standing behind processes of photosynthesis, cellular mitosis, and the engineering of petroleum-based consumer goods.[56] Such knowledge about the structure of the entire universe is based upon a scripturalist assertion that the Jewish canon is itself unquestionably self-authorizing, inerrant, internally consistent, and comprehensive. As succinctly formulated by Rabbi Mordechai Gifter (1915–2001), head of the Telz Yeshiva in Cleveland, Ohio, and a foremost Haredi authority of the post–World War II period, "God's Torah may be explained only in light of Torah."[57] This repudiation of "non-Jewish" sources of authoritative knowledge can also be characterized as one of the founding motives of the ArtScroll press. As Rabbi Zlotowitz argued, in his preface to *The Megillah: The Book of Esther,* the very first ArtScroll publication:

It must be made clear that this is not a so-called "scientific" or "apologetic" commentary on the Megillah [The Book of Esther]. That area has, unfortunately, been too well-covered, resulting in violence to the Jewish faith as well as to correct interpretation. It is in no way the intention of this book to demonstrate the legitimacy or historicity of Esther or Mordechai to non-believers or doubters. *Belief in the authenticity of every book of the Torah is basic to Jewish faith, and we proceed from there.* It comes as no surprise to me—nor should it to any Orthodox Jew—that the palace of Shushan, as unearthed by archaeologists, bears out the description of the palace in the Megillah in every detail; nor do we deem it necessary to prove, by means of "Persian borrow-words," nor by whatever means, that the Book was, indeed, written in that contemporary period. Rather, the aim was a traditional commentary reflecting the Megillah as understood by Chazal [the ancient sages]. No non-Jewish sources have been consulted, much less quoted. *I consider it offensive that the Torah should need authentication from the secular or so-called "scientific" sources.*[58]

As Rabbi Zlotowitz's text makes clear, *scripturalism* refers not only to the unchallengeable authority of sacred Jewish texts as sources of knowledge but also to the ways Haredi knowledge seekers have accorded a commensurate form of authority to their teachers, the most trusted readers of those texts. In fact, the master-disciple relationship cultivated in the yeshiva provides a model for the spread of what in Haredi circles is known as *da'at Torah* (knowledge of Torah): a specifically charismatic source of religious, intellectual, and legal authority that permeates the Haredi enclave. Having been trained in the traditions of the yeshiva, and having proven themselves as masters of textual exegesis, leading teachers and scholars of the Haredi world are seen to possess esoteric knowledge that authorizes them to issue ex cathedra pronouncements in the realm of halakhah and in all other matters of everyday conduct, "their sole authority being their position as rabbis immersed in the study of Torah."[59] They are known as the *gedolim:* the great Torah sages of the yeshiva world, who stand at the pinnacle of an army of students, cultural brokers, and other agents responsible for mediating their *da'at Torah* through the production, promotion, distribution, explication, translation, vulgarization, application, and defense of Haredi interpretations of Jewish sacred texts.

We shall have occasion later to consider more carefully the tacit assumption that scripturalism is typically a product of great social upheaval: a response to the lived experience of such things as wars, political revolutions, colonial conquests, or the industrialization of rural economies, or, in the case under consideration here, a product of the destruction wreaked by the Nazi Holocaust and the transplantation of survivors to a new location in the Jewish diaspora. Future chapters will also shed light on the communicational, technological, and institutional conditions, and the lived experiences, that shape this apparent "victory of the academy over the laity."[60] Among other things, I shall devote particular attention to the contexts of reception, where this laity is imagined, constituted, and daily reproduced as a reading public through the work of negotiation among authors, readers, and intermediary agents, such as teachers, booksellers, librarians, pulpit rabbis, and, not least, the material agency of the books themselves. In the remainder of this chapter, I wish to clarify the conditions under which this scripturalist social logic has come into being.

To understand the rise of scripturalism within Orthodox Judaism and, more broadly, within the transnational Jewish public sphere, one might begin by tracing the institutional development of the modern Haredi yeshiva. Its prototype is found in the yeshivot of nineteenth-century eastern Europe, most famously the model academy founded by Reb Chaim of Volozhin (Lithuania) in 1802.[61] The Volozhin yeshiva was revolutionary in its efforts to accumulate knowledge based on the intensive study of canonical Jewish texts, to accord such study the highest possible religious significance, and, on these terms, to precipitate a dramatic transformation in the aim and purpose of Jewish education.[62] For much of Jewish history, Jewish education and scholarly pursuits took place in local houses of study that catered to the needs of the immediate environment, producing a lay population and its religious and intellectual leadership on a local scale.[63] The traditional institution of the *heder* (primary school) aimed principally at integrating students into the life of the synagogue and the community, providing familiarity with the basic elements of religious obligation and conformity with communal law.[64] By contrast, the Volozhin yeshiva drew in students, teachers, and financial support from widely dispersed sources, yet was directly responsible to none of them. It housed a relatively autonomous coterie of male students and scholars, insulated from the everyday material world, whose loyalties lay, not with neighbors, parents, or the local rabbinate, but rather with the yeshiva itself and its hierarchy of teachers and learned sages.[65]

As a center for cultivating the uninterrupted, unending work of *Talmud Torah lishma* (the study of Torah for its own sake), the yeshiva provided an infrastructure for the production of what Menachem Friedman has described as "a tempered elite which saw its aim and purpose in absolute— 'heroic'—dedication to the ideal of Torah study as expressing Judaism in its fullness, and to the yeshiva as the core from which Jewish existence would draw sustenance."[66] Having arrogated onto themselves the responsibility to define all matters of legitimate conduct, yeshiva teachers proclaimed they were simply upholding historically sanctioned approaches to the Jewish canon. In practice, this often entailed identifying what they regarded as Jewishly inauthentic, inadequate, or corrupt: not least, the customs, rituals, and standards of observance of Jewish law as practiced in the communities from which students originated.[67] By subjecting local custom to systematic critique, Haredi rabbinic elites at the same time elevated the political and even the cosmic significance of everyday behavior. Even the most mundane acts could now be defined as potential expressions of loyalty to the authority of the yeshiva and commitment to its ongoing struggle to remain "Torah-true."

Over the course of the nineteenth century, Volozhin provided a model for the spread of yeshivot in Lithuania and thence across much of eastern Europe.[68] After World War II, the surviving members of these yeshivot were transplanted to new contexts in Israel and in the English-speaking diaspora, where they established new academies, often named after those institutions that had been destroyed in the war.[69] One striking trend that developed in the aftermath of this transplantation was the rapid growth in number and size of yeshivot: in part a product of the high fertility rate among the Haredim, but also a reflection of the changing function of the yeshiva within these reconstituted communities of "Torah-true" Jews. Whereas in times past the yeshiva had been considered the purview of only a small, scholarly elite, after World War II it became a mechanism for broad social inclusion, designed to accommodate the expressed desire of Haredi leaders that *all* boys should dedicate their lives to studying Talmud in yeshiva, moving from the *yeshiva ketana* (the "little *yeshiva*," i.e., primary school), to the *mesivta* (secondary school), to the *kollel* (the yeshiva for adult men). A parallel development in Jewish education for girls and women saw the rapid growth of institutions devoted to the rudiments of religious life and observance of Jewish law, on the argument that modern Haredi women could not be trusted to have received adequate instruction from parents or other informal sources. In both Israel and the diaspora, this included institutions such as Bais Yaakov (a.k.a. Beth Jacob), a federation of primary and secondary schools for Haredi girls closely affiliated with Agudat Israel, as well as *midrashot* (seminaries for adult women's education in Torah), and women's study circles and other types of part-time instruction sponsored by local synagogues and community institutions.[70]

An unsurprising consequence of this ever-expanding circle of students devoted to the study of sacred literature was a new premium placed on the written text. For yeshiva students, their families, and growing numbers of Jews within and beyond the Haredi community, Jewish books increasingly came to be seen as guarantors of instruction and as sources and touchstones of all forms of religious authenticity. In an influential study of contemporary Orthodox Judaism, Haym Soloveitchik has described this transformation in terms of a larger shift from "mimetic" to "textual" modes of pedagogy. Knowledge and patterns of practice acquired from parents, friends, or neighbors—and even from local rabbis—by imitation and through habituated practice has been supplanted by knowledge codified in texts, particularly texts produced by and for the yeshiva world. Such texts epitomize and dynamically shape the Haredi community's "tireless quest for absolute accuracy . . . [and for] faultless congruence between conception and performance," as evident in the efforts of Haredi scholars to systematically organize and fix in written form the entire range of mandatory, acceptable, and forbidden forms of Jewish behavior, including the routine practices of eating, dressing, working, and praying.[71]

In the case of the contemporary English-language Jewish diaspora, ArtScroll can be singled out as perhaps the most important purveyor of such works, although it is by no means the only publisher devoted to this literary output (other significant publishers in this field are Feldheim, Kehot, and Targum Press, not to mention the publishers in Israel whose Yiddish- and Hebrew-language works are exported abroad). In fact, ArtScroll has published dozens of texts that impart an understanding of the minutiae of Jewish law and legitimate conduct from a Haredi perspective. These include the press's popular "Halachah" series, featuring works that outline such things as the proper observance of the Sabbath and other Jewish festivals; the rules and procedures for keeping a kosher home; the proper care of religious articles; monetary issues, such as the regulations concerning accumulating interest or charitable giving; and summations of the laws of *niddah* (women's menstruation). Other ArtScroll texts offer advice to spouses, parents, adult children who must care for aging parents, and those experiencing bereavement or depression, along with many other guides to daily living. Such texts exemplify the way Haredism has developed as a mode of conceiving and performing all aspects of Jewish life "by the book," the contents of which are derived from and authorized by the scholarly elite of the yeshiva world.[72]

Of course, ArtScroll is not the first publisher to produce code books, and contemporary Haredi communities are not the first to make use of them.

Written works designed to distill the basic principles of Jewish law and to codify legitimate conduct have a long history in the Jewish tradition, most famously, perhaps, in the examples of Maimonides' twelfth-century Mishneh Torah or Rabbi Yosef Karo's sixteenth-century Shulhan Arukh, both of which became staples in the Jewish canon and still today are considered authoritative among both Haredi and non-Haredi Orthodox Jews. But as Soloveitchik argues, for much of history Jewish "custom was a correlative datum of the *halakhic* system [and] on frequent occasions, the written word was reread in the light of traditional behavior."[73] In support of the legitimacy of family routine and local custom, rabbinic authorities made frequent use of a Talmudic principle of legal reasoning that standards of acceptable behavior could be determined by going to "see what the people are doing."[74] In the contemporary situation, however, this relationship between the text and everyday experience has been reversed. Legitimate conduct is no longer measured against "what the people are doing" but only against increasingly rigid and stringent interpretations of textual codes. This posture of indifference (if not outright disdain) toward unreflectively received patterns of behavior is perhaps unsurprising in the light of Haredi society's experiences of displacement, the interruption of personal memories and familial traditions, and the proliferation of risks presented by the widening cultural opportunities and choices available in the new diaspora contexts. For yeshiva enclaves that had been transplanted and newly constituted in the aftermath of war, and faced threats from a larger culture of moral relativism, hedonism, and secular individualism, "the book took the place of the community, which had been left behind."[75]

We should add that what is unique about this form of text-centrism is not the Haredi community's sense of dislocation and precariousness, since, after all, Jewish history has been shaped by millennia of upheavals and migrations. Rather, the institutional and material conditions for the production and dissemination of text-based knowledge are what makes the contemporary situation so peculiar. One side of this story, we have already seen, can be traced through rising rates of literacy and textual competence among diverse Jewish constituencies, thanks in part to the spread and influence of educational institutions such as the yeshiva. The growth of Haredi yeshivot has in fact precipitated an increased likelihood that knowledge-seeking Jews will come into contact with Haredi interpretive approaches via the circulation of their texts and also through the diffusion of Haredi-trained teachers into non-Haredi institutional domains. Yet an equally important dimension of the rise of Haredi-based text-centrism is rooted in technological and material changes in the very modes of textual production and circulation, particularly with regard to print commodities and their reading publics. In fact, the past century, especially the post-World War II period, has seen a dramatic growth in the production and distribution of printed manuals, practical guides, and instructional handbooks explicating observance of religious codes, aimed explicitly at a lay audience.[76] Rising rates of production have not only extended such texts to new classes of readers but also precipitated new techniques, temporalities, and locations of reading, from houses of study and worship, to the domestic sphere, and even onto the human body in motion, such as through the creation of portable editions of code books that can be incorporated into "the 'worship gear' the devout carry with them as part of their prayer routines, to be read in the interstices of liturgy."[77]

Code books represent only one part of an even larger—and steadily growing—terrain of Orthodox Jewish book culture, encompassing diverse literary genres, fields of production, systems of circulation, and reading publics located both within and outside the Haredi enclave. The ArtScroll booklist, which currently boasts over one thousand titles in print, provides an ample illustration of this diversity. It includes the key sacred texts for which ArtScroll is best known, such as their prayer books, Bibles, rabbinic commentaries, and of course, the *Schottenstein Talmud,* each of which is available in a range of formats. But also included on the ArtScroll list are numerous encyclopedias, reference books, historical monographs, biographies, children's stories, cookbooks, adventure novels, self-help and pop psychology books, popular science books, and works of "ethical inspiration." As we shall see in greater detail in Chapter 2—where I shall paint a more detailed picture of the literary field of production and the public culture in which ArtScroll books are located—ArtScroll's embrace of this generic diversity throws into sharp relief the larger operative principles upon which Haredi intellectual and religious authorities must depend in their effort to infuse the entire universe with their Torah-true knowledge and to communicate this fullness to an indeterminate, mediated audience of insiders and outsiders.

Haredi scripturalism must therefore be viewed as more than simply a product of shifting attitudes toward the written word. It is also an effect of the expanding production and reach of the books themselves. As we have seen, in centuries past, the proportion of members of the Jewish community devoted to intensive textual study was greatly restricted. So too was their access to texts tightly circumscribed by such material factors as the high cost of paper and the limited technological capacities for reproducing, distributing, and preserving books. For much of the history of diaspora Jewry, local elites were able to study, interpret, and apply the Jewish canon only on the basis of what was available to them locally. Typically, this consisted of a limited library collection, supported by wealthy patrons of the community and augmented by the occasional arrival of new books transported by merchants and itinerant students or by other textual matter that circulated through available epistolary networks and postal systems.[78] Without the benefit of a mass print industry, the spread of Jewish books was thus arduous, fragmentary, and highly selective.[79] Starting in the nineteenth century, however, with the introduction of mass-reproduction print technologies, Jewish readers were afforded access to increasingly extensive bodies of material that would have been unknown or at best vaguely familiar—but in any event largely inaccessible—to previous generations of readers.[80] By the post-World War II period, the industrialization of book production had reached such a level that Orthodox publishing houses could begin to make their names by anthologizing, redacting, and widely distributing Talmud commentaries and other rabbinic literatures. It has in fact been one of the principal aims of ArtScroll to make available a vast range of Jewish religious texts—from the very familiar to the very rare—enabling local institutions, families, and even individuals to have direct possession of a library, the contents of which could rival, and even surpass, any of the great historic libraries of Jewish centers of learning.

In this expanding field of production and circulation, it has become possible for readers to gain access to texts that hitherto were available only in archives, university libraries, or private collections, thereby "reclaiming much that has been forgotten in both the Sephardi and Ashkenazic Talmudic heritages."[81] Such reclamations have led, quite literally, to a reconstruction of the Jewish canon itself. By forging new modes of connection between the present and the past, they have made "forgotten" or "lost" Jewish texts readily available to contemporary readers (a process that has been even more dramatically accelerated since the rise of computer-based technologies for digitizing texts and making them available on searchable electronic databases), thereby opening up a "universe of Talmudic commentaries to those who are unable to devote a lifetime to visiting libraries and examining manuscripts around the world."[82] This combination of comprehensive breadth and ease of access has defined the emergent conditions of possibility for the circulation of knowledge and the exercise of religious authority. Specifically, it demarcates the ways Haredi forms of authority can be felt beyond the direct presence of rabbis, teachers, and other visible agents, by being sedimented into the structured activities of collecting, preserving, and reading Jewish books. As Heilman astutely observes, "The current book-oriented generation, inundated by and possessing more and more texts—both virtual and printed—has a far more direct encounter with these books. Surrounded by them in their homes and their synagogues and even on their computers, so proud of their competence in them, which is enhanced by the translations and new access points, this new book-oriented class of Orthodox Jews is not likely to mount a revolt against their own libraries."[83]

FROM ENCLAVE TO PUBLIC CULTURE

We must ask ourselves how many neshomos [souls] have we lost because we have refused to use more effectively the weapons that have been used against us. Just as in modern war, rifles are not an adequate defense against aircraft, so too must we arm ourselves with the same weapons used by the enemy.

ALEXANDER ZUSHA FRIEDMAN

"The Fundamentals of Agudath Israel"

As we have seen, the yeshiva provides the key institutional setting for the propagation of Haredi religious authority, concentrated in the hands of its cadre of elite Talmud sages, the *gedolim*. By virtue of their occupation as disinterested scholars, working in a restricted field of intellectual production, the *gedolim* are accorded the greatest respect, and their word carries the greatest authority as the purest possible distillation of the meaning of Jewish sacred texts. In the words of the Chofetz Chaim (Rabbi Yisrael Meir Kagan, 1838–1933), the Polish *rosh yeshiva* and one of the most important founding figures of Agudat Israel and of the Haredi movement as a whole, "The person whose view [*da'ato*] is the view of the Torah [*da'at Torah*] can solve all worldly problems, both specific and general. However, there is one condition attached. The *Daas Torah* [*da'at Torah*] must be pure, without any interest or bias. However, if there is a person who possesses *Daas Torah* but it is intermingled even slightly with other views from the marketplace or from the newspapers, then this *Daas Torah* is turbid, intermingled with dregs. Such a person cannot penetrate into the heart of the matter."[84] However, to communicate this putatively pure and disinterested knowledge, Haredi intellectuals must avail themselves of the existing terms of social address. To have influence, their words must be able to forge sustainable bonds with diffusely located students, followers, interested lay audiences, and even intellectual and religious competitors. This constraint is symptomatic of the structure and character of all modern fields of politics and culture, where the industries, technologies, and symbolic economies of mediated communication delineate the horizons of action in which "the masses" are made to appear. The very possibility of having influence is tied to the performative principles of becoming visible and of reaching out to others and winning their assent within a cacophonous arena of competing voices and images and within generalized conditions of spectacle, distraction, and of readily dissolving attentions.[85] This is the public culture within which Haredi scholars and intellectual producers must labor to attract and retain a following and to legitimate their intellectual, religious, and cultural authority.

The strategic importance of being able to control the resources of mediated communication has been acknowledged within Haredi circles for some time. As succinctly stated by one contributor to an early edition of the *Jewish Observer* (the English-language journal of Agudath Israel of America), "The ability . . . to master the new media has become the key to success—or failure—to win the allegiance of the masses. . . . Jewish leadership is in the hands of those who can best make use of the new techniques of communication."[86] The mastery to which this author refers depends, in the first instance, on the success of Haredi Jews to redefine the terms by which they have been represented in the larger public sphere. Through polemical modes of address, Haredim seek to rescue Orthodoxy from the obloquy heaped upon it by its detractors. So, for instance, Rabbi Avi Shafran, public affairs director for Agudath Israel of America, calls upon his fellow Haredim to "utilize the Anglo-Jewish press—through carefully written letters to editors and articles—to reach the non-Orthodox laity and counter what their leaders are telling them and to present Torah-perspectives clearly and properly. . . . The larger Jewish world needs to hear our voices."[87] Through such forays into the public sphere, Haredi intellectuals have proven themselves equally aware of the ideolects, styles, and modes of address that are necessary for competent participation in modern media fields. This is colorfully illustrated in an anecdote recounted by Rabbi Nisson Wolpin, a former editor-in-chief of the *Jewish Observer:*

> When I was new at the desk of *The Jewish Observer,* I had the privilege of driving one of our leading *Roshei Yeshiva* home from a meeting of the

Moetzes Gedolei HaTorah [the supreme governing body of Agudat Israel]. At the session, the members had deliberated over a very sensitive topic, and during the ride home, I asked my esteemed passenger how I should treat the subject in the pages of the magazine. He replied: "It's important that your message be read, and that it be fully and clearly understood. Use the methods of advertisers. Copy advertising style: short articles, short paragraphs, words that are not too difficult." At first, I was taken aback. It struck me that the *Rosh Yeshiva,* celebrated for his intellectual genius and poetic gift of expression, was talking down to me. After some thought, however, I realized the justice of his counsel. Advertisers constantly check themselves as to whether their message is reaching the people. If they buy, then the message is being read and understood. If not, it's back to the drawing board. No other area of writing is exposed to such constant testing and evaluation.[88]

To "reach the people," Rabbi Wolpin warns, authoritative proclamations must speak a language the people can readily understand, whether this be advertising or some other mode of popular address. Such an attitude stands on the shoulders of a more incremental, historical shift away from what might be construed as the more "traditional" attitudes toward mediated communication, and in particular the participation of Jews in larger fields of print-mediated publicity. Indeed, for much of the history of print, Jewish rabbinic elites stood Janus-faced, from one perspective lauding the promises of this technology to facilitate the production and dissemination of sacred works, and from the other bemoaning the ways print increased the opportunities for contact with a hostile world of "foreign ideas," threatened to undo the "customary" structures of communal, religious, and intellectual authority.[89] Nevertheless, despite the ambivalence of rabbinic authorities, it is possible to trace a steady and growing involvement of Orthodox Jewish intellectuals in print-mediated arenas of public culture, as reflected, for instance, in the initiatives to publish popular manuals, ethical works, biographies, and other printed works starting in the late eighteenth century. By the early twentieth century, sectors of the Orthodox intelligentsia were devoted to the production of a series of flourishing daily presses aimed at large sectors of the Orthodox population.[90] And by the post-World War II period, Orthodox involvements in the daily press, in periodical publications, and in book publishing had increased exponentially, especially in Israel and the United States, the two most important sites of production for Orthodox literature. This growth in production is directly related to the consolidation of an expanding, transnation-ally situated constituency of Orthodox Jewish consumers, able to express demand, not only for canonical texts, but also for newspapers, journals, and other forms of popular literature, such as history, fiction, popular psychology, and children's books.[91] In all these ways, a growing premium on accessibility—of "reaching the people," as Rabbi Wolpin puts it—has shaped the ways modern Orthodox intellectuals and religious leaders seek to legitimate and consolidate their authority.

The mission of publishing houses such as ArtScroll cannot be understood without reference to this longer history of privileging the "accessibility" of messages and of engaging both insiders and outsiders on such terms. Indeed, ArtScroll's massive output provides a compelling illustration of how Haredi cultural mediators today must negotiate between their urge to faithfully represent the "true" meaning of Jewish texts, as authorized by the Haredi yeshiva elite, and their need to make such meanings apprehensible among diverse readerships located both within and outside the Haredi world and encompassing a range of competencies and levels of familiarity with canonical Jewish literature, as well as varying degrees of reading ability in the original source languages. At the same time, the contemporary field of literary production imposes upon all Haredi publishing houses the expectation that they will reach their audiences by operating within the constraints of financial viability and reliable market conditions, in part by overtaking competing sources of religious and intellectual authority, embedded in the literatures produced under the auspices of modern Orthodox, Conservative, Reform, and secular Jewish institutions, as well as other academic, university, and trade publishers that cater to the modern Jewish reading public. As we have already seen in this chapter, with the release of the *Schottenstein Talmud* and its public consecration in such venues as libraries, museums, and mass rallies, ArtScroll has proven itself to be highly adept at handling the instruments designed to secure success in the media field. Of course, it is another matter altogether to say whether and how such campaigns to make Haredi messages both authoritative and accessible actually work on the ground, within an arena of competing publishers, literary agents, and authors and within the diverse, local contexts of reception for ArtScroll books. That is the subject of the next chapter.

TWO

ArtScroll's Public Life

AS WE HAVE SEEN, ArtScroll defines its mission as one of reaching beyond the Haredi enclave, addressing and reclaiming a universal class of Jews in search of authentic meaning. Through the production and dissemination of texts that have been authorized and approved by the elites of the Haredi yeshiva world, ArtScroll offers a comprehensive body of Torah-true literature, designed to inform, instruct, and emotionally uplift readers in all aspects of public and private life. The ideal readers are the ones who are able to fill up every dimension of their lives with ArtScroll books as sources of knowledge, as narrative models for ethical conduct, as partners in ritual performance, and as objects to collect and display.

Do such readers exist? Perhaps nowhere more clearly than in the imagination of ArtScroll's own stakeholders and supporters. After all, authors, publishers, and readers do not normally meet except through the medium of the market and according to the technological, material, and temporal conditions that allow for writing and reading to take place. Claims about the intentions of authors or, for that matter, publishers, as well as their effect on readers through the medium of their books, should always be tempered by a sober account of the spatial, temporal, and social distances between these agents. This is all the more pressing for an understanding of whether and how ArtScroll's editors and authors exert religious authority in the contemporary situation of Jewish public culture. As I argued in

Chapter 1, modern conditions of voluntary affiliation, and of easy access to vast storehouses of knowledge—thanks especially to accelerating rates of production of print matter—have dramatically altered the expression of religious authority, both for those who seek to assert it and for those who are presumed to fall under its sway. In the contemporary situation, the powers and privileges once enjoyed by the rabbinic elites of the traditional Jewish corporation have given way to a new public culture defined by increasingly frequent and dense interactions among strangers, often connected only by media, and by the crisscrossing of multiple, competing interpretive approaches to legitimate Jewish practice and to the meaning of Jewish texts.

This is not to say one cannot find the kind of consumer ArtScroll claims as its own. Consider the following interview with Aaron (a pseudonym), a forty-eight-year-old medical professional, a father of four, and an ardent ArtScroll fan. Aaron goes to a Toronto Orthodox synagogue "a few times a week." He defines himself as having lived a "strictly Orthodox" life for the past thirteen years. Before that, he was "totally secular," and growing up he received "only a minimal Jewish education."

JS: What's your opinion of the *ArtScroll Siddur* [basic prayer book]?

A: It's outstanding.

JS: How so?

A: It's by far superior for people who are, it's particularly constructed for people like us who perhaps didn't have a formal Jewish education but are serious about our *Yiddishkeit* [Jewishness], and who are coming back to *Yiddishkeit* seriously. So we're looking for something that gives us information, is easy to read and informs us, and is written with sincerity. And you get the sense with ArtScroll that there is an awful lot of sincerity on the part of those who wrote it. They clearly want to help you.

JS: That's interesting. How would you describe the difference between the ArtScroll and other Siddurim you have seen?

A: Well, ArtScroll has really good commentaries. And excellent cross-references. I mean, it cross-references virtually everything and it's really easy to find the references. But I suppose, I mean, most of all it's the English translation I like. I think it's closer to the Hebrew, or what the Hebrew is meant to be. And so those are the real strengths of the ArtScroll. Virtually no other Siddur has that combination. I only think they ought to price them down a bit. But aside from that I think they're really outstanding.

JS: What about other ArtScroll books? You know, they produce self-help books, history books . . .

A: Yeah, yeah. Well, we've got them all. There's virtually nothing put out by ArtScroll that we don't have. The *musar* [ethical guidance] books, the halakhah [books on Jewish law], the list goes on and on.

JS: You own all these books?

A: Yep. We bought them all.

JS: Do you have any particular favorites?

A: I can't say, to be honest. There are so many. I can't begin to count them, I read them all the time.[1]

Of course, not every consumer shares Aaron's uniformly glowing approval of everything ArtScroll has to offer, nor would it be accurate to describe ArtScroll's position in the book market as monopolistic. In fact, ArtScroll's reach into Jewish lives and into the spaces of local Jewish communities is far from ubiquitous. It would be more accurate to suggest that, through strategies to identify and supply carefully defined market niches, ArtScroll has managed to cultivate a committed customer base encompassing specific sectors of the Haredi world and also specific communities of readers located beyond the Haredi enclave and beyond the Orthodox world as a whole. Above all, ArtScroll's success is materialized in its growing share of the market for prayer books, Bibles, and other liturgical works, buttressed by its reputation as a "strictly Orthodox" and "traditional" publisher and at the same time as a purveyor of "beautifully crafted" print products. This hold on the market for liturgical works is further cemented by the innovative production and marketing strategies utilized by the publisher, as evident from ArtScroll's creation of multiple versions of each of its prayer books, at a range of prices, in different sizes and physical formats, designed for either daily or weekly usage, with translations aimed at either elementary or advanced readers of Hebrew, and reflective of specific differences of liturgical custom among Ashkenazi, Hasidic, and Sephardic congregations. Other works, such as ArtScroll's Bible translation, *The Stone Edition of the Tanach,* the previously discussed *Schottenstein Talmud, The Stone Edition of the Chumash* (Pentateuch), and even the best-selling cookbook *Kosher by Design,* have also been marketed successfully to a broad audience, including both religious and secular Jews and even non-Jewish readers, such as members of the American Christian evangelical community, who are attracted to ArtScroll's products as exemplars of authentic Jewish wisdom.[2]

All the same, it is important to note that ArtScroll's foray into the English-language book market has been neither random nor indiscriminate. On the contrary, as this chapter aims to show, its direction, scale, and pace have been determined by prevailing financial and technological conditions; by the relationships between the publisher, its authors, and competitors; and by the institutional affiliations and social locations of consumers, including their gender, class, type of education, nationality, age, and generation. ArtScroll's spread has also been shaped by the attitudes of local authorities and other intermediary figures—such as librarians or booksellers—toward the publisher and its various genres of writing. As we shall see from an examination of each of these factors, in contrast with some of the inflated claims about the "ArtScroll revolution," the publisher has succeeded in winning a foothold only within particular segments of the reading public that are receptive to the benefits that ownership of ArtScroll books appears to entail.

THE INSTITUTIONAL ORGANIZATION OF AUDIENCES

This analysis proceeds from the basic axiom that authors, editors, and other producers of textual matter never address such a thing as a universal audience. As the literary critic Mikhail Bakhtin teaches us, to communicate speakers and writers must cast their utterances in forms recognizable and appropriate to the concrete social situations in which they find themselves, and these forms of address—Bakhtin calls them "speech genres"—constitute the very basis upon which utterances are constructed and meaning is conveyed.[3] In the case of reading publics, we must also bear in mind that interlocutors do not join in directly reciprocal relationships for the production of meaning, as in the case of theatrical performances or everyday oral interactions. Instead, relationships between authors and readers are always complicated by the intervening presence of economic and material networks that make up the book industry, which, as Pierre Bourdieu puts it, "forms a protective screen between the artist and the market, [but is] also what links them to the market."[4] Writers and readers are also separated by the inescapable fact that every written text can exist only in a larger universe of intertextuality: the endless web of references, quotations, indices, classificatory schemata, and genres of reported speech that surrounds all acts of writing and reading. Not least among these intertextual relations one finds various "epitexts," shaping the terms of production and reception of texts themselves, as in the case of book reviews in journals, promotional material and advertising, or the documented protocols of school and library acquisition policies.[5] Each of these social structures of addressivity and receptivity contributes to the ways authors write, editors edit, and publishers market their books. By the same token, attention to such structures helps remind us that readers do not encounter texts as atomistic individuals, propelled by their own, self-fashioned standards of taste and intellectual expectations, picking and choosing from the heteroglossia of available texts and ignoring what does not suit them. Instead, customers, readers, and other users of books make their choices in relation to an array of products formed in advance of their arrival on the market. The very range and availability of such products are thus shaped by material conditions of production and circulation and by social modes of legitimation, sense making, and taste inhering in the aforementioned epitexts and related structures of intermediation. Because one cannot exercise demand outside the constraints of these complex intermediating networks, any act of choosing from among textual products available on the market is simultaneously an act of positioning oneself in relation to identifiable distinctions among already constituted social groups. In other words, to appropriate an ArtScroll book is to enter into a relationship of economic exchange but also to immerse oneself in a larger network of affiliations, shared styles, modes of circulating knowledge, and patterns of social behavior that help to define the very meaning of that book and therefore also its owner.

Nowhere are these processes of collective decision making and social distinction more palpable than in the context of Jewish communal institutions, such as synagogues, Jewish schools, community centers, and libraries. All such institutions are notable for the considerable economic and symbolic resources they invest to sustain the existence of their books and to make them routinely available to their employees, clients, and other stakeholders. The mere presence of a given book within any of these locations thus helps to consecrate its status as a part of "official" Jewish public culture (or, as we shall see presently in the case of ArtScroll liturgical works, as a lightning rod for public controversy). In the specific case of synagogues and their congregational communities, next to the Torah scroll itself, sets of Siddurim (basic prayer books) and Chumashim (an edited version of the Pentateuch, divided into fifty-two sections, for weekly readings) are the most important examples of such artifacts. Through their routine use in public ritual and for study, these works offer the congregation a means of reproducing itself in time and space according to the rhythms of the ritual calendar and through its networked affiliations with other congregations, in other places, engaged with the same books.

Such modes of collective engagement with prayer books are the product of a very long history of Jewish liturgy, in which locally variant practices based on memorization and oral recitation were sedimented into "official" versions and fixed in written form.[6] These pressures toward textualization and standardization were greatly increased with the introduction of techniques of mass reproduction and the circulation of ritual texts in the form of print commodities. By the late nineteenth century, such forces were starting to be consolidated into relatively stable relationships between the economic organization of the Jewish book market and the symbolic authority of rabbinic governing bodies. Today, most congregations in the English-speaking world are affiliated with one or another of these umbrella organizations. Such affiliation generally assumes commitment to the use of "established" liturgical texts, while at the same time binding local communities into relationships of economic exchange with the "authorized" publishers of such works (see Table 1).[7]

ArtScroll operates as a relative newcomer within this consolidated field of relations among institutions, local congregations, and users of Jewish liturgical texts. Moreover, as I have already indicated, ArtScroll is further distinguished as an independent publisher, without formal ties or obligations to any of the governing bodies with which most Jewish congregations, schools, and communal institutions are affiliated. This relative autonomy has allowed the press to cater to multiple communities at the same time, with considerable success. So, for instance, ArtScroll has produced slightly modified versions of its basic prayer book, *The Complete ArtScroll Siddur,* in cooperation with the Orthodox Union and the Rabbinical Council of America, the two largest modern Orthodox governing bodies in the English-speaking world. ArtScroll's institutional independence has also meant that the press does not operate under the constraints of cumbersome editorial processes mandated by most governing bodies, such as the election of liturgical committees, membership opinion surveys, and other modes of administrative oversight in the composition of prayer books, Bibles, and related works. Rather, editorial decisions, production processes, and marketing strategies are developed internally, according to the personal affiliations of ArtScroll's key editors with religious and intellectual authorities of the yeshiva world and according to their own conceptions of a prospective audience that cuts across the established divides of rabbinic governing bodies.

TABLE I

Principal governing bodies of Jewish congregations (U.S., U.K., and Canadian)
and their common liturgical texts

	Principal Governing Bodies	Common Prayer Books	Common Chumashim
Orthodox	Union of Orthodox Jewish Congregations of America (a.k.a. the Orthodox Union) (USA and Canada)	Daily Prayer Book (Birnbaum, 1949; reissued 1977)	The Pentateuch (Hertz 1929–36), reissued as the Hertz Chumash (Cohen, 1983)
	Rabbinical Council of America (USA and Canada)	Siddur: The Traditional Prayer Book for Sabbath and Festivals (de Sola Pool, 1960)	Soncino Chumash (Cohen, 1947; revised ed., 1983)
	National Council of Young Israel (USA)	Authorised Daily Prayer Book of the United Hebrew Congregations of the British Empire (Hertz, 1947)	Torah and the Haftarot (Birnbaum, 1983)
	Union of Orthodox Rabbis (Agudath haRabbanim) (USA and Canada)		The Living Torah, by Maznaim Press (Kaplan, 1981)
	Agudath Israel of America (USA and Canada)	Authorised Daily Prayer Book of the United Hebrew Congregations of the Commonwealth (Singer, 1992)	Books of the Bible, by Judaica Press (Rosenberg, 1993)
	Union of Orthodox Hebrew Congregations (UK)	Authorised Daily Prayer Book of the United Hebrew Congregations of the Commonwealth of Nations: A New Translation and Commentary (Sacks, 2006)	The Stone Edition of the Chumash, by ArtScroll (Scherman, 1993)
	United Synagogue (UK)		The Margolin Edition of the Torah, by Feldheim Publishers (Moore, 1999)
	Federation of Synagogues (UK)	The Complete ArtScroll Siddur (Scherman, 1984)	

Conservative/Masorti	United Synagogue of Conservative Judaism (USA and Canada) Rabbinical Assembly (USA and Canada) Union for Traditional Judaism Reform Synagogues of Great Britain (UK)	Daily Prayer Book (Birnbaum, 1949) Weekday Prayer Book (Silverman, 1946) Siddur Sim Shalom (Harlow, 1985; reissued 1998) Or Hadash (Hammer, 2004)	The Pentateuch (Rabbi Joseph Hertz, 1929–36, reissued as the Hertz Chumash, Cohen, 1983) Etz Hayim Chumash (Lieber, 2001)
Reform	Union of Reform Judaism (formerly Union of American Hebrew Congregations) (USA and Canada) Central Conference of American Rabbis (USA and Canada) Union of Liberal and Progressive Synagogues (UK)	Siddur Teflot Yisrael: The Union Prayer Book (CCAR, 1895; rev. 1940) Gates of Prayer (Stern, 1975; rev. ed., 1994) Mishkan T'filah (Frishman, 2006)	The Torah: A Modern Commentary (Plaut, 1981)

NOTE: Does not represent independent (unaffiliated) congregations (such as many Haredi synagogues and their communities). Also does not indicate the many instances where a rabbi is "more Orthodox" than the congregation itself.

These are the terms on which ArtScroll has orchestrated a decisive entry into the field of Jewish liturgical practice. Since the mid-1990s, ArtScroll prayer books have in fact been adopted as "official" editions for a growing number of Jewish communities across the English-speaking world, especially (but not exclusively) among so-called "modern" Orthodox congregations. In this way, they have increasingly displaced such works as Philip Birnbaum's *Daily Prayer Book,* David de Sola Pool's *Siddur,* Joseph Hertz's *Authorized Daily Prayer Book* and *Pentateuch and Haftorahs,* and the *Soncino Chumash,* all of which have been considered the "standard" works of liturgy for English-speaking Orthodox communities for the better part of the past century.[8] This trend is evident from data I collected between 2001 and 2004 regarding synagogues that had or had not recently acquired ArtScroll's most popular liturgical text, *The Complete ArtScroll Siddur,* in three major centers of the English-speaking Jewish world: London, Toronto, and New York City (see Table 2).[9]

As indicated in Table 2, ArtScroll's liturgical works have become especially popular among what might be characterized as "mainstream" Orthodox congregations (its offerings were found in two-thirds to three-fourths of the sample in each of the three cities under examination), whereas other communities—Sephardi, Liberal, Reform, Reconstructionist—showed no interest at all in acquiring or using ArtScroll texts. But there are two notable exceptions to this trend. The first is the existence of a minority of Conservative synagogues (located in Toronto and New York) that have recently adopted ArtScroll works, evincing an important cultural shift that I shall address presently. The second is the absence of ArtScroll texts within Haredi prayer houses. This latter occurrence is perhaps an indicator of a more tenacious attachment to older liturgical texts, or even ideological discomfort with the sorts of changes connoted by the ArtScroll "brand," but can just as readily be interpreted in light of other factors, such as the very high degree of command of Hebrew among Haredi readers (thereby precluding the need for ArtScroll's bilingual prayer books).

In conclusion, the collected data suggest that in the space of only a few years ArtScroll has ascended to a clear position of dominance in the institutional context of Orthodox ritual life (representing over 50 percent of "official" texts across all types of Orthodox synagogues throughout the sampled data in the three cities under consideration). Moreover, this dominance has begun to have an impact outside the Orthodox community, as the name ArtScroll becomes increasingly identified as the "standard" purveyor of Orthodox prayer books for English-speaking Jews—even among

TABLE 2

Use of ArtScroll prayer books in synagogues by city and denomination, 2001–4

| | Orthodox | | | | | Other | | | Total |
	Haredi	Independent	Modern	Total Orthodox	Conservative (Masorti)	Reform	Reconstructionist	Sephardi	
London n=26	0% (0/4)	75% (3/4)	70% (7/10)	55.5% (10/18)	50% (1/2)	0% (0/5)	0% (0/0)	0% (0/1)	42.3% (11/26)
Toronto n=29	0% (0/2)	100% (1/1)	75% (6/8)	63.6% (7/11)	22.2% (2/9)	0% (0/5)	0% (0/3)	0% (0/1)	31% (9/29)
New York n=66	0% (0/4)	50% (2/4)	62.5% (15/24)	53.1% (17/32)	14.3% (4/28)	0% (0/3)	0% (0/1)	0% (0/2)	31.8% (21/66)

NOTE: Indicates cases where ArtScroll prayer books have become the main (if not the only) edition available for congregants. Does not indicate cases where congregants own their own copies of ArtScroll texts for home use and/or use these during synagogue services.

those who choose not to purchase or use them. The size and reach of its operations further suggest that ArtScroll is likely to retain its commanding position within the liturgical field for the foreseeable future, as the publisher leverages economies of scale in its favor, making it increasingly difficult for competing Orthodox publishers to offer financially viable alternatives. Most strikingly, ArtScroll's influence has begun to be registered even among non-Orthodox publishers, who feel compelled to produce "answers to ArtScroll," that is, liturgical texts that offer features similar to those for which ArtScroll is well known, such as embossed coverings, innovative typography, or an abundance of instructions relating to the "choreography" of ritual performance.[10] Examples of this trend are the Conservative movement's recent prayer book, *Or Hadash,* and Bible, *Etz Hayim,* and the Reform movement's newest prayer book, *Mishkan T'filah,* all of which place a greater emphasis on reading Hebrew and offer far more instructional notes, historical commentaries, and citations than any of the previously existing Conservative and Reform liturgical texts.[11] That non-Orthodox Jewish organizations see fit to introduce their own "alternatives to ArtScroll" makes it tempting to speak of a more generalized process of "ArtScrollification" of the entire liturgical field for English-speaking Jews, regardless of their specific institutional affiliation. After all, behind every effort to distinguish oneself from one's competitors is a prior acknowledgment that they are "worthy adversaries," which is simply another way of conceding their power.[12]

THE POLITICS OF SWITCHING TO ARTSCROLL

Why have congregations switched to ArtScroll, and how ought we to assess these shifts? Supporters often hail ArtScroll's arrival as having provided a compelling opportunity to counterbalance trends toward liberalism and assimilation that purportedly have been plaguing the Jewish community and against which the "turgid prose" and "outdated scholarship" of the standard English texts, they claim, offers no compelling remedy. One London-based Orthodox rabbi, responsible for the incorporation of *The Complete ArtScroll Siddur* into his congregation, explained ArtScroll's importance for revitalizing the London Jewish community in this way: "The Masorti [Conservative] and the Reform movements don't seem to have the confidence of conviction to produce books like ArtScroll. They're always too diffident: '*x* says this and *y* says that.' ArtScroll, on the other hand, claim to have produced a *definitive* version. What's better? People won't observe Pesach [Passover] if they are presented with twenty opportunities not to observe it. People don't seem to get this message so clearly from Hertz or Singer [the "established" Orthodox prayer books in the United Kingdom—see Table 1, above]."[13]

For some, then, the acquisition of ArtScroll prayer books fits into a larger set of strategies aimed at retaining the integrity of Orthodox ritual practices in the face of growing threats of laxity. In other cases, with the arrival of ArtScroll prayer books in new institutional settings, formerly secure loyalties and patterns of observance are challenged, not confirmed, as new possibilities emerge to forge relationships across and around what were once taken to be hardened lines of communal affiliation. The power of ArtScroll to upset established patterns of ritual practice and assertions of communal identity is especially evident in the case of a small but growing number of North American Conservative Jewish congregations that have recently adopted ArtScroll prayer books and Bibles as their "official" liturgical texts, not to mention a much larger number of Conservative synagogues that over recent years have grown accustomed to individual congregants participating in prayer services with editions of ArtScroll prayer books in their hands. These recent converts to ArtScroll are typically members of an incipient movement popularly termed "Conservadox" Judaism, a trend institutionally expressed by the creation of its own governing body, the Union for Traditional Judaism, led by a breakaway group of "traditionalist" Conservative rabbis (representing many, but not all, Conservadox communities across North America). Conservadox Jews are united in their disaffection with what they perceive as a drift toward laxity in the observance of Jewish law, as reflected in the positions taken by the Conservative leadership (the Rabbinical Assembly and the United Synagogues of Conservative Judaism) and in the movement's "official" prayer books, such as the *Siddur Sim Shalom* and even its recent replacement, *Or Hadash*.[14] ArtScroll, it so happens, has been greeted by many members of the Conservadox community as an adequate representation of the more traditional liturgy they seek to embrace, and the adoption of ArtScroll prayer books is therefore a marker of ideological and cultural rapprochement between the right wing of Conservatism and the Orthodox mainstream. As summarized by one rabbi, originally trained in an Orthodox yeshiva, who leads a Conservadox synagogue in the greater New York area, "While [ArtScroll books] are predominantly associated with Orthodox institutions, they're not exclusively associated with Orthodoxy. There are other, traditional congregations, such as mine, which have reacted positively, where ArtScroll has created a bit of a niche."[15]

It is no small thing for a local community to flout the authority of the mainstream Conservative governing bodies by acquiring an unambiguously Orthodox prayer book, especially when one considers the expenses associated with such an acquisition and the length of time these artifacts can survive in institutional settings, often outlasting the generation involved in their purchase.[16] In this way, the act of "switching to ArtScroll" can be read as far more than the outcome of the search for a suitable text to guide the community in the performance of ritual practice. It is also a public statement of principles, a claim about what counts as legitimate Jewish conduct. Such shifts frequently result in tensions, for example, between local rabbis and lay leaders of the congregation, and they often invite more widespread controversy within the congregation as a whole, especially among generational cohorts, since older congregants tend to be more tenaciously attached to the prayer books they have known for most (if not all) their lives, whereas younger members are more receptive to change.[17] As communities become embroiled in these politics of brand switching, it is possible to map out the positions they stake within a volatile field of competing loyalties and public controversies. Consider, in this regard, the conversation I had in 2003 with Deborah (a pseudonym), a "sixty-plus-year-old observant Jew" affiliated with a large Conservative synagogue in Toronto, that could be characterized as symptomatic of the shift toward Conservadoxy. The synagogue had recently received a set of *The Complete ArtScroll Siddur* from a wealthy donor and had added the volumes to its existing stock of (Conservative) prayer books, much to Deborah's disapproval:

D: The print is too small, and I don't like the commentaries. And on the whole, ArtScroll is too triumphant.

JS: What do you mean by *triumphant*?

D: "Our form of Judaism is successful; others are withering away. Our form of Judaism includes deprecating other religions, and we're going to be the future." That's the agenda they're communicating.

JS: That's interesting you say that. So, why do you think that your shul [synagogue] brought in the ArtScroll?

D: Because it's convenient. And I guess for a lot of people it's attractive. I think they prefer it. Like when you walk into the synagogue. Now, ever since ArtScroll arrived, so many people, when they sit down, they look around to see if there's an ArtScroll.

JS: So it's not the only Siddur. What's the other one you are using besides the ArtScroll?

D: Yes, there's the big brown one.

JS: Would you say that there are any other people in shul who feel the same way you do?

D: Well some of the older women do, I think so.

JS: Hmm, so do you mean that maybe the men find a different aspect of ArtScroll . . .

D: . . . I don't know what the men think. I don't talk to them.[18]

It is striking that Deborah's assessment of ArtScroll, much like that of ArtScroll enthusiasts, attends to the material form of the books ("the print is too small") as well as their discursive content (the publisher's "triumphant agenda"), and these concatenated observations remind us that ArtScroll's arrival is typically registered at not only the intellectual but also the pragmatic and even the sensorial level.[19] For Deborah, as for many participants of routine institutional ritual practices, before the arrival of ArtScroll's Siddur in her synagogue, prayer books were relatively anonymous instruments for ritual conduct. Precisely because so much about the prayer book in her synagogue was *not* noteworthy it seems to have been seamlessly integrated into the categories, orders, and placement of objects that underpinned habitual and routine practices of ritual life. When she went to shul, Deborah used to look for, take hold of, read, and recite prayers from a book whose identity could sufficiently be recalled through the simple designation, "the big brown one."[20] ArtScroll, on the other hand, is explicitly identified here as a new arrival. As such, its very name references new possibilities for relating ritual practitioners and written texts and new ways of negotiating between the authority of local traditions and the authorizing power of a published work. For as Deborah intimates, those who pray with ArtScroll are transformed by their very engagement with the book. They are no longer part of the undifferentiated mass that made up her community, at least so far as their use of prayer books is concerned. Now they are the ones who affiliate with ArtScroll, the ones who "look around" to see if they can find a copy of the ArtScroll prayer book and in so doing also locate themselves within a new complex of intellectual, aesthetic, ideological, performative, and affective distinctions.

The foregoing analysis has given us a partial but telling picture of ArtScroll's penetration of the market for Jewish liturgical texts, and especially of the ways this trend has been aligned with shifts in institutional allegiance and cultural practice and the generation of public disputes for Jewish communities located in three major urban centers of the English-speaking diaspora. Anecdotal evidence points to a similar picture in many other cities across the United States, Canada, the United Kingdom, Australia, and South Africa. It remains to be seen whether a similar trend toward growing acceptance of ArtScroll will emerge among French-, Spanish-, and Russian-speaking Jewish communities, given the publisher's recent efforts to produce works in these languages, but it is worth noting recent reports suggesting that ArtScroll has also been gaining a strong foothold in Israel among modern Hebrew-speaking Jews.[21] Taking this larger field into perspective, we might also note that although institutional purchases of ArtScroll prayer books stage some of the most visible public dramas involving the publisher, its largest gains are registered more incrementally (and therefore less noticeably) in the context of the retail book market. Indeed, ArtScroll's strong foothold in this market was consistently evident in my repeated visits to several dozen bookstores specializing in Judaica in London, Toronto, and New York between 2000 and 2008, where I estimated ArtScroll's presence in terms of the proportion of total shelf space, the positioning of ArtScroll books in window and in-store displays, and promotional offerings (most significantly, participation in annual sales and other seasonal discounts organized by the publisher). In a few cases, ArtScroll books represented as much as 50 percent of the total stock available in the store. Although retail booksellers generally do not divulge data about sales, the heavy presence of ArtScroll books in their stores is a sufficient indication of steady demand. This demand includes sales generated simply by virtue of ArtScroll's imprimatur and its contagious effects as a brand name. As reported by one employee in a Judaica bookstore in New York City,

> ArtScroll has all kind of books. Right across the board. You know, all kinds of things. So much so that in the store we need to have an ArtScroll section now. Because people are coming in and saying, "I heard that ArtScroll has something new out on this subject, do you have it yet?" And we'd say, "Sorry, we don't, but we can put your name down and we'll

order it, and we'll call you when it comes in." Because with ArtScroll, you know, once someone found something by them, they would come back and say, "Do you have this?" Something else by them on a different subject. They're definitely the most popular thing going in the store.[22]

The fact that ArtScroll has risen to such prominence in the retail book market invites consideration of the larger field that assigns ArtScroll its position in relation to competing publishers and its comparative leverage vis-à-vis distributors, retail booksellers, and other agents involved in the dissemination of Jewish books. These interactions can productively be analyzed according to the logic and structure of what Pierre Bourdieu calls a field of cultural production. For Bourdieu, a given field of cultural production is defined by the practices of its actors, who are distinguished by their competitive struggles for control over the symbolic resources that circulate within the field, such as legitimacy, authority, recognition, honor, and fame. Through their interactions, actors position themselves, and are positioned by one another, according to their degree of access to these inherently scarce resources and also according to the hierarchical structure of the field as a whole. Actors thus have an interest in securing legitimacy, even if they often deny, repress, or misrecognize their role in this struggle, for example, by proclaiming the "disinterestedness" of their activities. By simply engaging in the practices of a given field, wittingly or unwittingly, actors enact strategies that reproduce and sustain the dynamically competitive structure of the social order in which they are situated.[23]

In the case of publishing houses, each such actor is differentiated according to its hierarchical position in the larger field of print-mediated cultural production. The assignment of a position within this field undergirds such things as the publisher's financial viability, the desire (and capacity) of the publisher to bring new products to market, the publisher's ability to dominate identifiable market niches, and the publisher's ability to receive recognition and legitimation from (often competing) cultural authorities. A publishing house, we should further note, is a peculiar sort of actor. It comprises, but cannot be reduced to, the authors whose names appear on the titles of its books. After all, authors represent only one portion of the institutional makeup of a publisher, alongside its business partners, investors and shareholders, editors, graphic designers, marketing agents, accountants, and various types of inventory and clerical staff.[24] Although these personnel are differentiated according to their function within the process of literary production (as well as their degree of commitment to the publisher, or access to and control over its various resources), and although it is thereby possible to treat each of these social groups as analytically distinct entities, they are nonetheless united within the institutional identity of the publisher itself. As we have already seen in the specific case of ArtScroll, this institutional identity is further distinguished by the porous walls dividing the business of producing an authentic and sacred literature from the business of producing and selling books. This porosity is evident in the close collaboration between ArtScroll and members of the yeshiva world, who are routinely engaged as researchers, translators, proofreaders, and "content providers," and also—in the case of more prominent rabbinic figures—as endorsers of the authenticity and legitimacy of ArtScroll's products. For the purposes of this discussion, the name ArtScroll must therefore be understood as a shorthand term of reference for the full range of formal and informal interactions among business associates, authors, employees, and other stakeholders, as well as the financial, technical, and legal resources that enable the publisher to function as a productive entity.

It is possible to analyze publishing houses in terms of these internal structures and operations, leading us to a greater understanding of such things as the processes of financial and editorial decision making or the work routines of their personnel. But one of the virtues of Bourdieu's analytical approach is that it emphasizes the *external* logic of mutual positioning and the ways such positioning shapes the strategies and prospects for the accumulation of both cultural and economic capital. In this spirit, Table 3 offers a representation of the competitive and hierarchical relationships among the key contemporary English-language Jewish publishing houses, distinguished by age and type of organization.

According to Bourdieu, fields of cultural production tend to be organized by a series of binary oppositions—such as that between purveyors of "high art" (the "subfield of restricted production") and purveyors of "mass art" (the "subfield of large-scale production"), or between "established" artists and "newcomers"—and these oppositions govern the strategies and trajectories of actors to define their audiences, innovate products, and accumulate rewards.[25] In the case of the field of production of English-language Jewish books, it is likewise useful to distinguish publishing houses in terms of the kinds of books for which they have developed a reputation (and therefore the types of consumers they try to address), but also in terms of their degree of "establishment" (determined by the age of the publishers, as well as their connection with other key institutions, such as universities or religious governing bodies) and, not least, their financial organization (e.g., as pub-

TABLE 3
English-language publishing houses devoted principally to Jewish books,
with date of founding

	Trade Presses	Institutional Presses	Independent Orthodox Presses
Established	• Bloch Publishing Co. (Chicago, 1885; New York City, 1901) • Jewish Publication Society (Philadelphia, 1888) • Behrman House (New York City,1921) • Ktav Publishing House (New York City, 1925) • Schocken (Berlin, 1931; New York City, 1945; acquired by Random House, 1987)	• Hebrew Union College Press (Cincinnati, OH, 1949)	• Hebrew Publishing Co. (New York City, 1901) • Soncino (London, 1929; Brooklyn, 1979) • Feldheim Press (New York City, 1939) • Prayer Book Press (New York City, 1933) • Kehot Publication Society (Brooklyn, 1942)
Newcomers	• Keter Publishing House (Jerusalem, 1960) • Jason Aronson (New York City, 1966; acquired by Rowman and Littlefield, 2003) • Jewish Lights (Woodstock, VT, 1985)	• Yeshiva University Press (New York City, 1980)	• Targum Press (Jerusalem, 1988) • C.I.S. Publications (Lakewood, NJ, 1985) • Judaica Press (New York City, 1963) • Koren Publishers (Jerusalem, 1961) • ArtScroll [imprint of Mesorah Publications] (Brooklyn, 1976) • Shaar Press [imprint of Mesorah Publications] (Brooklyn, 1990)

NOTE: Does not include "mainstream" trade and university presses that also maintain a "Jewish" booklist. The division between "Established" and "Newcomers" is a question of perspective. For the purposes of this discussion, the line has been drawn at 1960, marking the beginning of a publishing boom that has continued into the present.

licly traded companies or as nonprofit organizations). Table 3 suggests one way of identifying ArtScroll's position in terms of its differential relationships with other publishers along (at least) three axes: it is a relative newcomer; it is not affiliated with any other major Jewish institution; and it is dedicated exclusively to the production of recognizably "Orthodox" print commodities. As already noted in the Introduction, this publisher is further distinguished by the fact that, strictly speaking, ArtScroll is the imprimatur of Mesorah Publications, an entity that also has ties to the Mesorah Heritage Foundation, a nonprofit entity.[26] This position within the larger field of production of Jewish books helps to explain the opportunities as well as the pressures ArtScroll faces in its effort to develop print products hitherto unavailable on the market and to cultivate specific niches of consumers. By the same token, the logic of mutual positioning helps to explain how and why more established publishers have been obligated to respond in kind to ArtScroll's incursions, as we have seen in the case of the decisions of Conservative and Reform governing bodies to produce "alternatives" to ArtScroll's popular prayer books as a strategy to recapture lost audiences. In all these respects, the scale, scope, and focus of ArtScroll's market success, and the consequences of that success for the shape of the market as a whole, can be at least partially explained in terms of ArtScroll's location within the conditions and dynamics of competition that define the field of cultural production of print commodities addressed to English-speaking Jewish readers and users of books.

A further advantage of Bourdieu's method of field analysis is that it provides a context for understanding how symbolic value is generated and made to circulate, with particular attention devoted to intermediary institutions and actors that stand between authors, publishers, and their audiences. In this regard, it is important to note that cultural fields comprise not only the producers of cultural artifacts (in this case, publishing houses) but also the much larger "universe of belief" that contributes to a given artifact's meaning and assigns its value. In other words, just as cultural producers are distinguishable in terms of their differential access to symbolic capital and other valued resources, so too are the receivers of cultural products positioned in terms of hierarchical systems of classification—such as their type and level of education or their aesthetic tastes—that further constitute the stakes of symbolic struggle in the cultural field and often silently contribute to the reproduction of patterns of cultural and social domination.[27] In the case of the cultural field of Jewish books, questions of competence, taste, legitimacy, and symbolic value are determined through the competitive interactions of a multiplicity of agents, including academic scholars, rabbinic authorities, literary critics, journalists, and other producers of the epitexts in which literary products are assessed and distinguished. Indeed, prior to their arrival on the market, consumers face abundant opportunities to establish, confirm, or refine their preferences within the field of available products, for example, by consulting with any of aforementioned authority figures, by reading book reviews (ranging from those published in newspapers and journals to customer reviews on popular retail Web sites, such as amazon.com or barnesandnoble.com), or by participating in listservs, discussions on blogs, and other Internet-based public forums of discussion and debate.[28]

It is therefore important to note how consumers and readers exercise demand in and through their ongoing relationships with any number of these mediating agents. Mediation occurs in this field, not only through the circulation of epitexts (such as book reviews), but also at the local level in the form of identifiable "gatekeepers" and cultural brokers. These include pulpit rabbis, synagogue administrators, members of ritual committees, booksellers, librarians, teachers, educational professionals, and other figures situated within the interconnected institutions of synagogues, schools, libraries, community centers, and other places of gathering that shape Jewish public culture at the local level. Each of these actors plays a significant role in shaping the assessment and reception of books among local populations, and ArtScroll is certainly no exception to this rule. Although every local culture includes intermediaries with diverse attitudes to ArtScroll, ranging from indiscriminate enthusiasm to unvarying hostility, a typical pattern among local brokers has been to enforce a distinction between ArtScroll's "religious" texts—which are often praised as "valuable additions"—and all the other works on the ArtScroll booklist, which receive much less praise. Outside the Haredi enclave, the majority of local brokers are in fact quite selective in their approval of ArtScroll books, and some speak quite disparagingly about ArtScroll's history and self-help books in particular. One librarian, responsible for stocking and maintaining libraries at two "modern" Orthodox synagogues in London (both of which happen to use *The Complete ArtScroll Siddur*), put it thus:

> I think that any thinking, modern, educated Jew will find the whole ArtScroll ethos extraordinarily banal and sanitized. I think most people are aware of that. But again, I guess they accept that because of the parallel benefits of information that the books contain, and that they're generally well presented and well argued, and have a lot of useful material in them. So for example, the ArtScroll books on particular topics, like *kashrut* [kosher laws], or even explanations of parts of the service, stuff like that—all these specific books which give information about *halakhic* matters or liturgical matters—generally speaking, they're quite reasonably

received as being informative. The stuff on history is what people find the least interesting. I mean, I find it all amazingly bland and repetitive. Rabbis are seen in a uniformly pink glow; their human complexities are just not addressed in the ArtScroll texts. You can substitute one rabbi for another, and you could almost say the same about all of them. And all the stuff for young couples—the relationship books—that's amazingly banal. It's obviously written mainly for *yeshiva bochurim* [students], who don't know anything about girls. That comes through very clearly, I think.[29]

A partial opinion, no doubt. But let us not underestimate the influence librarians, booksellers, rabbis, and other intermediaries enjoy over "common" readers. Through policies of acquisition and distribution, whether explicit or implicit, they help to consecrate texts and to legitimate their use. This is indicative of the difficulty the ArtScroll cadre faces when trying to speak directly to its target audience, over the heads of local intermediary figures.[30] Sometimes, the selective reception of ArtScroll books among local brokers can be traced back to their ideological commitments, or to their personal intellectual and aesthetic sensibilities, but more often it is based on their knowledge about and sensitivity toward established patterns of consumption and use at the local level. This is evident from the decision-making process described by one New York–based bookseller in response to a query about whether and how he recommends ArtScroll books to his customers:

> Okay, for example, let's say a person comes in about a week before Rosh Hashanah [the Jewish New Year], and they know they are going to have to sit through two days of services, and they don't want this year to be like the past years of their life, where they're just sitting there, trying to get through it. They want to actually get something out of it, 'cause people realize that time is valuable and they don't want to just sleep through two days. So they come in for a *machzor* [special prayer book for the High Holidays], and the first thing I'd ask is, "What shul [synagogue] do you go to?" And if I happen to know what *machzor* that shul uses I'll recommend that, so they'll be on the same page when they call it out. But if someone wants to actually get into it beforehand, you know, to prepare themselves to find out what they're actually getting themselves into, well, then I'd recommend they get an ArtScroll.[31]

Functioning simultaneously as marketing agents, teachers, social psychologists, product "troubleshooters," and expert witnesses, local booksellers stand at a key crossroad in the nexus of production and consumption of print matter. Through their observations of and strategic interactions with customers, they exert considerable influence on sales. Consider, in this regard, the following interview with Rebecca (a pseudonym), a sales clerk at a Toronto Judaica bookstore:

JS: Do you recommend the ArtScroll Siddur to customers who come in the store?

R: Well, it depends. You know, a lot of the time, books sell by their name, not by, not just because they're ArtScroll. But on the other hand, that's another thing, ArtScroll just has very good writers. Somehow they've just managed to corner the publishing market on good writers. But not everything is equally popular. I mean, the least popular ArtScroll stuff, I would probably say, the biographies don't really go so well, the biographies. One thing that *is* very popular, though, is the children's Siddur. It's beautiful. It's illustrated. It costs a lot of money, but people still buy it.

JS: So, are there any ArtScroll books that you wouldn't try to encourage people to buy? Or maybe that you would only recommend depending on the person . . .

R: . . . Yeah, I know the kind of book you are referring to. There are one or two books that I can think of in the bookstore, but none of them are ArtScroll. I'm quite a supporter, like, I'm not very critical, just like, by nature, you can easily find people who would find, if not offensive, that it wouldn't be helpful. No, I can't think of anything really. Not by ArtScroll. But oh, wait, now that you mention it, you know, what is a really bad seller in the store are the novels. They stink; they absolutely stink. No one buys them. They're awful and they don't read well. Yeah, I guess I would have to change it and say that I wouldn't recommend the novels. They haven't got any flair.

JS: Okay, so who would you say are the majority of the people who come in and buy ArtScroll books? Are they people who are already *frum* [religiously observant, by Orthodox standards], or just starting to get into Judaism, or . . .

R: . . . Well it's all different types. Older men, they just go straight for the Talmud. All the way. Older women, they seem to like the self-help stuff a lot, that and other spiritually involved topics. The average

teenage guy, he'll also go for the Talmud, and if not, then he isn't really that religious and he probably doesn't shop here. Like, you know,
boys don't, um, they don't really get into buying books. They'll buy
music. And the girls buy stuff about women and relationships, and
women in the Torah. Stuff like that. And, you know, there are all kinds
of people who come in here who really don't know a lot. Like the ones
who come in with booklists from Aish haTorah [a major *kiruv* (outreach) organization catering to *ba'alei teshuva* ("converts" to Orthodoxy); see Chapter 1, above]. It's really funny, they can hardly say the
titles. They just hand us the list and, you know, a lot of them are
ArtScroll books. So, I guess, it's not, like, it's not a cool kind of thing,
not if you're happy at a kind of low observance level, then you
wouldn't go for ArtScroll. But if someone is currently at a low observance level, and looking to become more observant, or having crises in
faith, and they are looking to understand more, then they go for
ArtScroll.

JS: That's really interesting that you say that Aish haTorah sends people
      out with booklists. Is that something that happens often?

R: Uh huh, pretty often.[32]

Among other things it is striking how, despite her claim to be "quite a supporter" and "not very critical," Rebecca both observes and actively contributes to the differential reception of ArtScroll books along the lines of
gender, age, type of education, and degree of commitment to and competence in the practice of Orthodox Judaism. Rebecca's comments also remind us of the symbolic distinctions and selective appropriations enacted
by local figures in their relation to ArtScroll's total literary output. In Rebecca's store, the publisher is best known to customers for its "high-quality"
versions of the "Jewish classics" (such as their prayer books, Bibles, and Talmud), whereas the other genres seem to be relatively unpopular, notwith-
standing the generation of booklists by *kiruv* organizations like Aish ha-
Torah. This trend was further corroborated in my conversations with
employees in Judaica bookstores throughout the three cities of my field
research. They consistently reported to me that, except for a few "best-
sellers"—such as the aforementioned "Jewish classics" (Siddurim, Talmud
volumes, Bibles), Rabbi Berel Wein's three-volume, coffee-table-sized *History of the Jewish People,* a few of Rabbi Abraham Twerski's self-help titles,
and the very popular cookbook *Kosher by Design*—ArtScroll does not reach
a very broad audience.[33] The rest of its books, primarily historical biogra-

phies, halakhah instructional manuals, and "inspirational" literature, were frequently described as titles that "don't sell very well." In the context of the retail book trade, their principal customers were characterized by booksellers either as existing members of the Haredi community or as *ba'alei teshuva* "looking for background information," or "impulse shopping," as one Manhattan-based Jewish book merchant put it.[34]

In sum, one inference to be drawn from these observations about the local contexts of reception is that, despite the considerable generic diversity to be found on the ArtScroll booklist (spanning religious texts, novels, history books, children's literature, etc.), significant limits are placed on ArtScroll's ability to "fill up all of life" among its intended addressees. As purveyors of prayer books, Bibles, Talmud, and related works, ArtScroll has unambiguously become a major player in the field of English-speaking Judaica publishing, and the effects of this ascendance have already been noteworthy. Yet this success has not translated into the creation of very many consumers of the likes of Aaron, who try to acquire "everything" on the ArtScroll booklist. Indeed, beyond the narrow niches of readers and consumers situated within or directly adjacent to the Haredi enclave, or among (demographically small) populations of English-speaking *ba'alei teshuva,* it is quite hard to find examples of the readership ArtScroll imagines and claims as its own.

ARTSCROLL END USERS

Thus far our attention has been devoted to questions of marketing and strategic competition in the field of Jewish literary production and the interaction of intermediaries and mediating agencies as they relate to the circulation of ArtScroll books in the public sphere, in such contexts as synagogues, schools, or bookstores. But what can one say about the identity of ArtScroll's "end users," the identifiable individuals who purchase, borrow, or otherwise acquire these books and incorporate them into their daily lives? These end users compose a rather unstable conglomeration of people, making it exceedingly hazardous to invoke an image of the "typical" owner, reader, or user of ArtScroll books. For one thing, as I have already suggested, this constituency is differentiated according to sometimes overlapping and sometimes opposing distinctions of gender, age, class, geographic location, education, degree of knowledge of the Jewish canon, ability to read Hebrew, and ideological relationship with Haredi Orthodox Judaism (as some type of partisan, fellow traveler, critic, bystander, or enemy).

Moreover, as I have also noted, the appropriation of ArtScroll books depends on the varying responses to and assessments of the distinct genres that make up the publisher's literary output, which, we can recall, includes such diverse works as liturgical texts, Bibles, rabbinic and legal commentaries, instruction manuals, novels, pop psychology, primary and secondary curricular material, and even cookbooks. To account for ArtScroll's end users one would also need to consider the performative protocols, modes of concerted attention, and habituated practices that define the very possibility of participating in ArtScroll's reading public. If, for instance, I own an ArtScroll book but it sits on my shelf and is never opened, am I a member of its audience? What if I happen to rely on a book such as *The Complete ArtScroll Siddur* in my routine ritual practices but I never pay attention to this fact and am unable to identify its title or publisher? In other words, can I belong to ArtScroll's public without even knowing it? And what if I happen to read, interpret, or make use of ArtScroll books in ways not necessarily intended—perhaps even entirely unanticipated—by its author or publisher? Would that imply that ArtScroll's position is not nearly so dominant as suggested by its apparent market success? In the face of all these variables, I shall not attempt to paint a picture that will fully encompass the vastness and indeterminacy of membership to the category of ArtScroll's "audience," let alone all the times and places where audiences come into being. In what follows I offer observations that should be construed, if not as representative, then as symptomatic of the patterns of reception that define ArtScroll's place in the public culture of English-speaking diaspora Jews.

Read in English

One could make several tempting generalizations about the identity of ArtScroll end-users: their economic standing (possessing the disposable income to buy books), their access to available "reading time," or their shared interest in what they take to be reliably authentic and well-designed Jewish print products. To this one might add that the ArtScroll end user is typically an Anglophone. Although, as I have already pointed out, the publisher has made recent incursions into non-Anglophone Jewish communities through the introduction of French-, Spanish-, Russian-, and Hebrew-language editions of some of their best-known books, ArtScroll is overwhelmingly geared toward an English-speaking readership. Best known are its translations, transliterations, and elucidations of canonical Jewish works that include commentaries and instructions aimed at the English-speaking reader. Beyond this, one encounters a vast booklist encompassing diverse subgenres of "Jewish" literature, all written in English and framed by strict Orthodox sensibilities. Of course, this output is not terribly surprising for a publishing house located in New York City, one of the great world capitals of the English-language print industry and also, it so happens, home to the single largest concentration of Jews living outside Israel. It is in fact possible to trace the history of ArtScroll's progressive entry into the public sphere from its initial cultivation of a geographically contiguous audience—a Brooklyn-based publisher catering to the Brooklyn-based Orthodox community—through its gradual evolution into a publisher distributed across the United States, to its rise as a global purveyor of Jewish works, feeding markets around the world, wherever English-speaking communities of readers are found. ArtScroll's ability to have an impact on the global public stage is thus ineluctably tied to the fortuitous conditions of an internationally dispersed English-speaking community who have considerable buying power for Jewish books and are receptive to the literary, philosophical, and ideological orientations of writings that emerge from the Haredi enclave. One contributor to the industry magazine *Judaica Book News* has succinctly identified ArtScroll's special affinity with the

> two generations [that have] grown up in the United States, England, and other English-speaking countries that have been well educated Jewishly and that have placed Torah observance and knowledge at the top of their priorities. And there are countless others who are not particularly observant, but who have a Jewish pride that was hopelessly out of fashion in the 1930s and '40s. They all have in common that their mother tongue is English, even those who were yeshiva-educated. It is one thing to be trained in the scholarly analysis of difficult texts; it is quite another to be able to curl up with a complex Aramaic work or lean back on a recliner with five or six Hebrew commentaries on one's lap. So the ground was fertile and waiting for someone to plant the seeds. ArtScroll did it first.[35]

The "fertile ground" that lies beneath the demand English-speaking Jews express for ArtScroll books can be elaborated with reference to a much longer history conjoining the circulation of sacred texts and the shifting uses of vernacular tongues in diaspora Jewish communities. Indeed, one thing that distinguishes ArtScroll's audience as a specifically Jewish one, unlike other Anglophone textual communities, is the central and commanding presence of a non-English language of Jewish expression, that is, Hebrew. Strictly speaking, the term *English-language public sphere* is misleading here, since we are speaking about a communicational environment characterized by what sociolinguists call "diglossia": the complementary uses of two languages, hierarchically interrelated and often unevenly distributed among speakers and user contexts.[36] In the public culture addressed by ArtScroll, readers and speakers are thus distinguished according to their capacity to switch codes or translate between different linguistic registers. However, as in all forms of Jewish public culture, a special place is reserved for those who demonstrate mastery of Hebrew-language texts in ritual performance, in study, and in other contexts where familiarity with Hebrew is relevant. Even among Jews who speak or read virtually no Hebrew, the language serves as a powerful symbolic marker of identity and affinity.[37]

For most of history, Jews lived within some version of this diglossic situation. Even in antiquity, in the Mishnaic period (approx. 70–200 CE), Hebrew, the language of the Torah and Temple worship, had already ceased to function as a vernacular, having been replaced by Aramaic. Later, with the spread of Jewish diaspora communities throughout the Middle East and the Mediterranean basin and eventually across the European continent (and elsewhere), other Jewish vernaculars emerged, including Judaicized versions of Arabic, German, Spanish, and so on.[38] Of course, Jews also participated in the languages of their neighbors to engage in commerce or to interact with state officials and other outsiders. But a central feature of "traditional" Jewish society was the hierarchical and complementary distinction between Hebrew, or, better stated, *leshon ha-kodesh* (the holy tongue)—the (overtly masculinized) language of liturgy, scholarship, jurisprudence, poetry, and "official" correspondence—and a Jewish vernacular (such as Yiddish or Ladino) that was reserved for the mundane, everyday spheres of oral discourse, popular instruction, and entertainment. This hierarchy was preserved in the ways *leshon ha-kodesh* was represented as the authentic language of divine revelation, as well as in its restricted use among a narrow elite of male literati and religious authorities.[39] Indeed, while a rudimentary knowledge of *leshon ha-kodesh* was incumbent on all members of the Jewish community, mastery of its written texts was notoriously difficult.[40] The exclusivity and prestige associated with *leshon ha-kodesh* also contributed to a characterization of vernaculars such as Yiddish as "mere jargon": a reflection of the sensibilities, intelligence, and needs of the broad masses of unlearned people *('amei ha-aretz)* and women. Among eastern European Ashkenazi Jews, for instance, Yiddish was the most prevalent vernacular, but it was also rhetorically demoted and feminized as the *mame-loshn* (the "mother tongue"). Even with the rise of a substantial Yiddish literature in the nineteenth century, Yiddish writing, when compared to texts written in Hebrew, was still often regarded as an arena of "merely women's literature."[41]

The interlocking hierarchies of gender, class, and literacy helped to ensure the reproduction of religious, cultural, and intellectual authority among Jewish elites who mastered Hebrew, but they also had significant consequences for the exercise of text-centrism. This is especially evident in the ways Jewish literati expressed concerns about how "the masses"—who relied on vernaculars—should relate to sacred texts, including basic narratives, precepts, and prayers originally formulated in Hebrew. As noted by the literary historian Israel Zinberg, there is a long history of rabbinic debate over the question whether holy books could legitimately be written, elucidated, or recited in anything except the holy language. Some authorities, such as the thirteenth-century Catalan rabbi Yonah Gerondi and his Italian contemporary Rabbi Yehudah ben Benjamin, stressed the value of vernacular translations in order "to explain the Torah to women and unlettered persons who do not understand Hebrew," arguing that "prayer is the petition of the heart, and if the heart does not know what the lips say, of what avail can such a prayer be? Hence it is better that every man should pray in the language that he understands."[42] Such arguments also provided discursive legitimation for the composition of "helping books" that could be utilized by teachers to convey the meaning of sacred texts written in Hebrew, as in the case of glossaries of Hebrew terms translated and elaborated in Yiddish, examples of which can be found dating back to the fourteenth and fifteenth centuries.[43]

In light of this history, it is tempting to treat ArtScroll as simply the most recent manifestation of a long-standing tradition involving the vernacularization and "vulgarization" of sacred Jewish texts. Indeed, ArtScroll's efforts to translate, elaborate, elucidate, and otherwise diffuse such works in vernacular form can be set against a long line of historical precedents, including examples in English dating back to the eighteenth century.[44] This is not terribly surprising when one considers the macrohistorical context of Jewish migration, embourgeoisement, and progressive acculturation into the English-speaking world.[45] However helpful it is to recall this broad historical sweep, we must not lose sight of the important *discontinuities* between the symbolic status and functional uses of Jewish vernaculars in earlier times and today. It is beyond the scope of this book to provide a detailed account of the complex history of competing efforts to refashion the diglossic order of Jewish society, especially as they were worked out by Ashkenazi European Jews of the nineteenth and early twentieth centuries in the aftermath of Emancipation. It is nonetheless useful to think about the rise of English in relation to the other programs for modernization and linguistic reform proposed by Jewish religious and political authorities, poets and novelists, journalists, grammarians, translators, and other word-smiths. These included attempts to reconstruct and promote the use of a "pure" version of the Hebrew language, to encourage the replacement of vernaculars such as Yiddish with European languages of state (such as German, Russian, Polish, or French), or to endorse a properly Jewish linguistic nationalism, as in the case of Yiddish for Bundists and modern Hebrew for early Zionists.[46] We should also recall how such projects took shape at the same time that Jewish diglossia was being transformed in more unremarked ways on the ground, in the everyday spaces of both public and domestic life, thanks in no small measure to the industrialization of print media.

Over the twentieth century, these competing options for the linguistic organization of Jewish society were even more radically reconfigured, on the one hand, by the waves of migration that shifted the demographic core of diaspora Jewry to the English-speaking world and, on the other, by the founding of the state of Israel and the adoption of modern Hebrew as its official language, now extended into the "national" domains of science, law, commerce, journalism, and literature. One familiar and well-documented consequence of the rise of this new diglossic order, constellated around the use of English and modern Hebrew, was the fated "withering" of Yiddish as a viable Jewish vernacular. Whereas in the early part of the twentieth century, New York, the leading metropolitan center of Jewish society, could safely be characterized as the seat of a thriving Yiddish culture catering to an immigrant Jewish population (as one might measure by its output of Yiddish theater, literature, films, or newspapers that easily competed with their English counterparts in terms of circulation), beginning in the 1920s, and with increasing pace in the post-World War II period, American Jews progressively replaced Yiddish with English as their vernacular.[47] With their rising economic standing and growing participation in the "main-stream" institutions and social contexts of American public life, this community partook of numerous English-language newspapers, periodicals, books, and other forms of Jewish discourse. As English came to occupy ever-greater terrains of daily life—from commerce to comedy, and from politics to prayer—Yiddish was relegated to a position that Jeffrey Shandler suggestively calls "postvernacular," which does not at all refer to a "dead" language, but rather to its transference to new (more restricted) cultural contexts and arenas of activity.[48]

These are among the most important cultural, political, and economic forces that have enabled English to occupy many of the functions and uses formerly enjoyed by Yiddish and thereby to assume its position as the pre-eminent vernacular of diaspora Jewry, at least as far as Ashkenazi Jewish society is concerned. The core of this vernacular community is located in the United States, home to the largest population of diaspora Jewry and also the largest number of publishing houses and other media producers. But it extends to other places where a significant Anglophone Jewish population can be found: in Canada and the United Kingdom; in Australia and South Africa; in Israel (where English is widely used among immigrants as well as native Hebrew speakers); and, not least, among the virtual, deterritorialized communities one finds on the Internet. But the English-language Jewish public sphere is not simply the product of a shift from one Jewish vernacular to another. Nor should we think of it as the exchange of a specifically "Jewish" language for a language of state, since to do so would occlude the peculiar status of English in the world today. For unlike most other national languages (such as German, Polish, or Russian) or even other internationally distributed languages (such as French, Spanish, or Arabic), English can safely be characterized as the world's most "global" language. Enjoying an unprecedented and unmatched geographic and demographic distribution, English has indeed become the most privileged medium of international communication—in diplomacy, commerce, science, and entertainment, among other things—and in the eyes of many this preeminence is an expression of the technological, economic, political, and cultural dominance, first of the British Empire and then of the United States, within world affairs. At the same time, the "globality" of English is registered in the heterogeneous ways it is rearticulated, and even resisted, among local societies that adopt and adapt the language according to their own local needs and sensibilities.[49]

The Jewish English-language public sphere is one such arena, defined by the patterns of economic, cultural, and communicational exchange between the gravitational core of America and the transnational dispersion of English-speaking Jews. Within this context, ArtScroll is of course only one of numerous publishing houses, newspapers, and other media organs that operate within and daily help to reproduce this transnational English-language Jewish public sphere. As we have seen, just in the narrow case of book publishing, some of the currently operating agents are more than a century old.[50] Confronting this large and well-established field of production, and the circulation of a wide variety of English-language media products, the individuals who happen to become ArtScroll end users are poised between their high degree of literacy in English and their desire for, or need to rely on, discursive content that is religiously and culturally coded as Orthodox Jewish.[51] This Anglophone community is differentiated in various ways, not least by regional patterns of accent, vocabulary, and local styles of writing and speech. So, for instance, in the case of ArtScroll, in London books such as *The Complete ArtScroll Siddur* and *The Stone Chumash* are typically referred to as "American" publications, whereas in New York—and, most interestingly, also in Toronto—they are rarely identified as such, thus shedding light on the varying relationships with "America" across the English-speaking transnation. Another significant difference can be drawn along the frontiers of the Haredi enclave, dividing a population that has tended to receive a long and intensive education in Hebrew-language texts from one that has also been highly educated but is increasingly becoming less so in the case of sacred Jewish texts. We can now understand these differences in relation to the transformation of the "old" diglossic order—which was explicitly tied to the enforcement of hierarchies of gender, literacy, and class—into a new situation for assessing the cultural power of sacred texts originally composed in Hebrew. Because of the high degree of acculturation into English-speaking societies, and also because of the language's global power, the use of English breaks apart long-standing power relations in Jewish public culture, providing new opportunities, for instance, for both men and women who are highly literate, and unambiguously committed to living a Jewish life, but all the same "Jewishly ignorant."

For religious authorities, particularly in the Haredi world, literacy in English thus represents a threatening circulation of knowledge, narratives, and other discursive forms operating outside the orbit of rabbinic control, which was more readily assured, so they claim, in times and places when *leshon ha-kodesh* served as the sole gateway to authoritative writing. This helps to explain the ambivalence among contemporary Haredi elites with regard to the use of English within the Haredi enclave. On the one hand, we have already noted that male yeshiva students and female members of the Haredi community together make up the principal consumer base for English-language novels, pop psychology, history books, and other genres framed by Haredi sensibilities. This reading community has evolved in part thanks to the direct involvement of Haredi elites, who stamp such works with the imprimatur of "approved reading," as one can note in the reproduction of *haskamot* (official letters of approbation) in the prefaces of English-language publications, including many works on the ArtScroll booklist. On the other hand, even as they approve more and more books written in English, these same Haredi authorities continue to demote the value and legitimacy of English as a language of religious communication or study, as we have already seen (in Chapter 1) in the example of the awkward decision to describe ArtScroll's Talmud as an "elucidation," not a translation.[52]

As a translator, elucidator, and commentator of Jewish texts aimed at the Anglophone community, ArtScroll is framed precisely by these tensions with regard to language use, and in the next two chapters I shall attend to some of the ways these tensions operate within the books themselves. But let us note here that ArtScroll's end users are themselves shaped by the rivalry between Hebrew as the most authentically sacred language and English as the language of "comprehension." Even fully bilingual users who claim to be able to move freely between the Hebrew and the English passages in ArtScroll books often find themselves entangled in these linguistic tensions. Consider the observations of Menachem (a pseudonym), a fifty-seven-year-old printer who emigrated from Israel to the United Kingdom in the mid-1990s. Menachem attends a modern Orthodox synagogue in London that uses *The Complete ArtScroll Siddur.* In response to a query about his assessment of the book, Menachem stated:

> Honestly, I think it's a better book, there's no question about it. I mean, it gives you a lot of explanation. I may, sometimes, I wonder about certain things, and it gives me the answers right there. But I don't read the translations very much, because, you know, I am very familiar with the Hebrew. I really don't, to be very honest with you. But sometimes, what I do read, sometimes they explain what you have to do during the service, and I think it's very helpful. I mean, I know how to do certain things, but when I see that written there, it's a help. And I can also help others, and in fact, I've managed to convince other members of the shul here to use it, and they love it because of that. It explains so much; everything is there about why you do certain things.[53]

By highlighting his own competence in Hebrew, Menachem appears to set himself apart from other end users, who presumably rely either partially or entirely on the English translation and instructional notes found in ArtScroll publications. But something else is going on in the lived context of his ritual community, as when Menachem participates in the public reading and recitation of these books and thereby unwittingly helps to reproduce the conditions of text-centrism that are crucial to ArtScroll's success among Anglophone Jews. In those moments, Menachem helps to distribute a translation he himself does not require, thereby facilitating the collective reception of words that are not his own.

Knowledge Seekers

One measure of ArtScroll's success, we have seen throughout the foregoing discussion, is the publisher's ability to cultivate readerships both within and outside the Haredi enclave. Within the Haredi enclave, we have noted the rising success of ArtScroll (alongside other presses publishing in Hebrew as well as English) to supply markets for consumers in search of appropriate "substitute products" representing the full gamut of literary genres found outside Haredi society, including homespun versions of children's books, adventure fiction, and self-help guides that take into account specifically Haredi cultural sensibilities and religious requirements.[54] In this context, we can refer to a category of end users who are unambiguously located within the Haredi enclave and whose command of English makes ArtScroll products particularly attractive. For these readers, many titles on ArtScroll's booklist provide opportunities to participate in the aesthetic universe of modern literary styles, genres, and lifestyle patterns without ever appearing to "leave" the Haredi enclave, and to engage in what otherwise might seem to be frivolous or suspect cultural activities. Other works, such as ArtScroll's many halakhah manuals and code books, are equally attractive to Haredi end users in that they furnish detailed instructions about legitimate conduct in an ever-mutating modern world of new consumer products and bourgeois lifestyles, addressing such minutiae as the proper ways to handle disposable diapers, dental floss, and battery-operated devices, or to tie and untie shoelaces during the Sabbath, among many other things. In these respects, ArtScroll's diverse literary output appears to evince the "scripturalist" mode of address that resonates among English-speaking end users within the Haredi enclave, although, as we shall see in future chapters, many of these books are written, materially organized, and sometimes taken up by users in ways that do not straightforwardly confirm the religious authority claimed on behalf of the Haredi rabbinic elite.

ArtScroll's reception among end users outside the Haredi fold provides equally important insight into the ambiguous, and sometimes quite unanticipated, ways Haredi religious authority is exercised and experienced. Here, in the larger public culture of English-speaking diaspora Jewish society, ArtScroll's end users are still distinguished by their command of English, their high degree of literacy, and their economic standing. But unlike many of their Haredi counterparts they are also marked by their increasingly provisional loyalties to established institutional arrangements (as we saw in the case of Conservadox Jews) and by their apparent need to "supplement" their project to lead a Jewish life with written instruction—in particular, instruction whose authenticity has been authorized by Haredi rabbinic scholars—and other forms of knowledge circulated in English-language texts. These seemingly contradictory characteristics of affluence, intellectual autonomy, ignorance, and Jewish pride are not evenly distributed among ArtScroll end users either inside or outside the Haredi community. But when they are found in conjunction they throw into relief some of the most powerful cultural and social forces that have brought ArtScroll to such prominence in the contemporary English-language Jewish public sphere. One particularly receptive population consists of young professionals who either have disaffiliated from the Jewish attachments of their parents or grew up in unaffiliated homes but in one way or another as adults have "returned" to Judaism, typically with the help, and under the watchful eye, of Haredi Orthodox *kiruv* organizations. As liminal figures, heading toward but not yet fully immersed into Haredi society, these Jews tend to define themselves as knowledge seekers, and ArtScroll books—typically introduced by *kiruv* activists—provide the raw material to further their mission. Consider, for instance, the case of David (a pseudonym), a thirty-two-year-old *ba'al teshuva* ("convert" to Orthodoxy), a regular attendee of services at the Village Shul, a Toronto synagogue affiliated with the Aish ha-Torah, the *kiruv* organization David first encountered during an extended sojourn in Israel. Like many other Orthodox synagogues catering especially to a *ba'al teshuva* constituency, the Village Shul makes heavy use of ArtScroll prayer books, Bibles, and other works in their regular services, in Torah classes, and other activities. David describes the process that led him to join this particular "ArtScroll community" after having grown up in what he calls "your typical North American Jewish home":

> My family is definitely not religious. I don't know if I would go as far as saying antireligious. They're traditional, I guess, in that they know enough that Rosh Hashanah, Yom Kippur, you don't go places, you don't go to the beach that day. That is the day to go to shul, any shul. But some of them have issues with religious Jews. You know, like asking, "What has Judaism done for me?" Well, that's my family. And that's the environment where I grew up. I went to Hebrew school, you know, the one that goes on Tuesdays and Thursdays. What I call Jew Jail. That's because you really don't learn anything there, it's pretty much, you know, pretty much a prison. You go to public school, you make friends, and you want to go

after school, you want to play, whatever, and you're stuck in Jew Jail. So I pretty much did that up until my bar mitzvah, a little bit longer. And then I cut it out, and I kind of stopped doing anything until—well, now we're getting to my story—until I went to college, and one day I was driving north on the highway one morning and I had a rear tire blowout that totaled the car, but I walked out without a scratch. Nothing. And everybody said that it's a miracle, and I'm thinking, "Wow, you know what, there's something going on here." So I sort of had to start looking, searching, and I ended up going to Israel and doing some learning there. That's how I got involved with Aish, and that's how I got to where I am today.[55]

Such conversion narratives are familiar stock in the scholarly literature on the Jewish "return to tradition."[56] But it is not always evident what, precisely, *ba'alei teshuva* like David are converting *to*. For one thing, when members of such constituencies appropriate ArtScroll texts in their ritual practices, this does not automatically entail commitment to all the norms, precepts, and ideological positions articulated among elites of the yeshiva-based Haredi world, to which the ArtScroll cadre claims loyalty. ArtScroll books might just as readily serve as vehicles for bringing such end users into contact with textual sources that they seek to reclaim on their own terms. ArtScroll's Siddur in particular is made to function as a screen upon which local congregations can project their own representations of authentic Jewish practice and meaning. This position is defended by Rabbi Pini Dunner, a yeshiva graduate, radio DJ, and former head of the Saatchi Synagogue, an Independent Orthodox congregation founded in London by the advertising moguls Charles and Maurice Saatchi in 1998. Popularly known by its nickname, Coolshul, the Saatchi Synagogue has served as a leading institutional home for young professionals in the London Jewish community, offering an "authentic" Orthodox service but one that breaks with the established customs and atmosphere of the other Orthodox communities, as materialized in its controversial advertisements, its prominent public lecture series, and its idiosyncratic—and often ironically rich—innovations in Jewish custom, such as their "Tequila Megilla" parties, held during the Festival of Purim. But at the same time, the Saatchi Synagogue makes exclusive use of ArtScroll liturgical texts. When I discussed this curious combination with Rabbi Dunner in 2001, he explained:

> For me, ArtScroll is an extremely valuable resource, whether or not I subscribe to their ideology. I don't know why people are so resistant to ArtScroll publications just because they emerge from an agenda-driven

source. Why should people care? I think they [ArtScroll] have done an absolutely sterling job of opening up Jewish texts and Judaism to a wide audience. People can read it, not agree with it, and not have to worry about it. They take what they want to take. The publisher's agenda and the reader's agenda don't have to be the same. Readers aren't unintelligent, so let's not insult them.[57]

Rabbi Dunner's caution is well taken. But unauthorized use does not necessarily imply a rejection of religious authority per se. We must guard here against a naive populism that exaggerates the significance of the fact that "the masses" always engage in processes of selection and reinterpretation, extending the meaning of the products they consume into new, often unanticipated fields of semiotic productivity. In Rabbi Dunner's defense, one can make a good case that the mere availability of books on the market is no real determinant of their use and that their consumption always allows for creative reconstructions within social domains beyond the reach of the publisher. It does not follow, however, that such reconstructions are entirely without design or constraint. Nor is it the case that producers are denied the possibility of accruing other sorts of dividends from the apparently uncoerced expressions of demand by consumers: profits that may exceed the restricted economy of exchanging money for books. Let me elaborate this point by returning to my interview with David, the *ba'al teshuva* who belongs to a constituency not unlike that of the Saatchi Synagogue. After his account of how he came to "convert" to Orthodoxy, the discussion turned to David's daily routines in the present:

JS: You said you go pretty regularly to the Village Shul, is that right?

D: It goes in waves. I was just there this morning. Sometimes I go just for *shabbos* [the Sabbath]. But I meet my wife there pretty regularly. We both like it there. I mean, it's a very friendly, a very user-friendly place. I mean, I guess it's the same thing as ArtScroll. In a way, it falls into the same category as Aish. They're a perfect match for each other. They're both very user friendly. One is a very user-friendly service, and the other is a very user-friendly book. You know, I've moved around a bit to different shuls, but I always seem to keep coming back.

JS: What keeps bringing you back? Is it the way the service is conducted?

D: There's a phrase for a place like the Village Shul—TCB—taking care of business. What I mean is I don't like a shul that delves too far off the beaten track in terms of holistic remedies or long sermons about whatever. You know, I want to go, I want to *daven* [pray], I want to come home and eat my *shabbos* [Sabbath] lunch, and then I want to take a nap. You know, just taking care of business.

JS: Is that really it?

D: Well, that's part of it. Sure. But it's the community too, I guess. At this point in my life, I would say that the majority of the people I know are in the same situation as me. They didn't necessarily grow up religious, but they've come to it at a later time in their lives. A kind of *ba'al teshuvah* thing. And, of course, that's where a place like the Village Shul and ArtScroll come in very handy, especially now that they've come out with the interlinear translation. You know, very often you have Jews who didn't grow up learning Judaism, so their Hebrew is very bad, if at all, so you have to have something with a very good translation, translated for meaning as well, you know, what are the Hebrew words actually saying. I guess you could say that we're a more intellectual crowd, we want to understand what we're saying.

JS: Is that what do you think makes ArtScroll so popular?

D: Well, I guess that a lot of people, whether they're religious or not, they want to better themselves, they want to improve their minds. You know, I saw someone doing a study somewhere on the statistic growth of people joining health clubs. People want to better themselves physically. But what I've seen is people trying to improve their, shall we say, spiritual side. I was thinking—you're a sociologist, so you're going to love this— especially since September 11th. People are saying: "What's going on here?" And I've seen this urge in people, there's got to be more, what's going on in this world, what's this world really about. And they are look- ing to improve themselves. So, you know, you have stories about Holly- wood, where anything can happen, where famous movie stars or pop singers are studying Kabbalah. What they're actually studying you don't know, but you just mention the word *Kabbalah* and they're like, "Oooh." Why is that? Because they're looking for self-improvement.

JS: So you think that ArtScroll is especially valuable for someone who doesn't have much background, someone who's going to . . .

D: . . . Yeah. Exactly. You know, we have to do all kinds of things. But we still have to know why we're doing it. As a generation, we're actually getting into that.

JS: So you think this is a more recent trend?

D: More and more.

JS: Would you say . . .

D: . . . It's just about everything being easier. Again, it's the "taking care of business" thing. Even a person who doesn't keep kosher, for example. You know, maybe they don't really know how even to begin. But someone gives them an ArtScroll, it doesn't matter what. Or they can be in shul and looking at something. And the person may be thinking, "This makes sense." The minute that starts to happen, then they start thinking, and then a day later maybe they find themselves in a conversation, and then their brain will click back to what they read. And they'll tell it. And then their friend will say, "Oh, that's interesting." And then that person happens to be talking on the phone later in the week to a friend in Milwaukee, and so on.[58]

There is much in this interview that merits our close attention. First, we can note how David repeatedly places himself in a generational cohort that he describes as being dissatisfied with the knowledge and forms of Jewish observance they acquired as children and as being driven to improve themselves and to strengthen their religious consciousness—the spiritual equivalent to deciding to join a health club. Having grown up in "Jew Jail," David embarked on his own search for religious authenticity and knowledge, reliable signs of which he claims to have found in the Village Shul and also in ArtScroll's liturgical texts. Both synagogue and text are praised for their ability to communicate the more "traditional" form of Jewish practice David seeks: one that does not "delve too far off the beaten track." At the same time, as a member of a "more intellectual crowd," David subjects his search for "correct practice" to the criteria of transparency and reasonable justification. "You know, we have to do all kinds of things" to become an Orthodox Jew, David argues, "but we still have to know why we are doing it." There can be no interest in obedience here without the legitimating presence of textual explanation and justification. Quite unlike the exercise of *da'at Torah,* which (as we saw in Chapter 1) is said to define religious authority within the Haredi enclave, rules of correct conduct are legitimate in David's eyes because reasons, explanations, and justifications are provided in written form. But most remarkably, the intelligibility David seeks depends upon the removal of all ambiguity, equivocation, and even complexity. For David, the codified rules and protocols for Orthodox Jewish observance should be "easy to perform" and "businesslike," meaning explicit, definitive, and discursively organized for the sake of prompt execution. David's professed thirst for knowledge is thus tied to his desire for functional ease, captured in the colorful acronym TCB, "taking care of business." Stated bluntly, "TCB" is possible only when the conditions are "user friendly." And as it so happens, both ArtScroll and the Village Shul are noted for precisely such user-friendliness. This remarkable combination of performative and intellectual goals—functional ease, transparency, persuasiveness, reliability, and authenticity—stands at the heart of the ArtScroll's capacity to resonate with end users such as David.

David's interview also provides a further window from which one might survey the social locations of ArtScroll users, such as the institutional context of a synagogal community devoted largely to adult converts (the Village Shul, administered by the *kiruv* organization Aish haTorah), or the chains of interlocutors who speak on the telephone and recommend ArtScroll books to each other. As this chapter has aimed to demonstrate, ArtScroll books are in a sense made and remade through the conditions and dynamic forces that structure their appearance on such social stages. But beyond the negotiations of authors, publics, and their intermediary institutions there is another source of agency that has not yet been considered: the agency of the books themselves. This is the topic to which I turn in the succeeding two chapters: to identify first some of the key discursive features and then the material form and agency of selected ArtScroll books.

THREE

Prayer Books, Cookbooks, Self-Help Books

Designs for Kosher Living

A COMMON INTERPRETATION OF THE contemporary Haredi enclave points to a fundamental paradox. A society driven by the desire to safeguard its cherished traditions of knowledge, cultural practice, and moral outlook discovers it can achieve its ends only through cultural innovation. The more it wishes to uphold tradition, the more intensely it must engage with bodies of knowledge, forms of political power, lifestyles, and cultural products that lie beyond the designated boundaries of authentic Jewish society, in the dense interactions and circulations that constitute global modernity. Whether their attention is directed inwardly, toward followers, or outwardly, toward competitors and prospective allies, converts, and client groups, Haredi religious authorities, writers, publishers, and other cultural agents must defend the purity of the Haredi enclave through ever more elaborate arguments about the ethical and cosmological ordering of the universe and through ever more precise and disambiguated prescriptions governing both public and private life. Alien cultural practices, commodities, and lifestyles must be assessed, resisted, selectively appropriated, or replaced with acceptable substitutes. Outsiders must be won over, neutralized, or kept at a distance. Yet all such strategic efforts invariably require defenders of the Haredi enclave to master the use of speech genres, managerial techniques, and modes of cultural activity found in the "outerworld" domains of advertising, fundraising, political lobbying, secular scholarship, popular music, and fashion. Caught within this paradoxical logic, proponents of Haredism engage in ceaseless negotiations over where and how to draw the line dividing an embattled essence from the multiplying pollutants that surround it: an exercise that makes it increasingly difficult to distinguish means from ends, instruments from their users, or the essential from the peripheral elements of authentic Jewish expression. As stated succinctly by Yoel Finkelman in his study of Haredi adventure fiction—a rather surprising literary genre that has emerged over the past two decades, wonderfully illustrating the performative contradictions of the Haredi writing community—every appropriation of a new cultural form "runs the risk of profaning the sacred rather than sanctifying the profane."[1]

The most rigorous defenses of tradition thus often turn out to be radical reworkings of the customary practices, received texts, and historical modes of social, political, and economic organization that are said to identify that very tradition. Of course, this situation is hardly unique to Haredism, and one might even argue that precisely because we live in "modern" times there is no way for us to have a relationship with tradition that is not paradoxical. As indicated in its Latin root, *traditio* (meaning to transmit, hand over, surrender, or betray), the word *tradition* has a transitive function, referring to intergenerational exchanges of texts, art, biota, and other materialities of inheritance, heritage, and memory.[2] Strictly speaking, therefore, historical moments that are defined as revivals, renewals, or updated renditions of tradition can never be continuous with traditions themselves. Rather, they are "flashbacks": analeptical ways of sequencing time that imply a prior rupture and the acceptance of a line dividing the traditional past from the no-longer-traditional present.[3] Even what seems merely to be an act of preservation is a form of innovation, whereby "the old" is reorganized and re-mediated in order to secure its place in the protean context of "the new." For all these reasons, one cannot take at face value the claims of apologists who describe the contemporary Haredi community as the embodiment of an "unbroken chain of tradition" from Moses at Mount Sinai "down through the most violent and turbulent periods of the past, and to this very day."[4] On the contrary, as we have seen, Haredism is a product of cumulative ruptures, migrations, displacements, and social catastrophes, and as such, its situation is radically distinct from the technological, institutional, socioeconomic, and cultural arrangements of historical Jewish society. Located in the markedly "untraditional" contemporary public arena of competing sources of authority, divided attentions, and volatile allegiances, the Haredim are starkly separated from the forebears in whose names they speak and act.

Although these changes have been driven by social forces largely beyond the control of local Jewish communities, rabbinic authorities have had recourse to long-standing strategies, precipitated by the arrival of new technologies, new political arrangements, or new patterns of cultural practice, for redrawing the circle that would define legitimate Jewish conduct. Going all the way back to the Talmud, rabbinic authorities routinely confronted novel practices and alien products in order to domesticate them: to make them Jewishly familiar, halakhically acceptable, and usable within the framework of rabbinic modalities of authentication and control.[5] When "the new" could not be avoided or rejected outright, an alternative argument was readily available: what seems new is not really new at all, its arrival having already been anticipated and its meaning encrypted in sacred texts, perhaps even in the white spaces between the words of the Torah. Such attempts to frame the use of new technologies, institutions, and cultural practices arrogated to rabbinic authorities the role of gatekeepers, empowered to set rules and procedures for proper use, to define standards of excellence, and to validate bona fide techniques for creating and distributing the products and practices in question. Contemporary Haredi rabbinic authorities thus claim to act as direct successors to this long history of interpretation and legal adjudication, only "updating" what is necessary to address shifting circumstances of technological invention, cultural practice, and institutional arrangements originating from the "outside world."

But as we saw in Chapter 1, Haredi defenses of tradition are complicated by radical changes in the ways authoritative interpretations of sacred texts are rendered and acted upon. This was discussed in terms of the rise of "scripturalism" within Orthodox Jewish society, materialized in Haredi approaches to the canon of Jewish sacred texts as a self-authorizing, inerrant, and comprehensive guide to all matters of knowledge and conduct. Haredi scripturalism, we can recall, is characterized by its privileging of the written holy text over all other sources of knowledge and by the propagation of claims that the most trustworthy interpreters of that canon are the *gedolim* of the yeshiva world, whose esoteric *da'at Torah* (knowledge of the Torah) must not be amended, let alone rejected. This understanding of the relationship between Jewish texts and their authorized interpreters has also empowered Haredi cultural agents to reassess and, where need be, to overturn long-standing forms of conduct and sanctioned interpretation. Indeed, the Haredi investment in the text as the sole guarantor of legitimate conduct has been part and parcel with the movement's promotion of stricter norms within the framework of halakhic decision making, effecting what in halakhic language can be called a "swing toward *humra*" (stringency).[6] Haredi scripturalism has thereby served as the gateway to an ascendant form of asceticism within modern Jewish society: a reclamation of the pristine authenticity of divine revelation through uncompromisingly stringent interpretations of Jewish texts and an unqualified embrace of the "hard life" that such readings entail.

Of course, contemporary Haredi religious elites are not the first to have promoted interpretations of Jewish scripture that imply strict observance of halakhah. On the contrary, the canons of Jewish legal opinion and philosophical writings contain many pronouncements about stringency as a sign of religious piety and a passionate desire to serve God.[7] But as Sara Weinstein has noted, canonical sources were hardly uniform in their praise of stringency, particularly when self-imposed. The desire to fast for extra days, recite extra prayers, or in other ways engage in ascetic conduct was often seen to carry the risk of transforming genuine piety into arrogance and condescension, which would in turn undermine Jewish unity. In the Talmud, for instance, ascetic behavior is often framed by the opposing argument that "the Jew has been commanded to take good care of the body that was given by God. . . . Self-denial is criticized not only because it is wrong to deny that which is permitted, but because God wants human beings to actively pursue the enjoyment of the world that he gave them. These attitudes thus fit along a continuum that ranges from the position that self-denial is praiseworthy behavior, all the way to the opposite extreme that holds that enjoying all [kosher] foods is actually a religious obligation."[8] The contemporary Haredi enclave, by contrast, is said to eschew these long-standing restraints on ascetic practice, on the argument that the pervasive and often overwhelming temptations of laxity, hedonism, and other "un-Jewish" lifestyle options demand the rigid application of legal codes of conduct in every conceivable arena of public and private life. In their promotion of the strictest possible standards for assessing the range of mandatory, permitted, and forbidden actions and behaviors that constitute the covenant between God and his Chosen People, Haredi rabbinic authorities rhetorically ground their approaches to Jewish legal opinion in the maxim, as phrased by one observer, that "when the mean is perceived as unconscionable compromise, the extreme may appear eminently reasonable."[9]

Yet at the same time, as we have also seen, because Haredi agents are concerned to "democratize" this ascetic way of life—to bring it out of the confined religious culture of the yeshiva and onto a broader terrain of Jewish public culture—their assertions of legal extremes are often conjoined with equally powerful desires for influence among client populations (such as prospective *ba'alei teshuva,* or "returnees" to Orthodoxy, to name a particularly prominent case). But, like all pathways to "the people," the route chosen for the exercise of popular influence is paved with compromise. How, indeed, could Haredi cultural agents communicate their scripturalist tenets without taking into account the constraints of contemporary Jewish public culture, characterized by its conditions of voluntary affinity, divided attentions, and unreliable levels of literacy and competency in the pragmata of Jewish ritual life? While hardly representative of the full range of Haredi strategies for addressing questions of public influence, ArtScroll provides an instructive opportunity for tracking the operations of Haredi cultural agents in this context of competing pressures for internal legitimation and outward appeal. We have seen how, by defining itself as both an "authoritative" and an "accessible" purveyor of authentically traditional Jewish works, this publishing entity is structured by the paradoxical promises of delivering an "innovative preservation of tradition" and an "easy path to a hard life." Paradoxes also abound in the divergent vocabularies used to assess ArtScroll books, as we saw in Chapter 2 in our examination of some of the particular contexts of reception where ArtScroll books are appropriated, critiqued, or defended through the interaction of promoters, intermediaries, local authorities, and their respective market niches and client populations. Let us recall, for instance, how enthusiastic consumers such as David praise ArtScroll's liturgical texts as simultaneously modern and classic, intellectually challenging and businesslike, authoritative and user friendly.

That such dissonant terms might somehow belong together as an adequate description of ArtScroll books not only suggests the presence of a deep paradox but also provides an important clue for understanding how these texts work and why they resonate so powerfully with their addressees. The linked themes of, on the one hand, accessibility, functional ease, and convenience and, on the other, definitiveness and fidelity to tradition lie at the heart of ArtScroll's project to market and to publicly legitimate a version of Haredi Orthodoxy. What, then, is at stake in this desire to make Haredi-defined standards of knowledge and conduct "easier to understand" or "more convenient to execute"? Does the production of "helpful" (or even "enjoyable") points of entry into the prescribed life path of ever-greater stringency undermine the very idea of stringency? Is it tenable to suggest that ArtScroll simply presents "the ancient wine of Sinai in the vessel of today's vernacular"?[10] Or is it more likely that ArtScroll's embrace of the modern techniques and strategies for market success and, to that end, the publisher's appropriation of a range of authorial styles, formats, and literary genres make it impossible to disentangle antique from modern, tradition from innovation, or "vessel" from "wine"? In turn, are such paradoxes testaments to the fundamental inability of Haredi scripturalists to secure their authority and legitimacy within the cacophony of competing voices that make up the public culture of English-speaking diaspora Jewish society? Or, on the contrary, do the apparent paradoxes that we find in ArtScroll books serve as the means by which Haredi authority is in fact sustained? To begin to address these questions, we must first suspend the impulse that has driven critics to charge the Haredi enclave with the propagation of contractions, falsehoods, or even hypocrisies, all of which are intended to demonstrate that the Haredim are at odds with the modern world. Such conclusions appear sensible only if one chooses to ignore the many ways apparent paradoxes are also sites of intense cultural productivity. Indeed, what seems at first blush to be a question of contradiction or paradox is better approached as a matter of *design:* the application of creative energies in order to integrate diverse—even seemingly incommensurable and opposing—elements into a coherent form.

This chapter is devoted to an exploration of ArtScroll's paradoxical mode of address, tracing the way paradoxes are worked out in some of the key literary genres that bring the publisher into contact with diverse readerships and user contexts. In Chapter 2, my observations were for the most part restricted to ArtScroll's two main liturgical works, the *Complete ArtScroll Siddur* and the *Stone Chumash,* as I traced their patterns of reception in local markets and public institutions. But as I also pointed out earlier, these liturgical texts represent only a fraction of the publisher's total output, and it is therefore impossible to appreciate ArtScroll's successes and failures in the larger cultural field without attending to the diversity of this literary production. Table 4 offers a typology of the major literary genres found on the ArtScroll booklist, distinguished by their content, by modes of authorship and styles of writing, by the functional uses of these books, and by the types of legitimating discourses used to consecrate them as authentic expressions of Haredi Orthodox knowledge, moral outlook, and cultural practice.[11]

TABLE 4

Key literary genres in the ArtScroll corpus

	Mode of Address	Scenario	Legitimating Discourse
Prayer books (≈30 titles)	Procedural	Praying and performing rituals	Clear instructions that will reduce anxiety
Talmud and related commentary (≈180 titles)	Expository	Studying the law	Commentary that will elucidate the classical body of Jewish legal interpretation
Halakhah manuals (≈50 titles)	Expository	Executing the law	A detailed and methodical examination of mandatory, proscribed, and permitted conduct
Cookbooks (8 titles)	Procedural	Preparing food and decorating domestic space	Fun, fashionable, and easy cooking and entertaining
Self-help books (≈300 titles)	Hortatory	Fortifying the will to act through a positive self-image	Techniques for recovery
History books (~160 titles)	Narrative	Remembering, commemorating, and imagining the past	Inspiring, exemplary lives
Fiction and adventure (≈50 titles)	Narrative	Entering into a fantasy world	Wholesome entertainment

NOTE: The number of titles listed for each genre refers to the list of books in print in the 2009 catalog, not counting the varying sizes and bindings of individual editions.

These genres are organized so as to address divergent reading communities and to draw together diverse scenes of ritual practice, study, entertainment, and domestic life. Juxtaposing publishing initiatives that most unambiguously connote "scriptural purity," such as the prayer books or Talmud, with arguably "untraditional" genres, such as self-help books or adventure novels, the ArtScroll booklist demonstrates not only the breadth but also the vitality and dynamism of English-language Haredi publishing (and indeed, as we have also seen, ArtScroll is simply the most prominent and successful of a number of such publishing houses; see Table 3 in

Chapter 2, above). At the same time, the appropriation of so many literary genres also marks an implicit risk for ArtScroll in its stated ambition to provide a trustworthy vehicle for communicating Haredi intellectual and religious authority within the contemporary Jewish public sphere.

The diversity of this output also makes it exceedingly hazardous to make general pronouncements about the literary style or the ideological tone that typifies "an ArtScroll book," if indeed such a thing exists outside the orbit of individual authors and editors associated with the press. We are better served by focusing on particular examples, where it becomes possible to see in closer detail how specific genres of books bearing the ArtScroll imprimatur address their readers and what sorts of work they perform. In the following pages, I shall consider three such cases: prayer books, cookbooks, and self-help books.[12] When viewed in comparative perspective, prayer books, cookbooks, and self-help books instructively reveal how ArtScroll operates as a medium between the Haredi enclave and the larger public culture of English-speaking diaspora Jews. Functioning like hinges, each of these genres addresses a readership located on the borderland between the Haredi enclave and the outside world. ArtScroll's prayer books, cookbooks, and self-help books provide insiders to the Haredi enclave opportunities to engage with ideas and matters of concern that have been discursively framed in the outside world, all the while secure in the knowledge that they are engaging with "approved" readings. At the same time, through the medium of these same texts, non-Haredi readers are able to recuperate what they perceive as a more authentic form of Jewish meaning, one that has received the stamp of approval of the Haredi yeshiva world.

In this chapter I focus on prayer books, cookbooks, and self-help books for an additional reason, namely their performative dimension. These books are meant not only to be read but also to be acted upon. Beyond the narratives and information they contain, they articulate what performance theorist Diana Taylor calls *scenarios:* frameworks of meaning making that link together behaviors, social environments, and potential outcomes.[13] Through the communication of scenarios, these ArtScroll texts act upon and through the material medium of the body and its gestures, calling for the disciplining of concentration and attention, the governance of the emotional self, and the artful application of "recipes" for everyday living. Scenarios for praying, cooking, and even managing one's psychic well-being provide users of ArtScroll books with the means of reproducing themselves in the routine patterns of everyday life at home, among family and friends, and in the public spaces of modern cityscapes, workplaces, or houses of worship. By examining some of the scenarios presented by ArtScroll books, we can appreciate with greater precision how the ArtScroll cadre consolidates its grip on fellow Jews. As we shall see, rather than inculcating Haredi-defined standards of Jewish conduct by fiat or through polemical victories, these texts work on a more molecular level, materializing Haredi authority in detailed procedural instructions and in extended reflections on what constitutes a good performance. And because these ArtScroll books authorize scenarios of Jewish living in *textual* form—writing out what often were hitherto merely tacit or orally communicated bodies of knowledge—they rely on a mode of address that is quite distinct from the historical patterns of Jewish literary production.[14] By classifying, organizing, authorizing, and directing all manner of Jewish conduct, prayer books, cookbooks, and self-help books epitomize the scripturalist impulse that is said to have taken root in the contemporary Jewish public sphere. They also help us to see how scripturalism must be *designed* in order to have effect.

PRAYING WITH MEANING

ArtScroll publishes over thirty distinct editions of its basic prayer book, the Siddur.[15] It offers versions catering to distinct traditions of Orthodox liturgy (Nusach Ashkenaz and Nusach Sefard), with different modes of translation (the "standard" translation laid out on a facing page, interlinear translations, and transliterated editions), in different sizes (full sized, pocket sized, and special enlarged editions "for home and pulpit"), with different bindings (paperback, hardcover, and special handmade leather editions), and different typefaces (regular and large-type). There are also special editions packaged for use among particular Orthodox communities, such as those bearing the imprimatur of the major American Orthodox governing bodies, the Orthodox Union and the Rabbinical Council of the America. Recently, this diversity has grown even further, with the launching of a new line of Siddurim designed specifically for women users: the *Klein Edition Women's Siddur: Ohel Sarah,* which ArtScroll has marketed as a version of the classic text used by generations of women "in the spirit of the traditional Korban Minchah Siddur."[16] With only slight variation, each ArtScroll Siddur includes the same basic features (for sample pages, see Fig. 2):

· a comprehensive set of prayers, blessings, and Torah readings that constitute the "essentials" of Jewish liturgy and daily ritual practice, ordered into weekday and Sabbath readings, as well as the basic prayers

At this point, gather the four tzitzis between the fourth and fifth fingers of the left hand. Hold *tzitzis* in this manner throughout the *Shema*.

Bring us in peacefulness from the four corners of the earth and lead us with upright pride to our land. For You effect salvations, O God; You have chosen us from among every people and tongue.

Chazzan – *And You have brought us close to Your great Name forever in truth, to offer praiseful thanks to You, and proclaim Your Oneness with love. Blessed are You, HASHEM, Who chooses His people Israel with love.*

(Cong. – *Amen.*)

ᵉ⁊{ THE SHEMA }ᵉ꙰

Immediately before reciting the *Shema* concentrate on fulfilling the positive commandment of reciting the *Shema* every morning. It is important to enunciate each word clearly and not to run words together. See *Laws §46-60.*

When praying without a *minyan,* begin with the following three-word formula:

God, trustworthy King. *

Recite the first verse aloud, with the right hand covering the eyes, and concentrate intensely upon accepting God's absolute sovereignty.

Hear, O Israel: HASHEM is our God, HASHEM, the One and Only.*¹

In an undertone — *Blessed is the Name* of His glorious kingdom for all eternity.*

---

(1) *Deuteronomy 6:4.*

☐ At this point in history, HASHEM is only אֱלֹהֵינוּ, *our God,* for He is not acknowledged universally. Ultimately, however, all will recognize Him as ה' אֶחָד, HASHEM, *the One and Only* (*Rashi*; *Aruch HaShulchan* 61:4).

☐ ה' — HASHEM. God is the Eternal One, Who was, is, and always will be [הָיָה הֹוֶה וְיִהְיֶה], and He is אֲדֹון, *Master,* of all.

☐ אֱלֹהֵינוּ — *Our God.* He is All-Powerful (*Orach Chaim* 5).

אֶחָד — *The One and Only.* The word has two connotations: (a) There is no God other than HASHEM (*Rashbam*); and, (b) though we perceive God in many roles — kind, angry, merciful, wise, judgmental, and so on — these different attributes are not contradictory, even though human intelligence does not comprehend their harmony.

In saying the word אֶחָד, *the One and Only,* draw out the second syllable (חָ) a bit and emphasize the final consonant (ד). While drawing out the ח — a letter with the numerical value of eight — bear in mind that God is Master of the earth and the seven heavens. While clearly enunciating the final ד — which has the numerical value of four — bear in mind that God is Master in all four directions, meaning everywhere.

ᵉ⁊ **The enlarged ע and ד**

In Torah scrolls, the letters ע of שְׁמַע and ד of אֶחָד are enlarged. Together they form the word עֵד, *witness,* alluding to the thought that every Jew, by pronouncing the *Shema,* bears witness to HASHEM's unity and declares it to all the world (*Rokeach*; *Kol Bo*; *Abudraham*).

ᵉ⁊ בָּרוּךְ שֵׁם — *Blessed is the Name.* This verse is recited in an undertone because:

(a) At Jacob's deathbed his children affirmed their loyalty to God by proclaiming the verse *Shema* ["Israel" in that context refers to Jacob]. Jacob responded: *"Blessed is the Name ..."* The Sages taught: Should we say these words in our prayers because Jacob said them? Yes. But, on the other hand, Moses did not transmit them to us, for they are not found in the Torah. Therefore, let us say them softly (*Pesachim* 56a).

(b) Moses heard this beautiful prayer from the angels, and taught it to Israel. We dare not say it aloud, because we are sinful and therefore unworthy of using an angelic formula. On Yom Kippur, however, when Israel elevates itself to the sin-free level of angels, we do proclaim it loudly (*Devarim Rabbah* 2:36).

Figure 2. Sample pages from *The Complete ArtScroll Siddur,* pp. 90–91, presenting the Shema. Reproduced courtesy of Mesorah Publications (ArtScroll Series).

וַהֲבִיאֵנוּ לְשָׁלוֹם מֵאַרְבַּע כַּנְפוֹת הָאָרֶץ,
וְתוֹלִיכֵנוּ קוֹמְמִיּוּת לְאַרְצֵנוּ. כִּי אֵל פּוֹעֵל
יְשׁוּעוֹת אָתָּה, וּבָנוּ בָחַרְתָּ מִכָּל עַם וְלָשׁוֹן.

At this point, gather the four *tzitzis* between the fourth and fifth fingers of the left hand. Hold *tzitzis* in this manner throughout the שְׁמַע.

❖ וְקֵרַבְתָּנוּ לְשִׁמְךָ הַגָּדוֹל סֶלָה בֶּאֱמֶת, לְהוֹדוֹת לְךָ וּלְיַחֶדְךָ
בְּאַהֲבָה. בָּרוּךְ אַתָּה יהוה, הַבּוֹחֵר בְּעַמּוֹ יִשְׂרָאֵל בְּאַהֲבָה.
(.אָמֵן –Cong.)

❈ שמע ❈

Immediately before recitating the *Shema* concentrate on fulfilling the positive commandment of reciting the *Shema* every morning. It is important to enunciate each word clearly and not to run words together. See Laws, § 46-60.

When praying without a *minyan*, begin with the following three-word formula:

אֵל מֶלֶךְ נֶאֱמָן.*

Recite the first verse aloud, with the right hand covering the eyes, and concentrate intensely upon accepting God's absolute sovereignty.

שְׁמַע | יִשְׂרָאֵל,* | יהוה,* | אֱלֹהֵינוּ, | יהוה | אֶחָד:*[1]

בָּרוּךְ שֵׁם* כְּבוֹד מַלְכוּתוֹ לְעוֹלָם וָעֶד.—In an undertone

---

❈ שְׁמַע / THE SHEMA ❈

The recitation of the three paragraphs of *Shema* is required by the Torah, and one must have in mind that he is about to fulfill this commandment. Although one should try to concentrate on the meaning of all three paragraphs, one must concentrate at least on the meaning of the first verse (שְׁמַע) and the second verse (בָּרוּךְ שֵׁם) because the recitation of *Shema* represents fulfillment of the paramount commandment of acceptance of God's absolute sovereignty (קַבָּלַת עוֹל מַלְכוּת שָׁמַיִם). By declaring that God is One, Unique, and Indivisible, we subordinate every facet of our personalities, possessions — our very lives — to His will.

A summary of the laws of the *Shema* appears on pp. 982-983. For a full commentary and Overview, see ArtScroll *Shema Yisrael*. In the שְׁמַע we have included the cantillation symbols (*trop*) for the convenience of those who recite שְׁמַע in the manner it is read from the Torah. Nevertheless, to enable those unfamiliar with this notation to group the words properly, commas have been inserted. Additionally, vertical lines have been placed between any two words that are prone to be slurred into one and are not separated by a comma.

◆§ אֵל מֶלֶךְ נֶאֱמָן — *God, trustworthy King.* The Sages teach that there are both 248 organs in the human body and 248 positive commandments. This parallel number symbolizes that the purpose of physical existence is to obey the precepts of the Torah. The total number of words in the three paragraphs of *Shema* is 245. The Sages wished to convey the above symbolism in the recitation of the *Shema*, so they added three words to it. If a *minyan* is present, the congregation listens to the *chazzan's* repetition aloud of the three words ה' אֱלֹהֵיכֶם אֱמֶת. If there is no *minyan*, the three words אֵל מֶלֶךְ נֶאֱמָן are recited before *Shema* is begun. These words were chosen because their initials spell אָמֵן [literally, *it is true*], thus testifying to our belief in the truths we are about to recite.

The three words of the verse mean: He is אֵל, *God*, the All-powerful source of all mercy; He is the מֶלֶךְ, *King*, Who rules, leads, and exercises supervision over all; and He is נֶאֱמָן, *trustworthy*, fair, apportioning no more suffering nor less good than one deserves (*Anaf Yosef*).

◆§ שְׁמַע יִשְׂרָאֵל — *Hear, O Israel.* Although the commentators find many layers of profound meaning in this seminal verse, one should bear in mind at least the following points during its recitation:

Figure 2. (*continued*)

for major festivals, holy days, and other key events (e.g., prayers relating to death and bereavement); the selection and ordering of prayers follow the traditional format of Siddurim familiar to European Jewry for several centuries[17]

- an English translation of the Hebrew text (including diacritical information on pronunciation and ambiguities that are invisible to English-speaking readers), in some cases laid out on the opposing page, in others an interlinear translation, and in others still accompanied by a transliteration that presents the Hebrew text in Romanized script

- instructional notes (usually appearing immediately before the text of the prayer or blessing)

- footnotes (usually providing the biblical source text for specific names, words, and phrases)

- a running commentary on the bottom of each page, providing further references, glosses, and explanations of the origins, meaning, and purposes of the prayers, often (but not always) citing rabbinic authorities (selected according to the editors' preferred reading of the text in question), as well as information about when and why one must add, omit, or repeat specific passages in particular circumstances

- an appendix containing further information about the history, the correct interpretation, and details about the proper execution of ritual activities; in most editions, we find a reproduction of the twenty-four-page "General Laws of Prayer," compiled by Rabbi Hersh Goldwurm, first published in *The Complete ArtScroll Siddur*[18]

These combined features consecrate ArtScroll Siddurim as "definitive" representations of the form, order, meaning, and underlying purpose of Jewish prayer. Strictly speaking, ArtScroll pioneered none of these organizational features (such as providing an interlinear translation) or paratextual devices (such as footnotes, choreographic instructions, or commentaries). All such textual elements have existed in various forms for centuries of Jewish prayer book production.[19] Nevertheless, the ArtScroll texts stand out in two respects. The first (most frequently noted by the publisher's critics) is the distinctive selection of canonical sources in the commentaries, which purposefully and unapologetically exclude what ArtScroll editors deem to be "untraditional" or "un-Jewish" interpretations, such as those framed in the secular academic canons of philology, archeology, and higher criticism.[20] In this way, ArtScroll books are defined as representations of "traditional" Jewish ritual practice, authenticated by religious authorities who happen to be located in the Haredi yeshiva world. The second distinguishing feature of ArtScroll prayer books (most frequently noted by committed users) is the inclusion of detailed written instructions regarding the mechanics of ritual performance. Information that is left implicit or only briefly discussed in most other Jewish prayer books is meticulously laid out in the ArtScroll text. So, for instance, while other prayer books tell the reader that hands must be washed before reciting a prayer, the ArtScroll Siddur provides far more detailed instructions: "Wash the hands according to the ritual procedure: pick up the vessel of water with the right hand, pass it to the left, and pour water over the right. Then, with the right hand pour over the left. Follow this procedure until water has been poured over each hand three times."[21]

This procedural mode of address is repeated throughout the text, attending to all manner of routine, exceptional, and even quite extraordinary occasions. There are instructions on how to inspect a *tallis* (prayer shawl) to determine its validity; on when to bow to the right and when to the left while reciting the Kaddish (mourner's prayer); indications of the correct order of prayers to be recited while donning tefillin (phylacteries); and even listings of the correct *b'rucha* (blessing) to recite upon erecting a protective railing around one's roof, or upon seeing a rainbow. Often these instructions are quite brief and focus the mechanics of ritual performance, such as the correct gestures and movements of the body. Regarding the lighting of the Sabbath candles, for instance, the reader is simply and straightforwardly told: "Light the candles, then cover the eyes and recite the blessing. Uncover the eyes and gaze briefly at the candles."[22] In other cases, instructions expand outward to consider a range of ambiguities, local variations, and countermanding circumstances that are important to know in order to perform the ritual correctly. So, for example, in an extended note on how to determine the correct time to recite the Shacharis (the basic morning prayer), we read:

> Ideally, one should recite the *Shemoneh Esrei* of the morning prayer after sunrise, but if one cannot wait that long (e.g., he must hurry to work or to perform a *mitzvah* [good deed] that cannot be postponed) he may pray after dawn, i.e., before sunrise, when light appears on the horizon (*Orach Chaim* 89:1). However, if at all possible one should wait at least until the eastern

horizon is fully lit up. According to all views it is not permissible to put on *tefillin* [phylacteries] until there is sufficient daylight to recognize a casual acquaintance at a distance of four cubits (*Orach Chaim* 30:1). Since these times vary, competent authorities should be consulted on the exact time for each place and season. For example, in the northern United States, it varies from approximately fifty minutes before sunrise in March and September to as much as sixty-eight minutes (according to some) in June.[23]

Let us note here how courses of ritual action are plotted according to a hierarchy of variables and priorities, validated by canonical texts as well as by living "competent authorities" to whom the reader is asked to appeal in order to resolve any lingering doubts. The commentaries appearing in ArtScroll Siddurim extend this logic even further, weaving together discussions of the mechanics of ritual performance with reflections on the multiple layers of meaning of the ritual activity in question, so as to impart a "deeper understanding" of its purpose and function. The commentary on the ritual of lighting Sabbath candles is a good case in point, as it combines details about correct practice with a meditation on the representational function of the candles themselves:

> The Sabbath lights are kindled approximately eighteen minutes before sunset. Since women are generally found in the home more often than their husbands, and since women generally look after household matters, the *mitzvah* of kindling the lights has devolved upon the mistress of the house *(Rambam)*. Nevertheless, a man living alone, or with other men, is required to kindle the lights and recite the proper blessing. Similarly, if a woman is too ill to light, her husband should light the candles and recite the blessing.
>
> There should be some light in every room where it will be needed—and indeed this is a halachic requirement—nevertheless, the blessing is recited upon the flames that are kindled in the dining room *(Mishnah Berurah)*. A brightly-lit festive table represents one form of fulfillment of the prophet's instructions: *If you proclaim the Sabbath "a delight"; the holy one of Hashem "honored" . . . then you shall be granted delight with Hashem . . .* (Isaiah 58:13–14). The lights "honor" the Sabbath by brightening, and thereby imparting dignity and importance to, the festive meal *(Rashi)*.[24]

Other commentaries combine procedural statements with utterances that are best described as hortatory and homiletical in that they aim, not only to ensure that ritual participants perform correctly, but also to inspire them to adopt sentiments commensurate with the dignity and solemnity of the prayer. This is well illustrated in Rabbi Goldwurm's commentary on the correct way to perform the most basic Jewish prayer, the Shemoneh Esrei:

> During the *Shemoneh Esrei* one's eyes should be directed downward (*Orach Chaim* 95:2). His eyes should either be closed or reading from the *Siddur* and not looking around (*Mishnah Berurah* 95:5). One should not look up during the *Shemoneh Esrei,* but when he feels his concentration failing he should raise his eyes heavenward to renew his inspiration (*Mishnah Berurah* 90:8). . . . It is important that one should know the meaning of his prayers. If he had an audience with a human ruler he would take utmost care in his choice of words and be aware of their meaning. Surely, therefore, when one speaks before the King of Kings Who knows one's innermost thoughts, he must be careful how he speaks. . . . Thus it is of utmost importance that one learns the meaning of the prayers in order to develop his power of concentration.[25]

What is at stake in the inclusion of these minutiae of ritual conduct? Is it simply a matter of validating correct practice and "guarding against error"? Why do ArtScroll prayer books focus on instilling the forms of competence, confidence, understanding, and appropriate sentiments deemed necessary for participation in Jewish ritual life? For his part, Rabbi Scherman explains the inclusion of choreographic instructions in the ArtScroll Siddurim as follows: "It's all part of the concept of making the Siddur user friendly. If our goal was to bring to classics to 'every man,' to make the classics available and accessible to people of limited background, then it's part of it. It's obvious when you come into a shul [synagogue] and you have strangers there and they can't follow the service, and they're looking around to see when everyone else is standing. So, we felt that we had to do this. We felt that it was as important as the commentaries."[26]

ArtScroll prayer books thus address readers for whom successful conduct in prayer is tied to a presumed need for clear and succinct instruction about the mechanics of ritual performance, especially in the context of publicly performed rituals in synagogue. By lowering of thresholds of competence and ability required for participation in Jewish ritual, ArtScroll's prayer books are designed to reach an audience that cannot be relied upon to know enough or to be sufficiently or properly motivated in the execution of their prayers. This key theme of user-friendliness is echoed among numerous users of ArtScroll Siddurim. In the words of one rabbi at a "Conservadox" synagogue in Teaneck, New Jersey,

I think that [the reason why our congregation switched to ArtScroll] can be attributed to the congregants' desire to learn, to receive instructions. Not necessarily about the "why," but more about the "what" and the "how." How do I go about praying? What choreography is one expected to perform? For instance, I mean, it's nice to hear a rabbi discuss the philosophical implications about washing one's hands before prayer, but how do I go about washing my hands? All of these instructions—and ArtScroll is focused in on that, with lots of instructional information—it makes it more of a handbook than anything else. It's more pragmatic.[27]

Similarly, as worded by "Marty" (a pseudonym), a twenty-something *ba'al teshuva* living in Toronto and an enthusiastic ArtScroll fan:

I really like the way the ArtScroll is laid out. It all just seems very easy. Like, for example, my mother is remarried and her husband, I mean, he was a member of a Reform synagogue for years and years, but he really has no affiliation whatsoever, and he would really have no clue what to do when he's making *kiddush* [the blessing over wine to commence the Sabbath or festival meals]. So, he needs a Siddur that can really lay it out for him and explain it, like, "Put down the cup now and recite this *b'rucha* [blessing]." For me, I guess I kind of know what to do, but I still really like the way, like, how it basically assumes you're an idiot without treating you that way. That's the way I would put it. It basically gives you everything from the beginning without making you feel like you're a complete moron for needing it. I also like the way ArtScroll gives a preface to everything, they way they set you up for what's about to happen. Because if you're willing to spend a few minutes to read it, it really clears things up. Sometimes you wouldn't really understand what's going on, but now you do.[28]

Many users of ArtScroll books thus agree with the editors that "meaningful prayer"—the feelings of confidence, satisfaction, and pleasure associated with competent ritual performance—cannot reliably be secured by memory or by the example of family, friends, and neighbors. Only through scrupulous attention to written instruction can one hope to overcome the feeling that one is "a complete moron," and only on terms provided by the text can the mystery of ritual be "cleared up" so that one knows what to do and why. The genius of the ArtScroll Siddur, it seems, lies in its ability to anticipate such ignorance, and also the anxiety about one's own ignorance, communicating to readers in a helpful yet respectful tone: "assuming you are an idiot without treating you that way." The procedural language of the text is thus crafted to address a range of interlocutors, providing instructions and commentaries of service to all ritual participants, even those who already "kind of know what to do."

This concern about "user-friendliness" and the achievement of "meaningful prayer" is highly ironic, if not paradoxical, in the case of a prayer book that claims to recapture the "traditional" experience of Jewish ritual practice. Indeed, canonical Jewish sources have long emphasized that comprehension, while certainly a good thing, is not at all a prerequisite for compliance with Jewish law, following rabbinic interpretations of Exodus 24:7 ("All that God has said, we will do and we will listen"). A lower priority placed on "understanding" (as opposed to "doing") is likewise evidenced in debates concerning the legitimacy of prayers recited in Hebrew (which the person reciting might not be able to understand), as opposed to the vernacular.[29] This "traditional" attitude to the performance of ritual conduct is well summarized in Shulhan Arukh, a sixteenth-century compendium of Jewish law (later annotated and abridged) that continues to enjoy authoritative status among present-day Orthodox Jews: "Whoever learns Torah aloud fulfills the command of studying Torah, even if he does not understand. Therefore, an unlearned person can say the blessing for the Torah in the morning before reading the scriptural verses and when he is called to the reading of the Torah. Whoever studies Torah, but is unable to understand it, will merit to understand it in the world to come."[30]

But the suggestion that "understanding" might be deferred to the afterlife seems a far cry from ArtScroll's stated desire to make ritual conduct more "meaningful" for Jews engaged in ritual practice here and now. This difference is not lost on ArtScroll's principal editors, who readily acknowledge the challenges they face by trying to promote "correct" ritual conduct in an age of heightened expectations, dissolving forces of attention, and the increasingly provisional status of individual commitments. As Rabbi Scherman concedes, "It's harder to get people's attention nowadays. People are better educated secularly, but at the same time their faith has been weakened. Sincere people thus find it more important to understand the meaning of what they are doing."[31] And here, precisely, is the break with tradition that ArtScroll texts are designed to repair. No longer secure in the knowledge derived from their education, family traditions, or even their personal memories, contemporary Jews are characterized here as restless seekers of textual confirmation and legitimation for all aspects of their conduct as Jews. Rabbi Zlotowitz explains this demand for written instruction through the following anecdote: "Look, when I was young, when you got sick, you went to the doctor, and he gave you some medicine. It was just something in a bottle. You didn't really know what it was, but you took it, because you trusted the judgment of the doctor. Nowadays, you get a prescription from your doctor and you go onto the Internet to find out what it means, what are the ingredients, their side effects, and so on."[32]

Zlotowitz brings into focus an audience that is imagined as well educated but Jewishly ignorant, reluctant to cede authority yet hungry for clear guidance. On these terms, the popularity of ArtScroll prayer books seems to epitomize the rise of scripturalism in Jewish public culture, where the text itself, not the guardians of collective memory, becomes the guarantor of reliable knowledge and legitimate practice in all matters of ritual conduct. By anticipating and addressing all possible confusions, errors, or deviations from what are proclaimed to be the "authentic" and "traditional" forms of Jewish prayer, ArtScroll prayer books do more than simply furnish readers with "missing" knowledge. They also reorganize the long-standing Jewish hierarchies of understanding, obedience, and action that underpin one's willingness to adopt and execute these more "correct" forms of ritual practice. In the highly literate public culture of contemporary English-speaking diaspora Jewry, ArtScroll prayer books offer procedural knowledge as a legitimate, indeed a necessary, step toward making prayer "meaningful."

HIDDUR MITZVAH AND DESIGNER LIVING

Susie Fishbein is the author of a series of popular kosher cookbooks, beginning with *Kosher by Design*.[33] These works are among the best-selling products on the entire ArtScroll booklist, making Fishbein a key author for the publisher. Indeed, from its first appearance in 2003, *Kosher by Design* has been a runaway success within the Orthodox Jewish community, and well beyond it, as we can note in the marketing of this book in the U.S.-based Williams Sonoma home decor retail chain, in Fishbein's public career as "the Kosher Diva" and "the Jewish Martha Stewart" on the American television daytime talk show circuit, and, most strikingly, in the growing popularity of this text among Christian evangelical booksellers in the United States.[34] *Kosher by Design* presents "an engaging and elegant new cookbook that delights the senses and feeds the soul."[35] Comprising 250 recipes, 120 full-color photographs, and distinctive organizational features (such as holiday menu guides, complementary wine lists, and a special index indicating recipes appropriate for Passover), all encased in a laminated cover with a sturdy "concealed wire" binding, this cookbook is designed for both ease of use and "inspiring" visual pleasure. Is this too an instance of scripturalism? How elastic is the notion of scripturalism if it can include the works of Susie Fishbein? What are the underlying assumptions about authorial intent, editorial prerogative, and brand-naming that allow us to make such comparisons?

Jewish cookbooks, I suggest, offer an instructive point of entry into the study of scripturalism. They are particularly valuable for shedding light on the materialization of religious sensibilities, in this case the staging of scenarios for domestic living through a mode of address that artfully combines literary genres of recipes and lists, advice on etiquette and kitchen management, and expert opinion on *kashrut*, the Jewish laws of diet. More generally, cookbooks operate on the understanding that food is a key medium conjoining the individual and the social body, precariously situated between sustenance and pollution, desire and taboo, and governed by complex rules of taste, commensality, and etiquette. Food, after all, is a necessary condition for physiological and social reproduction, on the scale of both intergenerational transmission and everyday continuity. It is through food that we express our inescapable relationships of dependence with others, first as children requiring nutrition from caregivers and then as individuals situated within the institutions and action networks that govern its cultivation, harvesting, production, distribution, preparation, consumption, storage, and disposal. These routines of labor and exchange—predominantly, the labor of women—also provide occasions for the religious imagination to penetrate into the habitus of everyday life, especially domesticity and family life. In this respect, it is important to note that cookbooks typically provide, not only technical instructions about food preparation, but also advice on the attainment of social grace through the cultivation of culinary elegance, good manners, and firm management of the kitchen and the dining table as centerpieces of the domestic sphere. Borrowing from the long-standing genre of the etiquette manual, they seek to "civilize" social conduct through the disciplined practice of good dining.[36] Drawing upon the original sense of the word *etiquette*—an eighteenth-century neologism for *la petite éthique,* the "small ethics"—we can note how cookbooks mediate a form popular religion: a "minor tradition" of aesthetic sensibilities, techniques, and performative principles framed within, but never reducible to, the abstract formulations of Jewish law.[37]

As Barbara Kirshenblatt-Gimblett has shown, the genre of the Jewish cookbook both reflects and helps to constitute local culinary practices. It does so by presenting expert opinion on how to prepare and eat Jewish food and by staging imagined scenes of commensality and domestic sociability, while at the same time mediating large-scale patterns of technological and economic change, such as the creeping presence of the commercial food industry in the kitchen.[38] Through their recipes, commentaries, prefaces, illustrations, and, where they exist, photographs, cookbooks reproduce regional notions of "traditional" cuisine (defined by locally available ingredients and established methods of preparation), while at the same time extending the repertoire of legitimately "Jewish" food into new domains. Like its non-Jewish counterpart, the history of Jewish cookbook writing mirrors discrete stages of incorporation of new technologies and techniques, ingredients, styles, and dietary principles, innovated by expert knowledge producers, elite tastemakers, and popularizers of trends emanating from the world of haute cuisine. This history also encapsulates an evolving set of relationships between author and reader, whereby, among other things, faith in locally acquired, unwritten knowledge has steadily been eroded as a sufficient basis for the successful (re)production of Jewish food. By supplementing, if not replacing, culinary competencies that would otherwise have been acquired interpersonally—such as recipes or techniques passed down from parent to child, or among one's immediate community of neighbors and friends—Jewish cookbooks have increasingly come to evince the new, "scripturalist" role for the text as a sui generis voice of instruction. This is especially evident in the case of cookbooks that are marketed as strictly Orthodox, as in the case of ArtScroll's offerings.

Susie Fishbein was inspired to write *Kosher by Design* by what she claims (quite groundlessly) to have been a glaring hole in the kosher cookbook market[39]: "I wanted to do something like what Martha Stewart does—meals that are easy to prepare, and elegant and healthful, and that appeal to all the senses."[40] In other words, her goal was to realize "a gourmet potential in kosher cooking never dreamed possible in Grandma's day."[41] Like many of her predecessors, Fishbein made her entree into cookbook writing through charity fundraising initiatives. And like many cookbook authors, she derives her authority from her experience as the head of her household, in this instance as a mother of four children.[42] But Fishbein supplemented her authorial voice with a team of "experts": Larry Sexton, the florist at the New York Plaza Hotel; Renee Erreich, a "world class" party planner; and John Uher, a professional food and lifestyle magazine photographer. Working together, they produced a series of cookbooks that offer the reader not only recipes but also table setting plans, ideas for floral arrangements, party themes, wine lists for holiday menus (featuring "cutting-edge" kosher wines), resource guides for purchasing exotic kosher ingredients, and even corporate tie-ins, where the cooking tools and housewares featured in the photographs are also promoted for sale at the back of some of the books.

These features seem innovative, but many of them are variations on the genre of Jewish cookbook writing as it has existed since at least the eighteenth century. Fishbein's recent success was in fact prepared by a *longue durée* of sedimented social patterns of distinction and habit with regard to print matter, as well as patterns of leisure and economic upward mobility that secured an expanding consumer base for "Jewish products," including food, clothing, ritual objects, artwork, music, memorabilia, and the like.[43] The history of this advancing Jewish embourgeoisement was staged, among other things, through a succession of cookbooks that addressed readers who were assumed to be familiar with the basic laws of *kashrut*, and presumably with Jewish specialties, but not with the techniques and aesthetic standards required to produce culinary elegance. By "upgrading" the cuisine, they promised a means of overcoming the social embarrassment of kosher food as "not stylish." By the mid-twentieth century this mode of address was well ensconced within an expanding market—especially in the United States—emphasizing the importance of style and artistry, including the aesthetics of ritual performance, such as key festival meals that were accompanied by floral arrangements, color schemes, table decor, and other details of display that signaled elegant dining.[44] In this context, kosher cookbooks aimed to articulate the continuity of Jewish dietary requirements and to materialize the "spirit" of Jewish rituals (particularly rituals of commensality) through the pleasurable stimuli of fashionable food, with special attention devoted to its visual presentation. This trend in cookbook publishing was also closely tied to a broader pattern of evolution in the kosher food industry that enabled Jewish consumers to enter into a seemingly boundless gastronomic universe, enhanced by advances in technologies of food production and the consolidation of new global distribution chains of both raw and prepared ingredients, as well as an expanding culture of culinary spectacle created by professional kosher caterers at weddings, bar mitzvahs, and other events.[45]

In all these respects, *Kosher by Design* not only follows a well-worn path of predecessors in the genre of kosher cookbook writing but also epitomizes a more recent publishing trend extending far beyond the Jewish world: a proliferation of cookbooks exhibiting high production values, at the far extreme of which one finds the large-format, "coffee-table" style books, featuring the work of an expanding cult of cooking and home design celebrities such as Nigella Lawson, Jamie Oliver, and Martha Stewart. In such books, culinary elegance is conveyed by sophisticated recipes, as well as the material elements of bookbinding, typeface, illustration, and above all, full color photographs printed on coated stock, depicting prepared dishes artfully arranged according to professional techniques of lighting and composition. One of the most recognizable leaders of this food fashion trend is Martha Stewart, renowned food and home design mogul and purveyor of a wide range of media and consumer products, from her award-winning magazine, *Martha Stewart Living,* to her internationally syndicated TV and radio shows, to her brand-name household products, including lines of house paint, linen, and drapery sold in retail chain stores. In their ensemble, Stewart's products promote the realization of fantasies of an aristocratic, elegant, and well-ordered lifestyle through skilled technique and attention to detail (rather than through mere possession of great wealth), appealing especially to women readers who wish to make changes in their home environment but do not necessarily possess the time or money for extended projects or hired help. Through cascading images of immaculate homes, gorgeous landscaping, handmade gifts for the holidays, and flawless dinner parties, Martha Stewart's audiences are offered the means of producing an aristocratic lifestyle through skilled techniques of display, substituting the "look" of luxury for a much less easily attained class ascension, while at the same time validating domesticity as an arena of infinitely improvable beautification: an aesthetic project that both transfigures and overcomes the drudgery of cooking and cleaning.[46]

But *Kosher by Design* does far more than simply impart the requisite knowledge for producing elegance. It is also designed, as Susie Fishbein puts it, "to help families incorporate more of Judaism into our most important Jewish institution of all time: the home."[47] Recipes, menus, and sample table decor furnish the reader with instructions and models whereby the aesthetics of desirable food is cast as a positive outcome of scrupulous attention to Jewish law, and innovation in cuisine is presented as legitimate variation on religious custom. Throughout the book, one thus finds religious instructions juxtaposed with cooking techniques, advice on food presentation, and other suggestions for aesthetically elevating the dining experience. In addition to the recipes themselves, there are sections describing the major Jewish holidays, as well as suggested menu options for each such event. Text boxes appearing beside or beneath recipes offer such diverse instructions as how best to hard-cook eggs; how to *kasher* a chicken liver; how to create innovative but easy-to-do floral arrangements; how to serve soup in edible bread bowls; how to zest a lemon with a microplane; how to determine whether Worcestershire sauce is religiously permissible for use in meat recipes; and how to make a *bouquet garni,* among many other things.[48]

One important thread within the fabric of this "designer cuisine" is a Jewishly specific subgenre that one might call the *balebatish* style.[49] With its deployment of courtly signs—crushed velvet and golden tassels, white lace, silverware and crystal—the *balebatish* style connotes a mood of elegance and dignity, while at the same time invoking long-standing Jewish metaphors of the Torah as a king, adorned with a crown, or of the setting of the Sabbath table as preparation for the arrival of a queen (Fig. 3). Thus it is not luxury per se that is the object of desire. Through the visual language of the *balebatish,* signs of luxury function within Fishbein's texts as an index of a higher order of things, embodied in the sacred covenant between God and his Chosen People. Fishbein is a *Jewish* Martha Stewart not simply because she happens to be Jewish but more precisely because she draws upon the stock of *balebatish* images and styles, artfully rearranging and "updating" familiar elements to meet the aesthetic standards of the contemporary bourgeois home. And because these same elements are understood as legitimate modes of artistic production within the framework of Jewish laws concerning food and domestic life, an even better title for Susie Fishbein might be "the *kosher* Martha Stewart."

So, on the one hand, *Kosher by Design* offers a means of appropriating the "look" required for bourgeois self-representation by extending the circulation of expert knowledge about culinary elegance into the (ideally Orthodox) home. But at the same time, the lush sensorial repertoire of beautiful food and elegant dining is framed by strict interpretations of Jewish dietary requirements and custom in matters of ritual practice. Consider, for example, the kaleidoscopic combination of legal opinion, maternal advice, and fashion tips found in the section on the making of challah, a bread consumed on the Jewish Sabbath. The section opens with a discussion of the religious function of challah, constituted by the mitzvah (commandment) of *hafrashat challah.*[50] In a tone strikingly reminiscent of ArtScroll prayer books and other works addressing matters of correct conduct, Fishbein presents a detailed account of the ritual requirements governing challah production:

> The obligation begins when at least 2 lbs., 10 ounces of dough is kneaded,
> if it is made of one or more of five grains: wheat, barley, oats, rye, or
> spelt. A piece of dough the size of an olive is removed and burned. (You
> can wrap it in foil and put it in the oven until it is too charred to be

1 Bread and butter plate with butter knife	11 Fish knife
2 Coffee cup and saucer	12 Soup spoon
3-4 Dessert spoon and cake fork	13 Soup bowl
5 Red wine	14 Appetizer plate
6 White wine	15 Dinner plate
7 Water glass	16 Charger
8 Champagne and sparkling wine flute	17 Fish fork
9 Brandy snifter	18 Salad fork
10 Dinner knife	19 Dinner fork

Figure 3. The "Well-Dressed Table," *Kosher by Design,* p. 130. The term *well-dressed table* also references a canonical work of Jewish law, Shulchan Aruch, presenting a further layer of overlap between religious instruction and culinary elegance. Reproduced courtesy of Mesorah Publications (ArtScroll Series).

edible). If the batch is larger (legal opinions of the minimum amount range from 3 lbs., 10.7 ozs. to 4 lbs., 15.2 ozs.), a blessing is made before pulling off the dough. . . . Few people realize that the name for our special Shabbat bread derives from the *mitzvah* associated with it. By sanctifying our loaves, we demonstrate that we appreciate God's blessings; and in keeping alive the practice of reserving this portion of our food, we express our faith that someday the Jewish people will be able to return to the Temple and to the spiritual level that once was ours.[51]

Following this discussion comes Fishbein's challah recipe, forwarded by the comment:

I love the ease of baking challah in my bread machine. However, there are times that I love the experience of spending a Thursday night in the kitchen with my three daughters baking challah the old-fashioned way, the way its *[sic]* been done by mothers and daughters for generations. The kneading and mixing become a group effort with lots of giggling to go around. The anticipation of Shabbat fills the air. This is my family's favorite recipe.[52]

This scene of domestic conviviality and maternal aura, supplemented by the benefits of modern technology (cooks are free to choose between the convenience of a bread machine and the social benefits accrued from enlisting family members in collective labor), underscores the links between religious obligation and traditions of practice that stand at the heart of challah baking. But *Kosher by Design* does not rest here. The section on challah concludes with a second recipe, a variation on the "classic" mode of preparing and serving challah, in an innovative form Fishbein calls "challah napkin rings" (Fig. 4). "Could there be anything cuter on a Shabbos table than challah napkin rings? They serve a dual purpose by holding the napkins and providing dinner guests with their own challah roll."[53]

Challah napkin rings are located at the intersection of religious injunction, culinary tradition, and the impulse to "elevate" the dining experience through innovative aesthetic techniques. This artful combination of "cute" and "classical" modes of food preparation and presentation is echoed throughout *Kosher by Design,* especially in its presentation of holiday meals, which combine brief accounts of the legal requirements, suggested menus, wine lists, and table designs, all of which aim to convey the "spirit" of each holiday. For instance, in her introduction to the Jewish holiday of Simchat Torah (a celebration marking the conclusion of the

Figure 4. Challah napkin rings, *Kosher by Design,* p. 15. Reproduced courtesy of Mesorah Publications (ArtScroll Series).

yearlong cycle of reading the Torah), Fishbein writes: "Bursting with joy, our lively Simchat Torah table combines minimum fuss with maximum aesthetic impact. Begin with a floor-length orange tablecloth; then layer it with colored place mats and napkins (which are actually inexpensive dish towels and dish cloths). . . . A charming touch is to serve foods resembling Torah scrolls. In that spirit, we chose Chicken Negamaki to begin the meal [Fig. 5]. This rolled chicken dish, with its colorful pepper and scallion strips, offers an innovative angle on traditional fare."[54] Even for such an austere occasion as Yom Kippur, the Jewish Day of Atonement, Fishbein provides some helpful design hints:

> Yom Kippur is not about food. However, eating before the fasting begins is as much of a *mitzvah* [commandment] as the fast itself. It should be a full holiday meal. Spend a few minutes setting a beautiful table to help put you in the proper frame of mind for this holy day. We selected a simple white tablecloth because white is a symbol of Yom Kippur. . . . The simple menu omits salty and spicy foods because they cause thirst. . . . Time can run short, so we suggest store-purchased sorbets for dessert. Serving them in crystal martini glasses will elevate them to holiday elegance.[55]

chicken negamaki with red pepper chutney

appetizers

Figure 5. Chicken negamaki rolls, *Kosher by Design,* p. 21. Reproduced courtesy of Mesorah Publications (ArtScroll Series).

While Fishbein's variations on the traditional repertoire of Jewish cuisine and her suggestions for table decor would seem very familiar to Martha Stewart fans, rabbinic authorities are able to treat the same material as instantiations of a long-standing Jewish principle known as *hiddur mitzvah:* the enhancement or beautification of a religious commandment in order to exceed the minimum requirements of correct observance and to glorify God through practices of adornment or ornamentation. According to this principle, when Jews not only maintain the minimum effort required to correctly perform the observance of a *kiyum hamitzvah* (basic fulfillment of the mitzvah) but engage in "extra efforts" that will enhance that performance, a *hiddur mitzvah,* they glorify God. It is ritually sufficient, for instance, to drink wine mandated by certain prayers (e.g., the Kiddush) in a paper cup, but it is even better to drink the wine from a beautiful cup made of silver. In the rabbinic tradition, the principle of *hiddur mitzvah* has been applied to such diverse practices as the illumination of manuscripts, the refinement of ritual objects, and even the practice of circumcision.[56] By some interpretations, such acts of *hiddur mitzvah* also possess a theurgic function, whereby God is provoked to reciprocate "in kind" by providing the gift of a miracle.[57]

Through the legitimizing principle of *hiddur mitzvah,* Jewish history is replete with traditions of art and craft making, techniques of ornamentation, adornment, and other means of creating visual effects. Even the most rudimentary familiarity with this long history makes it untenable to regard ArtScroll's emphasis on the aesthetic as unprecedented, let alone to propose that it goes against the grain of what is in any event a much-exaggerated notion of Jewish aniconism.[58] Nevertheless, it is instructive to note the discontinuities, rather than the continuities, within religious frameworks of artistic production, since these often point to counterintuitive trends. In contemporary public culture, structured by unprecedented velocities and complexities in the flow of media, recognizably Jewish aesthetic practices risk disappearing within a vast universe of remediated texts, images, and styles of presentation. Returning to the case of *Kosher by Design,* we might ask what is and what is not "Jewish" about a challah napkin ring or a kosher chicken negamaki roll? The "religious" and the "aesthetic" dimensions of such products can be distinguished only by invoking one or another of a series of specious distinctions between essence and supplement, center and margin, form and content, or medium and message. Legal considerations and techniques for producing culinary elegance are thoroughly enmeshed here, and it is only in their combination that we can understand what is unique about this text.

Indeed, *Kosher by Design* does far more than simply provide a "script" for the performance of acts of *hiddur mitzvah.* Through techniques for elevating the dining experience, Fishbein's text participates in a broader process of reengineering the kosher home, where habits formed through religious discipline can be joined in new ways with an expanding culture of commodified leisure and practices and techniques of spectacle and display. However, once religious obligations are recast as opportunities for aesthetic expression, the terms of legitimate conduct and ritual observance risk undergoing significant change. Homemakers must now negotiate between competing sources of authority—the guardians of religious customs and laws and the experts on refined dining, interior decorating, and party planning—and learn how to accommodate their respective expectations. *Kosher by Design* thereby stages a remarkable reformulation of the balance of piety and pleasure in relation to religious conduct. As Fishbein puts it, in one interview, "The emphasis of *Kosher by Design* is on easy to do and enjoyable to do. With so many food-based events to prepare for in our communal and personal calendars, our team worked very hard so that you won't have to. We want you to spend more time being a gracious host than a chef who sweats it; but while you're wearing your chef's hat, we'll help you cook with confidence and inspiration."[59]

Here, once again, the requisite skills and knowledge are developed in the text, which is designed to anticipate ignorance, confusion, and error, and—standing behind the text—the team that "worked very hard so that the reader won't have to." The minimization of unregulated (and therefore potentially misdirected) activity not only reduces "sweat" but also instills personal confidence, which in turn secures a more "inspired" dining experience. In one interview following the release of *Kosher by Design,* Fishbein strikingly defines her mode of address as that of a "personal coach."[60] By invoking this figure, who functions not only as a guarantor of knowledge but also as a palliative and a psychological motivator, Fishbein signals the reordering of a much older Jewish economy of pleasure and pain. Indeed, to the extent that virtuosity and competence in religious conduct require effort, sacrifice, devotion, and training, religious instruction has always been defined in terms of its techniques and technologies for disciplining the self through the constitution of bodily regimens, the ordering of time and space, and the attentive focusing of the mind to transcend the ever-present threats of inertia, self-indulgence, and laxity. From the ancient monastic regimens of athletics, exercise, fasting, and diet to contemporary biopolitical practices of regularization and control of the body, or for that matter, of competent exercise of the laws of *kashrut* within the modern domestic sphere, it is possible to trace the history of a relatively continuous definition of "training" in terms of an economy of pleasure and pain, and of pleasure *in* pain, and the rewards of purification that accompany virtuosic performance, rigorous application, and self-denial.[61] But with the intrusion of Fishbein's "personal coach," the *reduction of effort* emerges as a new organizing principle for the successful replication of authentic Jewish practice, directly paralleling the emphasis on user-friendliness and functional ease that we have already seen at work in ArtScroll prayer books. Thanks to the clear instructions, the comforting tones, and the pleasurable visual stimuli that infuse the text, the hallowed experience of, for instance, the Passover seder meal becomes, in Fishbein's words, "a time to celebrate our historic liberation, not to feel oppressed by the cruel taskmaster of the menu."[62]

GETTING BY WITH A LITTLE HELP FROM HASHEM

"Every person needs a recovery program, and for the Jew, that recovery program is Torah."

ABRAHAM TWERSKI

Self-Improvement? I'm Jewish! Overcoming Self-Defeating Behavior

Praying and cooking, we have seen, materialize the metaphor of the "recipe" in different arenas of Jewish conduct. ArtScroll's prayer books provide instructions on the iterative requirements, the gestures, the bodily carriage, and the mechanics of ritual performance, while their cookbooks are concerned with techniques for producing desirable food and an elegant dining experience, which in turn are presented as positive outcomes of scrupulous attention to Jewish law. Both genres share a common mode of address that anticipates the possible anxieties, concerns, and knowledge gaps of their readers, seeking to overcome these impediments through detailed instruction. By concentrating on procedural matters—how to recite, how to pray, how to cook, how to decorate, how to ascertain whether a given course of action is religiously permissible—these texts communicate expert knowledge on Jewish conduct, the success of which depends in part on a displacement of the authority of informal sources of knowledge, such as family members, neighbors, or even local rabbis and teachers. As we have also seen, ArtScroll prayer books and cookbooks are further distinguished by their explicit concern with the conditions that shape one's willingness to learn, master, and apply these same instructions. Sensing that they cannot simply assume their readers to know how, let alone to want, to adhere to the stringent regulations that govern Haredi practice, the authors, editors, and marketing agents of ArtScroll books repeatedly emphasize that their recommended courses of action are in fact "easy to do" and that when properly executed they will engender more "meaningful" and "inspirational" experiences. Such promises point to a principle of human psychological satisfaction as a legitimate precondition, and also compensation, for accessions to Haredi rabbinic authority and to prescriptions of Jewish law as interpreted from a Haredi standpoint.

Prayer books and cookbooks are not the only texts concerned with the psychological underpinnings of Haredi-defined conduct. The ArtScroll booklist is in fact replete with works gathered under the rubrics of "Dating and Marriage," "Death and Bereavement," "Inspiration," "Ethical Insights," "Parenting," and "Psychology," all of which establish this publisher as a major purveyor of self-help literature for the English-speaking Orthodox Jewish reader. ArtScroll's most famous author in this domain is Rabbi Abraham Twerski, who has penned over thirty works for the press, including the perennial best-sellers *Self-Improvement? I'm Jewish! Overcoming Self-Defeating Behavior, Angels Don't Leave Footprints: Discovering What's Right with Yourself,* and his most recent publication, *The Sun Will Shine Again: Coping, Persevering, and Winning in Troubled Economic Times.*[63] Beyond Rabbi Twerski's offerings, ArtScroll has published roughly three hundred self-help books, bearing such diverse titles as Zelig Pliskin's *Anger! The Inner Teacher: A Nine-Step Program to Free Yourself from Anger,* Meir Wikler's *Partners with Hashem [God]: Effective Guidelines for Successful Parenting,* Dov Brezak's *Chinuch [Education] in Turbulent Times: Practical Strategies for Parents and Educators,* or Roiza Weinreich's *There Will Never Be Another You! Developing a Customized Plan to Reach Your Potential.*[64] Not unlike the prayer books and cookbooks, ArtScroll's self-help books present scenarios of Jewish conduct that have been authorized by Haredi rabbinic elites as reliable and morally appropriate. A wide range of scenarios of Jewish living are embedded in the expert advice given on such matters as managing anger, recovering from addictions, overcoming depression, and cultivating improved relations with one's spouse, parents, children, friends, and neighbors. Through their hortatory mode of address, ArtScroll self-help texts also offer encouragement and motivation to a readership imagined as battling—or at risk of succumbing to—the emotional traumas of anxiety, stress, low self-esteem, self-doubt, depression, or interpersonal conflict. On these terms, readers are offered tools designed to secure the psychic conditions necessary for leading a contented, emotionally enriched, and healthy life, all the while adhering strictly to Haredi-defined ethical standards and legal norms of conduct.

It is not terribly surprising that ArtScroll has devoted such energy to the publication of self-help literature, given the omnipresence of a "therapeutic" culture that is characteristic of most advanced liberal societies: especially the United States, but also other host countries of the English-speaking

Jewish diaspora, including Canada and the United Kingdom. In fact, although they are framed by the particular vocabularies, sensibilities, and legal requirements of Orthodox Judaism, ArtScroll's self-help books are familiar renditions of a much larger public circulation of expert knowledge about psychic well-being, interpersonal and professional success, and the art of emotions, as proffered by a growing breed of "spiritual directors" and "engineers of the soul," including international celebrities like Deepak Chopra, Anthony Robbins, Stephen Covey, and Helen Gurley Brown.[65] ArtScroll's contributions to the elaboration of self-help advice for the Orthodox Jewish reader can therefore be treated as a local variant of this widespread interest in pop psychology, both within and beyond the English-language Jewish public sphere.

We should also bear in mind that the publications under consideration here represent only one part of an ongoing effort among pop psychologists and public intellectuals to articulate Orthodox Jewish renditions of this larger self-help discourse. Indeed, ArtScroll's output is reflected, if not overshadowed, by the careers of prominent Orthodox public figures, such as Rabbi Shmuley Boteach—author of a string of bestsellers, including *Kosher Sex: A Recipe for Passion and Intimacy, Dating Secrets of the Ten Commandments,* and *Shalom in the Home*—and Rebbetzin Esther Jungreis—author of *The Committed Life: Principles for Good Living from Our Timeless Past* and *The Committed Marriage: A Guide to Finding a Soul Mate and Building a Relationship through Timeless Biblical Wisdom.*[66] Both Boteach and Jungreis are well known not only for their writings but for their regular appearances on the international Jewish lecture circuit, as well as on "mainstream" radio and television talk shows, making them interesting "crossover" figures who can speak effectively to both Jewish and non-Jewish audiences.[67] Placed in this larger context, the popularity of ArtScroll's self-help books would appear to epitomize a growing hunger among diverse audiences for new information and practical advice about how to heal pains and overcome bad habits, for which the "traditional" genres of religious instruction are often perceived as too vague or not grounded in firm scientific principles. However, because they insistently are presented as advice that is continuous with the "traditional" forms of Jewish discourse about ethical conduct, these particular self-help books do not precisely replicate the genre as it is found in the non-Orthodox Jewish world. Rather, the ArtScroll self-help series instantiates what Bakhtin would call a "hybrid construction": the dynamic, unstable, but richly suggestive conjunction of a "native" religious discourse about ethical conduct and the "foreign" vocabularies of psychology, psychotherapy, and self-help.[68]

Although its roots go back to the eighteenth century, if not further, the genre of self-help today represents a booming cultural industry of expert opinion giving that has enjoyed an increasingly prominent place in advanced liberal societies, addressing every conceivable arena of both public and private life, from financial planning to marital advice, time management, and soul-searching.[69] Self-help writings take many forms, but they are generally distinguished by their emphasis on processes of transforming the self through productive applications, whether these be external improvements in one's environment or the reformation of one's deep psychic predispositions, in order to allow a "new and improved" self to emerge. By offering clear, comprehensive, and (what is often proclaimed as) scientifically grounded advice on the cultivation of strategically effective techniques, self-help books promise to impart reliable means for achieving personal growth, self-esteem, psychologically enriching experiences, and healthy interpersonal relations. At the same time, as suggested by the very name "self-help," this genre also emphasizes the *voluntary* nature of all such enterprises. Rather than relying on coercive measures, the discourse of self-help suggests that changes in behavior are a product of personal responsibility. With the guidance of expert advice, readers must tap their own inner reservoirs of strength and probe their own behavior to understand and then transform themselves and their environments. In particular, through the elaboration of action models—such as countless variations on the "Twelve-Step" program originally developed in the 1930s by Alcoholics Anonymous—self-help authors provide detailed plans that show how to effect lasting changes in behavior, making their readers cognizant of the challenges of inertia, habit, or unconscious resistance that stand in the way of the "recovery" of one's true self and the path leading to a happier and more healthy way of life.[70]

An extensive scholarship has traced the origins of self-help literature, and the "therapeutic" culture of which it is a part, through the historical transformation of older vocabularies, representations, and techniques for ethical living—in particular, those found in religious texts and oral folk traditions—into modes of conduct that are grounded in the modern, Western conception of the "authentic self."[71] As Charles Taylor argues, unique to Western philosophical modernity (and, in particular, a tradition of Romantic thought beginning with Herder) was the growing acceptance of the imperative that to be "human" we must be "true to ourselves," which requires each of us to embark on the journey to discover, articulate, and cultivate our unique, original essence.[72] It is a matter of debate how much influence to ascribe to this philosophical tradition at the level of popular culture. But Taylor's description of the growing concern with the "self" provides a useful point of entry into contemporary Haredi self-help literature, where, it so happens, a high premium is placed on the discovery, fulfillment, and improvement of the self, even in what seem to be the most "selfless" domains of religious obligation, such as prayer. Consider, for instance, the following argument by Rabbi Noah Weinberg, the founder of Aish haTorah and author of the ArtScroll self-help title *What the Angel Taught You: Seven Keys to Life Fulfillment:*

> For most people, prayer is either a laundry list of requests to "remind" Him of what it is we need most (absurd), or a "wake-up call" to God to let Him know that we need some help down here (beyond absurd). . . . We would do well to remember two major points about God and our relationship with Him. We are praying to a Being that is, at the same time, All-Knowing, All-Powerful, and All-Loving. . . . Does He really need your reminders of what you think you need? Not only is God eminently capable of knowing and providing for your every need, but, more importantly, He also wants to give those things to you even more than you want them yourself! That is precisely why He created you. . . . So, it should be clear that prayer is neither a reminder nor a wake-up call to the Supreme Being. What then is it all about? It is all about YOU! That's right, you. Prayer is actually not for God at all. . . . Your prayers are not needed by God. . . . Prayer, logic insists, can only be an exercise for your own benefit. It is a process of introspection. It helps you clarify and refine who you really are, who you should be, and how to achieve the transformation. Prayer, therefore, is actually a sophisticated vehicle for self-knowledge and self-improvement. And to the extent that we improve ourselves through prayer, we become more capable of absorbing and incorporating God's blessing.[73]

Rabbi Weinberg's characterization of prayer as a "self-benefiting exercise" and a "sophisticated vehicle for self-knowledge and self-improvement," designed to "clarify and refine who you really are" and "who you should be," epitomizes the broad cultural preoccupation with the self that Taylor has described. These terms of reference are also mirrored in the historical development of a complex of sciences, techniques, and institutions that gave birth to the modern disciplines of psychology and psychotherapy and that enabled the spread of psychology into virtually every corner of social life. As a body of scientifically accredited analytical procedures and interventionist techniques, psychology offered new ways to conceive and manage one's self, supplanting the formerly uncontested authority of theological discourse in such matters as the moderation of carnal appetites, the calibration of conduct for the attainment of spiritual grace, and the expiatory power of confession. In the American context, the late nineteenth century marked the beginnings of a rapid uptake of these psychological modes of discourse about personal life and the growing authority of psychotherapeutic and psychopharmacological techniques for alleviating malaise, as evidenced in the penetration of psychological expertise into a wide range of medical, educational, penal, and juridical institutions, as well as the expanding market for books, magazines, news reportage, and other popular mediations addressed to lay audiences.[74] For more than a century, psychology has developed into one of the most powerful sources of expert opinion, cementing what has increasingly come to be seen as a self-evident assumption that there is a psychological root to all human problems. Indeed, psychological questions of personal satisfaction, desire, motivation, and fear point to the "core" of what it means to be human. It is especially but by no means uniquely proper to the contemporary public culture of Western modernity that we are ceaselessly called upon to transform ourselves: to work upon our emotional world, to improve our domestic arrangements, to refine our techniques of pleasure, and to reform our styles of living, at each stage binding ourselves ever more tightly to the language and norms of psychological expertise.[75]

These are the terms on which modern psychology is said to have supplanted religious instruction in matters of virtuous conduct, giving a sharp twist to "classical" religious notions of human willpower, sinfulness, and the calculus of rewards and punishments in the afterlife. Over the course of the past century, religious authorities have found themselves increasingly obliged to accept (if not explicitly reproduce) the more technically precise analytical vocabulary of professional psychology, and especially the latter's accounts of the dynamics of repression and denial, of unconscious motivation, and of the maintenance of psychological equilibrium. But as Andrew Heinze has shown with particular regard to the Jewish case, this confrontation between religious discourses on ethical conduct and modern psychology is not simply a story about the "replacement" of the former with the latter.[76] Rather, their encounter is rooted in a complex history of intellectual collaboration and competition centered on questions about human temperament and its challenges to ethical behavior, as evident in texts belonging to the Jewish literary genre known as *musar* (ethical instruction) and their shifting vocabularies, assumptions, and styles of reasoning over the course of the nineteenth and twentieth centuries.[77]

Rabbi Abraham Twerski is a notable exemplar of this hybridization of the discourses of *musar* and of modern psychology and psychotherapy, and his success in cultivating Haredi, non-Haredi, and even non-Jewish readerships is a testament to the influence of the self-help literature published by ArtScroll. As a trained psychiatrist, a rabbi, and a prolific *musar* author, Twerski has expounded in detail on the origins of low self-esteem and the practical tools that one can use to overcome it, presenting a defense of "traditional" *musar* ethical precepts with reference to a decidedly "untraditional" image of the moral self.[78] Indeed, on the one hand, Twerski frequently insists that modern methods of psychotherapy are merely supplementary to the ethical requirements of Jewish living, as ordained in scripture and in the long traditions of Jewish canonical writings. So he argues, "It is common practice that if one acquires a complex apparatus, one reads the manufacturer's instructions to know how to operate it and maintain it properly. Deviating from these instructions can result in malfunction and damage to the apparatus. Inasmuch as the Torah was given to us by the Creator, it constitutes the 'Manufacturer's instructions,' and by adhering to these instructions, one should avoid any and all maladjustments."[79]

Adherence to the "manufacturer's instructions," however, is not as straightforward as it used to be. Echoing a sentiment found among many Orthodox self-help authors, Twerski repeatedly avers that modern bourgeois living has made the Jewish soul weak and that it has become increasingly difficult for those who wish to obey Jewish law to actually perform that obedience. Even for those firmly ensconced within the Orthodox community, moral conduct is riskier nowadays because tendencies toward laxity and hedonism are more pervasive, insidious, and seductive than ever before. "Let us not fool ourselves," Twerski cautions his reader. "There may be nothing wrong with enjoying glatt [strictly] kosher Chinese cuisine or pizza with all the trimmings. However, we can hardly claim such pleasures enhance our progress toward angelic spirituality."[80] But for Twerski, the greatest danger for authentically Torah-true ethical conduct does not lie in the seductions of modern material comforts. It lies rather in the fundamental precariousness of human intention itself, as evidenced in the ease with which even the most well-intentioned and morally upright Jew can fall prey to self-destructive, unconscious patterns of thought and behavior. In a veiled critique of the conventional notions of human willpower, as found in many Jewish canonical writings as well as those of the aforementioned *musar* authors, Twerski proposes:

> We should realize that we may be unable to prevent certain ideas from occurring to us, but we are far too good to indulge in such actions. . . . Unless we understand this, we may fall into a dangerous trap. If we react to an unacceptable impulse by thinking, "I must be an evil person to think or feel this," we are lowering our self-esteem. *But it is precisely a strong self-esteem that can enable us not only to resist but also to dismiss unacceptable impulses.* If we do not think well of ourselves, we lose that most potent weapon against the *yetzer hara* [evil inclination] which repeatedly brings such notions to mind.[81]

Calling for recognition of the involuntary nature of "evil thoughts," Twerski not only complicates classical *musar* descriptions of the *yetzer hara* but also establishes the need for "more refined" techniques that will overcome "self-defeating behavior" and secure "strong self-esteem." In this vein, Twerski frequently invokes the Twelve-Step method of Alcoholics Anonymous, an interventionist technique that he considers fully compatible with both the professional standards of modern psychiatry and the demands of religious law, and in particular, given the AA movement's ecumenical vision of personal salvation, a legitimate elaboration of Jewish ethical conduct.[82] So, for instance, Twerski recommends that if his readers wish to improve their ethical conduct they should form self-help groups, on the model of AA meetings. Located outside the direct orbit of control by rabbinic authorities, these forums will provide opportunities to perform acts of confession, mutual support, and collective healing that cannot easily or effectively be extracted from "traditional" modes of Jewish engagement with ethical teachings. As Twerski puts it,

> Why are [self-help] groups essential? Since the principles are all of Talmudic and *mussar* origin, why not just have the Rabbi offer more *shiurim* [lessons] on these subjects? The answer is simple. *Shiurim* are didactic, and if didactic methods would be all that effective, *klal Yisroel* [the Jewish people] would have done *teshuva* [repented] long since. We have been taught *mussar* didactically from the time of the prophets onward. *Shiurim* are indeed important, but the messages in the *shiur* may not penetrate sufficiently to bring about the desired behavioral changes. . . . When a group

of people who have each experienced the painful consequences of self-defeating behavior come together and share their experiences and look at their lives in the light of Torah teachings, this provides an opportunity for applying the theory in practice, and converting the abstract into the concrete.[83]

The premium placed here on "concrete strategies" toward "recovery," and in particular the argument that such strategies depend on an acknowledgment of the unconscious and involuntary dimensions of human motivation, is not unique to Rabbi Twerski. His concern to develop "psychologically appropriate" methods to reform personal conduct in fact resonates with many other texts in the ArtScroll self-help series. Not only is there a wide consensus among these Haredi advice givers that the human will is frail, but they also repeatedly emphasize that religious commandments cannot easily be enforced in the current circumstances of social life, where both Haredim and non-Haredim face eroding structures of parental and communal authority.

Consider, in this regard, a recent guide for Orthodox parents in which the author, Dov Brezak, expounds at length on the need for parents to develop "strategically effective" interventions into the lives of their children. "Those who wish to enable their children to find the strength to resist the ubiquitous pull away from Torah that pervades our society must redouble their efforts," Brezak cautions. "Nowadays more than ever before, parents' calculated involvement in their children's emotional and spiritual development is absolutely necessary."[84] "Calculated involvement," according to Brezak, depends on an appreciation of the fundamental distinction between coercion and persuasion. Armed with the psychologically grounded knowledge that in the long run "it is impossible to influence anyone by force," parents must cultivate more refined methods to elicit desired behavior in their children.[85] The "conventional methods of rearing children are no longer enough," since they assume that obedience to Jewish law can be secured through rote learning, imitation, prohibition, or, where need be, corporal punishment.[86] As Brezak writes,

So many times, wayward boys have told me that they were never given any "flavor" in Torah observance. There was no beauty there; all they recall being taught was, "Don't do this, don't do that." Thus their observance, being but an empty shell, was not strong enough to protect them from the temptations of a decadent society. The way to cultivate a desire for Torah is not through force or pressure, but rather through enjoyment and a feeling of satisfaction. The more enjoyment a child finds in Torah and mitzvos [religious commandments], the more he will *want* to keep them. It follows then that we should invest a great deal into making the Torah and mitzvos more enjoyable for our children.[87]

Consonant with Rabbi Twerski's account of the insidious dangers of modernity, Brezak argues that contemporary social conditions have transformed Jewish law into a matter of voluntary assent, and he therefore argues that conformity with the law cannot be secured without proper motivation. In this scheme, Torah observance functions not only as a divine ordination but also a necessary condition of psychic well-being. Jewish law is hereby subordinated to the "feelings of satisfaction" promised to its lawful subjects: a calculus that children will most reliably master through a systematic pedagogy of "positive reinforcement." In Brezak's words,

> What is encouragement? In general, encouragement is anything—whether it takes the form of words or actions—that will empower the recipient to achieve more. It will give him the courage to strive and to push forward, and to overcome any obstacles he might encounter. Specifically, encouragement points out to someone the success that he is already having. If we want our children to succeed, and to be happy and motivated in life, we must point out what they are already doing right. Even in areas where children are experiencing difficulty, we must search for even the smallest measure of their success. By calling it to their attention and showing that we appreciate it, we are writing a powerful message on their hearts. "I can do it!" Writing such messages can result in truly amazing changes.[88]

Orthodox Jewish parents must therefore work to ensure that their children's "experiences in religious matters are *positive* experiences. They must be experiences that the children themselves view as positive and pleasurable. It is only such experiences that will instill in children—or in anyone—a love for Torah and mitzvos, and that will keep them strong and growing in the long run."[89] During the activity of prayer, for instance, parents "can insist that our child come to shul [synagogue] and sit near us—but *we should not try to force him to pray.* . . . We can make the time he spends in shul an even more pleasurable experience for our child by smiling at him now and then during the course of the prayers."[90]

In short, Brezak's emphasis on motivational psychology and the cultivation of "emotionally satisfying" experiences epitomizes the ArtScroll self-help series as a whole. Addressing a readership for whom the effort to live a "Torah-true" lifestyle is forever plagued by insecure loyalties, unpredictable interactions, and risky temptations, authors such as Brezak and Twerski present psychological well-being as both a prelude to and a reward for one's willful submission to Jewish law. Through their hortatory mode of address, these writings aim to fortify the will to act, arming the reader with the tools needed to plumb the hidden depths of unconscious motivation and its mechanisms of repression. On these terms, ArtScroll self-help books cast ethical living as a matter of psychological equilibrium, and vice versa.

SCENARIOS OF SCRIPTURALISM

A superficial analysis of ArtScroll's emphases on meaningful prayer, designer living, and the cultivation of inner happiness would have recourse to a variation of the familiar claim that modern, late capitalist, "Americanized" culture infects all things with its fantasies of self-invention and self-sufficiency. The false promises of atomistic individualism, it has often been said, constitute the hallmark features of "secular" modernity, produced by the weakening of communal solidarities, the erosion of "traditional" sources of parental and religious authority, and an advancing cultural logic of consumer sovereignty and commodified lifestyles. In this scheme, products of popular culture, including such things as "designer" prayer books, cookbooks, and self-help books, present themselves as items available for discretionary consumption, providing the entertaining stimulus, the incidental cultural and intellectual capital, or potentially useful information that individuals freely incorporate (or freely reject) in the cultivation of their own self-governing projects for everyday living. There is no doubt some explanatory value in this line of analysis. What, indeed, sounds more suspiciously "untraditional" than a Jewish Martha Stewart, a "user-friendly" prayer book, or a set of guidelines for Jewish ethical conduct modeled on the Twelve-Step program of Alcoholics Anonymous? Are these not signs of a creeping ethos of individualism and consumerism in Orthodox Jewish popular culture? If so, do they not further indicate a deep-seated pattern of contradiction, compromise, or corruption in "traditional" forms of religious and everyday conduct, thereby undermining Haredi proclamations that the lives they lead are fully inscribed within an authentic Jewish tradition? Perhaps. But as I have suggested throughout this chapter, it is not enough simply to point out the existence of these paradoxical tensions. We must move beyond such wide-eyed observations to examine more carefully how, for instance, the vocabulary of therapeutics and the embellishment of domestic routines constitute textual scenarios of action and to explore the ways such scenarios resonate with their intended readers.

Stated bluntly, at the heart of the scripturalist impulse are the *scripts* that define Haredi action and govern its execution. Exemplifying the rule that a good performance requires a carefully designed script, ArtScroll prayer books, cookbooks, and self-help books manifest Haredi scripturalism in some particularly ingenious ways, hybridizing elements of discourse and modes of address that have been drawn from a wide range of Jewish and non-Jewish literary traditions. As we have seen, ArtScroll prayer books provide a model for technically correct but also *meaningful* prayer: a scenario that transforms every act of praying into an opportunity for the psychological enrichment of the individual supplicant. ArtScroll cookbooks offer scenarios of "designer living," appropriating, classifying, and making Jewishly familiar evolving fashions in culinary products, techniques, styles of presentation, and rules of etiquette. ArtScroll self-help books elaborate scenarios of willed obedience to Jewish law and ethical conduct, whereby "recovery" is figured as a key metaphor and model for deepening one's commitment to Torah observance. In each case, scripturalist messages are manifested through carefully plotted scenarios, anticipating a startling range of circumstantial particularities, practical impediments, and motivating factors facing the prospective reader. Promising the acquisition of authentic experience and the knowledge of how to navigate between cultural innovations and religious obligations, ArtScroll prayer books, cookbooks, and self-help books thus provide the raw material readers can use to construct themselves as Haredi subjects. Through them one learns how to pray correctly, how to apply legal precepts, how to service the body and calibrate one's carnal appetites, and how to interact well with others in the ongoing performance of everyday life as a Haredi Jew. On these terms, we might say that ArtScroll scenarios are designed above all to "soften" the reader's entry into the "hard" life that Torah-true commitments presumably entail.

All the same, no script, however well designed, can fully anticipate its performance. On the contrary, performances require improvisational skills and tacit bodies of knowledge that are almost impossible to communicate in writing. No prayer book can adequately describe how precisely to hold one's body or to project one's voice in the performance of public rituals.

No cookbook can teach its reader how precisely to distinguish between the tastes of scalded and burnt milk. No self-help book can anticipate precisely the psychological or interpersonal particularities facing its individual reader. These limits should recall for us a larger lesson about the communication of scripturalism. Precisely because scenarios are meant not only to be read but also to be performed, scripts can never completely encompass their range of intended actions. Not everything in the relationship between authorial intent and readerly response can be worked out through (written) words. Other agents and other modes of distributed action are also at work in the communication of ArtScroll's scripturalist messages. In the following chapter, I expand further on the notion that the scripturalist impulse has nondiscursive dimensions, turning my attention to the agency of ArtScroll books as material artifacts.

FOUR

Materializing Authenticity

ARTSCROLL BOOKS, I have suggested, can be thought of as a kind of hinge that joins the cultural milieu of the Haredi yeshiva world with the broader realm of the English-language Jewish public sphere. Chapter 3 examined how some of ArtScroll's best-known works provide a connective tissue between the life-world of the author and that of the reader through the communication of scenarios—for praying, cooking, or the management of one's emotional life—written in extraordinary detail and exhibiting carefully calculated anticipation of the reader's potential misunderstandings or misgivings about the actions to be performed. Playing on the definition of *design* as an intended plan or blueprint, I have described ArtScroll scenarios as vehicles for designing an Orthodox Jewish life-form, providing a large storehouse of procedural knowledge about "correct" conduct in both ritual and everyday contexts. These scenarios appear to resonate with their readers precisely because they promise a comprehensive mastery of practical action, faithful to the firmest traditions of rabbinic authority, while at the same time sensitive to evolving cultural, social, and technological conditions, scientific knowledge, and literary styles. By furnishing their readers with an exhaustive account of what constitutes permissible, healthy, stylish, and psychologically rewarding conduct, ArtScroll prayer books, cookbooks, and self-help books thus epitomize the waxing text-centrism that is said to grip the contemporary Jewish imaginary. The mere fact that these texts are able to command the attention of a diverse readership—located, as we have seen, both within and outside the Orthodox world—lends much support to the thesis of Haredi scripturalism as a mode of religious power and authority mediated through written texts.

But as I have also stressed, even the most carefully designed script cannot fully predict or control the actions of even the most willing and obedient actor. Standing between the author who composes written instructions and the reader who carries them out are a host of intermediating market conditions, institutional gateways, and local patterns of reception that shape whether and how written communications reach their intended addressees. Moreover, to execute a given course of action, the reader cannot rely on the script alone but must also bring into play forms of mental and bodily discipline and practical knowledge acquired through repeated performance and from the direct example of others. Even acts of reading, consulting, or simply being in the presence of a text depend upon the operation of what might be called nondiscursive agencies. These include such things as the practical skills required to handle written materials, as well as the spatial and temporal arrangements and the technological supports that make it possible to engage with texts in the first place. In this chapter I conduct an inventory of selected forms of nondiscursive agency associated with ArtScroll books. The agencies in question are not apparent if we treat ArtScroll as the name for a body of texts, or even as an institutional entity encompassing authors, editors, and managerial staff. Instead, we need to approach ArtScroll as an assembly of material artifacts: more specifically, of industrial print commodities. As I shall argue in the coming pages, through their material properties ArtScroll books can be seen to possess forces that structure and constrain the ways they are stored, read, displayed, or otherwise used in their designated social settings. This agency, embedded in the material design of the books themselves, is hardly incidental to the centrality ArtScroll texts are said to enjoy, whether in everyday life situations or in the ways ArtScroll is publicly imagined, discussed, embraced, or even rejected.

Let us first concede that there is much to be lost by ignoring the materiality of ArtScroll books. Indeed, the assumption that serious readers would never stoop to judge a book by its cover is readily belied by the comments of ArtScroll enthusiasts and detractors alike, who, as we have already seen, frequently dwell on the physical features of the books, such as their typography, layout, or covers. Through their comments on the beauty or the functional practicality of an ArtScroll book's design elements, public commentators, collectors, and other end users demonstrate the impossibility of disentangling an assessment of the text from its material embodiment. Consider, in this regard, the following reflection on the materiality of books put forth by Roiza Weinreich, author of a popular self-help guide published by ArtScroll, *There Will Never Be Another You!*:

> The most common complaint I hear from mothers is that they intended to learn [study] but were delayed because they could not find the *sefer* [holy book] they needed. Our time is so limited that if we have to spend time searching for something, there won't be time left to use it. If the *sefer* is there when you have a spare moment, you will pick it up and look inside. If you have to go and get it, you will put it off and forget about it. Those little bits and snatches of learning are lost opportunities. . . . It is not only useful to have the *sefarim* we learn from on hand. It feels good. Seeing the *siddur* or *sefer* on the kitchen shelf as I pass it while doing other things reminds me of my goals. . . . Do you have a *siddur* on hand in your kitchen? Do you carry one with you in your pocketbook? Make what you need available now.[1]

In her advice to "busy mothers," Weinreich highlights the agency of religious books as material objects that announce their own presence in the home, offering opportunities to engage in the act of reading, and demanding particular forms of care. A book's convenient location thus helps to secure good study habits on the part of the reader. Even the mere sight of a holy book—on a kitchen shelf, for instance—can jog the memory of previous acts of reading, thereby eliciting meritorious behavior in the present. Through such observations, Weinreich underscores the simple point that without its materiality no text could exist, and consequently there could be no text-centrism. After all, interactions between humans and texts cannot occur without some form of material and bodily engagement. Acknowledgment of these material conditions should provoke a reassessment of the previously discussed terms *scripturalism* and *text-centrism,* which can now be seen to refer not only to the production and circulation of linguistic utterances but also to the physical properties and the dynamic interactions of devices, techniques, and habits that lie beneath and within a given text, defining the conditions for its perceptual apprehension. These material agencies include such things as the layout of a text on the page, the suppleness of the paper on which a text is inscribed, the durability of its binding, its size and weight, and even (as we shall see later) its touch, not to forget the relationship between a book and its complementary technologies of transportation, storage, or artificial illumination.[2]

A further lesson to be derived from the image invoked by Weinreich—of a holy book that calls upon its human cohabitant to take it down from the shelf and read it or that inspires action simply by remaining in plain view—is that the materiality of a text constitutes a sort of agency in the sense that the text as artifact performs work, such as making demands on its human users to acquire the skills required for participation in the various activities of textual communication. Put otherwise, it is only through the networked, recursive processes of commingling of humans, written documents, inscription technologies, systems of circulation, and environments built for reading that texts can be said to have a social life. This insight is well grounded in the analytical approach of actor-network theory, which invites us to treat a written text as a durable materialization of coordinated interactions between and among human and nonhuman actors. By attributing agency to the text *qua* material artifact, actor-network theory does not seek to discount the importance of human agency in the production, consumption, and routine use of books (or any other nonhuman artifact, for that matter). This approach simply demands an acknowledgment of the fact that the terms *agency* and *action* refer to a broad range of transformative relationships and events, many of which do not have to be rooted in the notion of an intending (human) subject. Consequently, ArtScroll books and their users can be defined as members of a cascading series of dyads—such as author/text, publisher/book, bookseller/commodity, library/librarian, text/reader, or artifact/user—that exist only, as Bruno Latour puts it, in *hybrid* form. These hybrids of part-human and part-nonhuman actors are created in and through a process of delegation and coordination of the pragmatic skills and productive forces necessary for action.[3] So, for example, the "busy mother" and the "conveniently located book" exist only in their mutual determination, springing to life as two halves of a single, coordinated action system that governs the ways such books are stored, displayed, transported, opened, and read by "busy" women.

Returning to the larger theme of text-centrism and its role in the organization of Jewish cultural life, it should now seem obvious that an analysis of the ideological, symbolic, and discursive architecture of Jewish texts is a necessary but not a sufficient basis for understanding how books, as material agents, coordinate with their human users in the formation of hybrid actors and networked regimes of action. One reason why this analytical approach has yet to take firm root might have to do with a widespread definitional confusion between *text* and *book,* as if these terms could be used interchangeably. A book, as the material substratum of a given text, possesses characteristics that distinguish it from other possible materializations of textual communication. Consider, in this regard, the diverse ways texts have been materialized over the long course of Jewish history, ranging from authorized social practices of memorization and public recitation (the communication of oral texts); to techniques for inscribing texts onto stone, leather, or paper; to the gathering of paper inscriptions into the form of scrolls, codices, or much later, printed books; and even, in recent times, to the rendering of texts into computer-mediated digital formats. Each of these media forms brings the text to life through its own mode of distributed action, an understanding of which requires attention to its distinct material and technological properties.

It would take us far beyond the focus of this study to attempt to trace the history of materialization of Jewish texts in all its details. Suffice it to recall that this history encompasses diverse ways of integrating raw materials, technologies, and skilled techniques in the production, distribution, storage, and use of texts. One apposite example is found in the Torah scroll, which since antiquity has been subject to complex rules surrounding its production: that it be made of leather from a ritually purified animal, inscribed only with authorized ink recipes and writing instruments, and crafted only by a professionally ordained scribe (a *sofer*), who must purify himself in a ritual bath each day before beginning to write. Torah scrolls are also subject to detailed prescriptions about how they can legitimately be stored, displayed, carried, opened and closed, repaired, or even "buried" when no longer in use.[4] Printed books, on the other hand, package their sacred contents in ways that have been standardized through mechanical production techniques, moving the text away from the caring hand of the individual scribe and into much larger, coordinated networks of industrial design. Between the handwritten scroll and the mass-produced book stand a host of discontinuities, which especially since the mid-nineteenth century have been marked by a dramatic expansion in the capacities for producing and circulating print matter, according to rapidly evolving institutional frameworks (from the printer's shop to the bureaucratized publishing house), inscription technologies (from steam presses to compositing software), and market conditions (from colporteurs to e-commerce). In short, the prominence of ArtScroll books cannot be separated from their condition as industrial products: reproduced in great numbers; distributed through efficient modes of circulation; and thereby commanding an expanded reach into new classes of readers, new public spaces, and new everyday habits relating to the use of print matter.[5]

The technological, economic, and social forces of mechanical standardization and efficient distribution that have shaped the modern book industry might also recall Walter Benjamin's famous discussion of the "liquidation of aura" in works of art. Mechanical reproducibility, Benjamin argued, detached individual artistic objects from their local contexts, emancipating them from their "aura": the "here-and-now-ness" upon which their power and authority were based. With the development of industrial techniques of reproduction and, more generally, the rise of a modern, industrial society characterized by the "permeation of reality with mechanical equipment," the aura of objects has been "liquidated," which is to say, no longer fixed in a unique time and space. Among other things, techniques of mass reproduction make it possible for objects to circulate in new ways, "to meet the beholder or listener in his particular situation."[6] The expanded reach of mass-reproduced art thus implies new possibilities for the generation of intimacy, in which the power of objects resides, no longer in the irreducible signature of the original, but rather in the mechanical provenance of the copy. Although Benjamin's analysis was framed in a philosophical, cultural, and political context that does not directly concern us here, his discussion invites us to explore the ways aura is communicated through ArtScroll books, not just as sacred texts, but also as industrial print commodities. In particular, as this chapter aims to show, a kind of aura is communicated in and through the design elements—such as typography, layout, and bindings—distinguishing ArtScroll books as "superior" products in the marketplace, as well as in the public and domestic lives of their users.

CAPTIVATING IMAGES

ArtScroll books are readily identified by their "look," materialized in such things as typography and layout as well as in the inclusion of diagrams, photographs, maps, and other illustrations. These design elements are part of a larger visual regime in which readers are both enabled and enjoined to undertake particular ways of "seeing" an authentic divine presence. We have already encountered some of the enthusiastic consumers and users of ArtScroll books, who repeatedly extol their *visual* beauty. ArtScroll editions of the Siddur, the Chumash, and the Talmud are celebrated for their "revolutionary" innovations in typography, layout, and even cover designs, displaying a remarkable craftsmanship commensurate with the dignity and austerity of sacred books.[7] This emphasis on good looks extends to other genres published by ArtScroll, not least the cookbooks authored by Susie Fishbein, which, as we have also seen, are notable for their inclusion of hundreds of professionally composed photographs, printed on coated stock. In the words of one reviewer, its illustrations make *Kosher by Design* "so beautiful . . . if the book was not so practical, I would suggest to place it in a display case in a museum."[8]

It is a testament to this publisher's dexterity that it has managed to brand itself as a purveyor of good-looking but nonetheless religiously serious books, a message that is powerfully signified by its very choice of the name ArtScroll. In a field of bookmaking perennially haunted by the specter of idolatry—the ancient Jewish suspicion of sacred images as "substitutive errors," in which the beholder confuses the divine itself for its mere representation—it is incumbent on all Orthodox publishers to design books in ways that not only are religiously permissible (i.e., by not violating any laws about image making) but also make use of visual cues that communicate the dignity of Jewish religious literature.[9] In the context of these larger cultural anxieties about how to ensure the dignity of images, ArtScroll has pioneered creative ways to incorporate illustrations, photographs, paintings, and other visual elements into its books without directly flouting the aesthetic conventions of Orthodox publishing. A remarkable instance is found in ArtScroll's edition of *Tractate Chullin,* the sixty-second volume of the *Schottenstein Talmud,* dealing with laws pertaining to the meat of nonsacred animals.[10] ArtScroll's edition of this Talmud tractate is a landmark in Jewish publishing, representing the first Talmud text to include full-color illustrations, over one hundred of which were produced on special contract by Howard S. Friedman, a prominent illustrator with the U.S.-based birdwatching association the Audubon Society. How can we understand the purpose and function of these images, and what can they tell us about the ways users engage with ArtScroll books?

According to the publisher's rhetoric, Howard Friedman's illustrations exist simply to provide visual representations conveying anatomically precise knowledge so that the reader can follow the complex legal reasoning contained in the text proper. So, for instance, illustrations are included in *Tractate Chullin* that indicate in detail the location of molar teeth in ruminant animals (such as cows and horses), or the shape of a desert locust's jumping legs (Fig. 6). These images are designed, in the words of the book's editors, to "add a significant measure of clarity to the many technical discussions of this volume."[11] Above all, they are addressed to readers

greater part of its body is kosher.[20]   רַבִּי יוֹסֵי אוֹמֵר – R' Yose says: וּשְׁמוֹ חָגָב – And its name must be *chagav*. [21]
The next category:

וּבְדָגִים – And among fish,   כּל שֶׁיֵּשׁ לוֹ סְנַפִּיר וְקַשְׂקֶשֶׂת – any type that has a *senapir* and a *kaskeses* is kosher.[22]
רַבִּי יְהוּדָה אוֹמֵר – R' Yehudah says: שְׁנֵי קַשְׂקַשִׂין וּסְנַפִּיר אֶחָד – It must have two *kaskasin* and one *senapir*. [23]
אֵלּוּ הֵן קַשְׂקַשִׂין – Which are the *kaskasin*?   הַקְּבוּעִין בּוֹ – Those that are affixed to [the fish], i.e. the scales;[24]
וּסְנַפִּירִים – And which are the *senapirin*?   הַשׁוֹרֵחַ בָּהֶן – Those with which it glides through the water, i.e. the fins.

Gemara

The Gemara cites a Baraisa that elaborates on the signs of kosher animals:

תָּנוּ רַבָּנָן – The Rabbis taught in a Baraisa: אֵלּוּ הֵן סִימָנֵי – WHICH ARE THE SIGNS OF A kosher ANIMAL?   ,,כּל־בְּהֵמָה – ANY ANIMAL THAT HAS A SPLIT HOOF etc. "   מַפְרֶסֶת פַּרְסָה וגו' – [that brings up its cud … it you may eat].[25]   כּל בְּהֵמָה שֶׁמַּעֲלַת

בְּיָדוּעַ שֶׁאֵין לָהּ שִׁנַּיִם – ANY ANIMAL THAT BRINGS UP its CUD   גֵּרָה – DEFINITELY DOES NOT HAVE UPPER FRONT TEETH, AND IS KOSHER.[26]   לְמַעֲלָה וּטְהוֹרָה

The Gemara proceeds to analyze this Baraisa:

וַהֲרֵי גָּמָל – Why, consider the camel,   וּכְלָלָא הוּא – But is this a valid rule?   דְּמַעֲלָה גֵרָה הוּא וְאֵין לוֹ שִׁנַּיִם לְמַעֲלָה –

NOTES

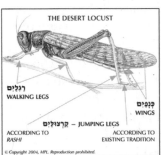

THE DESERT LOCUST

רַגְלַיִם
WALKING LEGS

כְּנָפַיִם
WINGS

קַרְצוּלַיִם – JUMPING LEGS

ACCORDING TO RASHI

ACCORDING TO EXISTING TRADITION

© Copyright 2004, MPL. Reproduction prohibited.

their bodies near the neck, above the walking legs. It is with these "jumping legs" that the grasshopper launches its peculiar spring (see also *Pirkei D'Rabbi Eliezer* Ch. 9).

It should be noted that in common grasshoppers and locusts, the jumping legs are *below* the four walking legs, toward the tail (see illustration). For this reason, R' Chaim ben Attar prohibited the consumption of all locusts in his time (see *Or HaChaim* to *Leviticus* 11:21, and *Pri Toar* 85:1 at length). In some Moroccan and Yemenite communities, however, there is a tradition as to the permissibility of a certain species of locust – אַרְבֶּה, the desert locust (*schistocerca gregaria*). According to their tradition, the קַרְצוּלַיִם are small footlike extensions at the ends of the jumping legs, which are present in the common desert locust (see the sources cited in *Encyclopedia Talmudis* vol. 12 p. 574, note 55).

20. The characteristics of four walking legs and two jumping legs are stated explicitly in the Torah (ibid.). The other two characteristics are derived exegetically by the Gemara below (65a-66a).

21. R' Yose stipulates that in addition to possessing these four characteristics, an insect must also be known to be called חָגָב, *chagav*, in order to be permissible. Although *chagav* is the name of a specific kosher species mentioned in the Torah (see the verse cited in note 18), it is also a more general term that includes all the kosher types. [In a similar vein, the word צֹאן can refer either specifically to sheep or more generally to flocks of sheep and goats] (*Meiri*; see also *Rashi* to 65b ד"ה ושמו חגב).

According to *Tosafos* (65a ד"ה רבי), R' Yose does not differ with the Tanna Kamma, but merely clarifies his ruling (see also *Yoreh Deah* 85:1; cf. *Rif* and *Ramban* to 65b).

[Nowadays, it is customary (in most communities) to refrain from eating even the grasshoppers that possess the four specified characteristics and are commonly called *chagav*, because we are not well versed in their names (*Taz* 85:1; see also *Rashi* to *Leviticus* 11:21, *Meiri* to 65a, and *Aruch HaShulchan* 85:5). As mentioned, however, to this day there are groups of Moroccan and Yemenite Jews who possess and rely upon traditions as to the kosher status of a certain species of locust (see *Kaf HaChaim*, *Yoreh Deah* 85:6; *Halichos Teiman* by R' Y. Kafich, pp. 218-221; and other sources cited by *Encyclopedia Talmudis* vol. 12 p. 577, note 74). For discussion of whether one whose community does not eat such a creature may rely on the tradition of the communities that do eat it, see *Yoreh Deah* 82:5 with *Shach*; *Maadanei HaShulchan* 85:9; *Teshuvos Yemei Yosef Basra* §3; *Teshuvos Divrei Chachamim*, *Yoreh Deah* §11; *Arichas HaShulchan* III p. 139.]

22. As the Mishnah proceeds to explain, a *senapir* is a fin and a *kaskeses* is a scale. The fish need not have two fins, nor must it have numerous

scales spread over its body. Even if it has only *one* fin and *one* scale, it is adjudged as a kosher fish (*Rambam, Maachalos Asuros* 1:24; *Yoreh Deah* 83:1). [Numerous kinds of fish (such as certain tuna species) have scales covering only minor portions of their bodies. *Ramban* (66a) states that he received a report about a type of fish that actually has but a single scale on its tail.]

The Torah (*Leviticus* 11:9, *Deuteronomy* 14:9) states that any fish that possesses קַשְׂקֶשֶׂת וּסְנַפִּיר, *a senapir and a kaskeses*, may be eaten. The Tanna understands the singular form to mean that a fish is permissible even on the basis of one fin and one scale (*Ran*, fol. 23a).

[The Rishonim raise the concern that when a fish has but one scale perhaps this scale became detached from a different fish and adhered to this one, which is actually nonkosher. Therefore, some state that the single scale must be located under the jaw, tail or fin, where it would not have adhered accidentally (*Ramban* ibid., based on *Tosefta*; see also *Rama* 83:1). Others, however, maintain that as long as the scale seems firmly attached to the fish's body, we can assume that it belongs to this fish, regardless of its location on the fish (*Ran*; see *Shach* 83:1).]

23. R' Yehudah maintains that since in the word קַשְׂקֶשֶׂת the syllable קש is repeated, there must be at least two scales (*Ran*; cf. *Meiri*).

24. Unlike the fins, which the fish is able to flap, the scales adhere to its skin and do not move unless something pulls them (*Rashi* to 66a). [*Ramban* (*Leviticus* 11:9) explains: The Mishnah's language should not be construed to mean that the scales are permanently attached and not removable. To the contrary, the scales that are a sign of kosherness are those that can be peeled off with the hand or a knife. Any fish that has scalelike protrusions that cannot be peeled off is *not* kosher. The Mishnah describes the scales as "affixed" only in relation to the fins, which flap freely. For further discussion, see *Noda BiYehudah II* §28-29, and *Pischei Teshuvah, Yoreh Deah* 83:1.]

25. *Deuteronomy* 14:6. A similar verse appears in *Leviticus* 11:3; see note 13 above.

26. The Baraisa introduces two novel points: (a) It sets down as fact that any animal that chews its cud has no upper front teeth; (b) it teaches that the lack of upper front teeth defines an animal as kosher. The Gemara will challenge each of these points.

[The ensuing discussion about upper teeth refers to incisors in the front of the mouth. Although the Gemara will cite several exceptions, it is generally the fact that ruminants (i.e. animals that chew their cuds) have no front teeth on their upper jaws. Ruminants, however, do have molars in the back of the upper jaw. The term שִׁנַּיִם, although generally translated simply as "teeth," actually refers specifically to front teeth; see *Tosafos* to 59b ד"ה נתור.]

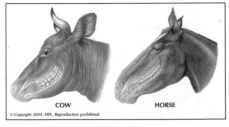

COW   HORSE

© Copyright 2004, MPL. Reproduction prohibited.

Figure 6. Illustrations on a page of *Tractate Chullin*, vol. 62 of the *Schottenstein Talmud*, p. 59a. Reproduced courtesy of Mesorah Publications (ArtScroll Series).

who are presumed to have little or no direct experience observing or handling animals and thus unlikely to possess mental images accurate enough to help them follow the technical details of the legal arguments spelled out in the text. In suggesting that the main purpose of the illustrations found in *Tractate Chullin* is to "add clarity," ArtScroll's editors also seek to assure their readers that such images are safely contained within the textual protocols that govern Talmudic study and debate and therefore pose no risk of violating the established aesthetics of a "serious" religious work. Surrounded by the editors' written elucidation of the Talmud text, they help to anchor meaning and in turn are anchored by the commentary in which they are embedded.

The assumptions made by ArtScroll's editors that images essentially exist in a subordinate relation to written texts can favorably be compared to the semiotic theory of the image famously postulated by Roland Barthes. According to Barthes, an image in itself exists in an indeterminate and unruly state, as a "message without a code," and it is chiefly through its accompanying text—such as a written caption—that the meaning of that image is "anchored" and its ideological content is fixed.[12] Barthes's theory of anchorage presents an optimistic account of the controlling power of words to engender preferred interpretations and to keep images in their place, so that, for instance, the drawing of the desert locust appearing on the Talmud page does not leap out of its own frame or in any other way distract the reader from the business of reading. However, the metaphor of anchorage as an account of how images function in relation to written texts has been the subject of intense critique in the field of visual culture studies. In fact, a growing consensus among scholars suggests that images in all their diversity, including ones that appear as illustrations in books, need to be analyzed as more than simply a plenum of representation that the producer encodes and the viewer decodes (with or without their discursive "anchors"). Images are also—and arguably more fundamentally—participants in vast networks of interaction involving visual stimuli, sensorially endowed human agents, and the complex technological and social environments that allow such interactions to occur. In this understanding, rather than trying to contain images within a linguistic model of meaning making—as "texts" to be "read"—we are called upon to explore the much wider range of perceptual, affective, cultural, and technological registers in and through which images are manifested and activities of "seeing" are performed.[13]

In this spirit of inquiry, I ask: What kinds of work do ArtScroll pictures perform in relation to their viewers? A partial answer can be found by returning once more to *Kosher by Design,* the most visually rich book in the ArtScroll corpus and perhaps, for this reason, a manifestation of the publisher's mode of visual address *in extremis.* I have already stressed (in Chapter 3) some of the remarkable ways *Kosher by Design* mediates visual effects through its instructions about how to plate food, arrange flowers, set tables, and related strategies for displaying culinary elegance. Let us note further how this emphasis on the visual culture of domestic life is both preceded and underpinned by the artistry and design of the book itself. Through the cascading images of prepared dishes and elegant dining, Susie Fishbein's food becomes, not just sustaining, not just ritually permitted, not just tasty, but *visually desirable:* food that is designed to be seen and good enough to be photographed. This transformation of food from a gustatory to a visual register is an outcome of the work performed above all by the book's photographs. Specifically, the photographs serve a function that is both iconic and indexical, referring at once to the prepared food that might appear somewhere on a "real" table and to the desired spectacular effects of such food on social gatherings and family life. As one anonymous reviewer observes, "The photo layout and designs of the dishes prepared are so beautiful and vibrant. It makes the reader feel like they are sitting at the table with the rest of the guests."[14] In other words, the photographs found in *Kosher by Design* not only convey information but also possess a cathectic power to transport their viewers into a virtual world of vibrant authenticity and harmonious fellowship, "at the table with the rest of the guests." To invoke a term developed by the anthropologist Alfred Gell, we might therefore speak of these images as "captivating." Their appearance is embedded in a realm of visual power—more specifically, a mode of spectacle making that seizes the viewer, producing experiences of sublimity, awe, or "cognitive indecipherability" that resemble the effects of a magical spell.[15]

As magical agents, *Kosher by Design*'s photographic images do far more than simply depict food; they captivate their viewers. Rather than referring to the photographs as aesthetic (in the narrow sense of "beautiful"), we might invoke here Christopher Pinney's term *corpothetic.*[16] In other words, these images present themselves as objects of pleasure, performing acts of seduction and offering a feast, not just for the disembodied eye, but for the whole body. In the preface to *Kosher by Design,* Fishbein herself stresses these visceral qualities of the photographs in her book:

> During the photo shoots for this book, my food stylist taught me that when we cook, we cook with all our senses. Listen for the sizzle as the

meat hits the pan, feel the food to determine its doneness, smell the nutty aroma of grains as they toast, behold with your eyes the plate's appeal, taste with your palate the delight of your creations. This is true about entertaining, too. It is not only what you serve, but how you serve it. A simple garnish, a beautiful table, an unusual floral arrangement, a colorful plate filled with assorted delicacies—all these things elevate the mundane to the magnificent. . . . Look around your house for things that can be used to achieve the ideas shown in this book. Mix and match concepts and adapt them to the various events of your lives.[17]

Food photography thus references a synesthetic experience, in which the apprehension of visual beauty is implicated in a larger economy of bodily senses, appetites, and desires. As Fishbein advises us, *Kosher by Design*'s images do far more than communicate discursive information, as in the popular saying "A picture is worth a thousand words." They also engage the viewer by referencing—and even exciting—the multiple sensory and somatic registers associated with the labor of cooking and serving and the pleasures of eating and dining. Operating at the level of the sensory organs and thereby eliciting bodily pleasures, photographic images of beautifully prepared and presented food also transmit to their viewers a sort of thaumaturgical energy, empowering them to act upon the world outside the text. As stated by one customer reviewer of *Kosher by Design* on the retail bookselling Web site amazon.com: "I haven't made a recipe I didn't like. It also turns out exactly as pictured in the book. I just made the white and dark chocolate mousse dessert and it looks incredible. My sister-in-law told me that my Sunken Apple and Honey cake looks so good it should be pictured on the cover of a magazine!" (Fig. 7).[18]

Rather than simply helping the reader to understand the written recipe "more clearly," an image of a sunken apple and honey cake or a white and dark chocolate mousse carries with it a more radical promise of perfect mimesis. By following the (easy) instructions in the text, one is guaranteed the precise reproduction of the referent to which the image points. Existing simultaneously as visual representations, objects of desire, and performative models, *Kosher by Design*'s images thus orchestrate a multitude of creative forces designed to bring the viewer into contact with an authentic presence. Locally made products can thus be assessed by the degree to which they look "exactly as pictured in the book," and even the written instructions are evaluated according to their ability to guide the cook at home toward achieving this visual goal. "If you can get past the blinding

Figure 7. Front cover of *Kosher by Design*. Reproduced courtesy of Mesorah Publications (ArtScroll Series).

beauty of this book and start cooking," writes another amazon.com re-viewer, "you would be even more impressed. I have shocked myself at what a great cook I have become because of this fabulous book."[19] On these terms, the images contained in *Kosher by Design*—and arguably, the images of all other ArtScroll books, including those found in *Tractate Chullin*—extend and further complicate the notion of Haredi scripturalism as something that rests specifically on the dissemination of written words. Images also contribute decisively to the production of text-centrism and to the authority invested in books.

DISCIPLINING THE EYE

Let us turn from photographs and illustrations to the visual organization of the written text itself, where we find many other hallmark features of ArtScroll books. Through such design elements as typeface and layout, ArtScroll books constitute a field of visual interaction that enables and encourages the reader to navigate the text in particular ways. When compositors block the pages of text, they must make multiple decisions about such things as spacing, alignment, and the size and shape of letters, and the overall design can therefore be understood as a strategy on the part of the publisher to achieve a range of cognitive as well as aesthetic effects. Such decisions are particularly complex in the case of writings that coordinate multiple texts, such as the bilingual editions of prayer books and other works for which ArtScroll is well known. As Stephen Lubell has argued, bilingual texts provide particularly complex challenges for a publisher, not only because they involve decisions about how to translate lexical and syntactic features of one language into the other, but also because they require the elaboration of strategies of typography and layout in order to help the reader move efficiently from the source text to its translation.[20] In this sense, the layout design of a bilingual text such as *The Complete ArtScroll Siddur* manifests the decisions undertaken by the publisher about how such a text "needs" to be visually organized in order to be read efficiently and correctly. Especially in the context of public ritual performance, in which prayer books not only are read but more importantly are recited aloud, the layout of the text prescribes and conditions acts of reading and reciting. ArtScroll's bilingual editions, especially their prayer books, reflect the publisher's strategy to address challenges of "efficient design," and as such they exemplify the ways intended courses of action are *transcribed* into texts designed specifically for liturgical performance.[21]

Of course, ArtScroll's bilingual prayer books are hardly unique among Jewish writings that lay out more than one text on a single page. In fact, many canonical Jewish texts are noted for coordinating multiple writings, including biblical passages and commentaries (as well as commentaries on the commentaries), as well as multiple languages. The best-known instance is the

Talmud, which allows—indeed, encourages—the attentive eye to move in multiple directions, thereby multiplying the possible interpretations of the text's meaning (Fig. 8). These layout designs have a long history stretching back to the dawn of Hebrew publishing, and even further back to the age of handwritten manuscripts.[22] As far as prayer books are concerned, ArtScroll's editions stand on the shoulders of an equally long history of relatively stable approaches to the layout of translations of sacred Hebrew texts, whether on facing columns, facing pages, or interlinearly.

All the same, prayer books containing interlinear translations of Hebrew into a vernacular language, such as English, offer a unique challenge for designers, and their layout sheds much light on the assumptions a publisher makes about the needs, abilities, and desires of its readers. This is because interlinear texts address readers who are presumed to require a translation in order to understand the meaning of the text and who also want to be able to read the original text without interruption. Interlinear prayer books are thus designed to assist the non-native Hebrew speaker to participate efficiently in public recitations of the text during synagogue worship. Rabbis Scherman and Zlotowitz describe the design challenges of interlinearity in the preface to their first interlinear publication, *Tehillim: The Book of Psalms:*

> Even someone fluent in Hebrew will often come across an unfamiliar word
> or phrase. To look at an adjoining column or facing page for the translation
> will solve the problem, but often at the price of a loss of concentration.
> Once the mind focuses away from the Hebrew text to the English transla-
> tion, one may find it difficult to return to the exact phrase of the prayer.
> Next time, the worshipper may well decide to forgo the translation in favor
> of continuing without a lapse. The result is a frequent, if not constant, tug
> of war between the desire for comprehension and the need not to interrupt
> the recitation, especially if one is praying with the congregation.[23]

As Scherman and Zlotowitz further note, the dangers inherent in this "tug of war" are particularly acute in the case of interlinear translations from He-brew, which is read from right to left, into vernaculars, such as English, that are read in the opposite direction. In their words, "The eye is confused, as it were, like an American stepping off a curb in England, and instinctively looking to his left, while traffic speeds toward him from the right."[24] Through such colorful metaphors as the "confused eye" and "speeding traf-fic," the ArtScroll editors acknowledge a problem that has persisted throughout the very long history of bilingual prayer books, including those with interlinear translations.[25] But these metaphors also set the stage upon which they announce ArtScroll's innovative solution: "In order to make this interlinear treatment convenient and practical, a way had to be found to solve the right-left problem. . . . After each English word or phrase, there is a barely obtrusive arrow, which directs the eye in the direction of the Hebrew. We have tested this device, and found that it solves the problem to an amazing degree. These arrows keep the reader's eye moving in the direction of the Hebrew without interfering with his reading of the English."[26]

Not unlike well-designed and well-placed traffic signs, ArtScroll's graphics icon—the "arrow"—is presented here as an efficient means of resolving the tensions between the temporal constraints of collective ritual performance, the desire for intelligibility, and the demand for concerted attention (Fig. 9). In the ArtScroll catalog, the introduction of the graphic arrow into ArtScroll's interlinear translations is repeatedly described as a "revolutionary new way to add meaning and understanding to prayer": "The translation is always in front of your eyes; your concentration is not disturbed; you never lose your place in the Hebrew; you never fall behind the congregation; you always know which English word fits which Hebrew word; you're never frustrated by that 'mysterious word.'"[27] On the artscroll.com Web site, the power of the arrow to "train the eye" is further elaborated. Prospective customers are invited to examine a sample page of a Hebrew prayer with its accompanying interlinear translation in English, in order to see for themselves how this technology works:

Read. Recite. Pray. Understand the words—and the flow. How much did you have to move your eye to look at the translation? Not a bit! How long did it take you to find the translation? No time at all! Did it interfere with your concentration? No—it improved it! Comprehension seeps in as you pray. The great difficulty in this kind of treatment is reading Hebrew from right to left, and English from left to right. How to keep the eye from wandering in both directions and falling prey to confusion? Look at the page again. The arrows unobtrusively direct your eye in the right direction. It's a tested, patent-pending method—and it works! But the syntax of Hebrew and English are different. Won't the sentences sometimes be incomprehensible? That's where the skill of the editors comes in. The comprehension is there. And wherever necessary, the commentary explains the flow of the verse. In addition, the commentary does what you expect an ArtScroll commentary to do: it explains and clarifies. Try this new Tehillim soon. You'll feel elevated![28]

praiseworthy; שְׁלִישִׁי שֶׁקָּרָא ד׳ מְשׁוּבָּח – **if the third [reader] reads four verses, he is praiseworthy.** I.e. any of the three readers may read the extra verse.[28]

The Gemara now demonstrates how it is known that special prominence can be assigned to the first, middle, or last in a series: רִאשׁוֹן שֶׁקָּרָא ד׳ מְשׁוּבָּח – If **the first [reader] reads four** verses **he is praiseworthy,** דְּתָנַן בִּשְׁלֹשׁ קֻפּוֹת שֶׁל שָׁלֹשׁ שָׁלֹשׁ סְאִין שֶׁבָּהֶן תּוֹרְמִין – **as we learned in a Mishnah:**[29] אֶת הַלִּשְׁכָּה – WITH THREE BASKETS OF THREE SE'AH EACH (WHICH WITH THEM)[30] THEY MAKE THE WITHDRAWAL FROM THE CHAMBER.[31] וְהָיָה כָּתוּב עֲלֵיהֶן אב״ג – AND ON [THESE BASKETS] WERE WRITTEN the Hebrew letters *ALEPH, BEIS, GIMMEL.*[32] רִאשׁוֹן – in order TO KNOW WHICH OF THEM WAS WITHDRAWN FIRST לֵידַע אֵיזוֹ מֵהֶן נִתְרְמָה רִאשׁוֹן לְהַקְרִיב מִמֶּנָּה in order TO OFFER sacrifices FROM THAT ONE FIRST, שֶׁמִּצְוָה בָּרִאשׁוֹן – SINCE IT IS PREFERABLE TO USE THE FIRST ONE first. This shows the importance of the first. Thus, it is praiseworthy for the first reader to read four verses.

The Gemara now proves the prominence of the middle one: אֶמְצָעִי שֶׁקָּרָא אַרְבָּעָה מְשׁוּבָּח – If **the middle** one, i.e. the second reader, **reads four** verses, **he is praiseworthy,** דְּתַנְיָא ,,אֶל־מוּל פְּנֵי הַמְּנוֹרָה יָאִירוּ׳׳ – **as it was taught in a Baraisa:** The verse states: *[THE SEVEN LAMPS] SHALL SHINE TOWARDS THE FACE OF THE MENORAH.*[33] מְלַמֵּד שֶׁמְּצַדֵּד פְּנֵיהֶם כְּלַפֵּי נֵר מֶעְרָבִי – THIS TEACHES THAT [THE *KOHEN*] MAKES [THE WICKS OF SIX LAMPS] FACE TOWARDS THE WESTERN LAMP, which is the middle one,[34] וְנֵר מַעְרָבִי כְּלַפֵּי שְׁכִינָה – AND THE WESTERN LAMP faces TOWARDS THE DIVINE PRESENCE, which rested on the Ark in the Holy of Holies.[35] וְאָמַר רַבִּי יוֹחָנָן – And R' Yochanan said: מִכָּאן שֶׁאֶמְצָעִי מְשׁוּבָּח – From here we see **that the middle one is praiseworthy.**[36] Accordingly, it is praiseworthy for the second reader, who is the middle reader, to read the four verses.

The Gemara now demonstrates the prominence of the last one: וְאַחֲרוֹן שֶׁקָּרָא אַרְבָּעָה מְשׁוּבָּח – And if **the last one,** i.e. the third reader, **reads four** verses, **he is praiseworthy,** מִשּׁוּם מַעֲלִין בַּקֹּדֶשׁ וְלֹא מוֹרִידִין – **because** of the general rule that **in matters of sanctity we elevate, and do not lower,** the degree of Sanctity. Thus, if the last reader reads more than those before him, he is praiseworthy.

The Gemara relates an incident regarding the aforementioned law: רַב פָּפָּא אִיקְלַע לְבֵי כְנִישְׁתָּא דַּאֲבִי גּוֹבֵר – **Rav Pappa happened to come to the synagogue of Avi Gover,** וְקָרָא רִאשׁוֹן אַרְבָּעָה – **and the first** reader **read four** verses, **and Rav Pappa praised him.**[37]

The Gemara cites another portion of our Mishnah: אֵין פּוֹחֲתִין מֵהֶן וְאֵין מוֹסִיפִין – WE MAY NOT DECREASE THEM NOR ADD TO THEM. [THE ONE WHO COMMENCES AND THE ONE WHO CONCLUDES the reading OF THE TORAH RECITE THE BLESSINGS BEFORE IT AND AFTER IT.][38] תָּנָא – **A Tanna taught in a Baraisa,** clarifying what is stated in our Mishnah: הַפּוֹתֵחַ מְבָרֵךְ לְפָנֶיהָ – THE ONE WHO COMMENCES the reading RECITES THE BLESSING BEFORE the reading, וְהַחוֹתֵם מְבָרֵךְ לְאַחֲרֶיהָ – AND THE ONE WHO CONCLUDES the reading RECITES THE BLESSING AFTER the reading.

However, the Gemara concludes: וְהָאִידְנָא דְּכוּלְּהוּ מְבָרְכִי לְפָנֶיהָ וּלְאַחֲרֶיהָ – But nowadays that **all the** readers **recite the blessings** both **before and after [the reading],** הַיְינוּ טַעְמָא דְּתַקִּינוּ רַבָּנַן – **the reason the Rabbis instituted** this גְּזֵירָה מִשּׁוּם הַנִּכְנָסִין וּמִשּׁוּם הַיּוֹצְאִין – was to **safeguard against** the misconceptions of **those who enter** the synagogue late **and of those who leave** the synagogue early.[39]

The Gemara introduces the next discussion with a quote from our Mishnah: בְּרָאשֵׁי חֳדָשִׁים וּבְחוּלּוֹ שֶׁל מוֹעֵד קוֹרִין אַרְבָּעָה וְכוּ׳ – ON ROSH CHODESH AND ON CHOL HAMOED FOUR people are called to READ etc.

The Gemara inquires: בְּעָא מִינֵּיהּ עוּלָּא בַּר רַב מֵרָבָא – **Ulla bar Rav inquired of Rava:** פָּרָשַׁת רֹאשׁ חוֹדֶשׁ כֵּיצַד קוֹרִין אוֹתָהּ – **The portion** read on **Rosh Chodesh, how is it read,** i.e. how is it divided among the four readers?

Ulla bar Rav elaborates on his inquiry, showing the problems of dividing the portion of Rosh Chodesh among four readers: ,,צַו אֶת־בְּנֵי יִשְׂרָאֵל וְאָמַרְתָּ אֲלֵהֶם אֶת־קָרְבָּנִי לַחְמִי׳׳ דְּהָוְיָין תְּמָנְיָא פְּסוּקֵי – **The section beginning with** *Command the children*

NOTES

28. When ten verses are read by three people, two will read the minimum three verses each, and only one will read an extra fourth verse. Rava informs us that whichever of the three readers avails himself of the privilege of reading that fourth verse is praiseworthy. Thus, if the first reader reads four instead of three, he is praiseworthy. If he read only three and the second reader reads four, then the second reader is praiseworthy. And if the second reader read only three and the third reader reads four, then the third reader is praiseworthy (Rashi). And if the portion being read is large enough so that all three read [at least] four verses, then all three are praiseworthy (ibid.; cf. Turei Even).

29. Shekalim 3:2.

30. The word שֶׁבָּהֶן, which with them, is deleted by Bach; neither does it appear in our versions of the Mishnah Shekalim.

31. This Mishnah refers to the annual half-shekel head tax, which was collected and placed in a chamber in the Temple. Three times a year, they withdrew funds from this chamber, to be used for public offerings. The Mishnah informs us that it was withdrawn in three baskets, each having the volume of three se'ah.

32. The concluding section that follows is not part of the Mishnah in Shekalim, but an explanation of the Mishnah presented in a Baraisa [Tosefta Shekalim 2:2, cited in Yoma 62a].

33. Numbers 8:2.

34. See next note.

35. See diagram. This Baraisa follows the view that the Menorah was positioned in

a north-south line. The Menorah consisted of a main trunk (topped by a lamp) and three branches on each side (topped by lamps). The verse states that the flames should be turned towards "the face of the Menorah," i.e. the main trunk, which held the middle lamp. Thus, the wicks of the three southern lamps were positioned on the northern side of their respective lamps, while the wicks of the three northern lamps were positioned on the southern side of their respective lamps. The wick of the middle lamp alone was positioned on the western side in order to face the Holy of Holies. Thus, the middle lamp is called the western lamp, since its wick was the most westward of all the wicks (Rashi).

36. [The prominence of the middle lamp is apparent from the fact that all the other lamps were made to face it.]

37. Certainly, Rav Pappa agrees that any of the three readers may read the four verses. Nevertheless, he praised the first reader for seizing the earliest opportunity to perform the mitzvah of reading the fourth verse (Maharsha).

38. The Gemara's next discussion involves this part of the Mishnah [in brackets], and it is indeed this part that is cited in Rif's version.

39. Under the original practice of only one blessing before the first reading and one after the last reading, one who comes late and arrives in middle of the Torah reading does not hear any preliminary blessing, and will assume that such a blessing is not necessary. Similarly, one who leaves before the end of the reading does not hear any concluding blessing, and will assume that such a blessing is not necessary. Therefore, the Rabbis ordained that each of the readers should recite a blessing before and after his reading (Rashi; see also Rashash, who offers a slightly different explanation [cf. above, 21a note 9]).

Figure 8. Sample Talmud page from *Tractate Megillah,* vol. 20 of the *Schottenstein Talmud,* p. 21b, with accompanying English "elucidation." Reproduced courtesy of Mesorah Publications (ArtScroll Series).

תנא מה שאין כן בתורה. פירוש שאין קורין קולא אלא אחד אחד מכאן קשיא למה שפירש רש"י לעיל דכ' גבי והקורין רבה (מגילה דף כ.) דסמכינן פסוקים שמותרין יחיד אחר יחיד לקרות אחד קורא שנים שפירש רש"י התם שנין יחיד קורא ולא אחד לקונוין קרא נראה כמו שפירש רש"י רס"י בתקונין יחיד קורא מפסיקין וקורין ולא יהיו אלא מפסקי פסוקים...

תנא מה מה שאין כן בתורה תנו רבנן בתורה אחד קורא ואחד מתרגם ובלבד שלא יהא אחד קורא ושנים מתרגמן ובלבד שלא יהו שנים קורין ושנים מתרגמן ובנביא אחד קורא ושנים מתרגמן ובלבד שלא יהו שנים קורין ושנים מתרגמן ובהלל ובמגילה אפילו עשרה קורין ועשרה מתרגמן מאי טעמא כיון דחביבה יהבי דעתייהו ושמעי:

מקום שנהגו לברך יברך: אמר אבי לא שנו אלא לאחריה אבל לפניה מצוה לברך דאמר רב יהודה אמר שמואל כל המצות כולן מברך עליהן עובר לעשייתן מאי משמע דהאי עובר לישנא דאקדומי הוא אמר רב נחמן בר יצחק דכתיב וירץ אחימעץ דרך הככר ויעבר את הכושי אביי אמר מהכא והוא עבר לפניהם ואיבעית אימא מהכא ויעבר מלכם לפניהם וה' בראשם:

כנגד תורה נביאים וכתובים:

Figure 9. Advertisement for the ArtScroll's Interlinear Siddur, demonstrating the patented use of arrows to direct the eye. Reproduced courtesy of Mesorah Publications (ArtScroll Series).

Figure 9. *(continued)*

ArtScroll's graphic icon is thus designed to compensate for (at least presumed) absences on the part of the reader, who cannot read the original Hebrew text without reference to a vernacular translation. Unlike a Talmud page, which, we have seen, is also designed to coordinate multiple texts on a single page, but for the purpose of lengthy study and discussion of Jewish law, the layout of the ArtScroll prayer book is designed to convey the full richness of the text's meaning within the relatively brief temporality of its recitation. In this performative context, the graphic arrow addresses a presumed desire on the part of the reader to understand what she or he is saying as it is being recited aloud. With the help of the graphic arrow, the meaning of the text can now "seep in as you pray," and the reader's risk is reduced that she or he will feel "frustrated by that mysterious word" or fail to "keep moving" and thus "fall behind the congregation." The arrow on the page and the eye of the reader thus come together to form a new hybrid actor: one who can focus attention on the meaning of the text without lingering or in any other way departing from the temporal rhythm of ritual performance.

In short, the interlinear arrow is far more than a prosthetic device. Not only does it perform the work of helping the reader follow the ritual, it also contributes to the transformation of ritual practice itself. By offering the ritual participant a way to coordinate and synchronize "deeper comprehension" and "correct performance," it anchors the experience of ritual in the expectation that such actions can and should be "meaningful" for those involved in its execution. Echoing the written instructions and procedural mode of address that one finds in the text proper (as we saw in Chapter 3, in the discussion of ArtScroll prayer books), the graphic arrow emphasizes intelligibility and informed consent, goals that contrast starkly with customary attitudes concerning the religious purposes of prayer and ritual performance. On these terms, the ArtScroll arrow illustrates the desire of the editors to address a much larger set of concerns and anxieties about the organization of collective ritual in an age of heightened standards of competence, dissolving forces of attention, and the increasingly provisional status of individual commitments.

HIDDEN DELEGATIONS

Located on the surface of the text, and performing the work of training the eye to read bilingually and bidirectionally, ArtScroll's graphic icon is explicitly described by the publisher as a "device" (and in fact, patent protection has been sought for its invention). But this is only one of numerous—often less explicitly noted—devices found in ArtScroll books. *Kosher by Design,* for instance, boasts a plasticized spiral metal binding that is attached to a hard cover so that it can be opened and closed without intrusion, a material arrangement that the publisher describes as a "concealed wire binding" (Fig. 10). Here, too, we encounter an example of nondiscursive agency that contributes to the formation of the action networks within which text-centrism is materialized.

Spiral bindings are popular devices in book manufacture, especially among small-scale or "desktop" publishers, including self-published cookbooks produced by local charitable organizations or individual authors. Very small press runs, where economies of scale prohibit the use of a more expensive binding, are more likely to use a cheap spiral binding. As such, spiral bindings connote not only affordability but also a certain degree of informality (or perhaps a lack of professionalism). Spiral bindings are also recognized as superior choices for books that need to lie flat when open: a priority in the kitchen, where one's hands are busy handling kitchen utensils and cooking ingredients. But ArtScroll's "concealed wire binding" suggests something altogether different. It marries the functionality of the spiral binding with the more dignified look of a traditionally hardbound book. Hardbound books, which are stitched together or glued at the spine and are bound by a leather-, cloth-, or buckram-covered rigid board, do not stay open very easily (unless the spine is forced, which can cause damage), but they are far better designed for storage and retrieval. When the book is resting on a shelf, for instance, its title, inscribed vertically along the spine, is easily readable. Most spiral-bound books, however, do not carry their titles on the spine. Moreover, with their "cheap" binding in full view, they call attention to themselves as "inferior" products. By concealing the binding—by making it appear as a "normal" hardbound book when viewed from the spine—*Kosher by Design* maintains the functionality of wire binding without sacrificing the desired "upscale look" of a hardbound book.

In this sense, *Kosher by Design*'s concealed wire binding encompasses a dual functionality: to be used and to be displayed. The wire binding, which is more durable than plastic, makes it easier for the user to routinely open and close the book, skim through its pages, or prop it up on a counter; the hard cover is designed to generate conspicuous attention to the book as an object of aesthetic contemplation when it is lying closed on a table or standing as a "valued addition" on a bookshelf. This dual functionality interlinks diverse social spaces and habituated practices within the domestic sphere:

Figure 10. Title page of *Kosher by Design,* displaying the "concealed wire binding." Reproduced courtesy of Mesorah Publications (ArtScroll Series).

places of labor and places of display. That *Kosher by Design*'s binding is "hidden" also reminds us how such technologies typically perform their work; they make themselves obscure precisely by succeeding in their actions.[29] Put otherwise, the book's binding cannot be reduced to a mere outward appearance, a superfluous, external dimension. Rather, the binding produces the book's interior not only in the sense that it quite literally holds the text together (and in ways quite different from a ring binder, recipe box, or online recipe collection) but also in the sense that these material constraints and enabling conditions delineate the range of possible interactions with that interior.

Book covers are significant not only because they physically hold pages together and allow for interactions in specific locales but also because they constitute what we might call a "surface mode of address." The closed book—even a book that is never opened—possesses communicative possibilities that are materialized on its outermost surface. To recall Roiza Weinreich's earlier comment, it makes her "feel good" simply to see a *sefer* (holy book) sitting on the shelf as she passes by.

In this spirit, it is important to distinguish ArtScroll books according to their distinct sizes, types of binding, and coverings, each of which is designed to enhance specific functions and uses and also to attract discrete categories of consumers. ArtScroll's editions extend from quite modest, pocket-size books (advertised as "travel editions") to large editions bound in hand-tooled leather. These latter versions are located on the high end of ArtScroll's product line and are clearly geared to the conspicuous consumption of religious artifacts. As such, they communicate a type of religious aura through the material form of their coverings. Consider, in this regard, an advertisement in the ArtScroll catalog for a line of hand-tooled leather prayer books under the trademark name Yerushalayim (Jerusalem) Leather (Fig. 11): "The rich scent of fine leather and the luxurious feel of hand-tooled workmanship give our Yerushalayim Leather volumes a distinction all their own. Unsurpassed gifts that will be used and cherished forever, their antique aura conveys a sense of tradition and warmth. Embossed with the Genuine ArtScroll sculpted emblem and specially designed endpapers arresting to their superior and authentic quality inside and out—Yerushalayim Genuine Leather superior reinforced bindings are timeless. They are an elegant expression of permanence and importance for all occasions or for one's own library."[30] It is striking how the associations of antique aura, elegance, permanence, and importance are conveyed here through the material presentation of the book, including the sculpted texture of its binding and its rich scent. Through the perceptual registers of seeing, touching, and even smelling, the leather book cover helps to secure the text contained within as "timeless" and of "superior and authentic quality."

The incorporation of expensive binding materials (such as leather) has long been understood as a marker of gentility and elegance, summoning a host of connotations that have little bearing on whether such books are actually read.[31] Even when produced on a mass scale, leather covers establish a line of continuity with religious print that can be traced back at least to

Figure 11. Advertisement for ArtScroll books bound in "Yerushalayim Leather." Reproduced courtesy of Mesorah Publications (ArtScroll Series).

the dawn of the printed book in the sixteenth century, if not further back to the venerated codex. As Paul Gutjahr has shown with reference to Bible production in nineteenth-century America, one of the significant changes in book production, beginning in the 1830s, was the introduction of new techniques and productive capacities for cloth bindings, allowing books to be produced and sold at significantly reduced costs.[32] However, long after cloth binding came to dominate almost every other area of the book trade, Bibles continued to be predominantly bound in leather.[33] The persistence of leather bindings, Gutjahr argues, indicates that publishers were concerned to reassert established cultural associations between the content and the covering of Bibles. Age-old techniques of leather binding, embossing,

Figure 12. Advertisement for a special edition of the ArtScroll Chumash, with handcrafted leather binding. Reproduced courtesy of Mesorah Publications (ArtScroll Series).

and tooling demarcated religious texts from their secular counterparts, emphasizing the "timelessness" of the text contained within. Leather bindings, were also important for the creation of material environments of spiritual edification and moral virtue that cut across the social divides of public and private. This was notably the case in the Victorian bourgeois home, where it was customary to have on display a lavish, leather-bound Bible as a prominent centerpiece within the carefully choreographed furnishings of the parlor, reminding family members as well as guests of God's eternal word.[34]

On similar terms, ArtScroll's leather-bound volumes reference a "classic" tradition of artisanal production, materializing religious works in ways that precious objects are supposed to look and feel. In an advertisement for a Special Limited Edition of the ArtScroll Chumash, retailing for $750.00, these associations are even more forcefully conveyed (Fig. 12). This special edition is presented not only as an expensive and beautiful acquisition—indeed, a "work of art"—but also as an "heirloom," endowed with the capacity to bind its owner into a chain of tradition. Through the inscription of a personal name onto a special page, the book directly interpellates its owner (and the owner's descendants) into the presence and the authorizing power of ArtScroll's editor-in-chief, Rabbi Scherman, behind whom stands the authority of Orthodox scholarship and its monopolistic claim over Jewish authenticity. As a limited edition, custom-crafted product, the book forms and sustains a select community of readers around it. The bonds of corporate sociability, matrimony, and domestic life are forged here in the presence of the book itself: "a corporate gift, a special gesture in honor of a wedding . . . the enhancement of a beautiful home."

For most consumers, however, ArtScroll's special editions are prohibitively expensive, and other means must be sought to achieve comparable results. In this regard, it is crucial to note that the great majority of ArtScroll books—the hundreds of thousands of prayer books, Bibles, Talmud tractates, and other canonical works that circulate throughout the contemporary English-language public sphere—are not leather bound. Rather, they are bound in a synthetic leather substitute: a polyurethane coating adhered to a fibrous base layer, colloquially known as "leatherette" or "pleather." Pleather products possess a range of properties, including a warm and comfortable touch to the hand, good abrasion resistance, high flexibility at extreme temperatures, and very good resistance to oils and fats. In all these ways, pleather provides the look and tactility of "traditional" leather at a significantly reduced cost, with the added advantage of greater durability and product uniformity. As such, the use of pleather bindings is tied to a principle of democratization: the production of affordable and durable books, and of an affordable book collection, which can still provide the correct look and feel associated with austere, dignified, and valued works of religious literature.

Echoing the dignified aura of genuine leather, ArtScroll's pleather-bound volumes function as what David Chidester, in a different context, has termed "authentic fakes."[35] The owners of ArtScroll books do not really believe that they are in possession of real leather-bound print commodities, yet this readily acknowledged subterfuge does not detract from the capacity of these books to generate bonds of sincerity and trust and to elicit from their users the seriousness and solemnity commensurate with the ownership and use of canonical Jewish works. They are, I suggest, works of "holy pleather." As material artifacts meant to communicate religious authenticity to their users, they are delicately poised at the intersection between the traditional and the modern and between competing demands for mass reproduction and an artisanal aesthetics.

READING ACCESSORIES

Just as the text cannot exist outside the material embodiment of the surface upon which it is inscribed, and the means by which multiple surfaces are held together, so the printed book (as one type of textual body) cannot exist outside its own networks of built environments and technical processes. These networks encompass and interlink the arenas where the activities of storage, private reading, or public recitation of books are carried out and where skilled users must coordinate books with complementary technologies, such as bookshelves, indexing and retrieval systems, seating arrangements, and sources of artificial illumination. In this regard, it is highly instructive to note that the ArtScroll brand name is closely tied, not only to specific categories of readers and places for reading, but also to a number of popular para-book technologies that we might call "reading accessories." Although these accessory items are produced by separate companies and cannot be defined as ArtScroll products *sensu stricto,* they occupy a prominent place in Orthodox Judaica stores, e-commerce, and even the ArtScroll catalog, where they are marketed as practical tools designed to supplement the repertoire of the discerning Orthodox consumer. Their close association with ArtScroll suggests an important synergy between the power of ArtScroll books, as valued print commodities, and the functionality of para-book technologies designed, among other things, to facilitate and enhance the experience of reading and to extend reading practices into new times and spaces. Two such technologies merit particular attention: the KosherLamp™, an artificial illumination device for use during the Sabbath, and SeferMate™, a collapsible and portable version of the bookstand commonly used in yeshivas for reading and studying religious texts (in Haredi circles, known by its Yiddish name, a *shtender*).

The KosherLamp™ is an invention of Kosher Innovations, a Toronto-based company founded in 2004 that markets itself as an "exclusive manufacturer and distributor of creative products for the Torah observant community."[36] It is widely available in Judaica stores in Canada and the United States, as well as being distributed internationally by Mesorah Publications through the artscroll.com Web site. The KosherLamp™ is a device that extends the use of artificial illumination in the domestic sphere, in accordance with the laws of Sabbath observance, as interpreted by the Orthodox rabbinic authorities who have officially endorsed this product.[37] This lantern-shaped light fixture contains an illuminated bulb and is encased by a movable sleeve that, when twisted back and forth, allows the user to cast or remove light in a room without violating Orthodox Jewish prohibitions against the use of electricity on the Sabbath. One of its functions, therefore, is to expand the temporal and spatial frontiers of reading activities, transforming otherwise inhospitable climates into places where books are made legible. SeferMate™ is another reading accessory sold in Judaica

Figure 13. Advertisement for the SeferMate™ *shtender.*

stores and through Internet-based retailers. It is a portable bookstand that can be collapsed into a compact briefcase, designed to transport and to hold in place an opened copy of a single Talmud volume (Fig. 13). Although not directly marketed by ArtScroll, SeferMate™'s associations with the publisher are unmistakable. Its dimensions are specifically tailored to the size of ArtScroll's Talmud editions, and its marketing literature alerts the buyer to the availability of two different models, designed to accommodate either ArtScroll's "Full Sized" or its "Daf Yomi" format. When put to use, Sefer-Mate™ supports an ArtScroll Talmud volume, while at the same time turning any horizontal surface—a dining room table, a countertop at work, a hotel room desk—into a potential place of study:. As such, it makes the Talmud text dramatically more portable, multiplying the reader's opportunities to open up and read ArtScroll books in new (and even hitherto impractical or inaccessible) places.

Accessory devices such as the KosherLamp™ and SeferMate™ serve a range of purposes, one of which is to make it easier to transport, store, open, and read books, and to undertake such activities at an expanding number of times and places. According to Rabbi Shmuel Veffer, the inventor of the KosherLamp™, "Our society is one that likes to come up with convenient things. And to make things more comfortable and convenient in terms of Jewish observance—why not?"[38] But these technologies should not be disregarded as merely superfluous appendages to the "real" activity of reading words on the page. Not only are they purveyors of convenience, but accessory devices also happen to provide examples of authorized objects, the laws for creation and legitimate use of which can readily be determined by consulting ArtScroll's detailed halakhah (legal) manuals.[39] As authorized objects, stamped with the seal of approval from prominent Orthodox rabbinic authorities, devices such as the Kosher-Lamp™ and SeferMate™ bring into alignment the materiality of the book and the discursive content of the text. By helping people, in Rabbi Veffer's words, "feel better about the commitments they make in terms of Jewish practice,"[40] they concretize the legal constraints, aesthetic protocols, and everyday habits central to Orthodox Jewish life, in the local settings and circumstances where religious meanings are inscribed, deciphered, materially instantiated, authorized, and performed. Even the most mundane accessory item, it seems, has the power to contribute to the manifestation of sacred aura. As Rabbi Veffer puts it, "Every time I twist the KosherLamp™ shade, it's a way to think about God in a way that I wouldn't during the week when flicking the switch on and off."[41]

MATERIALIZING AUTHENTICITY

Book bindings, covers, typefaces, illustrations, layout designs, and reading accessories demonstrate some of the ingenious ways that the ArtScroll brand name is tied to larger technological and stylistic advances in the production and circulation of Jewish religious print commodities, all the while affirming the publisher's identification with an artisanal tradition of bookmaking that "authentically" embodies sacred Jewish writing. Each of the design elements considered in this chapter contributes to the symbolic, aesthetic, cognitive, and performative dimensions of mediated interaction among consumers and collectors, lenders and borrowers, readers and listeners, and other users of texts, whether in the context of public ritual, kitchen labor, private reading, or the storage and display of books on a living room shelf. Through the study of such things as ArtScroll's "captivating" illustrations, "patent-pending" graphic icons, and "hidden" bindings, we have come to appreciate how these books possess a material agency and have noted some of the particular ways they populate and dynamically propel the networks of action, realms of imagination, economies of desire, and hierarchies of symbolic power that constitute text-centrism in contemporary Jewish culture. By acknowledging the material agency of ArtScroll books, we also add new wrinkles to the characterization of the Haredi scripturalist impulse within contemporary Jewish public culture. No longer is it tenable to treat text-centrism as a force resting exclusively on the power of linguistic meaning. Text-centrism must now be understood as a relationship manifested in the perceptual stimuli, affects, and embodied memories that together make books present in everyday life, whether one registers them in one's field of vision, touches them, skims their pages, or engages in the disciplined labor of intensively reading them at appointed times and places.

As the foregoing analysis also suggests, ArtScroll books win a foothold in the lives of their users not only because they are cleverly designed for easy access and reliable use—bearing the promises of interpretive clarity, portability, and convenience—but also because they carry with them the material signs of authenticity in and through which the power of Haredi rabbinic authority is communicated. Material form and written content collaborate to create "classic" works, in which ArtScroll books are simultaneously figured as authoritative representations of Jewish tradition and as valuable collectors' items, even family heirlooms. Through their look, their touch, and even their smell, these objects reference a world of "lost objects," associated with the artisanal techniques of book production from a preindustrial, prelapsarian past. By recognizing ArtScroll books as appropriately designed the way sacred books are "supposed" to look and feel, the users of these books place themselves in a temporal relationship in which "sacred text" and "authentic tradition" are located at the pinnacle of a cosmic order, descending down into the debased time and space of the reader/end user. On these terms, the authors and editors of ArtScroll books are further buttressed in their self-presentation as exclusive legatees of authentic Jewish tradition by having produced books that mediate the authority of contemporary Haredi rabbinic elites in a material form commensurate with this image of tradition.

At the same time, because ArtScroll books are reproduced mechanically on a mass scale, their "authenticity" is rife with contradiction, paralleling the fraught relationship with Jewish tradition that defines the position of contemporary Haredi rabbinic authorities. Let us recall how Haredim today present themselves as a remnant, the only remaining legatees and guardians of true faith and obedience to God's divine laws, but at the same time as a social enclave driven to innovate religious laws, codes of conduct, and mechanisms for legitimating cultural practice in order to "meet the challenges" of everyday life in the modern world. In a homologous position, ArtScroll books also simultaneously recuperate and transform the artisanal tradition of bookmaking associated with authentic experiences of Jewish text-centrism in times past. Through "revolutionary improvements"—better graphics and layout, stronger bindings, added illustrations, and more affordable (pleather) coverings—this publisher has restlessly "updated" the material form of sacred Jewish literature, all the while claiming to have preserved the aesthetics of the "traditionally" bound book. Here too we can learn something about how scripturalism is poised at the crossroads of innovation and conservation and how the material embodiments of Haredism connect images of prior times and places with the type of public they claim to form in the present.

FIVE

Gravity and Gravitas

A Concluding Reflection on Print Scripturalism
in the Digital Age

TOWARD THE END OF A wide-ranging discussion about ArtScroll's contributions to Orthodox Jewish publishing, editor-in-chief Rabbi Meir Zlotowitz put it to me that one of the press's best measures of success lay in the fact that ArtScroll books were increasingly being purchased all over the world through the Internet. As he stressed, "There is even this guy on the North Pole who orders all our books."[1] This striking image of a distant, solitary, and anonymous reader who furthers his Jewish education and secures an Orthodox way of life by building up his own ArtScroll library captures in condensed form two of the major themes with which this study has been concerned: the expanding presence of Haredi intellectuals and cultural producers in the contemporary Jewish public sphere; and the growing authority vested in written texts as a self-sufficient source of authentic religious knowledge. It also offers some food for thought about the shifting status of printed sacred works in a world increasingly defined by computer-mediated information flows.

In the first instance, Rabbi Zlotowitz's anecdote epitomizes the publisher's vision of global Jewry as a mission field encompassing even the most scattered and isolated individuals. Within this global space, ArtScroll books appear to circulate freely and independently and even to serve a prosthetic function, namely to act in place of face-to-face communities where they do not exist. Indeed, through his consumption of ArtScroll books, the "guy on the North Pole" is presumed to be able to erase the marginality of his location on the hinterland and to enter into a new type of community: the globally extensive English-language Jewish reading public. The ability of ArtScroll to address this diffuse reading public is therefore a mark of the success with which Haredi intellectuals and cultural producers overcome barriers of distance or local context and promulgate a form of religious authority grounded in the self-sufficient power of the text itself. As frequently claimed by the publisher's managers, contributing authors, financial backers, and legitimating authorities, ArtScroll books are designed to reach, instruct, inspire, and otherwise satisfy the needs of any Jew, anywhere. This rhetoric of infinite accessibility is suggestively aligned with ArtScroll's other performative goal: to fill up all the gaps and spaces in the lives of those touched by ArtScroll books. What drives the expansion of Haredi religious authority beyond its originating enclave society can thus be characterized as a scripturalist impulse, shaped by a vision in which everything from the complexities of ritual practice to the most mundane emotional states and everyday habits has been (or will soon be) anticipated, codified, and elaborated through written commentary and instruction. This is not to suggest that the ArtScroll cadre is somehow inattentive to the long-standing Jewish emphasis on ritual performance, study, and other reading practices as collective activities, ideally located within a face-to-face community, among teachers, rabbis, family, friends, and neighbors.[2] But where, unfortunately, such reading communities cannot be found—on the North Pole, perhaps—it would seem that ArtScroll books offer the best possible means of carrying on.

The flip side of Rabbi Zlotowitz's anecdote about extended reach is found in the curious fact that, despite his evident ease of access to the most advanced telecommunications technologies, the "guy on the North Pole" nevertheless exercises his demand for the comparatively primitive technology of the printed book. It seems that not just any kind of text will do, and the fact that ArtScroll has managed to consolidate its position as a premier purveyor of Jewish *books*—not electronic databases, handwritten scrolls, or other forms of textual media—is a crucial part of the story. This demand for printed works is partly a product of the book-centered traditions that have shaped the sensibilities and habits of religiously observant Jews, not least in the domain of ritual performance (where, for instance, the prohibition against operating electrical devices on the Sabbath would interdict the use of digitally mediated texts). But we also have good reason to suppose that the desire for printed works has something to do with the spiritual gifts that one acquires simply by being in their physical presence. For as we saw in Chapter 4, books can be said to possess a material agency whereby, for example, a leather covering has the power to convey an affective charge through its signifiers of dignity, solemnity, and artisanal authenticity. From this perspective, it would appear that the continued (and indeed growing) vitality of the market for printed books rests on a deeper set of cultural assumptions about what kinds of technologies and institutional frameworks are best suited to generate "authentic" religious experiences and to sustain the bonds of religious community. In the context of contemporary Jewish public culture, ArtScroll's success represents but one expression of what is in fact a broad consensus about the felicitous relationship between, on the one hand, the material agency of the printed book and, on the other hand, the ideas of origins, antique legacies, and even the notion of a direct, personal connection to God that is said to be central to Jewish religious experience.

In an attempt to further unpack Rabbi Zlotowitz's anecdote, I offer the term *gravity* as a means of describing the position ArtScroll books command both in public discourse and in everyday life. By one definition, *gravity* refers to weight and pressure; in another sense, it refers to dignity, solemnity, and seriousness. In both these senses, gravity is what links vertical relationships between the human and the divine with horizontal relationships of social life. It is gravity that pulls us down to earth and also enables relationships on the ground to cohere by anchoring individuals in relation to a center. So conceived, gravity suggests how it is possible for the printed word to retain its privileged status as a vehicle to communicate authoritative religious knowledge, despite (or perhaps precisely on account of) the ascendance of electronic media. Indeed, the printed book is not only a "time-tested" medium of Jewish communication, its ink and paper manifesting the residues of a centuries-old culture of book-centered activities. It is also a dynamic object in the present, a medial architecture unique in its ability to make distant social relationships *tangible*. Far from being rendered obsolete as "old" media, today's printed books have been reinvented as viable means of exercising authority and securing legitimacy through the particular disciplines and habits and the connective tissues that constitute text-centered religious community.[3] With their aura of trustworthiness and authenticity, and also their density and heft, printed works like those produced by ArtScroll act as counterweights to the vertiginous sense of weightlessness and rootlessness that is said to define contemporary Jewish public culture, cut loose from its traditional moorings and cast into a sea of mobile affinities, ephemeral connections, seductive distractions, and multiplying opportunities for reinvention of the self. In this sense, gravity delineates the shared desire on the part of both the publisher and its clients to locate themselves within a stable religious community, manifested in and through the circulation of uncompromisingly stringent, highly functional, and beautifully designed but nonetheless industrially produced print commodities. Likewise, to the extent that ArtScroll books succeed in directing particular courses of action—as suggested in Chapter 3's examination of "scripts" for kosher living—we can also think of the centrality of text-centrism precisely in terms of gravitational attraction to the printed word: a magnetic force that overpowers implicit or informal sources of knowledge. Even those who acidly disdain ArtScroll books—claiming to have no interest in receiving the intellectual and spiritual gifts offered by ArtScroll's authors, translators, and editors—nevertheless concede its dominant position in the current juncture as a uniquely powerful centripetal force in both the private and public lives of English-speaking religious Jews.

Of course, neither the theme of weightlessness and rootlessness nor that of the gravitational pull of text-centrism is new to Jewish religious and cultural history. As a stand-in for the lost Temple at Jerusalem, the Torah was long ago consecrated as the unifying symbol and gravitational core of the Jews' "portable homeland." For a community living in exile, the absence of fixity in territorial space was compensated through the consolidating powers and circulatory possibilities of the written text.[4] But as I have insisted in this book, it is specious to proclaim the existence of simple historical continuities among the various cultural, technological, and economic contexts of production, distribution, and consumption of written texts. The ArtScroll story is distinct from older patterns of Jewish text-centrism in that the power exercised by the publisher's various agents is circumscribed by the particular opportunities, challenges, and threats to customary arrangements augured by the rise of modern print markets, industrial production techniques, and the institutional organization of modern public spheres. ArtScroll's success in addressing interlocutors within contemporary public culture is also circumscribed by the constraints inhering in the medium of print itself. In this respect, let us not forget that there are limits to portability. Books can obviously be moved around more easily than temples, but their movements are still governed by the laws of inertia and gravity. Even a device such as the SeferMate™ *shtender,* designed to render ArtScroll Talmud tractates more portable, is still tied to the rather finite possibilities of mobility and interaction inhering in the object (the book) that it physically supports. In a similar vein, as we have seen in some detail, ArtScroll's vision of a universal reading public is belied by the sober realities of the publisher's limited market success, its ongoing struggles with competing publishers, the unabated criticism from non-Haredi intellectuals, and the divided attentions, ephemeral loyalties, and sometimes unruly habits of consumers themselves.[5]

In the preceding pages, I have offered a preliminary exploration of the gravitational powers that govern ArtScroll's mediation in Jewish social life, drawing upon diverse sources of evidence: survey data, interviews with interested parties (authors, editors, intermediary agents, end users), promotional materials, public testimonials, and, not least, an examination of the contents and material design of selected ArtScroll texts themselves. Even so, I freely admit to having barely scratched the surface of the life of ArtScroll as a publishing entity, as a community of authors, and as a corpus of circulating texts. No doubt much more can and should be said about the ways different genres of ArtScroll books are conceived, produced, marketed, and taken up in diverse user contexts and in the ever-shifting relations of complementarity and competition that locate ArtScroll among other publishers and other modes of mediated communication. But it is the conceit of this book that we have already been given adequate reasons to revise the notion of scripturalism as an account of the ways this community of writers and religious authorities enters public life and the ways their textual products are experienced on the ground. If *scripturalism* is to remain a useful term for describing something like the "ArtScroll revolution," I suggest that we need to distance ourselves from the rhetoric of both the publisher's advocates and its detractors. Indeed, public controversies surrounding ArtScroll as an index of a "slide to the right" in contemporary Jewish public life, or as an instance of "religious fundamentalism," have tended to focus on the ideological positions presumed to stand behind the specific words laid down in ArtScroll texts. It is hardly clear, however, how one is supposed to move from an interpretation of the *content* of a given text to an account of the political power presumably arrogated to its author or to the publicly recognized expert users of that text. In this respect, the concept of scripturalism seems to obscure more than it reveals about the gaps and bridges that divide and connect authors, texts, and readers. It does not provide a sufficiently robust account of the economic frameworks, institutional networks, cultural regimes of value, technologies, material agencies, and everyday habits that make up the social life of scriptural texts.

Having eschewed strictly formalist, hermeneutic, or philological approaches to ArtScroll books, I have, therefore, tried in this book to move the analysis in a different direction. My concern has been to show how *design*—as a phenomenon that transcends the dichotomies of style/function, form/content, and medium/message—navigates a path beyond the chasm dividing authorial intent and readerly response. Through the design of ArtScroll books, I have argued, scenarios of conception and production of texts get articulated with scenarios of their consumption and use. This is not to suggest that texts are always (if indeed ever) taken up by readers without modification, selective application, or, for that matter, wholesale reinterpretation. But it is to suggest that all acts of reception, including resistance and even outright disavowal, are predicated on the structured patterns of address already embedded in those texts. To elaborate that point, in Chapter 3 I inventoried a range of "action scenarios" that might be said to anchor their intended addressees in performative routines of ritual and domestic life and, more broadly, in the performance of one's everyday psychic self. In Chapter 4 I explored some of the ways embodied users and readers of books are also anchored in relations of material collaboration and exchange and linked into an interconnected series of action networks that structure the way books are stored, displayed, transported, handled, and read. These forms of address and patterns of use bring author and reader together in shared frameworks that encompass the design of books, the designs of their authors, and the opportunities to use such books to design a strict Orthodox Jewish lifestyle. By exploring the creative ways diverse ideas, affects, material forms, and habituated practices are integrated and interconnected in the lives of ArtScroll books, we can better appreciate how such mediations of Haredi religious authority need to be approached as something more than the expression of rigid (or even paradoxical) ideological positions or inexplicably contagious forms of charismatic power. Studying the constitution of Jewish Orthodoxy "by design," in other words, means trying to trace the many ways religious authorities, religious subjects, and other intermediating agents are entangled in the threads of knowledge and experience, public and domestic power, and mediated interaction that form the fabric of our global present.

NOTES

INTRODUCTION

The chapter epigraph is from *The ArtScroll Complete Catalogue* (Brooklyn, NY: ArtScroll/Mesorah Publications, 2006), 12–13, italics in original. The section epigraph for the anonymous reviewer of *The Chumash: The Stone Edition* posting on amazon.com, December 1, 1997, can be accessed at www.amazon.com/Chumash-Stone-Artscroll-Nosson-Scherman/product-reviews/0899060145/ref=cm_cr_pr_link_next_3?ie=UTF8&showViewpoints=0&pageNumber=5&sortBy=bySubmissionDateDescending.

1. The word *Haredism* is based on the Hebrew substantive *haredim*, which means "those who tremble," a scriptural reference to the righteous ones who fear the word of God (as in Isaiah 66:5). Unlike *ultra-Orthodox* and *Jewish fundamentalist* (which are ostensibly neutral but in fact subtly pejorative terms), the label *Haredi* is more readily recognizable among those so designated, although even this is not universal. In the social circles of the ArtScroll cadre of authors and editors, the preferred terms of self-identification are *Torah-True Jews* and *the Torah community.* Vexing problems of historical provenance, ideological variability, and cultural specificity have plagued scholars in their efforts to produce a consistent definition of Haredism. Given the considerable ambiguities and contestations surrounding the terms *Haredism, Haredi,* and *the Haredim,* the reader should understand their use here as figurative, referring to a loose constellation of cultural forms and ideas. For further details, see Chapter 1, below.

2. See, for instance, Amy Johnson Frykholm, *Rapture Culture: Left Behind in Evangelical America* (New York: Oxford University Press, 2004), and Heather Hendershot, *Shaking the World for Jesus: Media and Evangelical Culture* (Chicago: University of Chicago Press, 2004).

3. Charles Hirschkind, *The Ethical Soundscape: Cassette Sermons and Islamic Counterpublics* (New York: Columbia University Press, 2006).

4. Arvind Rajagopal, *Politics after Television: Hindu Nationalism and the Reshaping of the Public in India* (Cambridge: University of Cambridge Press, 2001).

5. An excellent overview of the burgeoning field of study in "religion and media" is *Key Words in Religion, Media and Culture,* ed. David Morgan (London: Routledge, 2008). See also Jeremy Stolow, "Religion and/as Media," *Theory, Culture, and Society* 22, no. 4 (2005): 119–45.

6. Of course, this question has relevance for the study of other forms of text-centrism, including those of Protestants, Muslims, and a host of book cultures that happen to define themselves as "secular."

7. Here, and throughout this book, I define *authority* as a mode of power articulated through the imposition of claims to legitimacy and the production of credibility and fidelity. This definition is loosely based on Max Weber's notion of legitimate domination, referring to that category of commands that are obeyed because there is "an interest in obedience." See Max Weber, *Economy and Society,* trans. Günther Ross et al (New York: Bedminster Press, 1968), 212; see also 31–38. It is also worth invoking here a long tradition of political philosophy that defines authority as the expression of political will: giving legal force, formally approving, etc., through representational practices or performative utterances. The close etymological connection between *author* and *authority* (both are derived from the Latin *augēre*) emphasizes the communicative dimension of this mode of power, in contradistinction to other means of inducing action, such as through coercive apparatuses or administrative systems of control of material space or the body.

8. Clifford Geertz, *Islam Observed: Religious Development in Morocco and Indonesia* (Chicago: Chicago University Press, 1968). Geertz's theory of scripturalism will receive more thorough treatment in Chapter 1.

9. Following the definition of *public* developed by Michael Warner, "Publics and Counterpublics," *Public Culture* 14, no. 1 (2002): 49–90.

10. For an insightful discussion of the history of the word *design,* particularly as it relates to the dichotomy of form and matter, see Vilém Flusser, *The Shape of Things: A Philosophy of Design* (London: Reaktion Books, 1999), 17–22 and passim. For useful overviews of the reigning theoretical and methodological assumptions within the fields of design history and design studies, see Clive Dilnot, "The State of Design History," *Design Issues* 1 (1984): 4–23, and Luz María Jiménez Narváez, "Design's Own Knowledge," *Design Issues* 16 (2000): 36–51. For a useful summary of theories of design from the perspective of

archaeology and material culture studies, see Margaret W. Conkey, "Style, Design, and Function," in *Handbook of Material Culture,* ed. Christopher Tilley et al. (Thousand Oaks, CA: Sage Publications, 2006), 355–72.

11. Bruno Latour, "Technology Is Society Made Durable," in *A Sociology of Monsters: Essays on Power, Technology and Domination,* ed. John Law (London: Routledge, 1991), 103–31.

12. Nosson Scherman and Nesanel Kasnett, "The Schottenstein Edition of the Babylonian Talmud: The Next Stage in Talmudic Elucidation," in *Printing the Talmud: From Bomberg to Schottenstein,* ed. Sharon Liberman Mintz and Gabriel Goldstein (New York: Yeshiva University Museum, 2005), 156.

13. A yeshiva (pl. yeshivot) is an academy of higher learning devoted to the study of Jewish classical texts and their commentaries, especially the Talmud.

14. More specifically, there are clear links—ideological, cultural, and social—between the ArtScroll cadre and Agudat Israel, one of the preeminent organizations devoted to the defense and cultivation of Jewish Orthodoxy as defined from a Haredi perspective. Many of the yeshivot related to the ArtScroll cadre also have close links with Agudat Israel. These include Mesivta Tifereth Jerusalem (in the Lower East Side of Manhattan, NY), Yeshiva Torah Vodath (in Brooklyn), the Yeshiva Gedolah (in Monsey, NY), the Beth Medrah Govohah (in Lakewood, NJ), the Telshe Yeshiva (in Wickliff, OH), the Mir Yeshiva (in Jerusalem), and the Ponevitz Yeshiva (in B'nei Brak, Tel Aviv). In Chapter 1 I discuss the role of the yeshiva in relation to Haredism in general and also with regard to specific institutions such as ArtScroll. For further discussion of Agudat Israel and its role within the contemporary religio-politics of transnational Jewish public culture, see Jeremy Stolow, "Transnationalism and the New Religio-Politics: Reflections on an Orthodox Jewish Case," *Theory, Culture and Society* 21, no. 2 (2004): 109–37. See also Chapter 1, n. 41, below.

15. This assessment of ArtScroll has been around for some time. See, for instance, Lawrence Kaplan, "*Daas Torah:* A Modern Conception of Rabbinic Authority," in *Rabbinic Authority and Personal Autonomy,* ed. Moshe Sokol (Northvale, NJ: Jason Arsonson, 1992), 1–60; Barry Levy, "Judge Not a Book by Its Cover," *Tradition* 19, no. 1 (1981): 89–95; Barry Levy, "Our Torah, Your Torah, and Their Torah: An Evaluation of the ArtScroll Phenomenon," in *Truth and Compassion: Essays on Judaism and Religion in Memory of Rabbi Dr. Solomon Frank,* ed. H. Joseph, Jack N. Lightstone, and M. D. Oppenheim (Waterloo, Ontario: Canadian Corporation for Studies in Religion/Wilfred Laurier University Press, 1983), 137–89; Alan Unterman, "The ArtScroll Mesorah Series: A Mixed Blessing," *Niv Hamidrashia: A Journal Devoted to Halacha, Jewish Thought, Education, and Literature* 18/19 (1985): 59–64. The characterization of ArtScroll as a Haredi or "fundamentalist" publisher is not restricted to academic circles; one finds similar assessments circulating widely in the Jewish blogosphere. "Wake up and smell the coffee!" asserts "Steve B.," a participant in

a blog devoted to discussion and debates about ArtScroll books. "ArtScroll's chief editors . . . strike me as front line representatives of the American Charedi world." From the blog Evanston Jew, October 31, 2006, http://evanstonjew .blogspot.com/2006/10/sociology-without-leaving-home.html.

16. Nosson Scherman, pers. comm., February 2004.

17. Although ArtScroll was initially created to serve the Anglophone Jewish book market, this audience is no longer its sole preoccupation. In recent years, the publisher has established markets for Spanish-, French-, Russian-, and also fluently Hebrew-speaking Jews, producing prayer books and other material in each of these languages and distributing them in various countries, including France, Mexico, Argentina, Russia, and Israel. Nevertheless, for reasons already stated (and that will become even clearer in Chapter 2), my principal concern is with ArtScroll's relation to the English-language Jewish reading public.

18. Meir Zlotowitz, preface to *The Megillah: The Book of Esther. A New Translation with a Commentary Anthologized from Talmudic, Midrashic and Rabbinic Sources* (Brooklyn, NY: ArtScroll/Mesorah Publications, 1976), ix.

19. Meir Zlotowitz, pers. comm., December 2003.

20. Quoted in Peter Ephros, "In 25 Years of Publishing, ArtScroll Captures Zeitgeist," *Jewish News of Greater Phoenix,* July 13, 2001, http://jewishaz.com/ jewishnews/010713/artscroll.shtml.

21. Anonymous reviewer posting on amazon.com, May 1, 2001, www .amazon.com/gp/product/customer-reviews/089906650X.

22. Anonymous reviewer posting on amazon.com, August 31, 1999, www .amazon.com/gp/product/customer-reviews/089906650X/.

23. Nosson Scherman, pers. comm., February 2004.

24. Nosson Scherman, pers. comm., December 2003. Of course, such claims about the lack of precedents cannot be taken at face value. Nor, for that matter, should it escape our attention that the principles of elaboration, simplification, and diffusion have a considerable history in Jewish textual practice. Among the many examples that could be cited here, one might invoke the Siddur *Iyyun Tefillah* (1855), edited by Jacob Mecklenburg, the rabbi of Königsberg, which, not unlike the *ArtScroll Siddur,* contained extensive commentaries in German. For details, see Cyrus Adler, "Prayer Books," *The Jewish Encyclopedia* (2002, unedited Internet edition of the original text from 1901–6), www.jewishencyclopedia.com. On related issues of design precedents, with a particular focus on the history of title pages, see Joseph Jacobs, "Typography," *The Jewish Encyclopedia,* www .jewishencyclopedia.com. One must nonetheless exercise caution when it comes to interpreting such precedents. Apparent continuities in content or form should not distract us from noting the *discontinuities* among differing cultural, technological, and economic contexts of production, distribution, and consumption of written texts.

25. Meir Zlotowitz, pers. comm., December 2003.

26. See, for instance, Janice Radway, *A Feeling for Books: The Book-of-the-Month Club, Literary Taste, and Middle-Class Desire* (Chapel Hill: University of North Carolina Press, 1997), and Joan Shelley Rubin, *The Making of Middlebrow Culture* (Chapel Hill: University of North Carolina Press, 1992).

27. Quoted in Rochelle Furstenberg, "Spirited Trade," *Jerusalem Report*, November 2, 1995, 47.

28. Zlotowitz, *Megillah*, ix.

29. Toronto interviewee, pers. comm., November 2002.

30. As we shall see in detail in Chapter 2, the spread of ArtScroll books has proceeded, not in a random fashion, but rather along a series of culturally and ideologically circumscribed routes, defined by differences within the community based on religious affiliation, national identity, and class location, as well as differences of generation, gender, and degree of command of Jewish canonical texts and of the Hebrew language in general.

31. Meir Zlotowitz, pers. comm., December 2003.

32. New York interviewee, pers. comm., November 2003.

33. This is a matter to which I shall return in Chapter 3.

34. Toronto interviewee, pers. comm., January 2003.

35. Here I follow the example of Bruno Latour's rethinking of the relationship between human and nonhuman (i.e., technological) forms of agency, whereby the former delegate specific skills and tasks for practical action to the latter through processes of inscription and transcription. See Latour, "Technology Is Society Made Durable," 103–31, and *We Have Never Been Modern* (Cambridge, MA: Harvard University Press, 1993). As I shall argue at greater length in Chapter 4, Latour's orientation to technology offers a productive framework for the analysis of texts as both artifacts and agents within larger networks of social interaction.

36. Nick Savage, "Why the Chicken Crossed the Road—A Jewish Response," Hazon.org, n.d., www.hazon.org/go.php?q=/readingroom/20-theFunnies/why TheChickenCrossedTheRoad.html, accessed February 24, 2009.

37. Nosson Scherman, pers. comm., February 2004.

38. Anonymous reviewer postings on amazon.com, March 16, 2000, August 29, 2000, and November 15, 2001, www.amazon.com/gp/product/customer -reviews/089906650X/.

39. New York interviewee, pers. comm., October 2003.

40. Toronto interviewee, pers. comm., December 2002.

41. The publisher does not divulge detailed information about sales, distribution, or records of profits. However, according to information collected by the Charity Navigator Rating Service, in 2007 the Mesorah Heritage Foundation (ArtScroll's "parent organization") declared a gross revenue of over $7.6 million and net assets of nearly $8.8 million. For details, see www.charitynavigator.org, accessed July 14, 2009. Coupled with the evidence of their large and continually

expanding booklist (now encompassing over one thousand titles in print) and the prominent visibility of ArtScroll products in retail bookselling outlets—as well as the high ranking of numerous volumes on major book retailing Web sites, such as amazon.com—it would be difficult to avoid the conclusion that ArtScroll is a very successful Judaica publisher.

42. Nevertheless, the United States remains ArtScroll's primary market, accounting for roughly 80 percent of its sales (Meir Zlotowitz, pers. comm., February 2004). According to one breakdown from the mid-1980s, reported in the industry journal *Publishers Weekly,* the Brooklyn community provided roughly 10 percent of Mesorah's business; 15 percent were already being shipped abroad, to Canada, the United Kingdom, Israel, and elsewhere. For details, see Eve Roshevsky, "Why Is This Publisher Different from Every Other Publisher?" *Publishers Weekly* 228, no. 13 (1985): 49. Today the publisher reports roughly similar figures, although since roughly 2002 there has been a rapid growth in direct Internet sales, which now account for roughly 15 to 20 percent of its business, through the ArtScroll Web site (www.artscroll.com), as well as via other Web-based distributors, including www.amazon.com and www.barnesandnoble.com.

43. As cited in Furstenberg, "Spirited Trade," 46.

44. Nelson Barber, "The ArtScroll Revolution," *Judaica Book News* 19 (1989): 15–16.

45. Quoted in Furstenberg, "Spirited Trade," 47.

46. Ibid., 46.

47. Nosson Scherman, "The Stone Edition of the Tanach: A View from the Inside," *New Standard* (Columbus, OH), January 1997, 62.

48. In 2003, Rabbi Zlotowitz reported that "our Siddurim [prayer books] in the various forms are now approaching a million copies sold. And the Chumash is now approaching 400,000 copies. There are also certain Talmud volumes that are also very popular; some have sold between 70 and 90,000 volumes. And our cookbook *Kosher by Design* has already sold about 70,000 copies in the half-year since it came out" (pers. comm., December 2003).

49. This includes different versions of their Siddur for Ashkenazi, Hasidic, and Sephardic congregations, as well as versions specifically designed for "modern" or "centrist" Orthodox congregations, including the Orthodox Union, and—for many observers, more surprisingly—an arrangement ArtScroll made with the Rabbinical Council of America (a decidedly non-Haredi Orthodox organization) to produce a slightly modified version of the ArtScroll Siddur with the RCA imprimatur. These modified versions include prayers for the state of Israel and the Israeli army, which are lacking in ArtScroll's original Siddur, an "omission" reflective of the uncomfortable historical relationship between Haredism and Zionism. For further details, see Chapters 2 and 3, below.

50. Although this is hailed as a unique strategy among Jewish publishers, it has numerous historical precedents. For instance, a Siddur published at Venice

in 1524 was produced in two volumes in order to overcome its "cumbersome" deficiency for carrying into synagogues. Similarly, the first Dutch translated Siddur (1791–93) was issued in various sizes and formats, from folio to 32mo, and in varying numbers of volumes. For details, see Adler, "Prayer Books."

51. Roshevsky, "Why Is This Publisher," 48.

52. ArtScroll developed its own bindery to address the general demise of the bookbinding industry in the greater New York area and the difficulty the publisher had to find a company that could meet its specific needs for high-quality leather binding at a marketable cost. For details, see Barber, "ArtScroll Revolution," 79.

53. The Mesorah Heritage Foundation's Library Enrichment Program, for instance, has furnished several hundred American colleges and universities with free copies of Talmud and other Jewish classics in order to encourage the use of their texts in undergraduate Jewish studies programs.

54. Under U.S. regulations, Mesorah is defined as a 501-C3 Charitable Foundation, which exempts the publisher from federal taxes in key domains of fundraising, publishing, and distribution. The trustees of this foundation have included Rabbis Zlotowitz and Scherman, and also Rabbi David Feinstein (son of the world-renowned halakhic authority Rabbi Moshe Feinstein), Dr. Joel Fleischman (the recently retired vice-president of Duke University), James Tisch (of the Loews Corporation), and Rabbi Lord Immanuel Jakobovits (Emeritus Chief Rabbi of the British Commonwealth, deceased in 1991). Irving Stone, founder and chairman of American Greetings Co., underwrote several publishing projects of ArtScroll, including their Chumash and Tanach. Jay Schottenstein of Columbus, Ohio (owners of a host of retail businesses, including department and furniture stores and casual clothing outlets), is another major player in the foundation, most noted for his extensive financial support for the translation of the Babylonian Talmud.

55. Although again, one must be cautious making overblown claims about the unprecedented nature of such arrangements. A telling precedent can be found in the publication of the *Daily Prayer Book* of the United Hebrew Congregations of the British Empire, authorized by Chief Rabbi N. M. Adler in 1891. The cost of producing this text was defrayed by Mrs. Nathaniel Montefiore, enabling distributors to sell the book for one shilling, both within the British Empire and also as an inexpensive export to the United States. For details, see Adler, "Prayer Books."

56. Although I speak in the following pages about the history of print, my principal focus is on the printed book and not the broader realm of print culture, which includes such things as newspapers, broadsheets, almanacs, magazines, calendars, legal documents, posters, postcards, stamps, and money. In so doing, I do not mean to suggest that the encounter with printed books, either historically or in the present, can be fully detached from the practical

engagements and ways of knowing that emerge in this larger, print-mediated universe, to say nothing of the intersection of print matter with other media forms that inscribe, store, reproduce, or disseminate images and sounds through audio recording, photography, radio, cinema, video, or digital technologies. I shall return to this point in Chapter 5.

57. On the social organization of production of written texts in antiquity, see Harold Adam Innis, *Empire and Communications* (Oxford: Oxford University Press, 1950). Innis was an early contributor to what has become a vast area of scholarship dealing with premodern modes of production of written materials. For details on the production of Bibles and other sacred works in the ancient Near East, see Louis J. Greenspoon, "Jewish Bible Translation," in *The Biblical World,* ed. J. Barton (London: Routledge, 2003), 397–412; Ernst Würthwein, *The Text of the Old Testament: An Introduction to the Biblia Hebraica,* 2nd ed. (Grand Rapids, MI: Eerdmans, 1995). On the history of papermaking, see Jonathan Bloom, *Paper before Print: The History and Impact of Paper in the Islamic World* (New Haven: Yale University Press, 2001). For useful accounts of manuscript culture in medieval Europe and in the Mediterranean world, see George N. Atiyeh, ed., *The Book in the Islamic World: The Written Word and Communication in the Middle East* (Albany: State University of New York Press, 1995), and Brian Stock, *The Implications of Literacy: Written Language and Modes of Interpretation in the Eleventh and Twelfth Centuries* (Princeton: Princeton University Press, 1983). On medieval Jewish manuscript culture, see Brigitte Bedos-Rezak, "The Confrontation of Orality and Textuality: Jewish and Christian Literacy in Eleventh and Twelfth-Century Northern France," in *Rashi, 1040–1990: Hommage à Ephraim E. Urbach,* ed. G. Sed-Rejna (Paris: Cerf, 1993), 541–58; Shelomo Dov Goitein, *Letters of Medieval Jewish Traders* (Princeton: Princeton University Press, 1973); Sophia Manache, ed., *Communication in the Jewish Diaspora: The Pre-modern World* (New York: E. J. Brill, 1996); Raphael Posner and Israel Ta-Shema, eds., *The Hebrew Book: An Historical Survey* (Jerusalem: Keter Publishing House, 1975); Stefan Reif, "Aspects of Mediaeval Jewish Literacy," in *The Uses of Literacy in Early Mediaeval Europe,* ed. R. McKitterick (Cambridge: Cambridge University Press, 1990), 134–55; Norman Roth, "Jewish Collaborators in Alfonso's Scientific Work," in *Emperor of Culture: Alfonso X, the Learned of Castile and His Thirteenth-Century Renaissance,* ed. Robert I. Burns (Philadelphia: University of Pennsylvania Press, 1990), 59–71; David Stern, "The First Jewish Books and the Early History of Jewish Reading," *Jewish Quarterly Review,* 98, no. 2 (2008): 163–202.

58. The technological capacity for printing is itself much older. Wood blocks were used to print written texts in the early T'ang dynasty of seventh-century China, and the techniques spread to Korea, Japan, Persia, and westwards in the ensuing centuries. For details, see Thomas F. Carter, *The Invention of Printing in China and Its Spread Westward,* 2nd rev ed. (New York: Ronald Press, 1955).

Gutenberg's innovation was to develop a technology based on movable type, using separate letters cast on a uniform pattern in a mold—the "original" model of the standardized, replaceable part. On the impact of Gutenberg's technology, see Lewis Mumford, *Art and Technics* (New York: Columbia University Press, 1952), 67–79, and Lucien Febvre and Henri-Jean Martin, *The Coming of the Book: The Impact of Printing, 1450–1800* (London: Verso Books, 1990), 49–76. The most influential account of the print revolution and the rise of print culture in early modern Europe is Elizabeth Eisenstein, *The Printing Press as an Agent of Change: Communications and Cultural Transformations in Early Modern Europe* (Cambridge: Cambridge University Press, 1979), although this pioneering work has been the subject of heated debate, centered on accusations that Eisenstein's narrative harbors a latent technological determinism. See, for instance, the exchange between Eisenstein and Adrian Johns in *American Historical Review* 107, no. 1 (2002): 84–128. More recent approaches to book history and the spread of print culture include Peter Burke, *A Social History of Knowledge: From Gutenberg to Diderot* (Cambridge: Polity Press, 2000); Adrian Johns, *The Nature of the Book: Print and Knowledge in the Making* (Chicago: University of Chicago Press, 1998); Sabrina Alcorn Baron, Eric N. Lindquist, and Eleanor F. Shevlin, eds., *Agent of Change: Print Culture Studies after Elizabeth L. Eisenstein* (Amherst: University of Massachusetts Press, 2007).

59. On the relationship between the printing press and the Protestant Reformation, see especially Eisenstein, *Printing Press,* 303–450. For detailed analysis of Luther's diverse range of "media strategies," including pamphleteering, Bible translation, and the production of standardized hymnals, see M. U. Edwards Jr., *Printing, Propaganda, and Martin Luther* (Berkeley: University of California Press, 1994); Robert W. Scribner, *For the Sake of Simple Folk: Popular Propaganda and the German Reformation* (Cambridge: Cambridge University Press, 1981); and Jean-François Gilmont, ed., *The Reformation and the Book* (Aldershot: Ashgate, 1998).

60. Readers will no doubt hear echoes in this account of Benedict Anderson's description of the rise of "print capitalism" and its social consequences. See Benedict Anderson, *Imagined Communities: Reflections on the Origin and Spread of Nationalism* (London: Verso Books, 1991), 37–46.

61. On the development of Jewish presses in early modern Europe, see Joseph Jacobs, "The Book Trade," *The Jewish Encyclopedia* (2002, unedited Internet edition of the original text from 1901–6), www.jewishencyclopedia.com. On reading habits among Renaissance Jews, see Shifra Baruchson, *Books and Readers: The Reading Interests of Italian Jews at the Close of the Renaissance* (Tel Aviv: Bar-Ilan University Press, 1993). For eighteenth- and nineteenth-century developments, see Zeev Gries, *The Book in the Jewish World, 1700–1900* (Oxford: Littman Library of Jewish Civilization, 2007).

62. As described by Radway, *Feeling for Books,* 135–37. See also Kevin Sharpe, *Reading Revolutions: The Politics of Reading in Early Modern England* (New Haven: Yale University Press, 2000); Wendy Wall, *The Imprint of Gender: Authorship and Publication in the English Renaissance* (Ithaca: Cornell University Press, 1993). On the structural organization of preindustrial print culture through class- and gender-based hierarchies of restricted literacy, see the monumental study by Harvey J. Graff, *The Legacies of Literacy: Continuities and Contradictions in Western Culture and Society* (Bloomington: Indiana University Press, 1987).

63. On the industrialization of print production in the nineteenth century, see especially Scott Casper et al., eds., *A History of the Book in America,* vol. 3, *The Industrial Book, 1840–1880* (Chapel Hill: University of North Carolina Press, 2007). See also John William Tebbel, *Between Covers: The Rise and Transformation of Book Publishing in America* (Oxford: Oxford University Press, 1987). On the industrialization of British publishing, see John Feather, *A History of British Publishing* (London: Routledge, 1988), 123–205. For Canadian developments, see Yvan Lamonde, Patricia Lockhart Fleming, and Fiona A. Black, eds., *History of the Book in Canada,* vol. 2, *1840–1918* (Toronto: University of Toronto Press, 2005).

64. See, for instance, Richard D. Altick, *The English Common Reader: A Social History of the Mass Reading Public, 1800–1900,* 2nd ed. (Columbus: Ohio State University Press, 1998); David M. Henkin, *City Reading: Written Words and Public Spaces in Antebellum New York* (New York: Columbia University Press, 1998); David Vincent, *Literacy and Popular Culture: England, 1750–1914* (Cambridge: Cambridge University Press, 1989).

65. With regard to the last of these oppositions, see Isabel Hofmeyer, *The Portable Bunyan: A Transnational History of the Pilgrim's Progress* (Princeton: Princeton University Press, 2003).

66. See the pioneering (but now dated) study by Lewis Coser, Charles Kadushin, and Walter Powell, *Books: The Culture and Commerce of Publishing* (Chicago: University of Chicago Press, 1982). For subsequent developments, especially with regard to the impact of computers on the publishing industry, see Albert N. Greco, *The Book Publishing Industry,* 2nd ed. (London: Routledge, 2005); Albert N. Greco, Clara E. Rodríguez, and Robert M. Wharton, *The Culture and Commerce of Publishing in the Twenty-first Century* (Stanford: Stanford University Press, 2007). On the evolution of the publishing industry in the first half of the twentieth century, see Carl Kaestle and Janice Radway, eds., *A History of the Book in America,* vol. 4, *Print in Motion: The Expansion of Publishing and Reading in the United States, 1880–1940* (Chapel Hill: University of North Carolina Press, 2009). At the time of writing, the fifth volume of this monumental series, dealing with the history of the book in the postwar period, has not yet been published: David Paul Nord, Joan Shelley Rubin, and Michael

Schudson, eds., *The Enduring Book: Print Culture in Postwar America* (Chapel Hill: University of North Carolina Press, 2009).

67. "Religious publishing" is of course a highly ambiguous and contested category, since no one can say with confidence what precisely constitutes a "religious" as opposed to a "nonreligious" book. See, for instance, Tebbel, *Between Covers*, 449–52. For publishing industry perspectives on the definition of religious publishing, see Lynn Garrett, "Bibles and Sacred Texts: Betcha Can't Own Just One," *Publishers Weekly* 246, no. 41 (1999): 33; Jana Riess, "Tracking the Mega-Categories (Religion Update)," *Publishers Weekly* 247, no. 22 (2000): S16–S18; Jana Riess, "New Genres, Emerging Audiences (Religion Update)," *Publishers Weekly* 247, no. 34 (2000): S4–S8; Kimberly Winston, "Bibles and Sacred Texts: Of the Making of Many Scriptures," *Publishers Weekly* 246, no. 41 (1999): 34–41; Kimberly Winston, "You Can Judge a (Good) Book by Its Cover," *Publishers Weekly* 250, no. 41 (2003): 32–38.

With this caveat in mind, it is instructive to review the data produced by organizations such as the Christian Booksellers Association, which suggest that by the mid-1990s the Christian book industry in the United States had developed into an industry worth over $2.5 billion per year, accounting for somewhere between 5 and 10 percent of the total U.S. book market, depending on what is being counted. For details, see Michael Kress, "Slicing the Market Pie (Religion Update)," *Publishers Weekly* 247, no. 13 (2000): S16–S18; Jim Milliot, "Do Religion Sales Add Up?" *Publishers Weekly* 242, no. 15 (2001): 25. This output— enormous by any reasonable standard of measurement—is abetted by the existence of a broad network of publishing houses, outreach organizations, church and para-church groups, retail sellers, and, it would appear, a large population of consumers willing to devote considerable sums of money on a regular basis.

68. On the global diffusion of Christian print in the nineteenth century, see, *inter alia*, Leslie Howsam, *Cheap Bibles: Nineteenth-Century Publishing and the British and Foreign Bible Society* (Cambridge: Cambridge University Press, 1991); Michael Ledger-Lomas, "Mass Markets: Religion," in *The History of the Book in Britain, 1830–1914*, ed. David McKitterick (Cambridge: Cambridge University Press, 2009), 324–58; John Lardas Modern, "Evangelical Secularism and the Measure of Leviathan," *Church History* 77 (December 2008): 801–76; David Morgan, *Protestants and Pictures: Religion, Visual Culture, and the Age of American Mass Production* (Oxford: Oxford University Press, 1999); David Paul Nord, *Faith in Reading: Religious Publishing and the Birth of Mass Media in America* (Oxford: Oxford University Press, 2004); Rasiah S. Sugirtharajah, *The Bible and the Third World: Precolonial, Colonial and Postcolonial Encounters* (Cambridge: Cambridge University Press, 2001); Peter J. Wosh, *Spreading the Word: The Bible Business in Nineteenth-Century America* (Ithaca: Cornell University Press, 1994).

Some have suggested that the diffusion of print not only facilitated the global spread of Christianity but also led to the "Protestantization" of non-Christian religions. Gananath Obeyesekere, for instance, famously referred to the rise of a form of "Protestant Buddhism" in nineteenth-century Sri Lanka, in which Buddhist intellectuals responded to missionary work by indigenizing print technologies and their modes of knowledge ordering and public making. See Gananath Obeyesekere, "Religious Symbolism and Political Change in Ceylon," *Modern Ceylon Studies* 1 (1970): 43–63.

69. To name but two studies dealing with non-Western developments: Yves Gonzalez-Quijano, *Les gens du livre: Édition et champ intellectuel dans l'Égypte républicaine* (Paris: CNRS Éditions, 1998); Maimuna Huq, "From Piety to Romance: Islam-Oriented Texts in Bangladesh," in *New Media in the Muslim World: The Emerging Public Sphere,* ed. Dale F. Eickelman and Jon W. Anderson (Bloomington: Indiana University Press, 1999), 133–61.

70. Paul C. Gutjahr, "The State of the Discipline: Sacred Texts in the United States," *Book History* 4 (2001): 338.

71. Jürgen Habermas, *The Structural Transformation of the Public Sphere: An Inquiry into a Category of Bourgeois Society* (Cambridge, MA: MIT Press, 1989). For critiques of the "secularist" bias of Habermas's public sphere model, see, *inter alia,* David Zaret, "Religion, Science and Printing in the Public Spheres in Seventeenth-Century England," in *Habermas and the Public Sphere,* ed. Craig Calhoun (Cambridge, MA: MIT Press, 1992), 212–35; Birgit Meyer and Annelies Moors, eds., *Religion, Media and the Public Sphere* (Bloomington: Indiana University Press, 2006).

72. Bereshit Rabbah 1:1, 8, as discussed in José Faur, *Golden Doves with Silver Dots* (Bloomington: Indiana University Press, 1986), 10–16. See also Susan Handelman, *Slayers of Moses: The Emergence of Rabbinic Interpretation in Modern Literary Theory* (Albany: State University of New York Press, 1982).

73. Moshe Halbertal, *People of the Book: Canon, Meaning, and Authority* (Cambridge, MA: Harvard University Press, 1997), 1.

74. Halbertal attributes the central role of scholars and scholarship to the sealing of the Jewish canon, at which point it was determined that no new "prophetic" text (or other testament of divine revelation) could legitimately be added to the existent set of religiously authoritative texts. The sealing of the Jewish canon, he argues, had specific historical consequences for the definition of religious meaning and authority in Judaism. It arrested prophecy as a legitimate activity and thereby effected a redistribution of authority onto interpreters. It endowed the existing texts with the status of exclusivity but also with new interpretative breadth, since the canon was thereafter expected to furnish answers to all sorts of new questions. And it spawned new social institutions (such as the *beit midrash,* or house of study) and a new literary genre—commentary—in and through which interpretative work could be carried out. See Halbertal, *People of the Book,* 18ff.

75. On modern-day Orthodox Jewish reading and studying practices, see Jonathan Boyarin, "Voices around the Text: The Ethnography of Reading at Mesivta Tifereth Jerusalem," in *The Ethnography of Reading,* ed. Jonathan Boyarin (Berkeley: University of California Press, 1993), 212–37; Tamar El-Or, *Educated and Ignorant: Ultraorthodox Jewish Women and Their World* (Boulder, CO: Lynne Rienner, 1994); Samuel C. Heilman, *The People of the Book: Drama, Fellowship, and Religion,* 2nd ed. (New Brunswick, NJ: Transaction Publishers, 2002); William B. Helmreich, *The World of the Yeshiva: An Intimate Portrait of Orthodox Jewry* (New Haven: Yale University Press, 1982).

76. On the expanding role of texts in Orthodox and Haredi Jewish society, see, *inter alia,* Menachem Friedman, "Life Tradition and Book Tradition in the Development of Ultraorthodox Judaism," in *Judaism Viewed from Within and from Without: Anthropological Studies,* ed. Harvey Goldberg (Albany: SUNY Press, 1987), 235–55; Samuel C. Heilman, *Sliding to the Right: The Contest for the Future of American Jewish Orthodoxy* (Berkeley: University of California Press, 2006), 127–39; Haym Soloveitchik, "Rupture and Reconstruction: The Transformation of Contemporary Orthodoxy," *Tradition* 28 (1994): 64–130. These are matters to which I shall return in Chapter 1.

77. In this sense, the present study builds upon but departs significantly from the institutional focus of earlier studies of Jewish publishing in the English-speaking world. See, for instance, Charles Madison, *Jewish Publishing in America: The Impact of Jewish Writing on American Culture* (New York: Sanhedrin Press, 1976); Jonathan D. Sarna, *JPS: The Americanization of Jewish Culture, 1888–1988* (Philadelphia: Jewish Publication Society, 1989).

78. For a trenchant critique of the dichotomies of form/matter and container/content, drawing upon the analogy of the post-Newtonian revision of the dichotomy of matter and energy, see Flusser, *Shape of Things,* 22–29. From the perspective of material culture studies, Margaret Conkey persuasively argues that style and function appear as distinct categories only at the expense of direct consideration of the objects themselves, when one focuses instead on the social contexts in which objects are talked about, exchanged, or otherwise put to use; "Style, Design, and Function," 355–72. For an influential (if controversial) critique of the distinction between medium and message, see Marshall McLuhan, *Understanding Media: The Extensions of Man* (New York: McGraw-Hill, 1964).

I. AUTHORITATIVE AND ACCESSIBLE

The section epigraph is from Alexander Zusha Friedman, "The Fundamentals of Agudath Israel," *Jewish Observer* 1, no. 9 (1964): 11–12, a translation and republication of Rabbi Friedman's keynote address at the 1923 Agudat Israel World Congress.

1. *Talmud Bavli: The Schottenstein Edition,* 73 vols., ed. Gedaliah Zlotowitz et al. (Brooklyn, NY: ArtScroll/Mesorah Publications, 1990–2005), hereafter referred to as the *Schottenstein Talmud.*

2. Nosson Scherman, *The Complete ArtScroll Siddur: Weekday/Sabbath/Festival Edition. Nusach Ashkenaz* (Brooklyn, NY: ArtScroll/Mesorah Publications, 1984); Susie Fishbein, *Kosher by Design: Picture Perfect Food for the Holidays and Every Day* (Brooklyn, NY: ArtScroll/Mesorah Publications, 2002). Both these texts will receive more thorough treatment in Chapters 3 and 4.

3. Each volume cost the Mesorah Heritage Foundation roughly $250,000 to produce, for a total of over $21 million for the entire project. See Joseph Berger, "An English Talmud for Daily Readers and Debaters," *New York Times,* February 10, 2005, www.nytimes.com/2005/02/10/books/10talm.html?_r=1&scp= 1&sq=joseph%20berger%20english%20talmud&st=cse.

4. The work we know today as the Talmud is the result of a complex evolution from a set of texts that were memorized, recited, analyzed, and passed on from master to disciple through living repositories of tradition, the *tannaim* (tradents), to a text that was fixed in writing. See Stern, "First Jewish Books," 163–202; Saul Lieberman, "The Publication of the *Mishnah,*" in *Hellenism in Jewish Palestine: Studies in the Literary Transmission, Beliefs, and Manners of Palestine in the I Century BCE—IV Century CE* (New York: Jewish Theological Seminary of America, 1950), 83–99. These developments occurred in two major centers of Jewish scholarship: Palestine and Babylonia. Correspondingly, two bodies of analysis developed, and two works of Talmud were created. The older text, the *Talmud Yerushalmi* (Jerusalem Talmud), was compiled during the fourth century CE, whereas the *Talmud Bavli* (Babylonian Talmud) was compiled around the year 500 CE. When used without qualification, the word *Talmud* usually refers to the Babylonian Talmud.

5. Vernacular translations of the Talmud began in the nineteenth century with Ephraim Moses Pinner (1800–1880), who wrote a German translation in the 1840s. Pinner argued that it was necessary to translate the Talmud because of "the present inability of the Jews to understand it in the original and the need to correct the distortions of the Talmud that had been created by its [Christian] opponents." Quoted in Adam Mintz, "Talmud in Translation," in S. Mintz and Goldstein, *Printing the Talmud,* 123. The first attempt to translate the Talmud into English, by Michael Levi Rodkinson (1845–1904), also dates back to the nineteenth century. It was followed by the mid-twentieth-century effort by Isodore Epstein, of Jews' College in London, who served as general editor for an edition published by Soncino Press between 1935 and 1952 and later a (never completed) edition edited by Rabbi Adin Steinsaltz (who initiated his English translation in 1989, on the heels of his very successful translation of the Talmud into modern Hebrew). For details, see A. Mintz, "Talmud in Translation," 127f. The only other translation of the Babylonian Talmud in English was undertaken

by Jacob Neusner (a professor of religion and theology at Bard College, New York): a twenty-two-volume edition completed in 1995, currently distributed by Hendrickson Publishers in both hardcover and CD-ROM versions.

6. By 2005, an average of twenty thousand copies of each volume of the Schottenstein edition had been printed, and some of the more popular tractates had sold over ninety thousand copies, as reported in Berger, "English Talmud." Individual volumes range in price from $34.99 to $49.99. Entire sets of the Schottenstein edition of *Talmud Bavli* are currently available through ArtScroll's Web site for a list price of $2,999.99. An entire seventy-three-volume purchase of the smaller, "Daf Yomi-sized edition" is listed at $1,999.99. The publisher is also in the process of publishing a seventy-one-volume modern Hebrew edition of the Talmud, also sponsored by the Schottenstein family, as well as a French translation, directed by Rabbi Aharon Marciano and sponsored by the family of Edmond Safra, the Sephardi Jewish banker and philanthropist. For details of the press's current Talmud offerings on the ArtScroll booklist, see www.artscroll .com/Categories/tlm.html.

7. See, for instance, the list of prominent Orthodox rabbis who issued *haskamot* (official letters of approbation) for the Schottenstein edition, including R. Shlomo Zalman Auerbach, R. Mordecai Gifter, R. Abraham Pam, R. Aaron M. Schechter, R. Yaakov Perlow, R. David Feinstein, R. Shmuel Kamenetzky, and R. David Cohen, as reprinted in the front matter of vol. 1 of the *Schottenstein Talmud.* Further evidence of the breadth of support for ArtScroll's Talmud project can be found in the very composition of the Mesorah Heritage Foundation's board of trustees, which over its history has included such religiously and culturally diverse figures as Rabbi David Feinstein (son of one of the foremost halakhic authorities of Orthodox Judaism in the twentieth century, and *rosh yeshiva* [headmaster] of the academy Mesivtha Tifereth Jerusalem), Dr. Joel Fleishman (the first senior vice president of Duke University), Lord Immanuel Jakobovits (the former chief rabbi of the British Commonwealth, d. 1991), and James Tisch (president of Loews Corporation, one of the largest diversified financial corporations in the United States). The membership of ArtScroll's board of trustees wonderfully illustrates the blurring of distinctions among distinct strains of Orthodoxy, as I shall discuss at greater length below.

8. Opposition to Talmud translation has always existed, not unlike earlier opposition to the translation of the Torah into the Septuagint some two thousand years ago. Various arguments have been put forth over the course of the past century, but their tenor is largely constant: a translation cannot capture the "full essence" of the original; translations will distort the meaning of the text as it should be understood; translations open the Talmud to a community of non-Jewish readers, who might make a mockery of its contents; and translations into the vernacular encourage and legitimate a secularization of the Jewish community by facilitating greater contact with non-Jews and by allowing Jews to "drift

away" from the true heritage embedded in their texts. See A. Mintz, "Talmud in Translation," 121ff. I shall return to this theme of vernacularization in Chapter 2.

One of the most vociferous modern-day critics of Talmud translation was Rabbi Elazar Menachem Schach (1898–2001), of the Ponevezh Yeshivah (in B'nei Brak, Israel), acknowledged by many as the supreme Haredi authority of the late twentieth century. In 1989, Rabbi Schach issued a ruling in opposition to both Steinsaltz translations of the Talmud—the completed modern Hebrew version, as well as his recently begun English—on the grounds that, even if translations helped to create a broader readership, the experience of such readers was meaningless because they would be engaging with a text that was now bereft of holiness and sanctity. While some of these criticisms have subsided, there is nonetheless an enduring sense among Orthodox intellectual elites that studying the Talmud in translation (whether into English or modern Hebrew) is like "cheating." See A. Mintz, "Talmud in Translation," 137–38. ArtScroll's efforts to define their edition as an "elucidation" (in which the translation is not supposed to stand on its own) is clearly aimed at forestalling any such criticisms.

9. Quoted in Adam Kirsch, "The Talmud in English, for Both Orthodox and Others," *New York Sun,* February 9, 2005, 1.

10. *Schottenstein Talmud,* 1:xxv–xxvi.

11. Quoted in Miriam Shaviv, "ArtScroll Readers of All Stripes Find Meaning in Translation," *Forward,* February 25, 2005, www.forward.com/articles/2999/.

12. *Library of Congress Dedication Ceremony,* Washington, DC, February 9, 2005, audiovisual recording courtesy of Chris Cross Photography, www .chriscrossphotography.com. My transcription.

13. Ibid.

14. See Adam Dickter, "Tens of Thousands Mark Talmud Completion," *Jewish Week,* March 4, 2005, www.thejewishweek.com/viewArticle/c36_a5666/ News/New_York.html; Andy Newman, "Orthodox Jews Celebrate End of a True Sabbatical," *New York Times,* March 2, 2005, http://query.nytimes.com/ gst/fullpage.html?res=9C03E4DD133DF931A35750C0A9639C8B63.

15. Readers should note that the name "Agudat Israel" generally refers to the international movement, while "Agudath Israel" typically references the American chapter, although often the differences between these two organizations are elided, and differences in spelling of terms transliterated from Hebrew are often overlooked within the Orthodox community.

16. See Marc B. Shapiro, "Talmud Study in the Modern Era: From *Wissenschaft* and Brisk to *Daf Yomi,*" in S. Mintz and Goldstein, *Printing the Talmud,* 109.

17. This is not to suggest that Daf Yomi received universal support among Orthodox Jews, especially in the early years, and especially among Hasidic groups that were opposed to Agudat Israel's larger political agenda. For instance, in the eyes of the Hungarian rabbi Hayyim Eleazar Shapira (1872–1937), the Daf

Yomi program was not only untenable ("How," he asked, "can one learn a page every day when the pages almost always end in the middle of a subject?") but also politically dangerous in that it encouraged the student to accept Agudat Israel's ideology, which included, from Rabbi Shapira's perspective, unacceptable compromises with the secular state (especially in Poland) and with Zionism. Rabbi Shapira even accused Agudat Israel of having initiated the Daf Yomi "in order to have at its disposal ready-made groups that could be used to colonize the Land of Israel," in violation of long-standing Orthodox proscriptions against returning to the Holy Land. Quoted in Shapiro, "Talmud Study," 109.

Leading up to the 2005 Siyum haShas, comparable criticisms were still being raised by (admittedly marginal) figures within the Haredi world. One such instance was penned by B. Rosenberg in the Yiddish-language Haredi newspaper *Der Yid,* who issued a shrill denunciation of the growing number of "professionals" now engaged in Talmud study, singling out the dangerous influence of the *Schottenstein Talmud* in particular: "The righteous are not impressed by sinners studying Torah. According to the Torah, one who does not follow the teachings is an unsuitable student, and brings only destruction on the Jewish people. Those studying Torah who possess secular educations are mixing good with evil. Particularly the English language Talmud, through its non-Jewish elements [*far'goyishte elementn*], brings a terrible evil to the Jewish people." In B. Rosenberg, "Holy Rabbis Oppose Daf Yomi," *Der Yid,* February 25, 2005, 21 (in Yiddish). My thanks to Chana Pollock for assistance with this translation.

18. "Jews around the Globe Celebrate Completion of Shas," in Dei'ah veDibur Information and Insight: A Window in the Chareidi World, March 9, 2005, http://chareidi/shemayisrael.com/archives5765/PKD65features.htm. For an insightful ethnographic account of the events of the Ninth Siyum haShas, held in 1990, see Samuel C. Heilman, "The Ninth Siyum haShas at Madison Square Garden: Contra-acculturation in American Life," in *The Americanization of the Jews,* ed. Robert M. Seltzer and Norman J. Cohen (New York: New York University Press, 1995), 311–18.

19. As detailed by Berger, "English Talmud."

20. Jonathan Rosenblum, "Technology in Torah's Service," *Hamodia,* February 16, 2005, www.jewishmediaresources.com/pfarticle.php?id=808.

21. Among the most popular Web sites are www.E-daf.com and http://dafyomi.org.

22. For details on these and other examples of the roughly 120 educational software titles produced by TES, see www.jewishsoftware.com, accessed February 25, 2009.

23. See Alex Mindlin, "2,000 Torah Tapes, or One Loaded iPod," *New York Times,* March 17, 2005, www.nytimes.com/2005/03/17/technology/circuits/17tora.html?scp=2&sq=2%2C000+Torah+Tapes&st=nyt. Further details about the ShasPod are available on the company's Web site, www.shaspods.com.

24. *The Eleventh Siyum haShas Interactive 5 CD-ROM Set* (New York: AD Publishers, 2005). My transcription.

25. Nosson Scherman and Nesanel Kasnett, "The Schottenstein Edition of the Babylonian Talmud: The Next Stage in Talmudic Elucidation," in S. Mintz and Goldstein, *Printing the Talmud*, 161.

26. Originally constructed in 1939 for the World's Fair, the Hilton is New York's largest hotel, located in the opulent heart of midtown Manhattan.

27. See Pierre Bourdieu, *The Field of Cultural Production: Essays on Art and Literature* (New York: Columbia University Press, 1993), 81 and passim.

28. S. Mintz and Goldstein, *Printing the Talmud.*

29. For details, see "Printing the Talmud," *Art Daily,* April 24, 2005, www .artdaily.com/indexv5.asp?int_sec=2&int_new=13377.

30. Silvia A. Herskowitz, preface to S. Mintz and Goldstein, *Printing the Talmud,* xi.

31. On the topic of museum displays, see Barbara Kirshenblatt-Gimblett, *Destination Culture: Tourism, Museums, and Heritage* (Berkeley: University of California Press, 1998), 17–78. We shall have occasion in Chapter 4 to discuss further the ways ArtScroll books, as material artifacts, participate in the circulation of meanings and practices that extend beyond the discursive surface of the texts themselves, as I have only begun to intimate here.

32. The story is further complicated by the fact that Jerome Schottenstein, in whose memory the Schottenstein family dedicated their sponsorship of the ArtScroll Talmud, had also served as a member of the board of trustees of Yeshiva University. This helps to remind us of the complex mediating role played by financial patrons such as the Schottenstein family, who presumably helped to broker a relationship between ArtScroll and the museum, and whose multiple attachments epitomized the new conditions of collaboration that have increasingly blurred the distinction between the "right" and "left" wings of Orthodox Judaism. This is a point to which I shall return presently.

33. On these terms, Haredi Jews have been inscribed—whether for good or ill—into larger historical and sociological narratives about the rise of religious fundamentalisms in the modern world. This is not the place, however, to review and assess the extensive literature concerning Haredism as a form of religious fundamentalism (if indeed such a thing as "fundamentalism" exists outside the context of the few Christian communities that explicitly identify themselves as such). Elsewhere, I have tried to suggest some lines of critique that might contribute to that debate. See Jeremy Stolow, "Here (We) Are the *Haredim:* Intertextuality and the Voice of Authority in the Representation of a Religious Fundamentalist Movement," in *The Invention of Religion: Rethinking Belief and Politics in History,* ed. Derek Peterson and Darren Walhof (New Brunswick: Rutgers University Press, 2002), 59–76.

34. See, *inter alia*, Etan Diamond, *And I Will Dwell in Their Midst: Orthodox Jews in Suburbia* (Chapel Hill: University of North Carolina Press, 2000); Yosseph Shilhav, "The Haredi Ghetto," *Contemporary Jewry* 10, no. 2 (1989): 51–64; Emmanuel Sivan, "The Enclave Culture," in *Fundamentalism Comprehended*, ed. Martin E. Marty and R. Scott Appleby (Chicago: University of Chicago Press, 1995), 11–63.

35. The notion of a *she'erit yisrael* (remnant of Israel) or *she'erit Yoseph* (remnant of Joseph) can be traced back to the prophecy in the Book of Amos (5:15, 9:8–15) where God announces his determination to annihilate all sinners and build a new kingdom with only a remnant of righteous and repentant Jews.

36. For further discussion of the Haredi impact on educational institutions in American Orthodox Jewish society, especially Jewish day schools, see Heilman, *Sliding to the Right*, 84–126; Jack Wertheimer, "Jewish Education in the United States: Recent Trends and Issues," *American Jewish Year Book* (1999): 52–59. On the history of the divide between "cosmopolitans" and "parochials" that informs the Haredi-modern Orthodox tension, see Samuel C. Heilman and Steven Cohen, *Cosmopolitans and Parochials: Modern Orthodox Jews in America* (Chicago: University of Chicago Press, 1989).

37. The relationship of the Haredi community with the modern Israeli nation-state, and with the very idea of the "promised land," is shaped by a complex history of competing narratives about the cosmic, political, and cultural significance of exile, as well as differing patterns of strategic alliance with (and at times struggles against) religious Zionists and involvement in Israeli institutions, including representation in governmental bodies, schools, welfare agencies, and even military service. For general treatments, see, *inter alia*, El-Or, *Educated and Ignorant;* Samuel C. Heilman and Menachem Friedman, "Religious Fundamentalism and Religious Jews: The Case of the Haredim," in *Fundamentalisms Observed*, ed. Martin E. Marty and R. Scott Appleby (Chicago: University of Chicago Press, 1991), 197–264; David Lehmann and Batia Siebzehner, *Remaking Israeli Judaism: The Challenge of Shas* (Oxford: Oxford University Press, 2006); Aviezer Ravitzky, *Messianism, Zionism, and Jewish Religious Radicalism* (Chicago: University of Chicago Press, 1996); Nurit Stadler, *Yeshiva Fundamentalism: Piety, Gender, and Resistance in the Ultra-Orthodox World* (New York: New York University Press, 2008). On the economic dependence of the Haredi community on the Israeli state, see Eli Berman, "Sect, Subsidy and Sacrifice: An Economist's View of Ultra-Orthodox Jews," *Quarterly Journal of Economics* 115, no. 3 (2000): 905–53. On the relationship between Israeli Haredim and the Israeli military and state security apparatus, see Nurit Stadler and Eyal Ben-Ari, "Other-Worldly Soldiers? Ultra-Orthodox Views of Military Service in Contemporary Israel," *Israel Affairs* 9, no. 4 (2003): 17–48; Nurit Stadler, Eyal Ben-Ari, and Einat Mesterman, "Terror, Aid, and Organization: The

Haredi Disaster Victim Identification Teams (ZAKA) in Israel," *Anthropological Quarterly* 78, no. 3 (2005): 619–51.

Although it is ultimately impossible to fully disentangle Haredi involvements in Israeli public life from their situation in the diaspora, the focus of this study is on the latter case, and particularly on the English-speaking Jewish diaspora, as I elaborate here and in Chapter 2.

38. See Salo Wittmayer Baron, "Ghetto and Emancipation: Shall We Revise the Traditional View?" *Menorah Journal* 14, no. 6 (1928): 515–26; Jacob Katz, *Tradition and Crisis: Jewish Society at the End of the Middle Ages* (New York: Schocken Books, 1993). On epistolary networks and other communications systems that interlinked *kehilot* in medieval European society, see Manache, *Communication*, 93–140 and passim.

39. Nineteenth-century Jewish modernization was shaped by considerable differences among national and regional contexts, competing political programs of assimilation and dissimilation, and gender-, class-, and cohort-specific experiences, a full accounting of which is far beyond the means of this study. With regard to experiences of Ashkenazi European Jews during these changes, exemplary studies include Salo Wittmayer Baron, *The Russian Jew under Tsars and Soviets*, 2nd rev. ed. (New York: Macmillan, 1976); Jonathan Frankel and Steven J. Zipperstein, eds., *Assimilation and Community: The Jews in Nineteenth-Century Europe* (Cambridge: Cambridge University Press, 1992); Paula Hyman, *Gender and Assimilation in Modern Jewish History: The Roles and Representation of Women* (Seattle: University of Washington Press, 1995); Michael Meyer, *Response to Modernity: A History of the Reform Movement in Judaism* (Detroit: Wayne State University Press, 1988).

The history of the "encounter with modernity" among non-Ashkenazi Jews—the Sephardim and the Mizrahim, living in such disparate locales as the Balkans, Asia Minor, North Africa, the Arabian Peninsula, and western Asia—falls outside the purview of the present study. This is because, when it comes to examining the English-speaking reading public of texts such as those produced by ArtScroll, it is impossible to ignore the fact that the participants in this cultural field are predominantly of Ashkenazi heritage. Moreover, it has been argued that the forces that have made contemporary Haredism ideologically and institutionally effective are of distinctly Ashkenazi provenance. See, for instance, Friedman, "Life Tradition," 252. But cf. Lehmann and Siebzehner, *Remaking Israeli Judaism*, for a compelling recent account of Shas, a Sephardi Haredi political movement in Israel. On the history of Sephardi Jewry and its encounter with modernity, see Esther Benbassa and Aron Rodrigue, *Sephardi Jewry: A History of the Judeo-Spanish Community, 14th–20th Centuries* (Berkeley: University of California Press, 2000); Harvey Goldberg, ed., *Sephardi and Middle Eastern Jewries: History and Culture in the Modern Era* (Bloomington: Indiana University Press, 1996);

Aron Rodrigue, *Jews and Muslims: Images of Sephardi and Eastern Jewries in Modern Times* (Seattle: University of Washington Press, 2003).

40. Key figures cited as progenitors of contemporary Haredism include Rabbi Samson Raphael Hirsch (1808–88); Rabbi Moses Sofer (1762–1839), author of the *Hatam Sofer;* Rabbi Hayyim ben Isaac (1749–1821); Rabbi Israel Salanter (1810–82); Rabbi Israel Meir Kahan (1835–1933), author of the *Hafetz Hayyim;* and Rabbi Avraham Yeshayahu Karelitz (1878–1953), author of the *Hazon Ish.* A voluminous literature has elaborated the distinct theological and ideological positions of these leading rabbis, as well as their cultural influence both within and outside the Orthodox world. See, *inter alia,* Friedman, "Life Tradition," 235–55; Heilman and Friedman, "Religious Fundamentalism," 197–264; Helmreich, *World of the Yeshiva,* 1–51; Kaplan, *"Daas Torah,"* 1–60. See also Mordechai Breuer, *Modernity within Tradition: The Social History of Orthodox Jewry in Imperial Germany* (New York: Columbia University Press, 1992); Immanuel Etkes, *Israel Salanter and the Mussar Movement: Seeking the Torah of Truth* (Philadelphia: Jewish Publication Society of America, 1993); Menachem Friedman, "Haredim Confront the Modern City," *Studies in Contemporary Jewry* 2 (1986): 74–96; Menachem Friedman, "The Lost Kiddush Cup: Changes in Ashkenazic Haredi Culture—A Tradition in Crisis," in *The Uses of Tradition: Jewish Continuity in the Modern Era,* ed. Jack Wertheimer (New York: Jewish Theological Seminary of America, 1992), 175–86; Hillel Goldberg, *Israel Salanter: Text, Structure, Idea. The Ethics and Theology of an Early Psychologist of the Unconscious* (New York: Ktav Publications, 1982); Jacob Katz, "Towards a Biography of the Hatam Sofer," in *From East and West: Jews in a Changing Europe, 1750–1870,* ed. Frances Malino and David Sorkin (Oxford: Blackwell, 1990), 223–66; Norman Lamm, *Torah Lishmah: Torah for Torah's Sake in the Works of Rabbi Hayyim of Volozhin and His Contemporaries* (New York: Yeshiva University Press, 1989); Allan Nadler, *The Faith of the Mithnadgim: Rabbinic Responses to Hasidic Rapture* (Baltimore: Johns Hopkins University Press, 1997); Michael K. Silber, "The Emergence of Ultra-Orthodoxy: The Invention of a Tradition," in Wertheimer, *Uses of Tradition,* 23–84.

41. On the history of Agudat Israel, see Stolow, "Transnationalism," 120–25. See also Gershon Bacon, *The Politics of Tradition: Agudat Yisrael in Poland, 1916–1939* (Jerusalem: Magnes Press, 1996); Alan L. Mittelman, *The Politics of Torah: The Jewish Political Tradition and the Founding of Agudat Israel* (Albany: SUNY Press, 1996). For an insider's history of the movement, see Joseph Friedenson, *A History of Agudath Israel: The First Fifty Years* (New York: Agudath Israel of America Publications, 1970).

42. This is not to suggest that all Haredi Jews saw themselves as potential members of Agudat Israel. On the contrary, large factions within the Haredi world, such as the Satmar Hasidim, have remained quite distant from Agudat

Israel both ideologically and institutionally from its very inception. Other Haredim parted company with Agudat Israel after the founding of the state of Israel, citing the "dangerous compromises" to which the Agudah had fallen victim in its decision to participate in routine Israeli political life, for example.by joining coalition governments.

43. The complex philosophical dimensions of the idea of *galut* (exile) cannot here be given the attention they deserve. Among other things, it would be necessary to note how the actuality of Jewish dispersion has for centuries served as a basis for elaborating numerous theories about the meaning of God's covenant with the Jews, the conditions under which the *galut* will be reversed (i.e., the timing of the messianic redemption), the degree of responsibility of Jews for their own exile, and even the possibility that the state of *galut* refers to a cosmic imbalance rooted in the structure of divine revelation itself. For a useful survey of ancient, medieval, and modern definitions of *galut,* see Arnold Eisen, *Galut: Modern Jewish Reflection on Homelessness and Homecoming* (Bloomington: Indiana University Press, 1986). On the influence of Lurianic Kabbalah on the meaning of exile and the possible means of its reversal, see Gershom Scholem, *Major Trends in Jewish Mysticism* (New York: Schocken Books, 1946), 244–86; Gershom Scholem, *The Messianic Idea in Judaism, and Other Essays on Jewish Spirituality* (New York: Schocken Books, 1971), 1–48. For a provocative account of Jewish notions of exile and diaspora, especially in relation to contemporary postcolonial theory, see Jonathan Boyarin and Daniel Boyarin, *Powers of Diaspora: Two Essays on the Relevance of Jewish Culture* (Minneapolis: University of Minnesota Press, 2002).

44. On the pre-World War II history of Orthodox Jews in the United States, see Jeffrey S. Gurock, *American Jewish Orthodoxy in Historical Perspective* (Hoboken, NJ: Ktav Publishing House, 1996); Jenna Weissman Joselit, *New York's Jewish Jews: The Orthodox Community in the Interwar Years* (Bloomington: Indiana University Press, 1990).

45. Friedman, "Haredim Confront," 77; Freidman, "Life Tradition," 250; Heilman and Friedman, "Religious Fundamentalism," 206–11.

46. On the relationship of Haredim and the Holocaust, see Heilman, *Sliding to the Right,* 24–29; Menachem Friedman, "The Haredim and the Holocaust," *Jerusalem Quarterly* 53 (1990): 86–114.

47. Although, as Etan Diamond has shown, the Jewish drive toward suburbanization in major centers (such as Toronto, the focus of Diamond's study) has not precipitated a wholesale disaffiliation with Orthodoxy. On the contrary, suburbanization has enabled Orthodoxy to thrive in new ways. See Diamond, *And I Will Dwell.*

48. Heilman, *Sliding to the Right,* 37–47.

49. I say "disproportional" because, demographically, the Haredim have never represented more than a fraction (at the highest count, one-third) of diaspora

Orthodox Jews, who in turn represent not much more than 10 percent of the total population of diaspora Jews. For a detailed analysis of Haredi demography in the United States, see Heilman, *Sliding to the Right,* 62–77. To date, no comparably detailed demographic analysis has been performed for the British, Canadian, and Australian Jewish communities, although it is safe to assume that Haredi Jews nowhere represent more than a fraction of the Orthodox community.

50. On conditions of work and economic survival in the Haredi community in Israel, see Berman, "Sect, Subsidy and Sacrifice," 905–53. On Israeli Haredi women's participation in the labor market, see Orna Blumen, "Criss-Crossing Boundaries: Ultraorthodox Jewish Women Go to Work," *Gender, Place and Culture* 9, no. 2 (2002): 133–51. For a thorough discussion of the situation in the United States, see Heilman, *Sliding to the Right,* 140–79.

51. See especially Nurit Stadler, "Is Profane Work an Obstacle to Salvation? The Case of Ultra-Orthodox (Haredi) Jews in Contemporary Israel," *Sociology of Religion* 63, no. 4 (2002): 455–74.

52. Discussions about the "divine obligation" to "rescue" "lost" (i.e., non-Orthodox) Jews have been held for a long time within Haredi circles. Among other places, they can be found in the numerous articles devoted to *kiruv* and the status of *tinokos shenishbu* in the *Jewish Observer,* the monthly English-language organ of Agudath Israel of America. See, for instance, David Gottlieb, "The Trials and Triumphs on the Road to Teshuva," *Jewish Observer* 19, no. 4 (1986): 7–13; Baruch Horovitz, "The Days Have Come: A Time to Reach Out," *Jewish Observer* 14, no. 9 (1989): 8–9; Zvi Markowitz, "The Generation of 'Captive Children,' " *Jewish Observer* 1, no. 2 (1963): 15–20.

53. The pioneering work of the *kiruv* movement was initiated in the late 1960s in Jerusalem through the creation of yeshivot geared specifically to young male Jewish tourists (predominantly from the United States), who were considered potential *ba'alei teshuva* but who lacked the means to overcome their ignorance about and hesitancy to enter into the Orthodox world. These early efforts laid the groundwork for what has grown into an international network of yeshivot and related Jewish learning centers catering to *ba'alei teshuva,* such as Aish HaTorah and Ohr Somayach, both of which run schools in Israel and throughout the Jewish diaspora that seek to impart a greater understanding of Jewish heritage, cultural pride, and ultimately dedication to Haredi-defined standards of observance of Jewish law. For details, see Aaron Tapper, "The 'Cult' of Aish Hatorah: Ba'alei Teshuva and the New Religious Movement Phenomenon," *Jewish Journal of Sociology* 44, no. 1/2 (2002): 5–29. Other major *kiruv* organizations include the Central Forum for Worldwide Jewish Outreach, Project Seed, the Association of Jewish Outreach Professionals, and the National Jewish Outreach Program. But the single largest *kiruv* network is doubtlessly the one managed by the Habad-Lubavitcher Hasidic group, which for decades has been

involved in a vast range of media-savvy outreach campaigns, in keeping with the movement's messianic mission to heal the Jewish nation and hasten the Redemption. On Habad's missionary work, see Menachem Friedman, "Habad as Messianic Fundamentalism: From Local Particularism to Universal Jewish Mission," in *Accounting for Fundamentalisms,* ed. Martin E. Marty and R. Scott Appleby (Chicago: University of Chicago Press, 1994), 328–57.

54. For studies of the rates of successful enactment of *teshuva* among non-Orthodox Jews and the dynamics of retention among such converts, see M. Herbert Danzger, *Returning to Tradition: The Contemporary Revival of Orthodox Judaism* (New Haven: Yale University Press, 1989); William Shaffir, "The Recruitment of Baalei Tshuvah in a Jerusalem Yeshiva," *Jewish Journal of Sociology* 25, no. 1 (1983): 33–46; William Shaffir, "Leaving the Ultra-Orthodox Fold: Haredi Jews Who Defected," *Jewish Journal of Sociology* 29, no. 2 (1987): 97–114.

55. Geertz, *Islam Observed,* 62, 69–74, 104–5. A strikingly similar account of the central, coordinating power of texts and their authorized interpreters is found in Brian Stock's account of eleventh- and twelfth-century western Europe, shaped by the formation of what Stock calls "textual communities." See Stock, *Implications of Literacy,* 88–91 and passim. These parallels between post-World War II Islamic and medieval Christian scholars serve to remind us that it would be at best hazardous to claim that the advent of scripturalism is a characteristic of modernizing societies. We are better served by trying to understand how, precisely, text-centrism is constituted in specific ways within each social context. This is certainly one of the goals of the present study.

56. Avrohom Katz, *Our Wondrous World: Wonders Hidden below the Surface* (Brooklyn, NY: ArtScroll/Mesorah Publications, 1999), xiii.

57. Quoted in Levy, "Our Torah, Your Torah," 180. Barry Levy has vociferous criticized this Judaicization of knowledge, with specific reference to the selection of commentaries in key religious works published by ArtScroll. He argues that ArtScroll's professed policy of citing only "traditional rabbinic sources" and excluding "untrustworthy" (i.e., "non-Jewish") sources ignores the fact that many Jewish sources themselves engaged with and depended upon non-Jewish texts, such as Josephus, who cited the Greek pagan Berosus, or Maimonides, who incorporated Aristotelian and neo-Platonic philosophy into his own work (139, 146–47, 155, 169–70, 174–75, 186–87).

58. Meir Zlotowitz, preface to *The Megillah: The Book of Esther. A New Translation with a Commentary Anthologized from Talmudic, Midrashic and Rabbinic Sources* (Brooklyn, NY: ArtScroll/Mesorah Publications, 1976), x, emphasis in original.

59. Jacob Katz, "*Da'at Torah*—The Unqualified Authority Claimed for Halakhists," *Jewish History* 11, no. 1 (1997): 43. See also Kaplan, *Daas Torah;* Lawrence Kaplan, "Rabbi Isaac Hutner's 'Daat Torah Perspective' on the Holocaust: A Critical Analysis," *Tradition* 18, no. 3 (1980): 235–48.

60. Heilman, *Sliding to the Right*, 136.

61. Strictly speaking, the yeshiva was not a nineteenth-century invention. Its basic structure was proclaimed as a revival of the academies of study that existed in antiquity, modeled in particular on the example of the yeshiva founded by Rabbi Yohanan ben Zakkai at Yavneh shortly after the destruction of Jerusalem in 70 CE. For a discussion of that academy, see Judah Goldin, "The Period of the Talmud," in *The Jews: Their History, Culture, and Religion*, vol. 1, ed. Louis Finkelstein (New York: Harper and Row, 1949), 146–52. A more immediate historical precedent is found in the circle of students of the renowned eighteenth-century scholar the Vilna Gaon (Rabbi Elijah ben Solomon Zalman, 1720–97). Nevertheless, the Volozhin yeshiva is distinguished by its unprecedented organizational features, requiring separate analytical treatment.

62. For details, see Lamm, *Torah Lishmah;* Nadler, *Faith of the Mithnadgim.*

63. Admittedly, this is a simplification of the complex and highly variegated relations of influence and intellectual exchange between local centers of authority and supralocal intellectual or administrative centers throughout Jewish history, as noted by Salo Wittmayer Baron, "Emphases in Jewish History," *Jewish Social Studies* 1, no. 1 (1939): 33. Jacob Katz has argued that the geographical spread of institutions of higher education in medieval European Jewish society was always *translocal:* ambitious or bright students often traveled great distances to study with noted Talmudic masters. Such arrangements required considerable communal and institutional support for the needs of the out-of-town students. As such, many schools were regulated by supracommunal institutions that raised funds, defined standards, and systematized the manner in which students would take up residence. See J. Katz, *Tradition and Crisis*, 164–66. What appears to set the Volozhin-type yeshiva apart from these earlier arrangements was its size and scale of operation. The nineteenth-century yeshivot could not depend on the financial resources of their immediate communities and by that token were all the less beholden to the prerogatives of local governing bodies.

64. *Heder* education consisted of learning to read the weekly portions of the Torah, translating them into the vernacular (for many European Jews, Yiddish), and mastering Rashi's commentary (the most familiar rabbinic interpretation). Only a small fraction of boys would be expected to progress to intensive Talmud study in advanced academies of learning. For details, see Shaul Stampfer, "*Heder* Study, Knowledge of Torah, and the Maintenance of Social Stratification in Traditional East European Jewish Society," *Studies in Jewish Education* 3 (1988): 271–89; Shaul Stampfer, "What Did 'Knowing Hebrew' Mean in Eastern Europe?" in *Hebrew in Ashkenaz: A Language in Exile*, ed. Lewis Glinert (Oxford: Oxford University Press, 1993), 129–40.

Jewish girls, for their part, were traditionally exempted from Talmud study and encouraged to focus instead on popular texts written in the vernacular. A prominent example of the latter was the *Tse'ena Urena*, a Yiddish text consisting of a free retelling of *aggadic* material. See Chava Weissler, *Voices of the Matriarchs: Listening to the Prayers of Early Modern Jewish Women* (Boston: Beacon Press, 1999). A common interpretation of this gendered hierarchy of educational practices is based on a selective reading of canonical sources, which putatively declare women to be "unfit" for Torah study. One frequently cited passage is from the Bablyonian Talmud (Sota 20a): "Anyone who teaches his daughter Torah taught her *tiflut* [indecency, folly, or pointless behavior]," quoted in Shaul Stampfer, "Gender Differentiation and Education of the Jewish Woman in Nineteenth-Century Eastern Europe," *Polin: A Journal of Polish-Jewish Studies* 7 (1992): 64. See also El-Or, *Educated and Ignorant,* 66–77. Daniel Boyarin, however, has challenged the assumption that canonical sources unequivocally barred women from access to religious study, offering instead a more complex reading of the dynamics of gender difference and power in canonical Jewish sources. See Daniel Boyarin, *Unheroic Conduct: The Rise of Heterosexuality and the Invention of the Jewish Man* (Berkeley: University of California Press, 2006), 152ff.

65. Friedman, "Haredim Confront," 77–80; Friedman, "Life Tradition," 236–42.

66. Friedman, "Haredim Confront," 80.

67. J. Katz, *Tradition and Crisis,* 66; Stampfer, "What Did 'Knowing Hebrew' Mean," 134.

68. This included yeshivot established at Minsk, Radin, Telshe, Slabodka, Slutsk, Lomza, Eyshishok, Kamenetz, and Nevardok, and further afield. For details, see Shaul Stampfer, "Hungarian Yeshivot, Lithuanian Yeshivot, and Joseph Ben-David," *Jewish History* 11, no. 1 (1997): 131–41.

69. Some of the most significant and influential of the yeshivot established in the post-World War II period include Mesivta Tifereth Jerusalem (in the Lower East Side of Manhattan, NY), Yeshiva Torah Vodath (in Brooklyn), the Yeshiva Gedolah (in Monsey, NY), the Beth Medrah Govohah (in Lakewood, NJ), the Telshe Yeshiva (in Wickliff, OH), the Mir Yeshiva (in Jerusalem), and the Ponevezh Yeshiva (in B'nei Brak, Tel Aviv). For details on these and other Haredi yeshivot in the United States, see Helmreich, *World of the Yeshiva,* 26–51.

70. For a general treatment of Haredi education in Israel, see Michael Rozenak, "Jewish Fundamentalism in Israeli Education," in *Fundamentalisms and Society: Reclaiming the Sciences, the Family, and Education,* ed. Martin E. Marty and R. Scott Appleby (Chicago: University of Chicago Press, 1993), 374–413. On adult education for Haredi women in Israel, see El-Or, *Educated and Ignorant.*

71. Soloveitchik, "Rupture and Reconstruction," 73.

72. For a full list of titles, see www.artscroll.com. I shall return to the topic of "codes" in greater depth in Chapter 3. At that time, we shall see that they do not so straightforwardly carry out the work of regulating everyday behaviors that is implied here.

73. Soloveitchik, "Rupture and Reconstruction," 67.

74. B. T. Berachot 45b, quoted in Heilman, *Sliding to the Right,* 136. One might further turn to the debates in Jewish antiquity regarding the legitimacy of written as opposed to memorized texts, most famously in the case of debates over the transcription of the Oral Law (Talmud). Talya Fishman has likewise pointed to medieval European Jewish society as another instance of a time and place in which the status and function of the written word underwent significant change. See Talya Fishman, "Rhineland Pietist Approaches to Prayer and the Textualization of Rabbinic Culture in Medieval Northern Europe," *Jewish Studies Quarterly* 11, no. 4 (2004): 313–31; Talya Fishman, "The Rhineland Pietists' Sacralization of Oral Torah," *Jewish Quarterly Review* 96, no. 1 (2006): 9–16. See also Stern, "First Jewish Books," 163–202.

75. Heilman, *Sliding to the Right,* 132.

76. Soloveitchik, "Rupture and Reconstruction," 68, 83–84. See also the section "Religion in Print," in the Introduction, above.

77. Heilman, *Sliding to the Right,* 137.

78. See Manache, *Communication.*

79. Hillel Goldberg, "Review of Israeli Intellectual Life: Evaluating the Book-Publishing Explosion," *Tradition* 19, no. 2 (1981): 164f.

80. The rapid growth of Hasidic literary enterprises across eastern Europe provides one useful measure, with the publication of rebbes' biographies, apothegms, and other works. See Glenn Dynner, *Men of Silk: The Hasidic Conquest of Polish Jewish Society* (Oxford: Oxford University Press, 2006), 197–226; Zeev Gries, "The Hasidic Managing Editor as an Agent of Culture," in *Hasidism Reappraised,* ed. Ada Rapaport-Albert (London: Littman Library of Jewish Civilization, 1996), 141–55.

81. Hillel Goldberg, "Review," 168.

82. Ibid., 166. A striking example is Otzar Hahochma, a virtual library of over twenty-three thousand digitally reproduced "Torah books," including a vast list of ancient and rare manuscripts. Roughly fifteen thousand of the texts in this electronic database are keyword searchable. See www.otzar.biz/index_e .php, accessed February 25, 2009. Another important digital library is the Bibliography of the Hebrew Book, claiming to cover over 90 percent of books printed in the Hebrew language between 1470 and 1960: www.hebrew-bibliography .com/, accessed February 25, 2009. See also the Responsa Project, a searchable, hypertexted database containing all the major Jewish sacred texts, managed by Bar Ilan University in Israel: www.biu.ac.il/jh/Responsa/.

Hillel Goldberg insightfully attributes one of the motivating factors for such initiatives to the specific cultural conditions of post-World War II Jewry, specifically to the aftermath of the Holocaust, when "many private and public collections of Jewish books and manuscripts were burned." This fueled "an enormous desire to reprint every manuscript or rare volume for which financing could be found. What is more, notes of, and even memories of, lectures *(shiurim)* by *rashei yeshivot* [headmasters] found their way into print. *Seforim* of all sorts flooded bookstores. There was, and there remains, the strong feeling that every manuscript of some worth must be printed, for no one knows whether now is the last chance or whether the urge to remember will recede." Hillel Goldberg, "Review," 165.

83. Heilman, *Sliding to the Right,* 138.

84. Quoted in Kaplan, *"Daas Torah,"* 8.

85. On the rise of visibility as a performative principle in modern, mediated public spheres, see John B. Thompson, "The New Visibility," *Theory, Culture and Society* 22, no. 6 (2005): 31–51. On the problematization of "attention" and the constitution of attentive subjects as crucial sites of disciplinary power and knowledge in such public arenas, see Jonathan Crary, *Suspensions of Perception: Attention, Spectacle, and Modern Culture* (Cambridge, MA: MIT Press, 1999).

86. David Mykoff, "Are We Preparing Torah Communicators? Salesman or Sage—Who Will They Listen To?" *Jewish Observer* 4, no. 10 (1968): 3–4.

87. Avi Shafran, "Seizing the Silver Lining: Opportunity in the Pluralism Controversy Raging in Israel and America," *Jewish Observer* 31, no. 1 (1998): 7. See also Nahum Duker, "Legators and Heirs," *Jewish Observer* 21, no. 9 (1988): 30.

88. Nisson Wolpin, "Assignment: Covering Page One," *Jewish Observer* 16, no. 2 (1988): 33.

89. It is significant that fixed codices of Jewish law that appeared in the sixteenth century, such as the Zohar, Joseph Karo's Shulhan Arukh, and Moshe Isserles' Torat ha-Hattat, were explicitly legitimated by their authors as necessary responses to the "proliferation of books," and consequently the spread of superficial halakhic opinions, once printed works began to fall into the hands of those without the requisite interpretive expertise. See Halbertal, *People of the Book,* 118, 164.

90. In Poland, at the behest of commanding Orthodox figures like the Gerer Rebbe, newspapers such as *Dos Yidishe Vort* (starting in 1916), *Der Yid* (1919–29), and *Dos Yidishe Togblat* (1929–39) appeared and were consumed in quantities that rivaled any of their secular counterparts, presenting an "Orthodox viewpoint" on current events and issues of the day. Similar periodicals proliferated across Europe: *Der Heint* (Riga), *Dos Vort* (Vilna), *Der Israelit* and *Nachlas Zvi* (Germany), and the *Yiddishe Presse* (Vienna). For details, see Andrzej Paczkowski, "The Jewish Press in the Political Life of the Second Republic," *Polin: Studies in Polish Jewry* 8 (1994): 176–93; C. Shmeruk, "The Yiddish Press in Eastern Europe," *Jewish Quarterly* 33, no. 1 (1986): 24–28. See also Alan Mintz and David Roskies, eds., "The Role of Periodicals in the Formation of Modern Jewish Identity," special issue, *Prooftexts: A Journal of Jewish Literary History,* 15, no. 1 (1995).

91. It is, of course, misleading to refer here to a single, homogeneous Orthodox reading public. This is evident in the structure of the book-publishing industry but even more, perhaps, in the existence of multiple, competing Orthodox

newspapers and their distinct readerships. Just to take the case of religious news-papers in Israel, in addition to the larger dailies, *Hamodia* (the organ of Agudat Israel in Israel) and *Yeted Neeman,* there are a plethora of minor periodicals, each identified with distinct sectors of the Haredi community. These include *Hamahaneh Haharedi* (the weekly of the Belz Hasidim), *Hahomah* (identified with the *Neturei Karta*), *Kfar Habad* (the organ of Habad-Lubavitcher Hasidim), and *Az Nidberu* (the paper of the Vishnitz Hasidim). On the rise of the Haredi press in Israel, see Amnon Levi, "The *Haredi* Press and Secular Society," in *Religious and Secular: Conflict and Accommodation between Jews in Israel,* ed. Charles Liebman (Jerusalem: Keter Publishing House, 1990), 21–44; M. Michelson, "The Ultra-Orthodox Press in Israel," *Qesher* 8 (November 1990): 12e–21e.

2. ARTSCROLL'S PUBLIC LIFE

1. Toronto interviewee, pers. comm., October 2002.

2. Nosson Scherman, *The Complete ArtScroll Siddur: Weekday/Sabbath/Festival Edition. Nusach Ashkenaz* (Brooklyn, NY: ArtScroll/Mesorah Publications, 1984); Susie Fishbein, *Kosher by Design: Picture Perfect Food for the Holidays and Every Day* (Brooklyn, NY: ArtScroll/Mesorah Publications, 2002); Nosson Scherman, *The Stone Edition of the Tanach: Torah/Prophets/Writings: The Twenty-Four Books of the Bible Newly Translated and Annotated* (Brooklyn, NY: ArtScroll/Mesorah Publications, 1996); Nosson Scherman, *The Stone Edition of the Chumash: The Torah, Haftaros, and Five Megillos, with a Commentary Anthologized from the Rabbinic Writings* (Brooklyn, NY: ArtScroll/Mesorah Publications, 1993).

3. According to Bakhtin, every utterance, including a written text, is consti-tuted by its "quality of being directed to someone, its *addressivity.* . . . Each speech genre in each area of speech communication has its own typical concep-tion of the addressee, and this defines it as a genre." Mikhail M. Bakhtin, *Speech Genres and Other Late Essays,* ed. Caryl Emerson and Michael Holquist (Austin: University of Texas Press, 1986), 94–95. Bakhtin defines speech genres as hetero-geneous (but nonetheless conventionalized) ways of constituting the world through language, such as gossip, military commands, political speeches, scientific and professional jargons, and so on. They consist of relatively stable categories of utterances "knit together with specific points of view, specific approaches, forms of thinking, nuances and accents." Mikhail M. Bakhtin, *The Dialogic Imagination* (Austin: University of Texas Press, 1981), 289. Speech genres are inherently collec-tive in character, although they are not reducible to specific social groups per se. As Bakhtin puts it, speech genres are "the drive belts from the history of society to the history of language" (*Speech Genres,* 65). They are, in other words, *mediating* structures between social formations and the specific signifying practices in which the members of those social formations engage.

4. Bourdieu, *Field of Cultural Production,* 79.

5. The term *epitext* is derived from Gérard Genette, *Paratexts: Thresholds of Interpretation* (Cambridge: Cambridge University Press, 1997), 344–403. According to Genette, an epitext is any of the category of written materials that accompany or are related to a given text but are physically removed from it, as in the case of book reviews, advertisements, inventory reports, authors' diaries, corrections for manuscript proofs, etc.

6. On ancient Jewish memory and oral preservation of texts, see Saul Lieberman, "The Publication of the *Mishnah*," in *Hellenism in Jewish Palestine*, 83–99. On the textualization (and consequent homogenization) of Jewish prayer, beginning with the redaction of the first prayer books in the ninth and tenth centuries CE, see Stefan Reif, *Judaism and Hebrew Prayer: New Perspectives on Jewish Liturgical History* (Cambridge: Cambridge University Press, 1993), 122–51.

7. The terms *established, authorized, official,* and *standard* must be used with caution here, since there are no universally recognized mechanisms for asserting such categories, as in the case, say, of the Roman Catholic Church. This is especially relevant for Orthodox Judaism. One of the striking features of Table 1 is that, despite their smaller numbers, Orthodox communities are divided into more umbrella organizations than their Conservative and Reform counterparts, and there are also more "independent," unaffiliated synagogues in the Orthodox camp. This discrepancy indicates a higher degree of competition and flux in the recognition of religious authority among Orthodox Jews, and also a stronger attachment to "minor" traditions of ritual and cultural practice, which in turn is reflected in the existence of a larger range of liturgical texts catering specifically to these discrepant Orthodox communities.

Lastly, we should note that in many synagogues—not just Orthodox ones—it is typical to find copies of more than one edition of liturgical works, both new and old (not least because of the complicated religious regulations surrounding sacred books, which cannot simply be destroyed or thrown away). Thus, even when a synagogue invests in the purchase of a new set of Siddurim or Chumashim, this does not automatically translate into its exclusive use in daily practice.

8. Philip Birnbaum, *Daily Prayer Book* (New York: Hebrew Publishing Co., 1949 [2nd ed., 1977]); Joseph H. Hertz, *The Pentateuch and Haftorahs: Hebrew Text, English Translation and Commentary,* 5 vols. (Oxford: Oxford University Press, 1929–36); Joseph H. Hertz, *The Authorised Daily Prayer Book of the United Hebrew Congregations of the British Empire, Revised Edition with Commentary* (London: Shapiro Vallentine, 1947); David de Sola Pool, *Siddur: The Traditional Prayer Book for Sabbath and Festivals* (New York: Behrman House, 1960); A. Cohen, ed., *The Soncino Chumash: The Five Books of Moses, with Haphtaroth* (Hindhead: Soncino Press, 1947 [rev. ed. 1983]).

9. I present this table with the following caveats. First, the distinctions I draw here between Haredi, Independent Orthodox, and Modern Orthodox are not

emic categories and are thus always contestable. Second, the sample is relatively small and therefore not amenable to hasty generalizations. I selected synagogues on the basis of their geographic location, size, age, and affiliation with governing bodies, with the aim of representing the breadth of the institutional Jewish community, but in no way should my selection be interpreted as a "comprehensive" sample. Finally, the data in this table present a synchronic snapshot of what is in fact a field undergoing rapid change. I do not doubt that subsequent surveys would present a different picture of the penetration of ArtScroll texts in the liturgical field of the three cities under examination—perhaps demonstrating an even tighter grip on the modern Orthodox community. Future research would also have to account for the growing popularity of ArtScroll's "Hebrew-only" editions among congregations across the English-speaking world.

10. These are features I shall examine in greater detail in Chapters 3 and 4.

11. David Lieber, *Etz Hayim: Torah and Commentary* (Philadelphia: Jewish Publication Society, in cooperation with the Rabbinical Assembly and the United Synagogue of Conservative Judaism, 2001); Reuven Hammer, *Or Hadash: Siddur Sim Shalom, with a New Commentary* (New York: Rabbinical Assembly/United Synagogue of Conservative Judaism, 2004); Elyse Frishman, *Mishkan T'filah: A Reform Siddur* (Cincinnati: Central Conference of American Rabbis Press, 2006).

Etz Hayim and *Or Hadash,* produced as joint ventures between the Rabbinical Assembly, the United Synagogue of Conservative Judaism, and the Jewish Publication Society, have been explicitly defined as measures aimed at curtailing the spread of ArtScroll books within the Conservative community. According to Rabbi Jerome Epstein, executive president of the United Synagogue, "Some [Conservative Jews] have felt that the ArtScroll really provided them with information that they needed. But its approach doesn't represent what we are or what we stand for." The recent texts were thus introduced as "Conservative alternatives" that would be able to "rival ArtScroll in its lucidity and comprehensiveness," a remarkable statement of concession to ArtScroll's influence in the larger liturgical field. All quotes from Ami Eden, "Conservatives Taking a Page from Orthodox Prayer Book," *Jewish Forward,* March 28, 2003, www.forward .com/articles/8465/.

Mishkan T'filah, produced under the auspices of the Central Conference of American Rabbis (CCAR), the principal organization of Reform rabbis in the United States, was introduced as the replacement the earlier, "standard" prayer books of Reform liturgy, *Siddur Tefilot Yisrael,* the "Union Prayer Book," and its successor, *Gates of Prayer.* See *Siddur Tefilot Yisrael: The Union Prayer Book,* ed. Central Conference of American Rabbis (Cincinnati: Central Conference of American Rabbis Press, 1895 [2nd rev. ed., 1940]); *Gates of Prayer: The New Union Prayerbook. Weekdays, Sabbaths, and Festivals Services and Prayers for Synagogue and Home,* ed. Chaim Stern (New York: Central Conference of American

Rabbis/Union of Liberal and Progressive Synagogues, London, 1975). It is striking that the new prayer book aims to reflect forms of ritual practice that, in the words of one (anonymous) CCAR representative, involve "more traditional, more participatory, and more tactile forms of worship," as well as a greater emphasis on being able to recite prayers in Hebrew, as opposed to English (pers. comm., March 2004). Unlike earlier Reform prayer books, *Mishkan T'filah* offers an abundance of instructional notes. As the CCAR representative explained, "Nowadays individuals want to have something that will provoke prayerful meditation. That opportunity is provided [in the new prayer book] on each facing page. There's also a horizontal line across the bottom of each page, which in some cases provides further instructional notes" (pers. comm., March 2004). While Reform authorities are loath to concede it, it is important to note here that many of *Mishkan T'filah*'s layout designs and instructional elements were pioneered by ArtScroll, and their adoption in a Reform prayer book sheds interesting light on the ways ArtScroll has influenced even Jewish communities that otherwise stand in stark ideological opposition to the former's "strict Orthodoxy." For further details on the release of the new Reform Siddur, see Laurie Goodstein, "In New Prayer Book, Signs of Broad Change," *New York Times,* September 3, 2007, www.nytimes.com/2007/09/03/us/03prayerbook.html.

12. The two latest "answers to ArtScroll" emerged in 2006 in the United Kingdom, with the release of Jonathan Sacks's *Authorised Daily Prayer Book of the United Hebrew Congregations of the Commonwealth of Nations: A New Translation and Commentary by Chief Rabbi Jonathan Sacks* (London: Harper-Collins, 2006), and most recently in 2009 in the United States and Canada, with the release of a modified version of Sacks's translation and commentary by the Jerusalem-based publisher Koren, in conjunction with the Orthodox Union: Jonathan Sacks, *The Koren Siddur: Hebrew and English Edition* (Jerusalem: Koren Publishers Jerusalem, 2009). In the British case, Sacks's new prayer book has been presented as a replacement for the "standard" Orthodox Jewish liturgical works for British congregations: Hertz, *Authorised Daily Prayer Book;* and S. Singer, *The Authorised Daily Prayer Book of the United Hebrew Congregations of the Commonwealth. Centenary Edition, with a New Translation and Introductions,* ed. Lord Immanuel Jakobovits (Cambridge: Cambridge University Press, 1992). With an explicit aim to recapture markets that have been "lost" to ArtScroll, the Sacks text contains abundant instructions and commentary, pronunciation guidelines, and a new translation in "more accessible" English—all of these being features for which ArtScroll is the acknowledged pioneer. The text has also been distributed together with a CD containing synagogue music and lectures by Rabbi Sacks on the meaning and nature of Jewish prayer. The *Koren Siddur,* for its part, combines the elegance of Sacks's translation and commentary—written from a Modern, not a Haredi Orthodox, perspective—with a sparse and aesthetically striking typography and layout, based on designs originally developed by

the publisher's founder, Eliyahu Koren (the German-born designer, noted for the creation of numerous prominent Israeli symbols, including the seal of the city of Jerusalem and Israel's first postage stamp, in addition to the Hebrew-language typefaces he developed for his own Bible and Siddur publications in the 1960s and 1970s). Unlike the standard edition of the ArtScroll Siddur, the *Koren Siddur* is also explicitly Zionist in tone, as evidenced by the inclusion of prayers for the state of Israel and its army. At the time of writing, it is impossible to determine whether this latest publication will succeed in displacing ArtScroll from its current position of dominance among Modern Orthodox congregations in the United States and Canada, although numerous observers are predicting that ArtScroll will experience a significant challenge in the coming years.

For details on the release and marketing of Sacks's prayer book in the United Kingdom, see "New Siddur Comes with CD," *United Synagogue,* December 8, 2006, www.theus.org.uk/the_united_synagogue/media_centre/press_coverage/archive/c-582/new-siddur-comes-with-cd/. For its reception in Australia, see "A New Siddur Reflects the Changing Times," *Australian Jewish News,* April 13, 2007, www.ajn.com.au/news/news.asp?pgID=2963. For readers' reviews posted on the U.K. version of the amazon.com Web site in the immediate aftermath of the Siddur's release, see www.amazon.co.uk/Hebrew-Daily-Prayer-Jonathan -Sacks/dp/0007200935, accessed January 6, 2008. For details on the release of the *Koren Siddur,* see Ben Harris, "ArtScroll Facing Challenge from Modern Orthodox," *JTA: The Global News Service of the Jewish People,* April 5, 2009, jta.org/news/article/2009/04/02/1004210/orthodox publisher-challenged-by-modern-orthodox; Raphael Ahren, "Storming the Siddur Scene," *Haaretz,* May 15, 2009, www.haaretz.com/hasen/spages/1084026.html; Joshua Friedman, "Prayer Type: How Eliyahu Koren Used Typography to Encourage a New Way to Pray," *Tablet,* June 30, 2009, www.tabletmag.com/life-and-religion/8297/prayer-type/.

13. London interviewee, pers. comm., June 2001.

14. Jules Harlow, *Siddur Sim Shalom: A Prayerbook for Shabbat, Festivals, and Weekdays* (New York: Rabbinical Assembly/United Synagogue of America, 1985 [2nd ed., 1998]); Hammer, *Or Hadash.*

15. New York interviewee, pers. comm., March 2004.

16. The political edge in these "switches" is further sharpened by the fact that acquisitions are often not the outcome of a collective decision-making process for the congregation as a whole but rather the result of a gift from an individual congregant.

17. This division was especially pronounced during my field research in the London Jewish community. ArtScroll enthusiasts were typically a generation younger than those who expressed opposition to the arrival of ArtScroll liturgical texts in their local communities. My older informants frequently decried ArtScroll as an unwelcome "Americanization" of traditions of ritual practice

local to British Orthodox Jews (a claim that was often based on little more than the knowledge that the publisher happens to be based in the United States), whereas those under forty frequently characterized ArtScroll books as "clearer," "better organized," and written in "modern language," in short, as a "breath of fresh air."

18. Toronto interviewee, pers. comm., January 2003.

19. The interaction of material and discursive registers of ArtScroll books will be analyzed further in Chapter 4.

20. The name of the prayer book Deborah was unable to recall was Harlow's *Siddur Sim Shalom,* the "official" liturgical text of Conservative Judaism, which had been commissioned by the Rabbinical Assembly of America as a replacement for the then-standard "Silverman" prayer book: Morris Silverman, *Weekday Prayer Book* (New York: Prayer Book Press, 1946). A year after my conversation with Deborah, the American Conservative movement issued its new prayer book, Hammer's *Or Hadash.*

21. ArtScroll is in the process of producing a French-language edition of their Talmud, directed by Rabbi Aharon Marciano and sponsored by the family of the late Edmond Safra, the French Jewish banker and philanthropist (at the time of writing, December 2009, fourteen volumes have appeared). The publisher has also recently issued Russian- and Spanish-language versions of *The Complete ArtScroll Siddur* (Ashkenazi ed.). In 2006, ArtScroll launched a massive advertising campaign in the Israeli press, as well as through direct mail, distributing over 120,000 brochures and promotional offerings of free copies of their new, "entirely Hebrew" Siddur, *Ner Naftoli.* According to one report, sales for ArtScroll's Hebrew-only works—in particular the Siddur and the Hebrew-only version of the *Schottenstein Talmud*—have been brisk, and the publisher has planned major advertising campaigns for the near future. See "ArtScroll Advertising Heavily in Eretz Yisroel [the Land of Israel]," *Yated Ne'eman,* May 17, 2006, Dei'ah veDibur: Information and Insight, http://chareidi.shemayisrael .com/archives5766/BHR66artscrll.htm.

22. New York interviewee, pers. comm., March 2004.

23. Bourdieu, *Field of Cultural Production,* 76–82 and passim.

24. In most cases, authors are affiliated with publishing houses only on the basis of contractual agreements (either by producing manuscripts that have been solicited by the publisher or by marketing their own, independently produced manuscripts), and some authors "belong" to more than one publisher. In the case of ArtScroll, a noted example is Rabbi Abraham J. Twerski, who is one of the publisher's best-selling authors, with over thirty books (loosely described as "self-help" works) on the ArtScroll booklist, but who has also published extensively with other trade presses, including St. Martin's Press, Henry Holt, Prentice Hall, Harper, and Macmillan. Rabbi Twerski's self-help writings will be examined in greater detail in Chapter 3.

25. Bourdieu, *Field of Cultural Production,* 53, 60, 83–84, 97–98, 106–8.

26. Ironically, this financial structure brings ArtScroll into closer alignment with many of the institutional publishers from which it seeks to distinguish itself, such as university presses. Unfortunately, however, the full details of these financial and legal arrangements are not publicly available and therefore are to some degree a matter of speculation. See the Introduction, note 41, above, for the scant available details concerning the finances and operating scale of the Mesorah Heritage Foundation.

27. This, loosely speaking, is the argument of Pierre Bourdieu's *Distinction: A Social Critique of the Judgement of Taste* (Cambridge, MA: Harvard University Press, 1984).

28. See, for instance, the blog What's Bothering ArtScroll?, http://elucidation -not-translation.blogspot.com/, which contains extensive discussions and debates about ArtScroll texts. Likewise, in the Internet-based encyclopedia Wikipedia, the entry for "ArtScroll" contains a very lengthy debate: http://en.wikipedia .org/wiki/Talk:ArtScroll, accessed February 25, 2009. See also the numerous entries relating to ArtScroll translations and commentaries in the Orthodox listserv Mail Jewish Home Page, http://mail-jewish.org/, accessed February 25, 2009. A keyword search with the term *ArtScroll* in the Mail Jewish archive produced over two hundred distinct discussion threads, spanning over fifteen years. Further examples of Internet-based forums for assessing ArtScroll can be found on the Web sites of major retail distributors, such as amazon.com (including the Canadian and British versions), where (often anonymous) readers post their own book reviews.

29. London interviewee, pers. comm., June 2001.

30. For the past several years, ArtScroll has been working to shift this balance of power by expanding its efforts at direct marketing through the Internet. Unfortunately, no reliable data are available to determine how successfully the publisher has been at generating sales to customers who would not have the opportunity to come into contact with specific ArtScroll titles by other means.

31. New York interviewee, pers. comm., March 2004.

32. Toronto interviewee, pers. comm., January 2002.

33. Fishbein, *Kosher by Design;* Berel Wein, *Triumph of Survival: The Story of the Jews in the Modern Era, 1650–1990* (Brooklyn, NY: Mesorah Publications/ Shaar Press, 1990); Berel Wein, *Herald of Destiny: The Story of the Jews in the Medieval Era, 750–1650* (Brooklyn, NY: Mesorah Publications/Shaar Press, 1993); Berel Wein, *Echoes of Glory: The Story of the Jews in the Classic Era, 350BCE–750CE* (Brooklyn, NY: Mesorah Publications/Shaar Press, 1995). Rabbi Twerski's self-help literature will be discussed in Chapter 3.

34. Likewise, in my field research, I have found that outside ArtScroll's "classics" (i.e., the canonical religious texts), most titles on the publisher's booklist are not systematically acquired by Jewish libraries (although a scattering of their

volumes can always be found) and they are rarely incorporated into the curriculum of Jewish day schools.

35. Nelson Barber, "The ArtScroll Revolution," *Judaica Book News* 19 (1989): 16.

36. The classic definition of *diglossia* is found in Charles Ferguson, "Diglossia," *Word* 15 (1959): 324–40. Max Weinreich pioneered the study of "internal bilingualism" in Ashkenazi Jewish society, on terms that sociolinguists would today characterize as diglossic. See Max Weinreich, "Internal Bilingualism in Ashkenaz," in *Voices from the Yiddish,* ed. Irving Howe and Eliezer Greenberg (New York: Schocken Books, 1975), 279–88.

In at least one scholarly tradition, *diglossia* refers, not to the coexistence of languages in their lexically and grammatically pure forms, but more broadly to the diverse speech situations and the patterns of flow and exchange that sustain the living threads of dialogue among social groups and in their use of different languages, argots, jargons, and other speech genres. Bakhtin's notion of "heteroglossia" provides an especially rich analytical framework for such an approach. See, e.g., Bakhtin, *Dialogic Imagination,* 271–72, 289–92, 328–42, 416; Bakhtin, *Speech Genres,* 78–79, 87–88. In a similar vein, the linguistic historian Henri Gobard speaks, not of diglossia, but of "tetraglossia," a hierarchical language system consisting of four functionally distinct groups: the vernacular (local, often only oral, and typically identified as "maternal"); the vehicular (the language of commerce and interaction with the state); the referential (the language of science and of literary expression); and the mythic (the language of sacred discourse, including prayer). See Henri Gobard, *L'aliénation linguistique: Analyse tétraglossique* (Paris: Flammarion, 1976), 31–51. While that study focuses on the particularities of French history, Gobard's model is productive for drawing attention to the relationships among linguistic form, user, and socio-spatial context that are found in all speech communities, including that of Jewish public culture.

37. For discussion of the relatively restricted use of modern Hebrew in the English-speaking world, both historically and today, see Michael Brown, "All, All Alone: The Hebrew Press in America from 1914 to 1924," *American Jewish History Quarterly* 59, no. 2 (1969): 139–78; Alan Mintz, introduction to *Hebrew in America: Perspectives and Prospects,* ed. Alan Mintz (Detroit: Wayne State University Press, 1993), 13–26; Gilead Morhag, "Language Is Not Enough," in Mintz, *Hebrew in America,* 187–208.

38. Israel Zinberg, *A History of Jewish Literature,* vol. 7, *Old Yiddish Literature from Its Origins to the Haskalah Period,* trans. Bernard Martin (Cincinnati: Hebrew Union College Press, 1975), 4–13.

39. *Leshon ha-kodesh* must not be confused with either classical or modern Hebrew. It consists of a distinctively postbiblical form of Hebrew, infused with Aramaic and ordered by specific traditions of composition, as found in the Talmud and other rabbinic writings. See Weinreich, "Internal Bilingualism," 279–88;

Stampfer, "*Heder* Study," 271–89; Stampfer, "Gender Differentiation," 63–87; Weissler, *Voices of the Matriarchs,* 51–65. See also Iris Parush, "The Politics of Literacy: Women and Foreign Languages in Jewish Society of 19th-Century Eastern Europe," *Modern Judaism* 15, no. 2 (1995): 183–206; Naomi Seidman, *A Marriage Made in Heaven: The Sexual Politics of Hebrew and Yiddish* (Berkeley: University of California Press, 1997), 1–39 and passim; Chava Weissler, " 'For Women and for Men Who Are Like Women': The Construction of Gender in Yiddish Devotional Literature," *Journal of Feminist Studies in Religion* 5, no. 2 (1989): 7–24.

40. We cannot allow ourselves to be misled here by the commonly invoked claim that Jews enjoyed a uniquely high rate of literacy, for instance, within medieval and early modern European society. While it is true that nearly all male Jews learned the Hebrew alphabet in the *heder* (a traditional elementary school) in order to fulfill their religious duties, and thus possessed at least a rudimentary mastery of *leshon ha-kodesh,* "reading *per se* did not always imply more than mechanical reading of a given text or guarantee a full comprehension." Parush, "Politics of Literacy," 185. See also Stampfer, "What Did 'Knowing Hebrew' Mean," 130–36.

41. The cultural devaluation/feminization of Yiddish was buttressed by the fact that, until the consolidation of the secular Zionist movement in the early twentieth century, women were expressly discouraged, when not directly prevented, from learning to read key rabbinic texts written in *leshon ha-kodesh,* most notably, the Talmud. Women were of course expected to learn how to pray in Hebrew, as well as to read biblical narratives, although such works were often glossed into Yiddish. See especially Weissler, *Voices of the Matriarchs.* The Yiddish works that proliferated in the nineteenth century—autobiographies and memoirs, belles lettres, novels, etc.—were consumed by a broad mass of readers, most of whom were in fact women. See Iris Parush, "Readers in Cameo: Women Readers in Jewish Society of Nineteenth-Century Eastern Europe," *Prooftexts: A Journal of Jewish Literary History* 14, no. 1 (1994): 13–16. For more extended treatment of the gender politics of Yiddish and modern Hebrew, see especially Seidman, *Marriage Made in Heaven.*

42. Quoted in Zinberg, *History of Jewish Literature,* 7:21–22. Zinberg further points out that "it was not the text of the Torah alone that the translators and interpreters explained. We know that already in the era of the Second Temple [i.e., ca. 400 BCE—70 CE] complete sermons filled with moral lessons and directions for proper conduct were gradually produced out of the 'explanation' of the Torah. Such sermons were given by the teachers and guides of the people on the Sabbath and festivals in the synagogues and houses of study" (24). The relationship Zinberg notes between translation and commentary, and the underlying assumptions about what constitutes "effective" pedagogy, will be examined in greater depth in Chapters 3 and 4 with reference to specific ArtScroll texts.

43. Ibid., 29–33.

44. The first English translation of a Siddur was published in London in 1738 by Gamaliel ben Pedahzur (probably a pseudonym). For details, see Adler, "Prayer Books." Other significant precedents to ArtScroll can be found in nineteenth-century Germany; see note 24 in the Introduction, above. More generally stated, we should recall that translation into vernacular is as old as Hebrew prayer itself and that its history is commensurate with the long process of regularization and codification that accompanied the transformation of oral traditions into textual forms. For detailed discussion of this history, see Reif, *Judaism and Hebrew Prayer,* 122–25 and passim.

45. Although a Jewish presence in the English-speaking world goes back several centuries, the crucial shifts occurred in successive waves of migration—especially, but not exclusively, to the United States—from the 1880s up to World War I and then again in the immediate aftermath of World War II. For a useful overview of the migratory wave of the 1880s, see David Berger, ed., *The Legacy of Jewish Migration: 1881 and Its Impact* (New York: Columbia University Press, 1983). For more recent developments, see Daniel Judah Elazar and Morton Weinfeld, eds., *Still Moving: Recent Jewish Migration in Comparative Perspective* (Edison, NJ: Transaction Publishers, 2000). For a serviceable history of Jewish immigration in the United States from the seventeenth to twentieth centuries, see Hasia Diner, *The Jews of the United States, 1654–2000* (Berkeley: University of California Press, 2004). On the history of Jewish immigration in England and Great Britain, see Todd Endelman, *The Jews of Britain, 1656–2000* (Berkeley: University of California Press, 2002); Lloyd Gartner, *The Jewish Immigrant in England, 1870–1914,* 3rd ed. (London: Vallentine Mitchell, 2001); David S. Katz, *The Jews in the History of England, 1485–1850* (Oxford: Oxford University Press, 1994). On Canada, see Irving Abella, *A Coat of Many Colours: Two Centuries of Jewish Life in Canada* (Toronto: Lester, 1990); Gerald Tulchinsky, *Taking Root: The Origins of the Canadian Jewish Community* (Hanover, NH: Brandeis University Press, 1993). On Australia, see Suzanne D. Rutland, *The Jews in Australia* (Cambridge: Cambridge University Press, 2006). On South Africa, see Milton Shain and Richard Mendelsohn, *Memories, Dreams, and Realities: Aspects of the South African Jewish Experience* (Johannesburg: Jonathan Ball, 2002). Finally, on the development of the Anglophone community in Israel, especially since the 1970s, see Bernard Spolksy, "English in Israel after Independence," in *Postimperial English: Status Change in Former British and American Colonies, 1940–1990,* ed. Joshua A. Fishman, Andrew W. Conrad, and Alma Rubal-Lopez (The Hague: Mouton de Gruyter, 1996), 535–56.

46. For a particularly insightful discussion of the history of these language politics, see Israel Bartal, "From Traditional Bilingualism to National Monolingualism," in *Hebrew in Ashkenaz: A Language in Exile,* ed. Lewis Glinert (Oxford: Oxford University Press, 1993), 141–50.

47. The important exception is the Haredi enclave, where Yiddish is still widely used for oral instruction in the yeshiva, as well as in family life and everyday labor and market transactions. See Lewis Glinert and Yosseph Shilhav, "Holy Land, Holy Language: A Study of an Ultraorthodox Jewish Ideology," *Language in Society* 20, no. 1 (1991): 59–86. But even in the Haredi community one can trace a growing use of English, including among Haredim in Israel. See, for instance, the trends analyzed in Simeon Baumel, "Teaching English in Israeli Haredi Schools," *Language Policy* 2, no. 1 (2003): 47–67; Sarah Bunin Benor, "*Talmid Chachams* and *Tsedeykeses:* Language, Learnedness, and Masculinity among Orthodox Jews," *Jewish Social Studies* 11, no. 1 (2004): 147–70.

48. Jeffrey Shandler, *Adventures in Yiddishland: Postvernacular Language and Culture* (Berkeley: University of California Press, 2006).

49. See, for instance, David Crystal, *English as a Global Language,* 2nd ed. (Cambridge: Cambridge University Press, 2003); Braj Kachru, "The Power and Politics of English," *World Englishes* 5, no. 2/3 (1986): 121–40; Alistair Pennycook, "Beyond Homogeny and Heterogeny: English as a Global and Worldly Language," in *The Politics of English as a World Language,* ed. C. Mair (Amsterdam: Rodopi, 2003), 3–17.

50. English-language Jewish publishing is much older than that, of course. See Jacobs, "Book Trade" and Jacobs, "Typography," for details on early presses in England and colonial America.

51. A further dimension to the story of Jewish uptake of English concerns the ways various Jewish communities have "indigenized" the language through specific styles of speech, idiolects, accents, etc. See, e.g., Sarah Bunin Benor, "Do American Jews Speak a 'Jewish Language'? A Model of Linguistic Distinctiveness," *Jewish Quarterly Review* 99, no. 2 (2009): 230–69.

52. Strictly speaking, the "traditional" diglossic organization of the Haredi enclave was based on *leshon ha-kodesh* for "official" texts and Yiddish for daily interactions and oral instruction. The growing presence of English has disrupted both "holy" and "vernacular" language use within the Haredi enclave as Yiddish has become increasingly marginalized in everyday life and as English translations of religious literature have become increasingly popular. Contemporary Haredi authorities thus struggle to contain the spread of English on both fronts, as noted by Baumel, "Teaching English," 47–67; Benor, "*Talmid Chachams,*" 147–70.

53. London interviewee, pers. comm., March 2001.

54. See, for example, Yoel Finkelman's insightful studies of Haredi adventure fiction and parenting guides: Yoel Finkelman, "Medium and Message in Contemporary Haredi Adventure Fiction," *Torah u-Maddah Journal* 13 (2005): 50–87; Yoel Finkelman, "Tradition and Innovation in American Haredi Parenting Literature," in *Innovation and Change in Jewish Education,* ed. David Zisenwine (Tel Aviv: Tel Aviv University Press, 2007), 37–61.

Among other things, Finkelman documents the complex dialectic of grassroots pressures and marketing initiatives that has fostered the growth of new literary genres within the Haredi community—such as adventure fiction—that emerged in the mid-1990s, with the growing popularity of authors such as Yair Weinstock, who first wrote in Hebrew and then was translated into English and published in the United States. Haredi publishers began to release such titles only when it became apparent that there was a viable market for such work, largely in response to pressure from readers, and in some cases in tension with opinions of rabbinic elites, who have tended to regard both the reading and writing of fiction as an "un-Jewish" activity. Many of the fans of Haredi adventure novels belong to the first generational cohort to have grown up on a steady diet of Haredi-oriented children's books (which first began to appear in the 1970s) and subsequently of Haredi "teen fiction," all of which laid the groundwork for their desire for "adult" fiction that nonetheless caters to their Haredi sensibilities. See Finkelman, "Medium and Message," 53–56.

55. Toronto interviewee, pers. comm., February 2003.

56. A large body of scholarship is devoted to *ba'alei teshuva* and the dynamics of "conversion" to Orthodox Judaism, both in Israel and in the Jewish diaspora. See, *inter alia,* Danzger, *Returning to Tradition;* Shaffir, "Recruitment of Baalei Tshuvah," 33–46; Shaffir, "Leaving the Ultra-Orthodox Fold," 97–114; Tapper, "'Cult' of Aish Hatorah," 5–29. See also Janet Aviad, *Return to Judaism: Religious Renewal in Israel* (Chicago: University of Chicago Press, 1983); Lynn Davidman, *Tradition in a Rootless World: Women Turn to Orthodox Judaism* (Berkeley: University of California Press, 1991); Debra Renee Kaufman, "Patriarchal Women: A Case Study of Newly Orthodox Jewish Women," *Symbolic Interaction* 12, no. 2 (1989): 299–314.

57. Rabbi Pini Dunner, pers. comm., July 2001. Rabbi Dunner retired from the synagogue in 2005. See the Saatchi Synagogue's Web site, www.coolshul .org, accessed February 25, 2009. For further analysis of the Saatchi Synagogue and its relationship to ArtScroll, see Jeremy Stolow, "Communicating Authority, Consuming Tradition: Jewish Orthodox Outreach Literature and Its Reading Public," in *Religion, Media, and the Public Sphere,* ed. Birgit Meyer and Annelies Moors (Bloomington: Indiana University Press, 2006), 73–90.

58. Toronto Interviewee, pers. comm., February 2003.

3. PRAYER BOOKS, COOKBOOKS, SELF-HELP BOOKS

The section epigraph is from Abraham Twerski, *Self-Improvement? I'm Jewish! Overcoming Self-Defeating Behavior* (Brooklyn, NY: ArtScroll/Mesorah Publications, 1995), 111.

1. Finkelman, "Medium and Message," 59.

2. Hence the etymological connections between *tradition* and *translation,* as well as *treason.* Note also the transitive dimensions of the Hebrew cognates for the word *tradition, mesorah* (as in the phrase *mesoret beyadam me'avotehem* [they possess a tradition from their ancestors]) and *kabbalah* (reception).

3. I am painting here with broad brush strokes an analytical approach to the invention of tradition that has been taken up, in different ways, by historians, sociologists and anthropologists of memory, and psychoanalysts, among others. See, *inter alia,* Maurice Halbwachs, *On Collective Memory,* ed. and trans. Lewis A. Coser (Chicago: University of Chicago Press, 1992); Eric Hobsbawm, "Inventing Traditions," in *The Invention of Tradition,* ed. Eric Hobsbawm and Terence Ranger (Cambridge: University of Cambridge Press, 1983), 1–14; Pierre Nora, "Between Memory and History," *Representation* 26 (1989): 7–25; Jean Starobinski, "The Idea of Nostalgia," *Diogenes* 55 (Summer 1966): 81–103; Jonathan Boyarin, ed., *Remapping Memory: The Politics of Timespace* (Minneapolis: University of Minnesota Press, 1992). With specific reference to Jewish memory and the Jewish past, see, *inter alia,* Israel Bartal, "True Knowledge and Wisdom: On Orthodox Historiography," *Studies in Contemporary Jewry* 10 (1994): 178–92; David N. Myers, *Re-inventing the Jewish Past: European Intellectuals and the Zionist Return to History* (Oxford: Oxford University Press, 1995); Yosef Haim Yerushalmi, *Zakhor: Jewish History and Jewish Memory,* 2nd ed. (New York: Schocken Books, 1989); Yael Zerubavel, *Recovered Roots: Collective Memory and the Making of Israeli National Tradition* (Chicago: University of Chicago Press, 1995).

4. Murray Friedman, "Understanding Jewish History," *Jewish Observer* 6, no. 5 (1970): 25.

5. I am indebted to Vanessa Ochs's insightful discussion of Jewish healing technologies, from amulets discussed in the Talmud to assisted reproductive technologies in contemporary Israel. See Vanessa Ochs, "Domesticating Healing Technologies, Making Them 'Jewish,'" unpublished ms., University of Virginia, 2007.

6. *Humra* (stringency) and *qulla* (leniency) together constitute a central, dynamic basis of halakhic interpretation, expressing a dialectical tension between the theoretical inclination to interpret legal codes without contradiction or compromise and the more practical need to temper religious stringency for the sake of social harmony and the everyday functioning of the local community. See Menachem Friedman, "Life Tradition," 236–39. See also Menachem Friedman, "The Market Model and Religious Radicalism," in *Jewish Fundamentalism in Comparative Perspective: Religion, Ideology, and the Crisis of Modernity,* ed. Lawrence J. Silberstein (New York: New York University Press, 1993), 196–99.

7. Haym Soloveitchik cautions that Jewish history has in fact seen a number of swings toward *humra,* or retreats into "the four cubits of the Halakhah" (i.e.,

a concentration on the controlling role of texts in social life), and he invokes as historical precedents the shift away from oral authority during the time of composition of the Mishneh Torah, the audit of contemporary practice in the late medieval period (and the dramatic swing toward stringency at that time), and similar trends within post-1492 Sephardic communities. See Soloveitchik, "Rupture and Reconstruction," 117 n. 40, cf. 110 n. 19. But although these historical moments of religious stringency are comparable, they are not identical, among other things because they are not based on a single, unchanging set of causes.

8. Sarah Epstein Weinstein, *Piety and Fanaticism: Rabbinic Criticism of Religious Stringency* (Northvale, NJ: Jason Aronson, 1997), 104–5.

9. Soloveitchik, "Rupture and Reconstruction," 72. See also Charles S. Liebman, "Extremism as a Religious Norm," *Journal for the Scientific Study of Religion* 22, no. 1 (1983): 75–86.

10. Nosson Scherman, *The Stone Edition of the Chumash: The Torah, Haftaros, and Five Megillos, with a Commentary Anthologized from the Rabbinic Writings* (Brooklyn, NY: ArtScroll/Mesorah Publications, 1993), xiii.

11. Written texts are almost invariably constituted as complex, compound discourses, combining a range of topics, communicative functions, referential and classificatory procedures, and literary conventions, and in this respect ArtScroll is no exception. The ArtScroll corpus is also internally differentiated by individual authorial styles and, in some cases, by the coordination of multiple authors and editors, as is most evident in the cases of compilation, translation, and presentation of "classic" works, such as Bibles, prayer books, and the Talmud. The table purports only to identify the dominant modes of address in the major literary genres represented on the ArtScroll booklist. These include *expository* genres (which logically order information to describe and explain a topic), *narrative* genres (which recount events unfolding over time), *procedural* genres (which outline the necessary steps for the performance of a given action), and *hortatory* genres (which issue commands, arguments, and expressions aimed at motivating the addressee to undertake action). My use of the terms *genre* and *mode of address* is meant to invoke the idea that discourses are shaped just as much by their content as by their orientation toward an imagined set of speakers. In this regard, see note 3 in Chapter 2, above, where I discuss the relevance of Bakhtin's notion of "speech genres."

12. Elsewhere, I have examined in detail ArtScroll's large corpus of historical works, including biographies, hagiographies, historical encyclopedias, memoirs, curriculum material, and other texts that deal with the Jewish past, not to mention ArtScroll's Bible and Chumash. See Jeremy Stolow, "Nation of Torah: Proselytism and the Politics of Historiography in a Religious Social Movement" (PhD diss., York University, 2000). For an analysis of Haredi adventure novels—in which ArtScroll has played a major role as the publisher of new au-

thors and the translators of Hebrew-language works prominent in Israel—see Finkelman, "Medium and Message," 50–87. For parenting advice manuals (again, well represented on the ArtScroll booklist), see Finkelman, "Tradition and Innovation," 37–61. Other genres published by ArtScroll—such as children's storybooks, fiction for young adults, popular science, Jewish holiday guides, reference works, and directories—have yet to receive the scholarly attention they deserve.

13. Diana Taylor, *The Archive and the Repertoire: Performing Cultural Memory in the Americas* (Durham: Duke University Press, 2003), 28–33.

14. To reiterate the argument made earlier in this book, I am not suggesting that ArtScroll's mode of address, let alone the "scripturalist" function of ArtScroll texts, is unprecedented in Jewish literary history. On the contrary, one finds many examples of code books, and other texts that "authorized" Jewish living, going back at least a millennium. I do contend, however, that the specific modes of address, the cultural contexts, and the performative function of ArtScroll scenarios are distinct from these earlier historical forms, as hopefully will become clearer in due course.

15. This is counting only English-language Siddurim (ArtScroll also produces French-, Spanish-, and Russian-language Siddurim), and only basic prayer books. Other liturgical works (e.g., the Makhzor, a special prayer book for High Holy Days of Rosh Hashanah and Yom Kippur, and the Hagaddah, the liturgical text used for the festival of Passover) also appear in multiple editions, in different sizes and bindings, with different types of translation, etc. For a full listing and descriptions of all these works, see www.artscroll.com.

16. Dovid Weinberger, Avrohom Biderman, and Nosson Scherman, *Siddur Ohel Sarah: The Klein Edition Women's Siddur,* Nusach Ashkenaz (Brooklyn, NY: ArtScroll/Mesorah Publications, 2005). The term *Korban Minchah* refers to "the prayerbook of the afternoon offering [in the Temple in Jerusalem]," and the term generally designates a "traditional" eastern European-style Siddur. ArtScroll's decision to release a Siddur designed specifically for women has been the subject of controversy, not least because the text purportedly emphasizes only the minimal requirements for women's participation in Jewish ritual life. Critical assessments of this latest offering from ArtScroll can thus be found in abundance in the Jewish blogosphere. For example, in the words of one critic, Rabbi Elli Fisher, "They've created an entirely new genre, an entirely new custom for women's prayer, and taken it upon themselves to present complex and disputed issues in a one-sided manner, ignoring age-old customs and halachic positions, and yet market the thing as though it's something that your *alter bubbe* [old grandmother] *davened* from." Elli Fisher, "The ArtScroll Women's Siddur: Men and Women, Dumb and Dumber," On the Contrary, July 18, 2005, http://adderabbi.blogspot.com/2005/07/artscroll-womens-siddur-men-and-women.html. For a summary of the controversies surrounding the publication

of *Siddur Ohel Sarah,* see Debra Nussbaum Cohen, "Feminists Object, but ArtScroll Rolls On," *Jewish Week,* November 10, 2007, www.thejewishweek.com/viewArticle/c36_a488/News/New_York.html.

17. For details on the history of Jewish prayer books, their composition, and the processes leading to their standardization, see especially Reif, *Judaism and Hebrew Prayer.*

18. Nosson Scherman, *The Complete ArtScroll Siddur: Weekday/Sabbath/Festival Edition. Nusach Ashkenaz* (Brooklyn, NY: ArtScroll/Mesorah Publications, 1984), 978–92.

19. I have already noted some of the most important precedents in the Introduction, notes 24 and 50.

20. Notably, the most common Siddurim used by English-speaking Orthodox Jews prior to ArtScroll, such as the Soncino and the Silverman, all cited a more diverse set of references and authoritative interpretations than what is found in the ArtScroll text. This shift is precisely one of the issues on which the charges of "Haredism," "fundamentalism," and "interpretive rigidity" have been based, as argued, for instance, by Barry Levy, "Judge Not a Book by Its Cover," *Tradition* 19, no. 1 (1981): 89–95; Levy, "Our Torah, Your Torah"; and Kaplan, *"Daas Torah,"* as well as numerous "amateur" assessors operating in the Jewish blogosphere (see Chapter 2, note 28, for representative examples).

21. Scherman, *Complete ArtScroll Siddur,* 2.

22. Ibid., 296.

23. Ibid., 979. The Shemoneh Esrei (the eighteen blessings), also referred to as the Amidah (standing prayer), is the central prayer of Jewish liturgy and must be recited at each prayer service of the day: in the morning (Shacharis), the afternoon (Minchah), and the evening (Ma'ariv).

24. Ibid., 296, emphasis in original.

25. Ibid., 978.

26. Nosson Scherman, pers. comm., February 2004.

27. New York interviewee, pers. comm., December 2003.

28. Toronto interviewee, pers. comm., February 2003.

29. B.T. Sotah 7.

30. Kitzur Shulhan Arukh 33:5, quoted in Gershon Appel, *The Concise Code of Jewish Law,* vol. 1 (New York: Ktav Publishing House, 1977), 128. Similarly, in the Talmud one finds the argument that even though "ignorant people" who attend religious services or a scholarly sermon on the Torah cannot enjoy all the fruits of Torah learning, their mere physical presence is a meritorious act (see, e.g., B.T. Berachot 6b). More generally stated, modes of participating in and experiencing religious ritual rarely hinge on questions of discursive intelligibility; it is more typical to characterize them in terms of their mysterious—and even inscrutable—emotional charge. This "classic" definition of ritual is found in Joachim Wach, *Understanding and Believing: Essays,* ed. Joseph Kitagawa

(New York: Harper and Row, 1967). See also Catherine Bell, *Ritual Theory, Ritual Practice* (Oxford: Oxford University Press, 1992).

31. Nosson Scherman, pers. comm., February 2004.

32. Meir Zlotowitz, pers. comm., February 2004.

33. Susie Fishbein, *Kosher by Design: Picture Perfect Food for the Holidays and Every Day* (Brooklyn, NY: ArtScroll/Mesorah Publications, 2002). To date, five more volumes in Fishbein's series have been published: *Kosher by Design Entertains: Fabulous Recipes for Parties and Every Day* (Brooklyn, NY: ArtScroll/Shaar Press, 2004); *Kosher by Design—Kids in the Kitchen* (Brooklyn, NY: ArtScroll/Shaar Press, 2005); *Kosher by Design, Short on Time: Fabulous Food Faster* (Brooklyn, NY: ArtScroll/Shaar Press, 2006); *Passover by Design* (Brooklyn, NY: ArtScroll/Shaar Press, 2008); *Kosher by Design Lightens Up* (Brooklyn, NY: ArtScroll/Shaar Press, 2008).

34. Within the first week of its publication, *Kosher by Design* had already sold twenty-four thousand copies, forcing ArtScroll to rush immediately to print a second run. By 2004, its sales surpassed the seventy thousand mark, a very high figure for the Jewish cookbook market (and even more remarkable for a text that is explicitly kosher). Fishbein's second cookbook, *Kosher by Design Entertains*, took only eight days after its release in 2004 to appear on amazon.com's Top 500 list. For details, see Gavriel Sanders, "Kosher Diva Outdoes Herself with Latest Offering," *Jewish World Review*, March 14, 2005, www.jewishworldreview.com/kosher/fishbein.php3.

To market *Kosher by Design* to Christian consumers (as an "authentic" representation of Jewish holiday food and its meaning), ArtScroll enlisted the Connecticut-based PR firm Martino & Binzer to attract attention among editors of national daily newspapers and through public book signings and cooking demonstrations, as well as to run advertising and promotionals on Christian cable television and at major conferences, such as the International Association of Christian Schools. The widespread availability of *Kosher by Design* on Christian booksellers' Web sites is one indicator of the success with which this text has "jumped tracks" into the non-Jewish book market. See, e.g., the advertisement posted on Dalton's Christian Books Web site, http://shop1.daltonschristianbooks.com/e/pdf/kosher/KosherAd.pdf, accessed August 30, 2005.

35. Fishbein, *Kosher by Design*, back cover.

36. The codification of culinary etiquette is quite old. In the European tradition, etiquette manuals can be found dating back to the sixteenth century, such as Erasmus's *De civilitate morum puerilium* [On Civility in Children] (1530), often cited as a progenitor of the genre. See Norbert Elias, *The Civilizing Process*, trans. Edmund Jephcott (Oxford: Blackwell, 1994), 42ff; Toby Miller and Alec McHoul, "Helping the Self," *Social Text* 57 (1998): 138–39; Cas Wouters, "Etiquette Books and Emotion Management in the Twentieth Century: Part One—The Integration of Social Classes," *Journal of Social History*

29, no. 1 (1995): 107–24. The tradition of European, and later American, Jewish writings on cooking and home management can be placed within this *longue durée* of authorizing and consecrating "good taste."

37. The term *popular religion* refers to one of a series of overlapping distinctions made between elite and popular, official and unofficial, religion as proclaimed (or prescribed) and religion as practiced. For a lucid analysis of these terms, see Stephen Sharot, *A Comparative Sociology of World Religions: Virtuosi, Priests, and Popular Religion* (New York: New York University Press, 2001), 14–16 and passim. For the purposes of this discussion, by *popular religion* I mean to refer to the overall complex of religious practices, habits, sensibilities, and ideas that represent local adaptations of a religious tradition (in this case, that of rabbinic Judaism) and that exist despite (and in certain respects also because of) the prescriptions of the elite.

38. Barbara Kirshenblatt-Gimblett, "Kitchen Judaism," in *Getting Comfortable in New York: The American Jewish Home, 1880–1950,* ed. Susan L. Braunstein and Jenna Weissman Joselit (Bloomington: Indiana University Press, 1991), 76–105. See also Barbara Kirshenblatt-Gimblett, "Playing to the Senses," *Performance Research* 4 (1999): 1–30.

39. There are in fact dozens of kosher cookbooks that are comparable to Fishbein's (although admittedly, few have enjoyed such public prominence). See, for instance, Esther Blau, *The Spice and Spirit of Kosher Jewish Cooking* (New York: Bloch, 1997); Trudy Garfunkel, *Kosher for Everybody: The Complete Guide to Understanding, Shopping, Cooking and Eating the Kosher Way* (San Francisco: John Wiley and Sons, 2004); Mildred Miller, *The Kosher Gourmet Cookbook* (New York: Galahad Books, 1983); Helen Nash, *Kosher Cuisine: Gourmet Recipes for the Modern Home* (New York: Jason Aronson, 1995); Judy Zeidler, *The Gourmet Jewish Cook* (New York: Harper Collins, 1999).

40. Quoted in Elaine Durbach, "Dining by Design," *New Jersey Jewish News,* October 30, 2003, www.njjewishnews.com/njjn.com/103003/ltdiningbydesign.html.

41. Quoted in Jennifer Seigel, "Why Has a New Kosher Cookbook Sold Over 24,000 Copies in a Week?" *Jewish World Review,* April 7, 2003, www.Jewishworldreview.com/kosher/living1.php3. It is worth noting how the theme of intergenerational crisis is linked to the recuperative powers of the text, which stands in here for a "lost tradition." See the Introduction, p. 10, above, for a related invocation of "the time of our grandparents."

42. Fishbein explains: "I love cooking and entertaining. I'm not necessarily the most talented cook. In fact, when I do cooking classes there's always a sigh of relief when I say I didn't go to cooking school. The appeal is that I'm just like the audience in my kitchen in New Jersey." Quoted in Suzi Brozman, "Not Your Bubbe's Cooking," *Jewish Times,* February 22, 2004, http://jewish.com/modules.phs?name=News&File=article&sid=1693. This quote may give us

pause for further reflection on the claim that Fishbein is a "Jewish Martha Stewart," since it is virtually unimaginable that Martha Stewart would ever attempt to efface her authority as a highly competent culinary expert (and thereby the symbolic power she enjoys over her "illiterate" audience). That said, I would argue that Fishbein and Stewart *do* enjoy comparable positions as what the Marxist critic Antonio Gramsci would call "organic intellectuals," in so far as both are devoted to the transformation of "common sense" into "good sense." See Antonio Gramsci, *Selections from the Prison Notebooks* (New York: International Publishers, 1971), 5–23 and passim.

43. Andrew Heinze, *Adapting to Abundance: Jewish Immigrants, Mass Consumption, and the Search for American Identity* (New York: Columbia University Press, 1990); Jenna Weissman Joselit, *The Wonders of America: Reinventing Jewish Culture, 1880–1950* (New York: Henry Holt, 1994).

44. Etan Diamond, "The Kosher Lifestyle: Religious Consumerism and Suburban Orthodox Jews," *Journal of Urban History* 28, no. 4 (2002): 488–505; Elliott Weiss, "Packaging Jewishness: Novelty and Tradition in Kosher Packages," *Design Issues* 20, no. 1 (2004): 48–61.

45. See Barbara Kirshenblatt-Gimblett's analysis of Betty Davis Greenberg and Althea Osber Silverman's *The Jewish Home Beautiful* (New York: Women's League of the United Synagogue of America, 1941), a kosher cookbook that epitomized the emerging emphasis on style and artistry. As Kirshenblatt-Gimblett notes, in the text Jewish religious experience was framed aesthetically by the set table—a trope indexing both the high bourgeois tradition of culinary elegance, *la table dressée*, and also one of the most important codices of Jewish law, the Shulhan Arukh (which also translates literally as "set table"). Together with its dialogic mode of address, *Jewish Home Beautiful*'s images of tables laden with food functioned as tableaux for a dramatic dialogue performed by mother and daughter: a script that was actually performed at various synagogues and churches, and even at the Temple of Religion at the New York World's Fair in 1939–40. Kirshenblatt-Gimblett, "Kitchen Judaism," 76–105.

46. Ann Mason and Marion Meyers, "Living with Martha Stewart Media: Chosen Domesticity in the Experience of Fans," *Journal of Communication* 51 (2001): 801–23.

47. Quoted in Sanders, "Kosher Diva."

48. Fishbein, *Kosher by Design*, 23, 32, 41, 64, 87, 98, 155.

49. *Balebatish* is a Yiddish adjective derived from the substantive *balebatim*, meaning persons of high standing. *Balebatish yidn* are respectable Jews, people of substance in the community (such as the board members of a synagogue or other distinguished figures). A *balebusteh* is a "top-notch" homemaker. My thanks to Barbara Kirshenblatt-Gimblett for pointing this out to me.

50. This refers to the ritual obligation to separate a piece of the dough as tithe for the Jewish priesthood, following Numbers 15:17–21.

51. Fishbein, *Kosher by Design,* 15.

52. Ibid., 16.

53. Ibid., 17.

54. Ibid., 125.

55. Ibid., 70.

56. In the case of the *milah,* the ritual cutting of the male foreskin, the Talmud mandates that only a certain portion of the foreskin, the *tzitzim ha'meacvim,* must be cut away to ensure the fulfillment of the *mitzvah* (Shabbat 137a). However, a *hiddur mitzvah* can be produced by cutting away a further part of the foreskin: the *tzitzim she'ainum meacvim.* See, for instance, Gedalia Hochberg, "Shmot 5759," 1998, Yeshivat Ohr Yerushalayim, www.yoy.org.il/article.php?id=125.

57. See, e.g., the interpretation of the miracle of Chanukah oil in Yosef HaLevi Loebenstein, "Days of Destiny: The Jewish Year under a Chassidic Microscope," *Sichos in English,* n.d., www.sichosinenglish.org/books/days-of -destiny/12.htm, accessed February 25, 2009.

58. As argued by Kalman Bland, *The Artless Jew: Medieval and Modern Affirmations and Denials of the Visual* (Princeton: Princeton University Press, 2001). For a related argument concerning the myth of Protestant aniconism, belied by rich traditions of artistic production and visual culture, see David Morgan, *Visual Piety: A History and Theory of Popular Religious Images* (Berkeley: University of California Press, 1998).

Wonderful evidence of the long history of Jewish image making within texts can be found in many places, including the *hagadot* (prayer books used for the Passover holiday) and *ketubot* (marriage contracts), which were typically (and sometimes lavishly) embellished and illuminated. See, for instance, Shalom Sabar, *Ketubbah: The Art of Jewish Marriage Contract* (New York: Rizzoli International Publications, 2000); Yosef Hayim Yerushalmi, *Haggadah and History: A Panorama in Facsimile of Five Centuries of the Printed Haggadah from the Collections of Harvard University and the Jewish Theological Seminary of America* (Philadelphia: Jewish Publication Society, 1997).

59. Quoted in Sanders, "Kosher Diva."

60. Quoted in Seigel, "Why."

61. See, for instance, Lawrence Fine, "Purifying the Body in the Name of the Soul: The Problem of the Body in Sixteenth-Century Kabbalah," in *People of the Body: Jews and Judaism from an Embodied Perspective,* ed. Howard Eilberg-Schwartz (Albany: SUNY Press, 1992), 117–42. For comparable discussions of bodily discipline and training in Christian and Islamic traditions, see Talal Asad, *Genealogies of Religion* (Baltimore: Johns Hopkins University Press, 1993), 125–67; Peter Brown, *The Body and Society: Men, Women and Sexual Renunciation in Early Christianity* (New York: Columbia University Press, 1988); R. Marie Griffith, *Born Again Bodies: Flesh and Spirit in American Christianity* (Berkeley:

University of California Press, 2004); Philip A. Mellor and Chris Shilling, *Reforming the Body: Religion, Community, and Modernity* (Thousand Oaks, CA: Sage Publications, 1997).

62. Quoted in Sanders, "Kosher Diva."

63. Abraham Twerski, *Self-Improvement? I'm Jewish! Overcoming Self-Defeating Behavior* (Brooklyn, NY: ArtScroll/Mesorah Publications, 1995); Abraham Twerski, *Angels Don't Leave Footprints: Discovering What's Right with Yourself* (Brooklyn, NY: ArtScroll/Mesorah Publications, 2001); Abraham Twerski, *The Sun Will Shine Again: Coping, Persevering, and Winning in Troubled Economic Times* (Brooklyn, NY: Mesorah Publications/Shaar Press, 2009).

64. Dov Brezak, *Chinuch in Turbulent Times: Practical Strategies for Parents and Educators* (Brooklyn, NY: ArtScroll/Mesorah Publications, 2002); Zelig Pliskin, *Anger! The Inner Teacher: A Nine-Step Program to Free Yourself from Anger* (Brooklyn, NY: ArtScroll/Mesorah Publications, 1997); Roiza Weinreich, *There Will Never Be Another You! Developing a Customized Plan to Reach Your Potential* (Brooklyn, NY: ArtScroll/Mesorah Publications, 1992); Meir Wikler, *Partners with Hashem: Effective Guidelines for Successful Parenting* (Brooklyn, NY: ArtScroll/Mesorah Publications, 2000).

65. See, *inter alia,* Micki McGee, *Self-Help, Inc.: Makeover Culture in American Life* (Oxford: Oxford University Press, 2005).

66. Shmuley Boteach, *Kosher Sex: A Recipe for Passion and Intimacy* (London: Hodder and Stoughton, 1999); Shmuley Boteach, *Dating Secrets of the Ten Commandments* (New York: Broadway Books, 2001); Shmuley Boteach, *Shalom in the Home* (New York: Meredith Books, 2007); Esther Jungreis, *The Committed Life: Principles for Good Living from Our Timeless Past* (New York: Harper Collins, 1999); Esther Jungreis, *The Committed Marriage: A Guide to Finding a Soul Mate and Building a Relationship through Timeless Biblical Wisdom* (New York: Harper Collins, 2003).

67. Rebbetzin Jungreis also writes a regular column for the New York-based periodical the *Jewish Press* and teaches Torah classes on cable TV. She manages her own Jewish outreach organization, Hineni, dedicated, according to its Web site, to "fighting the spiritual holocaust among Jews in the U.S. and around the world" (www.hineni.org/, accessed February 25, 2009). For further details on Jungreis, see Sam Apple, "A Rebbetzin's Advice," 2004, JBooks.com: The Online Jewish Books Community, www.jbooks.com/nonfiction/index/NF_Apple.htm.

68. For Bakhtin, a hybrid construction is "an utterance that belongs, by its grammatical (syntactic) and compositional markers, to a single speaker, but that actually contains mixed within it two utterances, two speech manners, two styles, two 'languages,' two semantic and axiological belief systems." Bakhtin, *Dialogic Imagination*, 304. See also 358–62.

69. In the English-speaking world, one finds significant precedents to the self-help genre in seventeenth-century morality tales and devotional guides,

such as Lewis Bayly's *The Practice of Piety* (1612) and John Bunyan's *A Pilgrim's Progress* (1678), but even more directly in popular eighteenth-century works, such as Cotton Mather's *The Christian and His Calling* (1701) and Benjamin Franklin's *Poor Richard's Almanac* (published annually from 1732 to 1758). By introducing ideas about "introspection" as a prelude to active goodness and about the need for prudent management of one's tangible and intangible resources (time, money, energy, friendship), both Mather and Franklin provided models for the genre of self-help as it developed in the late nineteenth century, when it began to acquire a more explicitly "psychological" tinge. For details of this history, see Roy M. Anker, *Self-Help and Popular Religion in Early American Culture: An Interpretive Guide* (Westport, CT: Greenwood Press, 1999), 106–31; John Cawelti, *Apostles of the Self-Made Man* (Chicago: University of Chicago Press, 1988); Andrew Heinze, *Jews and the American Soul: Human Nature in the Twentieth Century* (Princeton: Princeton University Press, 2004), 88–94.

70. On the incorporation of the Twelve-Step method into Haredi therapeutics, in particular through the work of Rabbi Abraham Twerski, see Andrew Heinze, "The Americanization of *Mussar*: Abraham Twerski's Twelve Steps," *Judaism* 48, no. 4 (1999): 450–69. More generally, on the history and (increasingly international) impact of the Alcoholics Anonymous movement and its techniques, see Carole Cain, "Personal Stories: Identity Acquisition and Self-Understanding in Alcoholics Anonymous," *Ethos* 19, no. 2 (1991): 210–53; Ernest Kurtz, *Not-God: A History of Alcoholics Anonymous* (Center City, MN: Hazelden, 1979); Mariana Valverde and Kimberley White-Mair, "'One Day at a Time,' and Other Slogans for Everyday Life: The Ethical Practices of Alcoholics Anonymous," *Sociology* 33, no. 2 (1999): 393–410.

71. See, inter alia, Anker, *Self-Help and Popular Religion;* Heinze, *Jews;* McGee, *Self-Help, Inc.;* Nikolas Rose, *Inventing Our Selves: Psychology, Power, and Personhood* (Cambridge: Cambridge University Press, 1998).

72. Charles Taylor, *Sources of the Self: The Making of Modern Identity* (Cambridge, MA: Harvard University Press, 1991), 28–29.

73. Noah Weinberg and Yaakov Salomon, *What the Angel Taught You: Seven Keys to Life Fulfillment* (Brooklyn, NY: Mesorah Publications/Shaar Press, 2003), 65–66.

74. As detailed in Anker, *Self-Help and Popular Religion;* Heinze, *Jews.*

75. See especially Rose, *Inventing Our Selves,* 95–96, 156–58.

76. Heinze, *Jews,* 40–49 and passim.

77. With firm roots in canonical sources—such as the many lists one finds in the Bible of praiseworthy behavior, beginning, perhaps, with the Ten Commandments—*musar* can be traced through a long history of written guides to moral conduct, culminating in the writings of Moses Chayim Luzzatto (1701–46), Menachem Mendel Lefin (1749–1826), and Israel Salanter (1810–83).

These authors advanced an understanding of the Jewish soul as governed by a constant and pervasive struggle between the inclination toward good *(yetzer tov)* and the inclination toward evil *(yetzer hara)*, and they promoted observance of Jewish law as the only effective means of combating the *yetzer hara* and the only secure path away from the hellish punishments that awaited the morally lazy soul. In particular, *musar* writers called on their fellow Jews to embark on a rigorous and unflinching examination of their own spiritual condition: to undertake an "accounting of the soul" *(heshbon hanefesh)* in order to confront the insidious and cunning presence of the *yetzer hara*. Nevertheless, even with their emphasis on self-introspection, *musar* writers relied on conventional notions of human willpower and thus had little appreciation of the reasons why "good" people might persist in "bad" habits. It was only with the rise of psychology that *musar* could be transformed into a modern discourse on ethical conduct, drawing in equal measure from the "religious" language of transgression and sin and the psychological language of unconscious motivation. On the history of *musar* and its relation to the rise of modern psychology, see Etkes, *Israel Salanter;* Goldberg, *Israel Salanter;* Heinze, *Jews.*

78. For an extended discussion of Twerski's biography and writings, see Heinze, "Americanization," 450–69.

79. Twerski, *Self-Improvement?* 26.

80. Twerski, *Angels Don't Leave Footprints,* 117.

81. Ibid., 150, emphasis in original.

82. See, for instance, Twerski, *Self-Improvement?* 83–111.

83. Ibid., 107–8.

84. Brezak, *Chinuch,* 18–19.

85. Ibid., 40.

86. Ibid., 98. As Yoel Finkelman has argued, Haredi authors of self-help books typically claim they are merely representing the "traditional" Jewish approach to intrafamilial relationships (as spouses and parents, among other things), but in practice they often ignore inconvenient statements found throughout the canonical literature, such as those regarding corporal punishment. In contrast with contemporary Haredi guides for parents, which often denounce both the immorality and the inefficiency of corporal punishment, there is, in fact, a long history of rabbinic commentaries that assumes the legitimacy of such measures, as reflected in the biblical passage, "One who spares the rod hates his child" (Proverbs 13:24). See Finkelman, "Tradition and Innovation," 45–49.

87. Brezak, *Chinuch,* 165.

88. Ibid., 89.

89. Ibid., 42.

90. Ibid., 44, emphasis in original.

4. MATERIALIZING AUTHENTICITY

1. Roiza Weinreich, *There Will Never Be Another You! Developing a Customized Plan to Reach Your Potential* (Brooklyn, NY: ArtScroll/Mesorah Publications, 1992), 138–39.

2. Genette, *Paratexts,* provides a useful taxonomy of what he calls "paratexts," which include footnotes, prefaces, afterwords, indexes, title pages, epigraphs, covers, and bindings, as well as external "epitexts," such as advertisements, book reviews, correspondence, and purchase and delivery orders. However, for the purposes of this analysis, Genette does not go far enough in his survey of paratextual devices in that he still restricts his attention to the level of discursive enunciations. What is missing is an account of the various nondiscursive technologies, devices, and materialities that surround, infuse, and sustain a given text and structure their possibilities for interaction, as I shall discuss in the coming pages.

3. For discussion of "hybrid actors," see Latour, *We Have Never Been Modern,* 1–12 and passim; Bruno Latour, *Pandora's Hope: Essays on the Reality of Science Studies* (Cambridge, MA: Harvard University Press, 1999), 176–98. For a comprehensive introduction to actor-network theory, see Bruno Latour, *Reassembling the Social: An Introduction to Actor-Network Theory* (Oxford: Oxford University Press, 2005). For an analysis of the material agency of texts, informed by actor-network theory, see François Cooren, "Textual Agency: How Texts Do Things in Organizational Settings," *Organization* 11, no. 3 (2004): 373–93.

4. On the production of Torah scrolls, see, for instance, Barbara Kirshenblatt-Gimblett, "The Cut That Binds: The Western Ashkenazic Torah Binder as Nexus between Circumcision and Torah," in *Celebration: Studies in Festivity and Ritual,* ed. Victor W. Turner (Washington, DC: Smithsonian Institution Press, 1982), 136–46. Importantly, while Jewish tradition has mandated the Torah to be committed to writing, other sacred texts, such as the Mishnah and the Talmud, were originally preserved only in oral form, transmitted by *tannaim* (tradents), the authorized individuals responsible for the text's memorization and public recitation. See Saul Lieberman, "Publication of the *Mishnah,*" in *Hellenism in Jewish Palestine,* 83–99; Stern, "First Jewish Books," 176–81 and passim. The decision to commit the Oral Law to writing (beginning in the third century CE) thus marked a key shift in the material organization of Jewish sacred texts, whereby a new premium was placed on written documents, as signaled by the development of new methods of logical and lexical analysis of Jewish texts and new procedures for repackaging, redacting, and ordering their contents. This process of textualization is especially well documented in medieval Europe, in the case of prayer books and other Jewish texts not yet fixed into stable written generic forms. See especially Reif, *Judaism and Hebrew Prayer.*

5. See the section "Religion in Print" in the Introduction, above.

6. Walter Benjamin, "The Work of Art in the Age of Its Technological Reproducibility: Second Version," in *The Work of Art in the Age of Its Technological Reproducibility, and Other Writings on Media,* ed. Michael W. Jennings, Brigid Doherty, and Thomas Y. Levin (Cambridge, MA: Harvard University Press, 2008), 21–24.

7. Skeptics, on the other hand, insist there is nothing at all "revolutionary" about the visual style for which ArtScroll has come to known. Indeed, it would behoove us to recall here that throughout the history of publishing (if not since the dawn of writing itself), compositors and book designers have always experimented with page layout and typefaces. The history of the design of the Jewish book is in part an expression of the diverse ways publishers have tackled pragmatic problems such as how best to organize the space of the page (in order to align discrete texts or to economize in the use of paper) or how to achieve desired effects on readers (such as guiding them through the order of a liturgical performance with the strategic use of blank spaces, lines, and differently sized fonts). One brief account of this history (including a rather uncharitable assessment of ArtScroll's typographical achievements) has been produced by Ari Davidow, a self-defined "Hebrew typesetter extraordinaire." See his Web site, "Ari Davidow, Hebrew Typographer," n.d., www.ivritype.com/hebrew, accessed February 25, 2009. See also Friedman, "Prayer Type."

8. Anonymous reviewer posting on the amazon.com Web site, May 5, 2003, www.amazon.com/gp/product/customer-reviews/157819707 4/.

9. On idolatry and aniconism in the Jewish tradition, see Moshe Halbertal and Avishai Margalit, *Idolatry* (Cambridge, MA: Harvard University Press, 1992). For a provocative reflection on the ways artists have negotiated religious protocols of this aniconism in the field of Jewish art making, see Bland, *Artless Jew.*

10. *Talmud Bavli: The Schottenstein Edition* (73 vols.), ed. Gedaliah Zlotowitz et al. (Brooklyn, NY: ArtScroll/Mesorah Publications, 1990–2005) (hereafter referred to as the *Schottenstein Talmud*), vol. 62 (*Tractate Chullin,* vol. 2).

11. Ibid., xxxv.

12. Roland Barthes, "The Rhetoric of the Image," in *Image-Music-Text,* ed. and trans. Stephen Heath (New York: Hill and Wang, 1978), 32–51.

13. The field of visual culture studies has been elaborated through a wide range of ideological and theoretical lines of discussion and debate, and also through engagement with diverse objects, and it is impossible to summarize these diverse strands in only a few words. Of particular note is the effort by art theorist W. J. T. Mitchell to effect a "pictorial turn" in the study of images: that is, a "postlinguistic, postsemiotic rediscovery" of the picture as an embodiment of complex interplay of "visuality, apparatus, institutions, discourse, bodies, and figurality." W. J. T. Mitchell, *Picture Theory: Essays on Verbal and Visual Representation* (Chicago: University of Chicago Press, 1994), 16. See also W. J. T. Mitchell, *What Do Pictures Want? The Lives and Loves of Images* (Chicago:

University of Chicago Press, 2005). This orientation has been particularly fruitful in the study of "religious" images and the techniques and technologies of the "sacred gaze," especially (but not uniquely) in the image-rich contexts of contemporary Hinduism, Christian evangelicalism, and Pentecostalism. See, for instance, Birgit Meyer, "Powerful Pictures: Popular Christian Aesthetics in Southern Ghana," *Journal of the American Academy of Religion* 76, no. 1 (2008): 82–110; Birgit Meyer, "Religious Revelation, Secrecy, and the Limits of Visual Representation," *Anthropological Theory* 6, no. 4 (2006): 431–53; Morgan, *Visual Piety;* David Morgan, *The Sacred Gaze: Religious Visual Culture in Theory and Practice* (Berkeley: University of California Press, 2005); Christopher Pinney, *Photos of the Gods: The Printed Image and Political Struggle in India* (London: Reaktion Books, 2004); Rajagopal, *Politics after Television.*

14. Anonymous reviewer of Fishbein's second book, *Kosher by Design Entertains,* posting on the amazon.com Web site, March 9, 2005, www.amazon.com/ Kosher-Design-Entertains-Fabulous-Recipes/dp/1578194474/ref=sr_1_6?ie=UTF8 &s=books&qid=1236025322&sr=1–6.

15. Alfred Gell, *Art and Agency: An Anthropological Theory* (Oxford: Clarendon Press, 1998), 68–95.

16. Pinney, *Photos of the Gods,* 19–23. Pinney's introduction of the neologism *corpothetic* resonates with the efforts of other scholars of visual culture to challenge the neo-Kantian tradition of aesthetics as the disembodied contemplation of an object's "beauty" and instead to recuperate the meaning of the ancient Greek term *aisthesis* as a corporeal, affective field of perception involving the conjunction of all the senses. See, for instance, Susan Buck-Morss, "Aesthetics and Anaesthetics: Walter Benjamin's Artwork Essay Reconsidered," *October* 62 (1992): 3–41; Laura Marks, *Touch: Sensuous Theory and Multisensory Media* (Minneapolis: University of Minnesota Press, 2002); Meyer, "Powerful Pictures," 82–110; Jojada Verrips, "Aisthesis and An-aesthesia," *Ethnologia Europea* 35, no. 1/2 (2006): 27–33.

17. Fishbein, *Kosher by Design,* 3.

18. Anonymous reviewer posting on the amazon.com Web site, September 26, 2003, www.amazon.com/gp/product/customer-reviews/1578197074/.

19. Anonymous reviewer of Fishbein's second book, *Kosher by Design Entertains,* posting on the amazon.com Web site, March 9, 2005, www.amazon.com/ Kosher-Design-Entertains-Fabulous-Recipes/dp/1578194474/ref=sr_1_6?ie= UTF8&s=books&qid=1236025322&sr=1–6.

20. Stephen Lubell, "Bilingualism in the Hebrew Text," *Visible Language* 27, no. 1/2 (1993): 163–204.

21. Here I follow Bruno Latour's sense of the verb *to transcribe:* to produce a nonperishable and transportable representation of human competencies and performative capacities that have been delegated onto nonhumans: in this case, onto texts. See Latour, *Pandora's Hope.*

22. Although the general structure of the Talmud page dates back several centuries, the specific layout and pagination of the *Schottenstein Talmud* are based on the Vilna edition, originally published by the Romm family during the 1880s, which has since been considered as the "standard edition." On the Vilna edition, see Michael Stanislawski, "The 'Vilna Shas' and East European Jewry," in S. Mintz and Goldstein, *Printing the Talmud,* 97–102.

For details on the early history of Talmud printing (including the standardization of page layout) see Edward Fram, "In the Margins of the Text: Changes in the Page of Talmud," in S. Mintz and Goldstein, *Printing the Talmud,* 91–96; Marvin J. Heller, *Printing the Talmud: A History of the Earliest Printed Editions of the Talmud* (Brooklyn, NY: Im Hasefer, 1992); Marvin J. Heller, "Designing the Talmud: The Origins of the Printed Talmudic Page," *Tradition* 29, no. 3 (1995): 40–51.

23. Menachem Davis, *Tehillim: The Book of Psalms, with an Interlinear Translation* (Brooklyn, NY: ArtScroll/Mesorah Publications, 2001), ix.

24. Ibid., x.

25. Texts bearing interlinear translations of Hebrew and other Semitic languages into European languages are found in antiquity, most notably the Septuagint. See Greenspoon, "Jewish Bible Translation," 397–412. See also Louis J. Greenspoon, "Traditional Text, Contemporary Contexts: English-Language Scriptures for Jews and the History of Bible Translating," in *Interpretation of the Bible* (Sheffield: Sheffield Academic Press, 1998), 2:565–75.

26. Davis, *Tehillim,* x.

27. *The ArtScroll Complete Catalogue* (Brooklyn, NY: ArtScroll/Mesorah Publications, 2006), 42.

28. *Interlinear Tehillim/Psalms,* product details, www.artscroll.com/Books/itehh.html, accessed February 25, 2009.

29. In social studies of science and technology, this is sometimes described as "blackboxing": the process whereby a device or machine appears to be working efficiently, its internal complexities having been rendered more or less invisible, so that all one tends to notice are the inputs and outputs relating to the work the machine performs. Only when machines cease functioning are their internal complexities made conspicuous. See, *inter alia,* Latour, *Pandora's Hope,* 304.

30. *ArtScroll Complete Catalogue* [2006].

31. For a fascinating discussion of seventeenth-century books as "talismans" rather than as texts to be read, see David Cressy, "Books as Totems in Seventeenth-Century England and New England," *Journal of Library History* 21, no. 1 (1986): 92–106. For a comparable study of the use of religious books as material artifacts among illiterate Christians in postcolonial Zimbabwe, see Matthew Engelke, *A Problem of Presence: Beyond Scripture in an African Church* (Berkeley: University of California Press, 2007).

32. Commensurate with this was a technological change toward a greater mechanization of the binding process and thereby a growing practice among publishers to bind books in house and to sell them as already bound texts, rather than as unbound sheets, a practice that, at least in the American context, had been customary up to the 1820s and 1830s. This required purchasers to pay the printer an extra cost to have the sheets bound or to hire an independent bookbinder to render this service. Paul C. Gutjahr, *An American Bible: A History of the Good Book in the United States, 1777–1880* (Stanford: Stanford University Press, 1999), 14–15. For the longer history, see Edward Walker, *The Art of Book-Binding: Its Rise and Progress* (New Castle, DE: Oak Knoll Books, 1984).

Publishers such as the (New York-based) American Bible Society, one of the most ambitious and important purveyors of Christian reading material for much of the nineteenth century, also recognized the opportunity to exert new forms of control over the text through the adoption of prefabricated bindings. As Gutjahr notes, one of the problems facing the Society was the tendency of independent bookbinders to bind "extra" material into Bibles, such as commentaries or apocrypha. So by integrating bookbinding into the Society's operations it was possible not only to increase the rate of production but also to secure greater control over the contents of the books themselves. Gutjahr, *American Bible*, 31.

33. Ibid., 42–43.

34. Ibid., 44–46.

35. David Chidester, *Authentic Fakes: Religion and American Popular Culture* (Berkeley: University of California Press, 2005). Although in antiquity the term *authentic* referred principally to a field of self-authorized actions (from the Greek *autos* "self" + *hentes* "doer, being"), in its modern sense it has incorporated the claim that the thing in question must be accepted as factual and not fictitious. According to Chidester, the Enlightenment established two key criteria for determining authenticity: *transparency* (for discerning genuine things and for speaking about them without recourse to jargon or other forms of obfuscatory discourse) and *control* (of the bodily senses, in order to elicit the requisite seriousness and solemnity attached to authentic experiences). In this context, the "authentication" of a cultural artifact refers to the effort to determine whether it is *truly* original, unadulterated, in conformity with the established facts—in short, not "fake." See ibid., 193ff.

36. The lamp was invented by the Torontonian Rabbi Shmuel Veffer, reportedly in response to a request from his wife "to hook up some kind of light for the bedroom so she could read on *Shabbos*." Quoted from the lampmaker's Web site, Kosher Innovations, www.kosherimage.com, accessed February 25, 2009.

37. The Kosher Innovations Web site reproduces several official letters declaring the permitted use of the KosherLamp on the Sabbath, including ones signed by Rabbi Shlomo Eliyahu Miller of Rosh Kollel Avreichim (Toronto),

Rabbi Yechezkel Roth of Beth Din—Kollel Bais Talmud L'horuah (Brooklyn), and Dayan Chanach Ha Cohen Ehrentreu of the Rosh Beit Din (high court) of London. See www.kosherimage.com, accessed February 25, 2009.

38. Quoted in Michael Kress, "Lighter Duty: New Devices Help Modern Jews Observe Ancient Sabbath Laws," *Dallas Morning News,* November 27, 2004.

39. See, for instance, Simcha Cohen, *Shabbos Kitchen: Hilkhot Shabat Ba-Mitbah: A Comprehensive Guide to the Preparation of Food and Other Kitchen Activities on Shabbos or Yom Tov* (Brooklyn, NY: ArtScroll/Mesorah Publications, 1991); Simcha Cohen, *The Shabbos Home: A Comprehensive Halachic Guide to the Laws of Shabbos as They Apply throughout the Home* (Brooklyn, NY: ArtScroll/Mesorah Publications, 1995); Simcha Cohen, *Muktzeh: A Practical Guide. A Comprehensive Treatment of the Principles and Common Applications of the Laws of Muktzeh* (Brooklyn, NY: ArtScroll/Mesorah Publications, 1999).

40. Quoted in Dave Gordon, "Inventions Make It Easier to Live Halachically," *Canadian Jewish News,* May 8, 2008, www.cjnews.com/index.php?option=com_content&task=view&id=14600&Itemid=86.

41. Quoted from the Kosher Innovations Web site, www.kosherimage.com/news.html, accessed February 25, 2009.

5. GRAVITY AND GRAVITAS

1. Meir Zlotowitz, pers. comm., February 2004.

2. In the Jewish tradition, the reading of sacred works has long been framed by regulations and legitimating structures that favor collective over individual reading. The Talmud, for instance, records the argument that, while solitary study of Torah is meritorious, studying with a partner adds something: the event is recorded in the celestial Book of Remembrance (B.T. Berachot 6a). Elsewhere it is emphasized that no individual should read the Bible more quickly than the congregation of which he is a member (B.T. Berachot 8a) and that students should always strive to live in the same town as their teacher (B.T. Berachot 8a). For rich ethnographic studies of the role of fellowship and collective study in Jewish reading practices, see J. Boyarin, "Voices around the Text," 212–37; Heilman, *People of the Book.*

3. Here I echo a growing scholarly suspicion of the grand metanarratives of media history as an evolutionary process, leading us to perceive changes in media technology (such as, in the present moment, the apparent "death of print" and its "replacement" with digital text) as a unidirectional progress toward ever greater efficiency and transparency. The current generation of media scholars has cast considerable doubt on the evolutionary model by exploring how old and new media continually confront and redefine one another, both historically and in the present. See, *inter alia,* Charles Acland, ed., *Residual Media* (Minneapolis: University of Minnesota Press, 2007); Jay David Bolter and

Richard Grusin, *Remediation: Understanding New Media* (Cambridge, MA: MIT Press, 2003); Lisa Gitelman, *Always Already New: Media, History, and the Data of Culture* (Cambridge, MA: MIT Press, 2006); Lisa Gitelman and Geoffrey Pingree, eds., *New Media, 1740–1915* (Cambridge, MA: MIT Press, 2003); David Thorburn and Henry Jenkins, eds., *Rethinking Media Change: The Aesthetics of Transition* (Cambridge, MA: MIT Press, 2003). For a prescient collection of essays addressing the prospects of the printed book at the cusp of the digital age, see Geoffrey Nunberg, ed., *The Future of the Book* (Berkeley: University of California Press, 1996).

4. See, for instance, Emanuel Maier, "Torah as Movable Territory," *Annals of the Association of American Geographers* 65, no. 1 (1975): 18–23; George Steiner, "Our Homeland, the Text," *Salmagundi: A Quarterly Journal of the Humanities and Social Sciences* 66 (1985): 4–25. For an influential analysis of the "powers of diaspora," see J. Boyarin and D. Boyarin, *Powers of Diaspora*.

5. Of course, the same can be argued about the putatively ethereal, disembodied, and instantaneous universe of electrically mediated communication flows, beginning with the telegraph and culminating in our present-day world of hyperlinked digital texts, mobile telephones, and satellite uplinks, among all the other technologies that are taken to index a communicative realm "freed from the constraints of geography." Indeed, despite all the rhetoric that suggests the contrary, electrically mediated communication never has been—and indeed cannot conceivably be—detached from its material infrastructure of cables, wires, microchips, keyboards, microphones, plasma screens, power generators, radio and microwave emitters, and other interlinked material agencies that organize the activity of communication. Only from the vantage point of the individual end user can one talk about experiences of disembodied, instantaneous communicative acts, somehow liberated from the laws of gravity. This observation should remind us that even if the distinction between "heavy books" and "weightless digital media" helps to make sense of the activities and settled assumptions of producers, marketers, and users of ArtScroll books, we are not speaking here of an absolute opposition, only of differences of degree, technological particularity, and structural organization. This point is well elaborated, among others, by Jonathan Sterne, "Transportation and Communication: Together as You've Always Wanted Them," in *Thinking with James Carey: Essays on Communications, Transportation, History*, ed. Jeremy Packer and Craig Robertson (New York: Peter Lang, 2006), 117–35.

SELECT BIBLIOGRAPHY

Abella, Irving. *A Coat of Many Colours: Two Centuries of Jewish Life in Canada.* Toronto: Lester, 1990.

Acland, Charles Acland, ed. *Residual Media.* Minneapolis: University of Minnesota Press, 2007.

Altick, Richard D. *The English Common Reader: A Social History of the Mass Reading Public, 1800–1900.* 2nd ed. Columbus: Ohio State University Press, 1998.

Anderson, Benedict. *Imagined Communities: Reflections on the Origin and Spread of Nationalism.* London: Verso Books, 1991.

Anker, Roy M. *Self-Help and Popular Religion in Early American Culture: An Interpretive Guide.* Westport, CT: Greenwood Press, 1999.

Asad, Talal. *Genealogies of Religion.* Baltimore: Johns Hopkins University Press, 1993.

Atiyeh, George N., ed. *The Book in the Islamic World: The Written Word and Communication in the Middle East.* Albany: State University of New York Press, 1995.

Aviad, Janet. *Return to Judaism: Religious Renewal in Israel.* Chicago: University of Chicago Press, 1983.

Bacon, Gershon. *The Politics of Tradition: Agudat Yisrael in Poland, 1916–1939.* Jerusalem: Magnes Press, 1996.

Bakhtin, Mikhail M. *The Dialogic Imagination.* Austin: University of Texas Press, 1981.

———. *Speech Genres and Other Late Essays.* Ed. Caryl Emerson and Michael Holquist. Austin: University of Texas Press, 1986.

Baron, Sabrina Alcorn, Eric N. Lindquist, and Eleanor F. Shevlin, eds. *Agent of Change: Print Culture Studies after Elizabeth L. Eisenstein.* Amherst: University of Massachusetts Press, 2007.

Baron, Salo Wittmayer. "Emphases in Jewish History." *Jewish Social Studies* 1, no. 1 (1939): 15–38.

———. "Ghetto and Emancipation: Shall We Revise the Traditional View?" *Menorah Journal* 14, no. 6 (1928): 515–26.

———. *The Russian Jew under Tsars and Soviets.* 2nd rev. ed. New York: Macmillan, 1976.

Bartal, Israel. "From Traditional Bilingualism to National Monolingualism." In *Hebrew in Ashkenaz: A Language in Exile,* ed. Lewis Glinert, 141–50. Oxford: Oxford University Press, 1993.

———. "True Knowledge and Wisdom: On Orthodox Historiography." *Studies in Contemporary Jewry* 10 (1994): 178–92.

Barthes, Roland. "The Rhetoric of the Image." In *Image-Music-Text,* ed. and trans. Stephen Heath, 32–51. New York: Hill and Wang, 1978.

Baumel, Simeon. "Teaching English in Israeli Haredi Schools." *Language Policy* 2, no. 1 (2003): 47–67.

Bedos-Rezak, Brigitte. "The Confrontation of Orality and Textuality: Jewish and Christian Literacy in Eleventh and Twelfth-Century Northern France." In *Rashi, 1040–1990: Hommage à Ephraim E. Urbach,* ed. G. Sed-Rejna, 541–58. Paris: Cerf, 1993.

Bell, Catherine. *Ritual Theory, Ritual Practice.* Oxford: Oxford University Press, 1992.

Benbassa, Esther, and Aron Rodrigue. *Sephardi Jewry: A History of the Judeo-Spanish Community, 14th-20th Centuries.* Berkeley: University of California Press, 2000.

Benjamin, Walter. "The Work of Art in the Age of Its Technological Reproducibility: Second Version." In *The Work of Art in the Age of Its Technological Reproducibility, and Other Writings on Media,* ed. Michael W. Jennings, Brigid Doherty, and Thomas Y. Levin, 19–55. Cambridge, MA: Harvard University Press, 2008.

Benor, Sarah Bunin. "Do American Jews Speak a 'Jewish Language'? A Model of Linguistic Distinctiveness." *Jewish Quarterly Review* 99, no. 2 (2009): 230–69.

———. "*Talmid Chachams* and *Tsedeykeses:* Language, Learnedness, and Masculinity among Orthodox Jews." *Jewish Social Studies* 11, no. 1 (2004): 147–70.

Berger, David, ed. *The Legacy of Jewish Migration: 1881 and Its Impact.* New York: Columbia University Press, 1983.

Berman, Eli. "Sect, Subsidy and Sacrifice: An Economist's View of Ultra-Orthodox Jews." *Quarterly Journal of Economics* 115, no. 3 (2000): 905–53.

Bland, Kalman. *The Artless Jew: Medieval and Modern Affirmations and Denials of the Visual.* Princeton: Princeton University Press, 2001.

Bloom, Jonathan. *Paper before Print: The History and Impact of Paper in the Islamic World.* New Haven: Yale University Press, 2001.

Blumen, Orna. "Criss-Crossing Boundaries: Ultraorthodox Jewish Women Go to Work." *Gender, Place and Culture* 9, no. 2 (2002): 133–51.

Bolter, Jay David, and Richard Grusin. *Remediation: Understanding New Media.* Cambridge, MA: MIT Press, 2003.

Bourdieu, Pierre. *Distinction: A Social Critique of the Judgement of Taste.* Cambridge, MA: Harvard University Press, 1984.

———. *The Field of Cultural Production: Essays on Art and Literature.* New York: Columbia University Press, 1993.

Boyarin, Daniel. *Unheroic Conduct: The Rise of Heterosexuality and the Invention of the Jewish Man.* Berkeley: University of California Press, 2006.

Boyarin, Jonathan, ed. *Remapping Memory: The Politics of Timespace.* Minneapolis: University of Minnesota Press, 1992.

———. "Voices around the Text: The Ethnography of Reading at Mesivta Tifereth Jerusalem." In *The Ethnography of Reading,* ed. Jonathan Boyarin, 212–37. Berkeley: University of California Press, 1993.

Boyarin, Jonathan, and Daniel Boyarin. *Powers of Diaspora: Two Essays on the Relevance of Jewish Culture.* Minneapolis: University of Minnesota Press, 2002.

Breuer, Mordechai. *Modernity within Tradition: The Social History of Orthodox Jewry in Imperial Germany.* New York: Columbia University Press, 1992.

Brown, Michael. "All, All Alone: The Hebrew Press in America from 1914 to 1924." *American Jewish History Quarterly* 59, no. 2 (1969): 139–78.

Brown, Peter. *The Body and Society: Men, Women and Sexual Renunciation in Early Christianity.* New York: Columbia University Press, 1988.

Buck-Morss, Susan. "Aesthetics and Anaesthetics: Walter Benjamin's Artwork Essay Reconsidered." *October* 62 (1992): 3–41.

Burke, Peter. *A Social History of Knowledge: From Gutenberg to Diderot.* Cambridge: Polity Press, 2000.

Cain, Carole. "Personal Stories: Identity Acquisition and Self-Understanding in Alcoholics Anonymous." *Ethos* 19, no. 2 (1991): 210–53.

Carter, Thomas F. *The Invention of Printing in China and Its Spread Westward.* 2nd rev. ed. New York: Ronald Press, 1955.

Casper, Scott, Jeffrey Groves, Stephen Nissenbaum, and Michael Winship, eds. *A History of the Book in America.* Vol. 3. *The Industrial Book, 1840–1880.* Chapel Hill: University of North Carolina Press, 2007.

Cawelti, John. *Apostles of the Self-Made Man.* Chicago: University of Chicago Press, 1988.

Chidester, David. *Authentic Fakes: Religion and American Popular Culture.* Berkeley: University of California Press, 2005.

Conkey, Margaret W. "Style, Design, and Function." In *Handbook of Material Culture*, ed. Christopher Tilley et al., 355–72. Thousand Oaks, CA: Sage Publications, 2006.

Cooren, François. "Textual Agency: How Texts Do Things in Organizational Settings." *Organization* 11, no. 3 (2004): 373–93.

Coser, Lewis, Charles Kadushin, and Walter Powell. *Books: The Culture and Commerce of Publishing.* Chicago: University of Chicago Press, 1982.

Crary, Jonathan. *Suspensions of Perception: Attention, Spectacle, and Modern Culture.* Cambridge, MA: MIT Press, 1999.

Cressy, David. "Books as Totems in Seventeenth-Century England and New England." *Journal of Library History* 21, no. 1 (1986): 92–106.

Crystal, David. *English as a Global Language.* 2nd ed. Cambridge: Cambridge University Press, 2003.

Danzger, M. Herbert. *Returning to Tradition: The Contemporary Revival of Orthodox Judaism.* New Haven: Yale University Press, 1989.

Davidman, Lynn. *Tradition in a Rootless World: Women Turn to Orthodox Judaism.* Berkeley: University of California Press, 1991.

Diamond, Etan. *And I Will Dwell in Their Midst: Orthodox Jews in Suburbia.* Chapel Hill: University of North Carolina Press, 2000.

———. "The Kosher Lifestyle: Religious Consumerism and Suburban Orthodox Jews." *Journal of Urban History* 28, no. 4 (2002): 488–505.

Diner, Hasia. *The Jews of the United States, 1654–2000.* Berkeley: University of California Press, 2004.

Dynner, Glenn. *Men of Silk: The Hasidic Conquest of Polish Jewish Society.* Oxford: Oxford University Press, 2006.

Edwards, M. U., Jr. *Printing, Propaganda, and Martin Luther.* Berkeley: University of California Press, 1994.

Eisen, Arnold. *Galut: Modern Jewish Reflection on Homelessness and Homecoming.* Bloomington: Indiana University Press, 1986.

Eisenstein, Elizabeth. *The Printing Press as an Agent of Change: Communications and Cultural Transformations in Early Modern Europe.* Cambridge: Cambridge University Press, 1979.

Elazar, Daniel Judah, and Morton Weinfeld, eds. *Still Moving: Recent Jewish Migration in Comparative Perspective.* Edison, NJ: Transaction Publishers, 2000.

Elias, Norbert. *The Civilizing Process.* Trans. Edmund Jephcott. Oxford: Blackwell, 1994.

El-Or, Tamar. *Educated and Ignorant: Ultraorthodox Jewish Women and Their World.* Boulder, CO: Lynne Rienner, 1994.

Endelman, Todd. *The Jews of Britain, 1656–2000.* Berkeley: University of California Press, 2002.

Engelke, Matthew. *A Problem of Presence: Beyond Scripture in an African Church.* Berkeley: University of California Press, 2007.

Etkes, Immanuel. *Israel Salanter and the Mussar Movement: Seeking the Torah of Truth.* Philadelphia: Jewish Publication Society of America, 1993.

Faur, José. *Golden Doves with Silver Dots.* Bloomington: Indiana University Press, 1986.

Feather, John. *A History of British Publishing.* London: Routledge, 1988.

Febvre, Lucien, and Henri-Jean Martin. *The Coming of the Book: The Impact of Printing, 1450–1800.* London: Verso Books, 1990.

Ferguson, Charles. "Diglossia." *Word* 15 (1959): 324–40.

Fine, Lawrence. "Purifying the Body in the Name of the Soul: The Problem of the Body in Sixteenth-Century Kabbalah." In *People of the Body: Jews and Judaism from an Embodied Perspective,* ed. Howard Eilberg-Schwartz, 117–42. Albany: SUNY Press, 1992.

Finkelman, Yoel. "Medium and Message in Contemporary Haredi Adventure Fiction." *Torah u-Maddah Journal* 13 (2005): 50–87.

———. "Tradition and Innovation in American Haredi Parenting Literature." In *Innovation and Change in Jewish Education,* ed. David Zisenwine, 37–61. Tel Aviv: Tel Aviv University Press, 2007.

Fishman, Talya. "Rhineland Pietist Approaches to Prayer and the Textualization of Rabbinic Culture in Medieval Northern Europe." *Jewish Studies Quarterly* 11, no. 4 (2004): 313–31.

———. "The Rhineland Pietists' Sacralization of Oral Torah." *Jewish Quarterly Review* 96, no. 1 (2006): 9–16.

Flusser, Vilém. *The Shape of Things: A Philosophy of Design.* London: Reaktion Books, 1999.

Frankel, Jonathan, and Steven J. Zipperstein, eds. *Assimilation and Community: The Jews in Nineteenth-Century Europe.* Cambridge: Cambridge University Press, 1992.

Friedman, Menachem. "Habad as Messianic Fundamentalism: From Local Particularism to Universal Jewish Mission." In *Accounting for Fundamentalisms,* ed. Martin E. Marty and R. Scott Appleby, 328–57. Chicago: University of Chicago Press, 1994.

———. "The Haredim and the Holocaust." *Jerusalem Quarterly* 53 (1990): 86–114.

———. "Haredim Confront the Modern City." *Studies in Contemporary Jewry* 2 (1986): 74–96.

———. "Life Tradition and Book Tradition in the Development of Ultraorthodox Judaism." In *Judaism Viewed from Within and from Without: Anthropological Studies,* ed. Harvey Goldberg, 235–55. Albany: SUNY Press, 1987.

———. "The Lost Kiddush Cup: Changes in Ashkenazic Haredi Culture—A Tradition in Crisis." In *The Uses of Tradition: Jewish Continuity in the Modern Era,* ed. Jack Wertheimer, 175–86. New York: Jewish Theological Seminary of America, 1992.

———. "The Market Model and Religious Radicalism." In *Jewish Fundamentalism in Comparative Perspective: Religion, Ideology, and the Crisis of Modernity,* ed. Lawrence J. Silberstein, 192–215. New York: New York University Press, 1993.

Frykholm, Amy Johnson. *Rapture Culture: Left Behind in Evangelical America.* New York: Oxford University Press, 2004.

Gartner, Lloyd. *The Jewish Immigrant in England, 1870–1914.* 3rd ed. London: Vallentine Mitchell, 2001.

Geertz, Clifford. *Islam Observed: Religious Development in Morocco and Indonesia.* Chicago: Chicago University Press, 1968.

Gell, Alfred. *Art and Agency: An Anthropological Theory.* Oxford: Clarendon Press, 1998.

Genette, Gérard. *Paratexts: Thresholds of Interpretation.* Cambridge: Cambridge University Press, 1997.

Gilmont, Jean-François, ed. *The Reformation and the Book.* Aldershot: Ashgate, 1998.

Gitelman, Lisa. *Always Already New: Media, History, and the Data of Culture.* Cambridge, MA: MIT Press, 2006.

Gitelman, Lisa, and Geoffrey Pingree, eds. *New Media, 1740–1915.* Cambridge, MA: MIT Press, 2003.

Glinert, Lewis, and Yosseph Shilhav. "Holy Land, Holy Language: A Study of an Ultraorthodox Jewish Ideology." *Language in Society* 20, no. 1 (1991): 59–86.

Gobard, Henri. *L'aliénation linguistique: Analyse tétraglossique.* Paris: Flammarion, 1976.

Goitein, Shelomo Dov. *Letters of Medieval Jewish Traders.* Princeton: Princeton University Press, 1973.

Goldberg, Harvey, ed. *Sephardi and Middle Eastern Jewries: History and Culture in the Modern Era.* Bloomington: Indiana University Press, 1996.

Goldberg, Hillel. *Israel Salanter: Text, Structure, Idea. The Ethics and Theology of an Early Psychologist of the Unconscious.* New York: Ktav Publications, 1982.

———. "Review of Israeli Intellectual Life: Evaluating the Book-Publishing Explosion." *Tradition* 19, no. 2 (1981): 163–70.

Goldin, Judah. "The Period of the Talmud." In *The Jews: Their History, Culture, and Religion,* vol. 1, ed. Louis Finkelstein, 146–52. New York: Harper and Row, 1949.

Gonzalez-Quijano, Yves. *Les gens du livre: Édition et champ intellectuel dans l'Égypte républicaine.* Paris: CNRS Éditions, 1998.

Graff, Harvey J. *The Legacies of Literacy: Continuities and Contradictions in Western Culture and Society.* Bloomington: Indiana University Press, 1987.

Gramsci, Antonio. *Selections from the Prison Notebooks.* New York: International Publishers, 1971.

Greco, Albert N. *The Book Publishing Industry.* 2nd ed. London: Routledge, 2005.

Greco, Albert N., Clara E. Rodríguez, and Robert M. Wharton. *The Culture and Commerce of Publishing in the Twenty-first Century.* Stanford: Stanford University Press, 2007.

Greenspoon, Louis J. "Jewish Bible Translation." In *The Biblical World,* ed. J. Barton, 397–412. London: Routledge, 2003.

———. "Traditional Text, Contemporary Contexts: English-Language Scriptures for Jews and the History of Bible Translating." In *Interpretation of the Bible,* 2:565–75. Sheffield: Sheffield Academic Press, 1998.

Gries, Zeev. *The Book in the Jewish World, 1700–1900.* Oxford: Littman Library of Jewish Civilization, 2007.

———. "The Hasidic Managing Editor as an Agent of Culture." In *Hasidism Reappraised,* ed. Ada Rapaport-Albert, 141–55. London: Littman Library of Jewish Civilization, 1996.

Griffith, R. Marie. *Born Again Bodies: Flesh and Spirit in American Christianity.* Berkeley: University of California Press, 2004.

Gurock, Jeffrey S. *American Jewish Orthodoxy in Historical Perspective.* Hoboken, NJ: Ktav Publishing House, 1996.

Gutjahr, Paul C. *An American Bible: A History of the Good Book in the United States, 1777–1880.* Stanford: Stanford University Press, 1999.

———. "The State of the Discipline: Sacred Texts in the United States." *Book History* 4 (2001): 335–70.

Habermas, Jürgen. *The Structural Transformation of the Public Sphere: An Inquiry into a Category of Bourgeois Society.* Cambridge, MA: MIT Press, 1989.

Halbertal, Moshe. *People of the Book: Canon, Meaning, and Authority.* Cambridge, MA: Harvard University Press, 1997.

Halbertal, Moshe, and Avishai Margalit. *Idolatry.* Cambridge, MA: Harvard University Press, 1992.

Halbwachs, Maurice. *On Collective Memory.* Ed. and trans. Lewis A. Coser. Chicago: University of Chicago Press, 1992.

Handelman, Susan. *Slayers of Moses: The Emergence of Rabbinic Interpretation in Modern Literary Theory.* Albany: State University of New York Press, 1982.

Heilman, Samuel C. "The Ninth Siyum haShas at Madison Square Garden: Contra-acculturation in American Life." In *The Americanization of the Jews,* ed. Robert M. Seltzer and Norman J. Cohen, 311–18. New York: New York University Press, 1995.

———. *The People of the Book: Drama, Fellowship, and Religion.* 2nd ed. New Brunswick, NJ: Transaction Publishers, 2002.

———. *Sliding to the Right: The Contest for the Future of American Jewish Orthodoxy.* Berkeley: University of California Press, 2006.

Heilman, Samuel C., and Steven Cohen. *Cosmopolitans and Parochials: Modern Orthodox Jews in America.* Chicago: University of Chicago Press, 1989.

Heilman, Samuel C., and Menachem Friedman. "Religious Fundamentalism and Religious Jews: The Case of the Haredim." In *Fundamentalisms Observed,* ed. Martin E. Marty and R. Scott Appleby, 197–264. Chicago: University of Chicago Press, 1991.

Heinze, Andrew. *Adapting to Abundance: Jewish Immigrants, Mass Consumption, and the Search for American Identity.* New York: Columbia University Press, 1990.

———. "The Americanization of *Mussar:* Abraham Twerski's Twelve Steps." *Judaism* 48, no. 4 (1999): 450–69.

———. *Jews and the American Soul: Human Nature in the Twentieth Century.* Princeton: Princeton University Press, 2004.

Heller, Marvin J. "Designing the Talmud: The Origins of the Printed Talmudic Page." *Tradition* 29, no. 3 (1995): 40–51.

———. *Printing the Talmud: A History of the Earliest Printed Editions of the Talmud.* Brooklyn, NY: Im Hasefer, 1992.

Helmreich, William B. *The World of the Yeshiva: An Intimate Portrait of Orthodox Jewry.* New Haven: Yale University Press, 1982.

Hendershot, Heather. *Shaking the World for Jesus: Media and Evangelical Culture.* Chicago: University of Chicago Press, 2004.

Henkin, David M. *City Reading: Written Words and Public Spaces in Antebellum New York.* New York: Columbia University Press, 1998.

Hirschkind, Charles. *The Ethical Soundscape: Cassette Sermons and Islamic Counterpublics.* New York: Columbia University Press, 2006.

Hobsbawm, Eric. "Inventing Traditions." In *The Invention of Tradition,* ed. Eric Hobsbawm and Terence Ranger, 1–14. Cambridge: University of Cambridge Press, 1983.

Hofmeyer, Isabel. *The Portable Bunyan: A Transnational History of the Pilgrim's Progress.* Princeton: Princeton University Press, 2003.

Howsam, Leslie. *Cheap Bibles: Nineteenth-Century Publishing and the British and Foreign Bible Society.* Cambridge: Cambridge University Press, 1991.

Huq, Maimuna. "From Piety to Romance: Islam-Oriented Texts in Bangladesh." In *New Media in the Muslim World: The Emerging Public Sphere,* ed. Dale F. Eickelman and Jon W. Anderson, 133–61. Bloomington: Indiana University Press, 1999.

Hyman, Paula. *Gender and Assimilation in Modern Jewish History: The Roles and Representation of Women.* Seattle: University of Washington Press, 1995.

Innis, Harold Adam. *Empire and Communications.* Oxford: Oxford University Press, 1950.

Johns, Adrian. *The Nature of the Book: Print and Knowledge in the Making.* Chicago: University of Chicago Press, 1998.

Joselit, Jenna Weissman. *New York's Jewish Jews: The Orthodox Community in the Interwar Years.* Bloomington: Indiana University Press, 1990.

———. *The Wonders of America: Reinventing Jewish Culture, 1880–1950*. New York: Henry Holt, 1994.

Kachru, Braj. "The Power and Politics of English." *World Englishes* 5, no. 2/3 (1986): 121–40.

Kaestle, Carl, and Janice Radway, eds. *A History of the Book in America*. Vol. 4. *Print in Motion: The Expansion of Publishing and Reading in the United States, 1880–1940*. Chapel Hill: University of North Carolina Press, 2009.

Kaplan, Lawrence. "*Daas Torah:* A Modern Conception of Rabbinic Authority." In *Rabbinic Authority and Personal Autonomy*, ed. Moshe Sokol, 1–60. Northvale, NJ: Jason Arsonson, 1992.

———. "Rabbi Isaac Hutner's 'Daat Torah Perspective' on the Holocaust: A Critical Analysis," *Tradition* 18, no. 3 (1980): 235–48.

Katz, David S. *The Jews in the History of England, 1485–1850*. Oxford: Oxford University Press, 1994.

Katz, Jacob. "*Da'at Torah*—The Unqualified Authority Claimed for Halakhists." *Jewish History* 11, no. 1 (1997): 41–50.

———. "Towards a Biography of the Hatam Sofer." In *From East and West: Jews in a Changing Europe, 1750–1870*, ed. Frances Malino and David Sorkin, 223–66. Oxford: Blackwell, 1990.

———. *Tradition and Crisis: Jewish Society at the End of the Middle Ages*. New York: Schocken Books, 1993.

Kaufman, Debra Renee. "Patriarchal Women: A Case Study of Newly Orthodox Jewish Women." *Symbolic Interaction* 12, no. 2 (1989): 299–314.

Kirshenblatt-Gimblett, Barbara. "The Cut That Binds: The Western Ashkenazic Torah Binder as Nexus between Circumcision and Torah." In *Celebration: Studies in Festivity and Ritual*, ed. Victor W. Turner, 136–46. Washington, DC: Smithsonian Institution Press, 1982.

———. *Destination Culture: Tourism, Museums, and Heritage*. Berkeley: University of California Press, 1998.

———. "Kitchen Judaism." In *Getting Comfortable in New York: The American Jewish Home, 1880–1950*, ed. Susan L. Braunstein and Jenna Weissman Joselit, 76–105. Bloomington: Indiana University Press, 1991.

———. "Playing to the Senses." *Performance Research* 4 (1999): 1–30.

Kurtz, Ernest. *Not-God: A History of Alcoholics Anonymous*. Center City, MN: Hazelden, 1979.

Lamm, Norman. *Torah Lishmah: Torah for Torah's Sake in the Works of Rabbi Hayyim of Volozhin and His Contemporaries*. New York: Yeshiva University Press, 1989.

Lamonde, Yvan, Patricia Lockhart Fleming, and Fiona A. Black, eds. *History of the Book in Canada*. Vol. 2. *1840–1918*. Toronto: University of Toronto Press, 2005.

Latour, Bruno. *Pandora's Hope: Essays on the Reality of Science Studies*. Cambridge, MA: Harvard University Press, 1999.

————. *Reassembling the Social: An Introduction to Actor-Network Theory.* Oxford: Oxford University Press, 2005.

————. "Technology Is Society Made Durable." In *A Sociology of Monsters: Essays on Power, Technology and Domination,* ed. John Law, 103–31. London: Routledge, 1991.

————. *We Have Never Been Modern.* Cambridge, MA: Harvard University Press, 1993.

Ledger-Lomas, Michael. "Mass Markets: Religion." In *The History of the Book in Britain, 1830–1914,* ed. David McKitterick, 324–58. Cambridge: Cambridge University Press, 2009.

Lehmann, David, and Batia Siebzehner. *Remaking Israeli Judaism: The Challenge of Shas.* Oxford: Oxford University Press, 2006.

Levi, Amnon. "The *Haredi* Press and Secular Society." In *Religious and Secular: Conflict and Accommodation between Jews in Israel,* ed. Charles Liebman, 21–44. Jerusalem: Keter Publishing House, 1990.

Levy, Barry. "Our Torah, Your Torah, and Their Torah: An Evaluation of the ArtScroll Phenomenon." In *Truth and Compassion: Essays on Judaism and Religion in Memory of Rabbi Dr. Solomon Frank,* ed. H. Joseph, Jack N. Lightstone, and M. D. Oppenheim, 137–89. Waterloo, Ontario: Canadian Corporation for Studies in Religion / Wilfred Laurier University Press, 1983.

Lieberman, Saul. *Hellenism in Jewish Palestine: Studies in the Literary Transmission, Beliefs, and Manners of Palestine in the I Century BCE—IV Century CE.* New York: Jewish Theological Seminary of America, 1950.

Liebman, Charles S. "Extremism as a Religious Norm." *Journal for the Scientific Study of Religion* 22, no. 1 (1983): 75–86.

Lubell, Stephen. "Bilingualism in the Hebrew Text." *Visible Language* 27, no. 1/2 (1993): 163–204.

Madison, Charles. *Jewish Publishing in America: The Impact of Jewish Writing on American Culture.* New York: Sanhedrin Press, 1976.

Maier, Emanuel. "Torah as Movable Territory." *Annals of the Association of American Geographers* 65, no. 1 (1975): 18–23.

Manache, Sophia, ed. *Communication in the Jewish Diaspora: The Pre-modern World.* Leiden: E. J. Brill, 1996.

Marks, Laura. *Touch: Sensuous Theory and Multisensory Media.* Minneapolis: University of Minnesota Press, 2002.

Mason, Ann, and Marion Meyers. "Living with Martha Stewart Media: Chosen Domesticity in the Experience of Fans." *Journal of Communication* 51 (2001): 801–23.

McGee, Micki. *Self-Help, Inc.: Makeover Culture in American Life.* Oxford: Oxford University Press, 2005.

McLuhan, Marshall. *Understanding Media: The Extensions of Man.* New York: McGraw-Hill, 1964.

Mellor, Philip A., and Chris Shilling. *Re-forming the Body: Religion, Community, and Modernity.* Thousand Oaks, CA: Sage Publications, 1997.

Meyer, Birgit. "Powerful Pictures: Popular Christian Aesthetics in Southern Ghana." *Journal of the American Academy of Religion* 76, no. 1 (2008): 82–110.

————. "Religious Revelation, Secrecy, and the Limits of Visual Representation." *Anthropological Theory* 6, no. 4 (2006): 431–53.

Meyer, Birgit, and Annelies Moors, eds. *Religion, Media and the Public Sphere.* Bloomington: Indiana University Press, 2006.

Meyer, Michael. *Response to Modernity: A History of the Reform Movement in Judaism.* Detroit: Wayne State University Press, 1988.

Michelson, M. "The Ultra-Orthodox Press in Israel." *Qesher* 8 (November 1990): 12e–21e.

Miller, Toby, and Alec McHoul. "Helping the Self." *Social Text* 57 (1998): 127–55.

Mintz, Alan, ed. *Hebrew in America: Perspectives and Prospects.* Detroit: Wayne State University Press, 1993.

Mintz, Alan, and David Roskies, eds. "The Role of Periodicals in the Formation of Modern Jewish Identity." Special issue, *Prooftexts: A Journal of Jewish Literary History* 15, no. 1 (1995).

Mintz, Sharon Liberman, and Gabriel Goldstein, eds. *Printing the Talmud: From Bomberg to Schottenstein.* New York: Yeshiva University Museum, 2005.

Mitchell, W. J. T. *Picture Theory: Essays on Verbal and Visual Representation.* Chicago: University of Chicago Press, 1994.

————. *What Do Pictures Want? The Lives and Loves of Images.* Chicago: University of Chicago Press, 2005.

Mittelman, Alan L. *The Politics of Torah: The Jewish Political Tradition and the Founding of Agudat Israel.* Albany: SUNY Press, 1996.

Modern, John Lardas. "Evangelical Secularism and the Measure of Leviathan." *Church History* 77 (December 2008): 801–76.

Morgan, David. *Protestants and Pictures: Religion, Visual Culture, and the Age of American Mass Production.* Oxford: Oxford University Press, 1999.

————. *The Sacred Gaze: Religious Visual Culture in Theory and Practice.* Berkeley: University of California Press, 2005.

————. *Visual Piety: A History and Theory of Popular Religious Images.* Berkeley: University of California Press, 1998.

————, ed. *Key Words in Religion, Media and Culture.* London: Routledge, 2008.

Mumford, Lewis. *Art and Technics.* New York: Columbia University Press, 1952.

Myers, David N. *Re-inventing the Jewish Past: European Intellectuals and the Zionist Return to History.* Oxford: Oxford University Press, 1995.

Nadler, Allan. *The Faith of the Mithnadgim: Rabbinic Responses to Hasidic Rapture.* Baltimore: Johns Hopkins University Press, 1997.

Nora, Pierre. "Between Memory and History." *Representations* 26 (1989): 7–25.

Nord, David Paul. *Faith in Reading: Religious Publishing and the Birth of Mass Media in America.* Oxford: Oxford University Press, 2004.

Nord, David Paul, Joan Shelley Rubin, and Michael Schudson, eds. *The Enduring Book: Print Culture in Postwar America.* Chapel Hill: University of North Carolina Press, 2009.

Nunberg, Geoffrey, ed. *The Future of the Book.* Berkeley: University of California Press, 1996.

Obeyesekere, Gananath. "Religious Symbolism and Political Change in Ceylon." *Modern Ceylon Studies* 1 (1970): 43–63.

Paczkowski, Andrzej. "The Jewish Press in the Political Life of the Second Republic." *Polin: Studies in Polish Jewry* 8 (1994): 176–93.

Parush, Iris. "The Politics of Literacy: Women and Foreign Languages in Jewish Society of 19th-Century Eastern Europe." *Modern Judaism* 15, no. 2 (1995): 183–206.

———. "Readers in Cameo: Women Readers in Jewish Society of Nineteenth-Century Eastern Europe." *Prooftexts: A Journal of Jewish Literary History* 14, no. 1 (1994): 13–16.

Pennycook, Alistair. "Beyond Homogeny and Heterogeny: English as a Global and Worldly Language." In *The Politics of English as a World Language,* ed. C. Mair, 3–17. Amsterdam: Rodopi, 2003.

Pinney, Christopher. *Photos of the Gods: The Printed Image and Political Struggle in India.* London: Reaktion Books, 2004.

Posner, Raphael, and Israel Ta-Shema, eds. *The Hebrew Book: An Historical Survey.* Jerusalem: Keter Publishing House, 1975.

Radway, Janice. *A Feeling for Books: The Book-of-the-Month Club, Literary Taste, and Middle-Class Desire.* Chapel Hill: University of North Carolina Press, 1997.

Rajagopal, Arvind. *Politics after Television: Hindu Nationalism and the Reshaping of the Public in India.* Cambridge: University of Cambridge Press, 2001.

Ravitzky, Aviezer. *Messianism, Zionism, and Jewish Religious Radicalism.* Chicago: University of Chicago Press, 1996.

Reif, Stefan. "Aspects of Mediaeval Jewish Literacy." In *The Uses of Literacy in Early Mediaeval Europe,* ed. R. McKitterick, 134–55. Cambridge: Cambridge University Press, 1990.

———. *Judaism and Hebrew Prayer: New Perspectives on Jewish Liturgical History.* Cambridge: Cambridge University Press, 1993.

Rodrigue, Aron. *Jews and Muslims: Images of Sephardi and Eastern Jewries in Modern Times.* Seattle: University of Washington Press, 2003.

Rose, Nikolas. *Inventing Our Selves: Psychology, Power, and Personhood.* Cambridge: Cambridge University Press, 1998.

Roth, Norman. "Jewish Collaborators in Alfonso's Scientific Work." In *Emperor of Culture: Alfonso X, the Learned of Castile and His Thirteenth-Century Renaissance,* ed. Robert I. Burns, 59–71. Philadelphia: University of Pennsylvania Press, 1990.

Rozenak, Michael. "Jewish Fundamentalism in Israeli Education." In *Fundamentalisms and Society: Reclaiming the Sciences, the Family, and Education,* ed. Martin E. Marty and R. Scott Appleby, 374–413. Chicago: University of Chicago Press, 1993.

Rubin, Joan Shelley. *The Making of Middlebrow Culture.* Chapel Hill: University of North Carolina Press, 1992.

Rutland, Suzanne D. *The Jews in Australia.* Cambridge: Cambridge University Press, 2006.

Sabar, Shalom. *Ketubbah: The Art of Jewish Marriage Contract.* New York: Rizzoli International Publications, 2000.

Sarna, Jonathan D. *JPS: The Americanization of Jewish Culture, 1888–1988.* Philadelphia: Jewish Publication Society, 1989.

Scholem, Gershom. *Major Trends in Jewish Mysticism* New York: Schocken Books, 1946.

———. *The Messianic Idea in Judaism, and Other Essays on Jewish Spirituality.* New York: Schocken Books, 1971.

Scribner, Robert W. *For the Sake of Simple Folk: Popular Propaganda and the German Reformation.* Cambridge: Cambridge University Press, 1981.

Seidman, Naomi. *A Marriage Made in Heaven: The Sexual Politics of Hebrew and Yiddish.* Berkeley: University of California Press, 1997.

Shaffir, William. "Leaving the Ultra-Orthodox Fold: Haredi Jews Who Defected." *Jewish Journal of Sociology* 29, no. 2 (1987): 97–114.

———. "The Recruitment of Baalei Tshuvah in a Jerusalem Yeshiva." *Jewish Journal of Sociology* 25, no. 1 (1983): 33–46.

Shain, Milton, and Richard Mendelsohn. *Memories, Dreams, and Realities: Aspects of the South African Jewish Experience.* Johannesburg: Jonathan Ball, 2002.

Shandler, Jeffrey. *Adventures in Yiddishland: Postvernacular Language and Culture.* Berkeley: University of California Press, 2006.

Sharot, Stephen. *A Comparative Sociology of World Religions: Virtuosi, Priests, and Popular Religion.* New York: New York University Press, 2001.

Sharpe, Kevin. *Reading Revolutions: The Politics of Reading in Early Modern England.* New Haven: Yale University Press, 2000.

Shilhav, Yosseph. "The Haredi Ghetto." *Contemporary Jewry* 10, no. 2 (1989): 51–64.

Shmeruk, C. "The Yiddish Press in Eastern Europe." *Jewish Quarterly* 33, no. 1 (1986): 24–28.

Silber, Michael K. "The Emergence of Ultra-Orthodoxy: The Invention of a Tradition." In *The Uses of Tradition: Jewish Continuity in the Modern Era,* ed. Jack Wertheimer, 23–84. New York: Jewish Theological Seminar of America, 1992.

Sivan, Emmanuel. "The Enclave Culture." In *Fundamentalism Comprehended,* ed. Martin E. Marty and R. Scott Appleby, 11–63. Chicago: University of Chicago Press, 1995.

Soloveitchik, Haym. "Rupture and Reconstruction: The Transformation of Contemporary Orthodoxy." *Tradition* 28 (1994): 64–130.

Spolksy, Bernard. "English in Israel after Independence." In *Post-imperial English: Status Change in Former British and American Colonies, 1940–1990,* ed. Joshua A. Fishman, Andrew W. Conrad, and Alma Rubal-Lopez, 535–56. The Hague: Mouton de Gruyter, 1996.

Stadler, Nurit. "Is Profane Work an Obstacle to Salvation? The Case of Ultra-Orthodox (Haredi) Jews in Contemporary Israel." *Sociology of Religion* 63, no. 4 (2002): 455–74.

———. *Yeshiva Fundamentalism: Piety, Gender, and Resistance in the Ultra-Orthodox World.* New York: New York University Press, 2008.

Stadler, Nurit, and Eyal Ben-Ari. "Other-Worldly Soldiers? Ultra-Orthodox Views of Military Service in Contemporary Israel." *Israel Affairs* 9, no. 4 (2003): 17–48.

Stadler, Nurit, Eyal Ben-Ari, and Einat Mesterman. "Terror, Aid, and Organization: The Haredi Disaster Victim Identification Teams (ZAKA) in Israel." *Anthropological Quarterly* 78, no. 3 (2005): 619–51.

Stampfer, Shaul. "Gender Differentiation and Education of the Jewish Woman in Nineteenth-Century Eastern Europe." *Polin: A Journal of Polish-Jewish Studies* 7 (1992): 63–87.

———. "*Heder* Study, Knowledge of Torah, and the Maintenance of Social Stratification in Traditional East European Jewish Society," *Studies in Jewish Education* 3 (1988): 271–89.

———. "Hungarian Yeshivot, Lithuanian Yeshivot, and Joseph Ben-David." *Jewish History* 11, no. 1 (1997): 131–41.

———. "What Did 'Knowing Hebrew' Mean in Eastern Europe?" In *Hebrew in Ashkenaz: A Language in Exile,* ed. Lewis Glinert, 129–40. Oxford: Oxford University Press, 1993.

Starobinski, Jean. "The Idea of Nostalgia." *Diogenes* 55 (Summer 1966): 81–103.

Steiner, George. "Our Homeland, the Text." *Salmagundi: A Quarterly Journal of the Humanities and Social Sciences* 66 (1985): 4–25.

Stern, David. "The First Jewish Books and the Early History of Jewish Reading." *Jewish Quarterly Review* 98, no. 2 (2008): 163–202.

Sterne, Jonathan. "Transportation and Communication: Together as You've Always Wanted Them." In *Thinking with James Carey: Essays on Communica-*

tions, Transportation, History, ed. Jeremy Packer and Craig Robertson, 117–35. New York: Peter Lang, 2006.

Stock, Brian. *The Implications of Literacy: Written Language and Modes of Interpretation in the Eleventh and Twelfth Centuries.* Princeton: Princeton University Press, 1983.

Stolow, Jeremy. "Communicating Authority, Consuming Tradition: Jewish Orthodox Outreach Literature and Its Reading Public." In *Religion, Media, and the Public Sphere,* ed. Birgit Meyer and Annelies Moors, 73–90. Bloomington: Indiana University Press, 2006.

———. "Here (We) Are the *Haredim*: Intertextuality and the Voice of Authority in the Representation of a Religious Fundamentalist Movement." In *The Invention of Religion: Rethinking Belief and Politics in History,* ed. Derek Peterson and Darren Walhof, 59–76. New Brunswick: Rutgers University Press, 2002.

———. "Nation of Torah: Proselytism and the Politics of Historiography in a Religious Social Movement." PhD diss., York University, 2000.

———. "Religion and/as Media." *Theory, Culture, and Society* 22, no. 4 (2005): 119–45.

———. "Transnationalism and the New Religio-Politics: Reflections on an Orthodox Jewish Case." *Theory, Culture and Society* 21, no. 2 (2004): 109–37.

Sugirtharajah, Rasiah S. *The Bible and the Third World: Precolonial, Colonial and Postcolonial Encounters.* Cambridge: Cambridge University Press, 2001.

Tapper, Aaron. "The 'Cult' of Aish Hatorah: Ba'alei Teshuva and the New Religious Movement Phenomenon." *Jewish Journal of Sociology* 44, no. 1/2 (2002): 5–29.

Taylor, Charles. *Sources of the Self: The Making of Modern Identity.* Cambridge, MA: Harvard University Press, 1991.

Taylor, Diana. *The Archive and the Repertoire: Performing Cultural Memory in the Americas.* Durham: Duke University Press, 2003.

Tebbel, John William. *Between Covers: The Rise and Transformation of Book Publishing in America.* Oxford: Oxford University Press, 1987.

Thompson, John B. "The New Visibility." *Theory, Culture and Society* 22, no. 6 (2005): 31–51.

Thorburn, David, and Henry Jenkins, eds. *Rethinking Media Change: The Aesthetics of Transition.* Cambridge, MA: MIT Press, 2003.

Tulchinsky, Gerald. *Taking Root: The Origins of the Canadian Jewish Community.* Hanover, NH: Brandeis University Press, 1993.

Valverde, Mariana, and Kimberley White-Mair. "'One Day at a Time', and Other Slogans for Everyday Life: The Ethical Practices of Alcoholics Anonymous." *Sociology* 33, no. 2 (1999): 393–410.

Verrips, Jojada. "Aisthesis and An-aesthesia." *Ethnologia Europea* 35, no. 1/2 (2006): 27–33.

Vincent, David. *Literacy and Popular Culture: England, 1750–1914.* Cambridge: Cambridge University Press, 1989.

Wach, Joachim. *Understanding and Believing: Essays.* Ed. Joseph Kitagawa. New York: Harper and Row, 1967.

Walker, Edward. *The Art of Book-Binding: Its Rise and Progress.* New Castle, DE: Oak Knoll Books, 1984.

Wall, Wendy. *The Imprint of Gender: Authorship and Publication in the English Renaissance.* Ithaca: Cornell University Press, 1993.

Warner, Michael. "Publics and Counterpublics." *Public Culture* 14, no. 1 (2002): 49–90.

Weber, Max. *Economy and Society.* Trans. Günther Ross et al. New York: Bedminster Press, 1968.

Weinreich, Max. "Internal Bilingualism in Ashkenaz." In *Voices from the Yiddish,* ed. Irving Howe and Eliezer Greenberg, 279–88. New York: Schocken Books, 1975.

Weinstein, Sarah Epstein. *Piety and Fanaticism: Rabbinic Criticism of Religious Stringency.* Northvale, NJ: Jason Aronson, 1997.

Weiss, Elliott. "Packaging Jewishness: Novelty and Tradition in Kosher Packages." *Design Issues* 20, no. 1 (2004): 48–61.

Weissler, Chava. " 'For Women and for Men Who Are Like Women': The Construction of Gender in Yiddish Devotional Literature." *Journal of Feminist Studies in Religion* 5, no. 2 (1989): 7–24.

———. *Voices of the Matriarchs: Listening to the Prayers of Early Modern Jewish Women.* Boston: Beacon Press, 1999.

Wertheimer, Jack. "Jewish Education in the United States: Recent Trends and Issues." *American Jewish Year Book* (1999): 52–59.

———, ed. *The Uses of Tradition: Jewish Continuity in the Modern Era.* New York: Jewish Theological Seminary of America, 1992.

Wosh, Peter J. *Spreading the Word: The Bible Business in Nineteenth-Century America.* Ithaca: Cornell University Press, 1994.

Wouters, Cas. "Etiquette Books and Emotion Management in the Twentieth Century: Part One—The Integration of Social Classes." *Journal of Social History* 29, no. 1 (1995): 107–24.

Würthwein, Ernst. *The Text of the Old Testament: An Introduction to the Biblia Hebraica.* 2nd ed. Grand Rapids, MI: Eerdmans, 1995.

Yerushalmi, Yosef Hayim. *Haggadah and History: A Panorama in Facsimile of Five Centuries of the Printed Haggadah from the Collections of Harvard University and the Jewish Theological Seminary of America.* Philadelphia: Jewish Publication Society, 1997.

———. *Zakhor: Jewish History and Jewish Memory.* 2nd ed. New York: Schocken Books, 1989.

Zaret, David. "Religion, Science and Printing in the Public Spheres in Seventeenth-Century England." In *Habermas and the Public Sphere,* ed. Craig Calhoun, 212–35. Cambridge, MA: MIT Press, 1992.

Zerubavel, Yael. *Recovered Roots: Collective Memory and the Making of Israeli National Tradition.* Chicago: University of Chicago Press, 1995.

Zinberg, Israel. *A History of Jewish Literature.* Vol. 7. *Old Yiddish Literature from Its Origins to the Haskalah Period.* Trans. Bernard Martin. Cincinnati: Hebrew Union College Press, 1975.

INDEX

Note: Page numbers followed by *f* or *t* denote figures and tables, respectively.

translations, 158; and Jewish public spheres, 9, 48–49, 78, 88–96; Talmud translations, 32, 38–39. *See also* vernaculars

epitexts, 67–68

Epstein, Isodore, 196n5

ethical conduct, 64, 133–135, 137–139. *See also musar*

etiquette, 121

Etz Hayim, 74

expository genres, 109t, 224n11

Feinstein, David, 189n54

fiction, 104, 109t

financial donors, 40, 42

Finkelman, Yoel, 104

Fishbein, Susie, 120–132, 151, 154–155

Fishman, Talya, 209n74

Fleischman, Joel, 189n54

Flusser, Vilém, 184n10, 195n78

food, 121, 154–155. *See also* cookbooks

footnotes, 114, 234n2

Friedman, Alexander Zusha, 60

Friedman, Howard S., 151

Friedman, Menachem, 54–55

fundraising, 45

galut, 204n43

gedolim 53, 60, 105. *See also Da'at Torah*

Geertz, Clifford, 5, 27–28, 52. *See also* scripturalism

Gell, Alfred, 154

Genette, Gérard, 212n5, 234n2

Gemara Tutor, 37

gender: in Haredi society, 50; and Hebrew, 94. *See also* women

genres: and ArtScroll books, 17, 87–89, 96, 109t, 108–110; and religious publishing, 22; speech, 67

Gerondi, Yonah, 91

Gifter, Mordechai, 52

Gobard, Henri, 218n36

Goldwurm, Hersh, 114, 117

graphic icons, 159, 162f, 164

gravity, 178–179

Gutenberg, Johannes, 19

Gutjahr, Paul, 168

Habermas, Jürgen, 23

"Halachah" series, 56. *See also* code books

halakhah: and decision-making 53, 57,106, 210n89, instruction manuals on, 87, 96, 109t, 173; Orthodox observance of, 47, 105; and Talmud, 31. *See also* code books; *humra; qullah*

Halbertal, Moshe, 194n74

Haredism and Haredi society: and authenticity, 174–175; defense of tradition in, 104–105; and English language, 94–95; and genres, 96; growth of, 1–2, 177; as mode of scripturalism, 14; rise of, 44–51; use of ArtScroll books in, 73t

Hasidic communities: within Haredi Orthodox society, 44, 203n42, 205n53; liturgical custom in, 66; and publishing, 209n80, 210n91, 211n91

Haskalah, 46

haskamot, 197n7

Hebrew language, 89–92, 114, 158

Heilman, Samuel, 49

Heinze, Andrew, 137

Hertz, Joseph, 72

hiddur mitzvah, 129–130

Hillel Goldberg, 209n82–210n82

Hinduism, 3

historical biographies, 86–87

history books, 86–7, 109t, 224n12

Holocaust, 48, 54

hortatory genres, 109t, 133, 224n11

humra, 106, 223n6, 223n7–224n7. *See also* halakhah; *qullah*

hybrids: and actor-network theory, 148, 164, 234n3; in discourse, 134, 231n68

idolatry, 151

illustrations, 151–153

images, 124–125, 150–157, 229n45, 230n58. *See also* visual culture

India, 3

The Infinite Sea (video installation), 42

inscription, 19, 148–149, 169, 187n35, 190n56

interlinear translations, 158–159, 162f, 164

intermediaries, 54, 67, 82–84. *See also* booksellers; librarians

Islam, 3, 52

Israel, 5, 45, 48, 50, 92, 201n37, 204n42, 205n50, 211n91; Anglophone community in, 15, 220n45, 221n47; marketing of ArtScroll prayer books in, 78, 216n21; and Holocaust, 48; prayers for in ArtScroll books, 188n49

Jakobovits, Immanuel, 189n54

Jewish public sphere, 4–5, 45–46, 50, 54, 60–63, 89–93, 177

The Jewish Home Beautiful (Greenberg and Silverman), 229n45

The Jewish Observer, 48, 61, 205n52

Jewish Orthodoxy. *See* Orthodox Judaism

"Judaicization" of knowledge, 52–53

Judaism, 24–25. *See also specific denominations*

Jungreis, Esther, 134. *See also* self help books

Kaddish, 115

Karo, Joseph, 25, 57

kashrut, 121, 123, 131

Katz, Avrohom, 52

Katz, Jacob, 207n63

kehila, 46

Kirshenblatt-Gimblett, Barbara, 121

kiruv movement, 50–51, 97. *See also ba'alei teshuva; tinokos shenishbu*

Klein Edition Women's Siddur, 111

Korban Minchah, 225n16

Kosher by Design (Susie Fishbein), 120–132; aesthetic of, 151; binding of, 165–166; marketing of, 66; photographs in, 154–156; success of, 30

KosherLamp™, 171–173

language(s): in bilingual texts, 157–158; of end users, 88–96. *See also specific languages*

Latour, Bruno, 7, 148, 187n35

layout, 150, 157

leather-bound books, 167–170

legitimacy, 79. *See also* authority

leshon hakodesh, 31, 90, 218n39, 219n40, 219n41, 221n52. *See also* Hebrew language

Levy, Barry, 206n57, 226n20

librarians, 44, 54, 83–84, 148

libraries, 59–60, 68, 167, 176

Library Enrichment Program, 189n53

Library of Congress, 33–35

"liquidation of aura," 150

literacy, 94. *See also* comprehension

lobby groups, 45

London, 44, 72, 73*t,* 74, 83, 94, 98

Lubell, Stephen, 157

Luther, Martin, 19

Maimonides, 25, 57, 206n57

market conditions, 149

marketing: and book design, 66; of *Kosher by Design,* 227n34

Masorti Judaism. *See* Conservative/Masorti Judaism

materiality, of ArtScroll books, 146–175; and authenticity, 169, 173–175, 178; binding in, 147, 165–170; and brand switching, 77; design elements in, 157–164; devices in, 164–166; images in, 150–157; and readers, 146–147; and reading accessories, 170–173; and text-centrism, 147–149, 173–174

mechanical reproducibility, 150

media. *See* intermediaries; publishing industry; religion and media

The Megillah: The Book of Esther, 16, 52–53

Mesorah Heritage Foundation, 18, 33, 39–40, 82, 187n41, 189n53, 189n54, 197n7

Mesorah Publications, 15–17, 82

middlebrow literature, 11

migration, 46, 48–49, 91–92. *See also* diaspora Jewish communities

mishkan T'filah, 74

Mishneh Torah, 57

Mitchell, W. J. T., 235n13

Modern Orthodox society, 42; growth of, 49; use of ArtScroll prayer books in, 72, 73*t*

Text: 11.25/13.5 Adobe Garamond
Display: Adobe Garamond and Perpetua
Compositor: Westchester Book Group
Printer and binder: Sheridan Books